COMING

CLEAN

Rhinos, Rats

and Runways

MIKE KELLY

Matador
9 Priory Business Park,
Wistow Road, Kibworth Beauchamp,
Leicestershire. LE8 0RX
Tel: 0116 279 2299
Email: books@troubador.co.uk
Web: www.troubador.co.uk/matador
Twitter: @matadorbooks

ISBN 978 1785892 424

British Library Cataloguing in Publication Data.
A catalogue record for this book is available from the British Library.

Printed and bound in the UK by TJ International, Padstow, Cornwall
Typeset in 11pt Aldine401 BT by Troubador Publishing Ltd, Leicester, UK

Matador is an imprint of Troubador Publishing Ltd

Coming Clean is dedicated to my wife Hilary and children Rachel and Christopher who put up with me through many years of regular absences from home and my unpredictable grumpiness on return, caused by jet lag.

I am grateful to my good friend Jenny Farrugia for her invaluable assistance in proof reading, editing and sorting out my execrable typing in the several variants of the book which I produced before this final version.

ABOUT THE AUTHOR

Mike Kelly trained in Environmental Health in Northern Ireland, graduating in 1967 and is a Fellow of the Chartered Institute of Environmental Health.

His career however didn't follow the normal route of progression upwards through Local Government. Instead he chose to venture further afield and having applied for a job through the Crown Agents went to Zambia in 1968 as a Government Health Officer on a three year contract working in remote areas of the African bush.

Returning to the UK in 1971 he joined the London Borough of Hillingdon where he worked in the Environmental Health department for four years, gaining invaluable experience and an insight into some of the more bizarre aspects of Local Authority work.

A move to British Airways in 1975 was intended to be for only a couple of years to gain commercial experience but the job proved so interesting that he stayed for more than thirty. Having started as a junior hygiene officer his career took him upwards via a Master's Degree in Business Administration, University of Bath, to being Senior Manager Catering Operations at BA London Heathrow then Head of Food Safety and Environmental Health with a small team covering the airline's worldwide operations.

He retired in 2006. In 2008 he was inducted into the President's Roll of Honour, International Flight Services Association, USA, for his "Outstanding contributions to the Flight Services Industry."

CONTENTS

PROLOGUE

At 39000 feet above Eastern Russia in 2005, flying home from another overseas audit, having just had a good meal and a glass of wine, I lapsed into a reverie and began to reflect on my life and what had been or might have been.

I hadn't planned any of it yet I had fallen into a career which had taken me from Ulster to Africa, Belfast to Bishkek, and into contact with elephants and Jumbos, pythons and pilots. A life so different, bizarre, amusing, and sometimes dangerous, worked out across all corners of the world, that most people reading the tales won't believe them.

However, I thought that it was worth recording some of my memories if only for my children to understand why it was that I was missing from home so often when they were young.

This is the result. My attempt to chronicle some of the history of my working life.

So when or where should I begin? Africa?

INTRODUCTION

The change in the engine note woke me from a deep sleep. For a few seconds I wondered where I was.

I glanced out of the window and was transfixed. A brilliant green landscape was visible in small patches through the breaks in the cloud as the VC10 turned steeply on its final approach into Ndola airport.

Africa!!

My first view, and not at all what I had expected. But what had I expected? Here I was, fresh out of Northern Ireland, newly qualified as an Environmental Health Officer, still wet behind the ears and very Provincial.

What must I have looked like when I eventually walked down the aircraft steps at my final destination, Lusaka, dressed in my blue Burberry raincoat, I squirm with embarrassment when I think about it now.

It had all seemed like a great adventure when I saw the advertisement in Environmental Health magazine. "Wanted by the Crown Agents, Environmental Health Officers for the Republic of Zambia. Two years post graduate experience required."

Never mind that I'd only been qualified for six weeks, it sounded like a much more exciting option than working as a junior officer in the mean terraced back streets of Belfast and if the alternative to that was to move away from home, then why stop at England?

I didn't expect to get an interview much less get the job, but then I didn't know how desperate they were for staff.

Sitting in the Crown Agents' offices in Millbank opposite the Houses of Parliament, I was somewhat in awe of the Saville Row suit questioning me on my qualifications and experience from behind the enormous oak desk standing on the thick pile carpet.

Not quite so impressive was the man seated beside him. Dressed uncomfortably in a blue serge suit he squirmed visibly when it was suggested that he ask me a question.

"Yes, Mr. Kelly" he started in a plummy accent, then cleared his throat loudly and started again. "Mr. Kelly, do you possess a dinner suit?"

I must have sat there for a minute with my mouth opening and closing like a goldfish for he then continued "We don't have any Moss Brothers in Zambia and one must keep up appearances you know."

Welcome to the Colonial Service or at least what remained of it in recently independent Zambia.

CHAPTER 1

EARLY DAYS

I must have looked a strange sight descending the steps of the aircraft at Lusaka. Still wearing the raincoat that had been the required garb at school, I collected my suitcase from the carousel and wandered somewhat apprehensively into the terminal.

A blaze of noise and colour greeted me and for a moment I was overwhelmed. Dozens of people thronged the concourse happily greeting their incoming friends and relatives.

Suddenly a Scottish twang spoke loudly and confidently in my ear. "Mr. Kelly?" A bright cheery face, well-tanned from years of working in the hot African sun was looking intently at me. "I'm Jim McPherson" he introduced himself. "I work for the Health Department and they've sent me over to pick you up and take you to the Government Hostel where you'll be staying for a couple of days."

"Once you've unpacked I've to take you to the office to meet Frank and John the Chief and Deputy Chief of the Department," he explained quickly on seeing the questioning expression on my face. "Is this all you've got?" he continued, looking at my somewhat incongruous grey suitcase, a gift from my colleagues at the Belfast City Health Department with whom I had worked for a scant four months. "Yes." "OK let's go".

I followed Jim to a dusty Land Rover parked outside the Terminal. Throwing my case into the back he clambered into the driver's seat. I climbed awkwardly into the front passenger seat hurriedly disposing of my Burberry into the seat beside me. It was the first time I had been in a Land Rover but it certainly wouldn't be the last, although I wasn't to know that at that moment.

Jim, dressed as he was in what would quickly become my standard uniform of open necked short sleeved shirt, shorts and knee length coloured socks above a pair of stout shoes, saw my embarrassment. "Och don't worry about that. I've seen people arrive with much stranger things in my time. Sometimes I wonder what they think they're coming to. I remember watching one guy coming down the steps of the aircraft carrying a hockey stick. When he came out of the baggage area and I met him I said what's that?" "It's a hockey stick" he said, looking at me as if I was a bit mad. "I know that" says I "but what are you expecting to do with it four hundred miles out in the bush? I suppose you could always chase the monkeys off the veranda with it."

We set off for the Government Hostel, one of three available in Lusaka to accommodate Government officials, arriving in or departing from the country or just coming into the city from their bush stations for a short time to attend meetings.

Effectively the hostel was a small hotel, run by the Government and staffed by a team of bright cheerful Zambians under the guidance of a European Manager. It was, I was told, the best of the three available, located in a pleasant part of the city, close to the cathedral.

I only had time to unpack rapidly, have a quick shower and change into an open necked shirt before jumping back into the Land Rover to be driven to the head office of the Department of Health, my new employer.

"Welcome to Zambia. Take a seat. This is John my deputy." Frank was slim, sharp faced and spoke with a distinctly English accent. John was shorter, more round in stature and Scottish. They immediately launched into what was effectively my induction into Environmental Health in Zambia.

I had been traveling for some thirty-six hours by this time, having left Northern Ireland at 8.00 am the previous morning. The vagaries of the Crown Agents were such that since they had a travel agreement with British United Airways to transport staff to Zambia I was forced to travel with that airline.

However, they only had two flights per day from Belfast to Gatwick, one in the early morning and one in the evening which meant that I had to be on their early morning flight as the evening flight wouldn't allow time for me to connect with the flight to Zambia.

I therefore had spent an entire day in Gatwick airport. Not exactly an exciting place since at that time, it was still a very small airport. Hence when I arrived in Lusaka after my long overnight flight, I was blitzed!!

The next day and a half passed in a blur. I had no idea when I had applied for the job that they were so desperate for staff that they would have taken anyone who was a qualified Environmental Health Officer. Zambia was a huge country compared to the UK yet there were only eight Environmental Health Officers (EHOs) employed in the regional areas.

The country was divided into provinces, each with a provincial Capital with one EHO positioned in each. The EHOs were responsible for a team of Zambian trained Health Assistants with each team working under the guidance of a senior assistant. I, because of my youth and inexperience, was to be deployed to Mazabuka in Southern province in the first instance, to be under the watchful eye of a more senior environmental health professional, John Muirden.

Mazabuka was only some eighty miles South of Lusaka and John was in Livingstone, some two hundred miles further south, so effectively I would be on my own. Frank and John carried on. "You have an office in Mazabuka. There hasn't been anyone stationed there for about six years so we don't know what you'll find. Go to the local hospital first. They are expecting you. I think they've organized a house for you but you'll find out when you get there. Check all the equipment in the stores at your office. There should be an inventory. Anything that doesn't work you'll need to get rid of. To do that you'll have to set up a board of enquiry to investigate and write it off then write up a new inventory."

They droned on and on. It was all a bit much on day one through a haze of tiredness.

Day two was marginally better. I had gone to bed early the night before to be awoken around six am the following morning by the chatter of a group of men outside my ground floor window. It was still dark but a quick investigation through a chink in the curtain revealed a shoe cleaning operation being carried out.

I turned on the bedside lamp only to shoot bolt upright at the sight of a very large and somewhat hairy spider grinning at me from the back corner of the bedside table. Spiders are not my favourite species and this monster (well it was at least three inches across!) was a great deal bigger than anything I'd ever seen before except in Belfast zoo.

I gingerly moved away from it, then rushed into the bathroom, grabbed a glass and bravely approached it with a view to trapping it in the glass and putting it outside. The spider would have nothing to do with it. It was not going to be co-operative. It watched my careful approach and just as I was

3

about to plunge the glass over its head it jumped acrobatically to the wall behind. I jumped just as rapidly backwards. I'd never come across a spider that jumped before. Irish spiders were comparatively docile and allowed themselves to be trapped and removed sensibly.

Deciding that discretion would be the better part of valour, I manoeuvred myself to a position where I could get to one side of the spider and with some dexterous waving at it with a large piece of paper shuffled it towards the door.

This time it got the message and before I could open the door to let it out it scuttled beneath it and disappeared.

Later when I related the story to Jim en route to the office he laughed. "You're going to have to get used to them and many a great deal bigger" he grinned. "Aren't some of them dangerous?" I asked. "Yes, but most of them are only nuisance value." "How do you know which are dangerous and which aren't?"

"You don't" was the less than comforting reply. "Some people will tell you that if they lie flat on the wall they are harmless but if they stand away from the wall on their legs they are more dangerous, or is it the other way round?" mused Jim.

I decided there and then to treat all of them with a great deal of respect although in future months I was to get more accustomed to them and even learned to live with some which were a great deal larger, but more of that later.

Day two at the office followed much the same pattern as day one. A continuation of the litany of do's and don'ts. Looking back at it now it was somewhat surreal. Although Zambia had been granted independence some four years previously, it was still very much in the death throes of its colonial past and old habits die hard. I was being inducted into the remnants of the old colonial regime with all the civil service routines which must have dated back to the nineteen thirties or earlier.

Once I was in post in my District I was expected stay there and could only leave with the permission of head office. Local leave would be taken appropriately through the year but I was supposed to stay in the country. I could leave the country at the end of my contract, which was initially for three years, but if I were renewing the contract I would return to England on six weeks paid leave before returning to work. However, this came with the qualification that whilst there I might be required to do a couple of days work with the Crown Agents in London, perhaps interviewing.

That explained the serge suit at my interview!! Some poor soul dragged in from his six weeks leave in the UK to interview people for a job about which it was likely that he knew absolutely nothing. My later experience with newly found friends was to confirm this. Many, particularly those recruited to be teachers, often in schools in remote areas were given an induction course at Farnham castle in suburban Surrey, where they were treated to some wonderful lectures often given by people who had never been to Zambia.

Statements such as "Chipata, the capital of Eastern province, is ideally situated between two railheads one four hundred miles to the South and the other three hundred miles to the East" were apparently the norm if I am to believe the stories that were doing the rounds amongst the expatriate community. My experience of the dinner suit now made reasonable sense in comparison!!

Meanwhile Frank expounded on the joys of an outbreak of serious infectious disease such as smallpox. "Let us know as soon as possible. Send us a telegram and advise what you are doing to control it."

Control it? I didn't have the faintest idea as to what it looked like, never mind control it! This wasn't part of my training in Environmental Health. There wasn't much in the way of smallpox to be found in East Belfast!

It appeared that Environmental Health in its UK connotation had little to do with the job in Zambia.

Each small town in every administrative district had its own council responsible for the day to day running of the basic amenities such as drinking water, electricity and waste disposal.

Each supposedly had qualified staff to organize and run the utilities. The reality however was that few, if any, of the councils had qualified staff so the Government Health Officer, which was my grand title, was expected to keep a watching brief on what was happening.

The main part of the job however was disease control. I along with my colleagues in other provinces was expected to organize and run vaccination campaigns to control smallpox, measles, tuberculosis etc.

Smallpox control was an international campaign organized by the World Health Organisation (WHO) and the entire country had to be vaccinated once every three years. This meant that one third of each province was vaccinated each year. A mammoth task considering the size of the country and the widely spread but sparse population.

Campaigns against measles and tuberculosis were local and involved visits to each school in the district. Measles was a serious killer of Zambian children and there was much work to do. Never mind. It would all become clearer in the fullness of time I thought.

"Well that's about it" said Frank. "Yes" agreed John as day two of my induction drew to a close. "We've got a Land Rover for you. It's waiting for you in Mazabuka. We'll meet again in three years at the end of your contract. Good luck."

I shook the outstretched hands of both Frank and John and made my way out.

Jim was waiting outside. "Got that over with then. You'll be glad to get away from here." It was a statement of fact rather than a question and implied that Jim wasn't overly keen on the bureaucracy that went with the job. "I'm to drive you down to Mazabuka to introduce you. I'll pick you up about eight o'clock in the morning."

CHAPTER 2

FINDING MY FEET

The morning dawned bright and clear. It was January and half way through the wet season. Dry season ran from April through to the end of October and wet season for the other half of the year.

I was soon to learn that the first couple of days of the wet season would bring heavy rain through the day. Thereafter the days would start bright and sunny with cloud building up in the afternoon culminating in heavy rain for an hour or two in late afternoon, then drying during the night. The temperatures were high as was the humidity.

Lusaka was awash with colour as we set off for the Great South road. I was amazed by the greenery. It was a city with acres of gardens surrounding the suburban houses. Bougainvillea abounded in masses of colour escaping over walls and fences and cascading like unkempt waterfalls into the streets. The jacaranda trees added their distinctive purple flowers to the palette. I hadn't really seen much of the city in daylight during my induction so I was only too glad to get out and get my first real look at Africa.

The Great South road was one of the four main highways leading out of the city, each geographically orientated, predictably North, South, East and West and leading equally predictably to Northern, Eastern, Southern and Western provinces.

The tarred surface in the City gave way rapidly to unmade laterite covered dirt roads which became more and more untamed the further away from the capital one drove, but I was to learn all this much later.

We were bowling merrily along a well-constructed highway which was to branch a few dozen miles south of the city with one route progressing towards Salisbury, the then capital of Rhodesia, now Harare, the capital of Zimbabwe, whilst the second turned more southerly and headed for Livingstone, the provincial capital of Southern province.

Livingstone is on the banks of the Zambesi river a short distance from the Victoria falls and the border with Rhodesia on the road to Bulawayo. I was to see and marvel at the falls on numerous occasions during my stay in Zambia and it is one of my abiding memories.

Just at the point where the road from Lusaka splits there was a motel, The Don Robin. Jim pulled into the car park. "Time for a cup of tea. It's a fair drive from here to Mazabuka and there isn't another stop along the way." We went into what was a fairly typical roadside café and were tucking into our scones and coffee when we were joined at an adjacent table by a group of males talking in strong South African or Rhodesian accents.

An animated conversation was taking place with one of the guys describing an accident in which he had been involved a little bit up the road a short time previously. "I was coming down the road at about 60 mph when this stupid muntu (in those days a White dismissive colloquial description of an African) stepped straight into the road in front of me. I couldn't miss him and bang he went over the top of my car. I stopped and got out and Jesus you should see the mess he's made of the front of my car!" There was a chorus of sympathy from the rest of the group.

I sat there stunned. What about the African? What had happened to him? Was life considered so cheap in this part of the world? It was a revelation to me and the first of many incidents which would awaken me from my Northern Irish naivety to the ways of the world.

Mazabuka, some eighty miles from Lusaka, was a small town set on a hillside astride the main road to Livingstone and the border with Rhodesia. It looked out over the Kafue flats, the flood plains of the Kafue river and the site of the newly started Zambia Sugar Company estate called Nakambala.

The road from Lusaka tipped sharply down the hill into the main street as I got my first glimpse of the place that was to become home for the next year. The view across the flats to the distant horizon was impressive. The street itself was busy. The Golf Club was on the left on the way down the slope, followed by a couple of streets of bungalow style housing, then came a general store, a garage and filling station. On the opposite side was more housing and Barclays bank almost facing its competitor the Standard Bank, an off shoot from its parent in South Africa.

Levelling out at the bottom of the hill the road turned sharply left to reveal more small general stores and the railway station on the right hand side. The street was full of people, Africans in their brightly coloured clothing, the women with babies held on their backs by a large towel wrapped around them in such a way as to keep the child firmly in place with no danger of falling.

Men in shorts and flat sandals or no shoes at all darted around the pavement, in and out of shops and trucks, loading and offloading. Overhead a canopy of jacaranda trees added more colour to the picture.

The road swept along then made a second sharp turn, this time to the right to cross the main railway line which ran all the way from South Africa to the Zambian copper belt cities from which the copper ore which supported the Zambian economy was mined and shipped out for smelting. Crossing the line we passed the local dairy then, heading out of town with the Catholic church on the left, turned right into the gateway of the hospital whose short driveway ended at a roundabout outside the main entrance.

The soft tones of a female Irish voice hit me as I climbed somewhat stiffly out of the Land Rover. "Welcome to Mazabuka."

A Nun was standing with a hand outstretched to greet me. "I'm Sister Agnes and I'm the matron here. I'll introduce you to the others in a moment but come inside and we'll have a cup of tea." She shooed away the collection of children who had gathered around me as an object of curiosity and led the way in.

The hospital was a single-storey bungalow style premises with a number of separate wings, painted in white which was discoloured at lower levels by the red sand which seemed to make up the local ground.

A number of what appeared to be gardeners were bent over the flower beds to one side of the main building, slowly weeding in the somewhat oppressive heat. A Bedford truck, painted white and with a large red cross on the side stood outside the door.

"Come in, come in." Sister Agnes swept imperiously into her small office. I followed meekly behind, somewhat overwhelmed. Despite my years of upbringing in Northern Ireland, or perhaps because of it, this was the first time that I had ever been in contact with a Nun. I wasn't really sure how I should deal with the lady.

She looked somewhat stern faced but I was soon to realize that there was a sparkle in the blue eyes behind her glasses and over the next few weeks she and her very small team of Irish Sisters of Charity, who formed the backbone of the nursing staff at the hospital, would go out of their way to ensure that I would be made comfortable and wouldn't feel too alone in this strange environment.

I sat down in the office, along with Jim who had followed me in and who had already organized the removal of my suitcase from the Land Rover. A line of people then appeared seemingly from nowhere, all wanting to shake my hand and introduce themselves. The first was a willowy Englishman with a slightly droopy moustache which gave him a somewhat foppish look. The hospital administrator, he welcomed me warmly and to my relief confirmed that they had been expecting me and a bungalow was available for me to move into that very day.

Next came a well-dressed Zambian gentleman who introduced himself as my Senior Health Assistant in charge of the team of staff spread across the area and who would report to me. Mr Mkele was to prove invaluable and a tower of strength to me in the following weeks.

The line seemed to go on forever as one after the other the main staff at the hospital were introduced. Smiling faces and unfamiliar names crowded upon me and I knew that it would take some time before I could get to grips with who they all were and what they did. However, all in good time and my first impression was one of friendliness and a warm welcome.

Jim decided that it was time he left. "Well that's it" he said cheerily. "I'd better be making my way back. You'll be OK now and no doubt I'll see you again before the end of your contract." "Good luck." He disappeared in a gentle cloud of red dust and with him went the only contact I had in Zambia outside those who stood around looking at me.

"Right then," said Matron. "It's time to get you organized. Malcolm, she pointed at the Administrator, has got your Land Rover round the back and he'll take you up to your house and get you settled in. Once you're organized, come back down here and we can sort out some of the other details." And so began my life in Mazabuka.

Mazabuka was a lively little town with a background of farming, situated as it was on the edge of the Kafue river, a tributary of the Zambezi. Zambia had only shaken off the mantle of British colonialism in the past four years and the local farmers were mainly of expatriate stock whose forebears had trekked into what was then Northern Rhodesia in the early part of the 20th century to carve out farms from the inhospitable bush.

Given the poor nature of the soil the farms tended to be large scale running into several thousand acres in many cases in order to support viable herds of cattle. As one farmer put it to me "In England you have 10 cows per acre of land, here in Zambia we have ten acres per cow."

Most of the farms were some distance from town and the farmers and their families only came in buy supplies and to socialize at the Golf Club, the Rugby Club or the bioscope, the South African name for the cinema. A regular weekly event the bioscope was held in the community hall and showed a film which had to be ordered from Lusaka.

Sometimes it would be collected by one of the local residents who was going up to Lusaka on business. This at least ensured delivery of the film which otherwise was in the hands of the postal service and might not appear on time.

The quality of the films varied and the film ordered wasn't always what was delivered since the system worked country wide and good films were greatly in demand. However, it satisfied the need for a social event.

Apart from farmers the population was a very mixed bunch. A number were long term residents, many of whom had arrived as early settlers and who now provided the higher level administrative back up in the Civil service, schools, hospitals, utilities etc. To add to that was a large number of contracted expatriate staff who, like me, had been recruited in the UK and sent out on three year contracts to provide the schoolteachers, agronomists, public works engineers, health professionals etc.

We were looked upon with some scorn by many of the long term residents and with good reason in some cases. We were better paid. Our contracts were based on short terms and high salaries, with a gratuity paid at the end of the contract in lieu of pension rights. Many of the expatriates were only there for the money and often never ventured far from their initial posting to look at the variety of life, scenery and wonders available in their adopted country. Not for them the wonders of the Victoria Falls or the nearby game reserves.

We were often described dismissively by the locals as "the VC tenners" this being the aircraft (Vickers VC10) which had transported most of us to Zambia.

Driving back through the town on my way to my new house I could see that the shops were a bit of a mixture covering as they did the needs of the entire community. They ranged from an approximation of a European department store through to a bakery which produced a variety of breads and cakes baked on the premises. These were interspersed by a garage which provided fuel and repairs and the two banks which I had spotted on my arrival.

Fruit and vegetables were in abundance, heaped in glorious cascades of colour on trestle stalls outside smaller shops whilst the butchery was evident not only by the flies which seemed to pervade the area in which it stood but also by the crowd of African women who seemingly permanently congregated outside the door trying to obtain the choicest pieces of meat for their families. Women adorned with children, hanging from their skirts, or attached to their backs by a large blanket or towel in which the baby was held safe, and sometimes attached to their fronts, hungrily sucking on often dry breasts. Many of the children exhibited signs of malnutrition, but as a total newcomer, I wasn't going to recognize this for a little while.

My house was half way up the hill, in a street running off the main road, positioned above the shops and below the golf course. Malcolm deposited me at the door and I was surprised to see a newly constructed European style bungalow set in its own garden and matched by similar properties running along the road.

Stepping inside I found myself in a lounge/dining room, off which was a kitchen on one side and a corridor on the other leading to the three bedrooms. Looking into the rear garden I noticed another building. "What's that"? I asked. "That's where your house boy and garden boy live with their families" said Malcolm. "House boy?" I queried somewhat incredulously.

"Yes. Everybody has house servants here. All your cleaning, cooking etc. will be done for you. You'll have to organize your own staff but I'm sure some of the local wives can help you with that." This was something that I hadn't expected and was a long way removed from what I was used to in my native Bangor.

The house was furnished with beds, dining table and chairs and a sofa and armchairs in a style which I was to become used to since it was replicated in every Government provided house in the country. I quickly recognized that I had no bed linen, curtains or other soft furnishings. Malcolm saw my problem. "Don't worry about the curtains and things.

Matron will help you organize those. Once you've unpacked your case we'll go back down to the hospital."

So off I went. Bed linen wasn't a problem as there was sufficient in the local store. Curtains and cushions would be sewn for me by the younger nurses, under the instruction of Matron who seemed to find it both challenging and amusing to have a young Irishman on the patch, albeit one who came from the North of Ireland rather than the Republic.

I soon settled to my new way of life. My office was down town, just off the main road and was fairly simple. A small brick built building with two adjacent offices, one for me and one for my team of Zambian technical staff under the leadership of a senior officer who rapidly took me under his wing.

Next to the office was a storeroom which when investigated yielded a supply of unlikely equipment, some of which must have dated back at least twenty-five years. It included such things as stirrup pumps, which I had never seen at close hand before and had no real idea as to what they might be used for but all would be revealed in good time.

In talking to my senior assistant I found out that I was part of a team of three Health Officers in Southern Province with my boss John being based in Livingstone, some two hundred miles to the South. He was to arrive in the near future to help me to set up but in the meantime I was on my own.

My district was around one hundred and fifty miles in length and probably some one hundred miles wide although I was never completely sure as to where it started and finished. The Western side was bounded by the Kafue flats, the flood plains of the Kafue river, which were in process of being developed as a sugar plantation by Tate & Lyle.

In the North East lay the Kariba dam where the mighty Zambesi had been contained in order to provide a hydroelectric scheme via an enormous lake. Siavonga, a small town close to the dam was my responsibility. To the South East lay the Gwembe valley which was my outermost point in that direction. Beyond the boundary of the valley and lake Kariba lay Rhodesia, tight in the grip of Ian Smith's unilateral declaration of independence and supposedly cut off from its neighbours by strict border controls.

Although I had been subjected to an induction in Lusaka I was very unsure as to what I was actually supposed to be doing. It appeared that I was responsible for all manner of things within the District, some of which such as water supplies and waste disposal I was familiar with, but others such as vaccinating the population against smallpox and the schoolchildren against measles and tuberculosis had not been on the agenda during my training in the UK and would normally have been the preserve of the Medical profession rather than Environmental Health.

I was soon to learn however that if you are the only pair of hands available you have to be prepared to do whatever is necessary at the time. More disconcerting was the fact that my team of amiable Zambian officers were very obviously waiting for their instructions and guidance from me. Life would however gradually take shape. My boss John arrived from Livingstone to give me some guidance. John was a laid back Scotsman who had been in Zambia for a long number of years and wasn't going to be fazed by the arrival of some snotty nosed youngster from Northern Ireland.

"It's all perfectly simple" he told me in his ripe Scottish accent. "You'll have to ensure that the population in one third of your District is vaccinated against smallpox this year. We vaccinate the entire population of the country every three years as that's as long as the vaccine remains effective."

"Och it's very straightforward. The vaccination is done by teams of lay vaccinators who will cover the district on bicycles. They're supplied by vaccine through your office and the hospital and they are overseen by Mkele, your Senior Assistant." John made it all seem so simple.

On top of this I was responsible for the school vaccination programme which I quickly learned I would carry out myself. I would soon become a dab hand at lining up a whole school population and vaccinating them all against tuberculosis and measles in a single morning.

Despite the fact that I had a Land Rover John was insistent that I should have my own car and we set about looking for something that would prove suitable. Once again I was very naïve and having looked with John at a number of cars he suggested that since he was leaving the country shortly on long leave and would wish to buy a new car on his return, I should buy his existing car from him. The car in question was a beautiful steel grey Rover 2000 with the distinctive number plate L77.

It was a lovely motor in my eyes but of course would prove to be totally useless in a country which had only a very limited amount of tarred roadway beyond which were dirt roads at best and bush tracks at worst.

Needless to say I agreed to buy it and John was delighted. Unfortunately my experience with the car was to prove short lived and somewhat disastrous, but more of that later.

Life in Mazabuka revolved around the Golf Club, positioned halfway up the hill from the town centre and just around the corner from my house. The club provided a nightly rendezvous for most of the expatriate male population, most of whom, like me were single, plus a few females who with few exceptions were either wives or in some cases daughters of expatriates or long term residents.

The majority of us worked for Government in some form or other, usually as teachers, medical staff, agronomists etc. There were a few lads who were employed by one or other of the two banks in town, and Barclays had a staff house in which all their male expatriates lived. All young and single they made a riotous contribution to the evenings in the Golf Club bar. I was made welcome and soon settled in.

My day usually started in my office which was shaded by a stand of high trees which I was told were milk trees. These seemed of little consequence until suddenly one morning whilst going through paperwork at my desk I was disturbed by a sudden outburst of shrieking and hullabaloo followed by raucous laughter. I ran out of the office to be confronted by the sight of one of my team racing off down the street waving his arms frantically whilst his erstwhile colleagues were falling about in laughter outside the office.

"What's happened?" I asked. "Oh a snake fell out of the trees and landed on Ndlovu's arms so he's running away trying to shake it off." This was the first of a number of similar incidents which would remind me that I was in Africa and not in Belfast.

I would also learn very quickly that most of my African colleagues had little or no idea as to how to identify the many indigenous poisonous snakes or spiders or how dangerous they were. It was somewhat different with the local farmers who had a great respect for the many animals, insects and snakes that they came across in their daily round.

One resident, Charles, better known as Chusky, who was in his twenties and had been born and bred in Mazabuka had an abiding love of snakes and was liable to pick up any that he happened to come across in his daily travels. He was quite happy to pop them into his car, which could best be described as having seen better days.

One of his larger snakes was a reticulated python which had been crossing the road as Chusky drove along. He leapt out of the car, grabbed the snake by the tail and wrestled with it for several minutes before finally getting the better of it and putting it in the car boot, subsequently keeping it in a large cool storage pit at the farm where he lived and where I later met it.

Smaller snakes were more likely to cause a problem however as Chusky was liable to forget that he had picked one up and put it in the car. This was to prove disastrous to his love life. One night whilst parked in a quiet spot with an attractive young lady, he was just getting to the high point of their encounter when suddenly and without warning a relatively small snake dropped out of a hole in the roof lining of the car straight on to the, at that moment, bare breasts of the girl.

Well all hell broke loose. She was out of the car like a greyhound out of a trap, running, screaming, half naked into the African night. "I don't know what the problem was" said Chusky recounting the tale some days later in the golf club bar. "It was a simple grass snake and totally harmless."

"Well what did you do?" the assembled males asked whilst crying with laughter into our beer. "I picked the snake off the floor and checked that it was all right of course."

Cause for more hilarity from the rest of us. As for the poor girl, she wouldn't ever go anywhere near Chusky again and even more so when she found out that he had told the tale in the Golf Club bar to almost the entire expatriate male community!!

CHAPTER 3

YOU MUST BE JOKING?

My work routine gradually became established as I got to know my working area and began to decipher what I was supposed to be doing. Some things, like the vaccination programme were very obvious and necessary. Others were a bit more daunting and seemed to be of little value but were probably the product of the "old colonial" way of doing things.

One of the problems with slow moving water and lakes in Africa is that they allow the breeding of a small snail which forms part of the life cycle of the debilitating disease Bilharzia. In order to eradicate this serious illness, it was decreed that where possible the snails should be destroyed in order to reduce the chance of infection. Destruction could be carried out by dosing areas of still water with copper sulphate.

Hence on one blistering sunny day I was in the rural village of Siavonga, in a boat being rowed along the edge of Lake Kariba, towing a sack of copper sulphate which was slowly dissolving into the water. The Kariba dam, completed during the late 1950's created an enormous lake around 140 miles long and 20 miles wide which was still filling and producing an inland sea nearly as big as the English Channel.

Can you imagine anything more ridiculous? Here was a lake as big as the English Channel containing who knows how many billions of gallons of water and I had been instructed to kill all the snails in my section of it using a sack of copper sulphate and a small rowing boat!!

A job for life I would suggest and likely to be fairly unrewarding. In fact, the biggest risks were that I would either catch bilharzia or if really unfortunate become a meal for a large crocodile or the victim of a hippo attack.

Similarly, the destruction of mosquitoes to reduce the risk of malaria.

Spraying all areas of lying water with a mixture of insecticide and oil was deemed to be effective in killing the insects but since our resources were very limited and the breeding areas and scale of both country and water available were enormous it made the exercise almost totally futile. But it still had to be done and heaven help me if my boss happened to visit part of my district and spot a rampant mosquito! At least I had found out what the stirrup pumps were for!

Despite this I was enjoying my life. It was very different and not only was I learning the basics of managing people but also taking responsibility for decision making.

I was also living a bachelor life in a totally new environment and with a very different lifestyle. Sport took up a lot of my spare time. Mazabuka had a thriving rugby team and although I hadn't played for some years I had been educated at a well-known Belfast rugby playing school where I had been taught the basics. Having stupidly volunteered this information to my new found friends at the golf club bar I was rapidly inducted into the local seven a side tournament to be played a couple of weekends hence.

Thus it was that I made an appearance on the rugby pitch on the due day. Two things I learned very quickly. Firstly, the local farmers and their sons were very large and secondly the ground was very hard despite the fact that we were still in the wet season and the pitch was well covered with grass.

I was playing as a centre back in one team and shortly into my first game was faced with an opponent who was breaking through our line. I was the last line of defence so nothing daunted I threw my full weight of nine stones into a flying tackle. My arms locked round his thighs and I executed the perfect tackle bringing down my man in full flight but in the process landing full stretch and at full speed horizontally on the ground. It was like hitting concrete! As I picked myself up shakily, feeling bruised all down one side, I was aware of the appreciative applause from the knowledgeable crowd. It didn't make the pain any easier but I had definitely made my best if not only contribution to the afternoon.

Worse still was the realization later in the day that spending time in the open sun had taken its toll on my fair skin and by 7.00pm I was the colour of an over ripe tomato on all areas which had been exposed through the afternoon. Bear in mind that this was long before the advent of the sun blocking creams which are the norm today.

Later in the evening I suffered the extreme agony of lowering myself into a hot bath where once the scream of pain subsided I lay long enough for some recuperative process to commence. This was the first of numerous brushes with sunburn which have resulted in my having to have numerous cancerous areas of skin removed in my later years.

This wasn't the end of my Mazabuka rugby career as I played in the full team on a couple of occasions when they were shorthanded. The most memorable of these was at Kalomo, a small town a hundred miles or so further South on the road to Livingstone. Similar to Mazabuka although smaller, they had a reasonable team whose greatest claim to fame was that one of their forwards was a former South African Springbok international rugby player.

More importantly, not only was he a giant of a man, but he was also famous for having killed a lion on his farm using only his bare hands. I never heard the whole story but I can vouch for the size of the man. He was enormous and showed across his body the scars of his battle with the lion including the fact that he was missing a few fingers.

We got into the game, playing on what had to be the worst pitch that I ever played on. It was regulation size but the grass had only recently been cut and a sizeable and very sharp stubble had been left behind. Hard to run in but even worse to tackle on as the stubble cut the skin off my legs every time I slid into it.

However worse was to come. Someway into the second half, I found myself in the middle of our half of the pitch, the last line of defence under a high dropping ball. Looking at the opposition I realized with some panic that heading towards me at a fair gallop was the man mountain. He had no right to be there! He was a forward for goodness sake. Why was he ahead of all the backs?

I knew what I had to do. I stood resolutely under the ball and waited as it dropped into my arms. A split second later he hit me in full stride, not just crushing me but nearly burying me in the ground. The next thing I remember was a soft South African accent. "Are you OK?" I then became aware that I was being held up off the ground by my opponent holding me by the waistband of my shorts. He was genuinely concerned for my welfare because eighteen stone versus nine wasn't a fair contest.

I was speechless. It took several minutes before I could reply. My breath, when it started to return, came in several large and painful gasps. My eyes were watering, my teeth still rattled and I felt as though I had been hit by a tank. However, I recovered to tell the tale and gained some kudos amongst my new friends by having been brave enough (or should it be stupid enough) to stand under the dropping ball whilst knowing what was likely to happen.

My work also provided some dangers which were unexpected. One afternoon I was driving into the Gwembe valley, a somewhat remote area in the Southern part of my District, leading down towards Lake Kariba. My Senior Hygiene Assistant Mkele was with me as we travelled towards one of our more remote Health Centres. Driving off road I wasn't really thinking as I drove the Land Rover rapidly through a large puddle in the middle of the rough track. The inevitable happened. Water showered into the air and almost instantly the engine died. I knew immediately that I had got water in the distributor so I would have to open it and dry it out.

"Damn" I thought as I climbed out into the hot humid air. I opened the bonnet and rapidly dismantled the distributor. Suddenly I was aware of a voice beside me "Bwana, bwana" it whispered. "What is it?" I said, not looking up from what I was doing. "Bwana, bwana" The voice, though still quiet, was much more insistent. I looked up to find myself staring into the barrel of a rifle.

Unknown to us we had strayed into a training camp of the guerillas who were attempting to overthrow Ian Smith from his seat of power in Southern Rhodesia. I smiled bravely at the man on the other end of the gun. He was accompanied by half a dozen friends, all similarly armed, and all of them showing a healthy interest in what I was doing. "Hello" I said, smiling again. "I've flooded the distributor" I added, hoping that they would understand English and would also be sympathetic. By the look that I got I wasn't being very successful.

Whether that was due to a lack of understanding or just a lack of sympathy I couldn't tell. I began to sweat a bit more than normal. At that moment Mkele spoke in the local dialect. I have no idea what he said but whatever it was the group broke into smiles and a few sniggers. It's likely that he had just explained that I was recently arrived from England and being a totally naïve idiot had just killed the engine of the "garrymotor" as the car was known locally.

Whatever, I was never more grateful for the diplomatic skills of my Assistant who was able to convince the ragged but heavily armed group of men who were surrounding us that I was there for the humanitarian benefit of the local population. The incident was soon resolved and we left with smiles all round but I certainly had a better understanding of local politics.

Many of my days were spent travelling into the local bush visiting schools and carrying out vaccinations against TB and measles. The schools were pretty basic by UK standards often having open "half walls" to the classrooms and little in the way of facilities but at least the children were getting an education and it was much prized.

Many children would walk for miles across country along the main roads to get to school and most schools ran a two shift system with one group of children being taught in the morning and a different group in the afternoon.

On my arrival with my small team I would be greeted by the head teacher then the entire school would line up in the sunshine in the yard to be vaccinated. Much smiling and giggling would take place as I worked my way through the rows of arms being proffered for my attention and rarely was there any hesitation on the part of the children coming forward. This was probably one of the most rewarding parts of my job in that I was doing something valuable for the children in helping prolong their life expectancy.

CHAPTER 4

TYPHOID!

Little did I know in these early days that I was soon to become much more practiced in the art of vaccination. Tate and Lyle the British sugar producing company had just opened their new sugar plantation on the Kafue flats just outside Mazabuka.

A vast area of land had been planted with sugar cane, a production factory had been built and a large number of workers had been brought from the island of Mauritius to run the operation and train local Zambians in the art. They were housed on site in a large village complete with its own facilities.

My first visit to the site was to look at the sewage disposal arrangements which had been constructed. These were of a new design and consisted of three large open lagoons in which the sewage was treated and purified by the action of bacteria, sunshine and oxygen. The lagoons worked in tandem with the first containing raw sewage, which, after a period of time purifying, flowed into the second which in turn flowed into the third. The principle seemed to work quite well since by the time the third lagoon was reached the water was virtually clean and had fish and ducks in it.

However, looking at the system I could see a major problem. Because the water table in the area was high the lagoons had been constructed on the surface of the ground rather than being dug into the ground. Unfortunately, the earthwork of each lagoon was leaking and water was oozing into the surrounding area.

At the lower end of the system this was a relatively minor issue as the waste water contained within the last lagoon was already well purified however the first lagoon contained raw sewage so any leakage was likely to be contaminated. The liquid was running across a pathway along which workers passed regularly and children ran barefooted.

I immediately contacted the site management to express my concern. Some time passed and nothing was done. Again I wrote to the site manager. Again nothing was done. Not surprising in some ways. There I was, a wet behind the ears newcomer, recently arrived in the country, trying to tell a grizzled old timer how to do his job. His engineer had told him that everything was OK so why should he believe me?

Whether or not the subsequent problem arose as a result of the sewage leakage I don't know but not many weeks later I was disturbed in my office by Lye Akerele running in.

Lye was the District Medical Officer. A Nigerian, a Fellow of the Royal College of Surgeons (Dublin), married to a Rhodesian girl he was a great character and working on contract like me.

"We've got a problem Mike" he said breathlessly. "What's happened?" I queried. "Typhoid fever" he replied. "On the sugar estate" he added.

Typhoid fever I thought quickly. I had read about it as part of my training but had absolutely no experience of the disease. I looked quickly at Lye for some guidance.

"We'll have to vaccinate the entire workforce" he said with a conviction that made me feel that he knew exactly what he was doing.

"OK. I presume you will need all my team to assist, I'll call Mkele." I went quickly to the room next door and explained the situation. "You had better come in and join us"

The two of us rejoined Lye and awaited instructions. "I've been in touch with Lusaka and they are going to send us the vaccine, the needles and all the necessary bits and pieces, we should have them in a couple of days. Apparently they have a stock which has been supplied from Japan" Lye told us. "Until it arrives I'll quarantine the estate and try to ensure that no-one either goes in or comes out to try to stop any spread into the town and surrounding area."

Well that was it then. All under control and ship shape. Thank God for Lye, a bit of experience coupled with a cool head, experience I was to benefit from many years later when back in England.

Three days later we had the vaccine and were ready to roll. Lye had told the estate management that the best way for us to proceed was for their entire population to be assembled at the beer hall in the employee housing area since it was the largest enclosed and sheltered space they had available.

Hence on the given morning I was standing in the cool of the beer hall alongside Lye, each of us in front of a table on which stood a pile of filled syringes prepared by my team of lay staff who were busy unwrapping them from boxes.

To my left I had an empty box into which the disposable syringe would be thrown when I had emptied the contents into the arm of a worker in front of me. Lye stood to my right similarly equipped.

Outside, a long line of workers and their families snaked into the distance as far as the eye could see. It was surreal. Lye had given me a two minute crash course on typhoid vaccination. "Hold the top of the arm tightly with one hand, pull the skin and muscle backwards then quickly insert the needle and push the end of the syringe to discharge it fully into the arm. Hopefully you won't hit the deltoid artery otherwise they'll bleed like a stuck pig." Very comforting I thought.

"We'll take them ten at a time, five each" he added.

We were ready to go. The first ten were brought in, a look of consternation on their faces, not sure as to what was actually about to happen. Four of my team were applying an alcohol rub to the upper arm of the workers as they shuffled hesitantly towards us. Four more were behind us busily sorting out the ready to use syringes and piling them on a table behind Lye and me. "Quickly, quickly," yelled Lye, "we haven't got all day."

And so it started and was to continue for the next three days until we had vaccinated all 7,500 employees and families. It became a living nightmare.

Ten in, arms clean and ready, five to Lye five to me. Grab the arm, pull it back, stick the needle in discharge the contents, pull the needle out throw it in the box grab the next one. By the time we finished not only were we exhausted but I could vaccinate in my sleep!!

Surprisingly we had very few problems. Many of those in the line broke into spontaneous giggles as the needle was withdrawn and they realized that they were still alive! I don't quite know what they were expecting.

The management staff were vaccinated separately in the offices and again we had few problems. I actually was complimented on my gentle touch by one of the women. A great surprise to me. The only amusement was provided by one of the South African managers. A tough, well-muscled, wiry guy, bronzed from working constantly outdoors and re-known as the scrum half on the Mazabuka rugby team he was full of bravado as I stuck the needle into him. He left immediately, jumped into his Land Rover and roared off down the track only to faint a few moments later and career straight into the sugar cane. Apparently he hated needles and the bravado had run out as fast as he had left the office.

His tougher South African and Rhodesian colleagues gave him a hard time for weeks afterwards. Unkind really as most of us have phobias of some sort but luckily we don't often have to face them in front of others.

Life went quite smoothly for the next couple of months before disaster struck. The road to Lusaka was typical of many in Zambia at the time in that it wasn't metalled across the entire surface width.

In order to save costs when building the road, it had a centre strip of tarmac, wide enough for one car, but the shoulders of the road were soft red laterite. The basic principle was that when meeting another vehicle, each moved to the side, placing the two nearside wheels on the laterite whilst keeping two on the tarmac. This enabled both cars to maintain a degree of safety.

The trouble arose when cars appeared suddenly round a bend or out of a severe dip in the road without being seen until the last minute. More so if they were cars containing a Government Minister, depicted by a small national flag fluttering from a flagstaff on the front wing of the car. They gave way to nobody and stayed resolutely in the centre of the road.

I was heading North along the Lusaka road when the car came out of a dip travelling very fast. I saw the fluttering flag way too late and realizing that the car wasn't going to give way I pulled sharply to the left and hit the laterite.

Too sharply as it turned out. Although I wasn't going overly fast the car started to slide with the tail swinging round. I corrected hard, spinning the steering wheel quickly in the opposite direction to the slide. The car came back across the road. The tyres bit into the metalled surface and the car lurched violently. There was a loud crunching noise, then silence.

I sat in my seat for what seemed like minutes but which could only have been a few seconds, then realization dawned. I was on my head. The car was upside down.

I climbed carefully out of the side window which had been open.

Looking down the road I saw the tail of the Ministerial car disappearing in a cloud of dust. He must have seen what had happened but was obviously unconcerned as to my fate.

I looked at what had been my pride and joy and could have wept. The beautiful gun metal grey car was totally on its roof which had been somewhat flattened by the impact with the road. What do I do next? I wondered.

Luckily the road was relatively busy so I only had to wait for about ten minutes before a vehicle came on the scene. The driver jumped out. "You OK?" he asked whilst surveying the scene. "What happened?" I told him the sorry tale. "Bastards." he said with feeling." You would think they owned the place." I smiled at the irony of his statement.

Half an hour later I was in the garage at Mazabuka relating the story. "Bad luck" said Dave, the owner. "I'll send out the recovery truck and get the car brought in. Your insurance will cover the repair costs but it will have to be transported to Lusaka for repair."

The car was a sorry sight when I saw it next day in the garage but looked little better next time I saw it in a repair yard in Lusaka some six months later after interminable negotiation with the insurance company and the repairers.

It had been straightened out but was now painted duck egg blue since the repairers couldn't get paint to match the original. Although I eventually got it back it was never the same again and I sold it a couple of years later at a considerable loss. It was ever thus with cars as I was to find out in later life.

There was much sympathy amongst the expatriate community in the Golf Club that evening as I was advised that the accident was part of the life of an expatriate.

"Didn't anyone tell you?" John said, looking quizzically at me over his pint of beer. "Tell me what?" I asked.

"It's one of the three things that happen to male expats during their contract." "What?" I asked again.

"You crash your car, your house will be burgled and you'll sleep with someone else's wife" John replied with a grin.

"What?" I was more than a bit incredulous. "You heard" John laughed.

"Well considering I'm not even married the last bit seems a bit extreme" "Sorry" John said, "it was just the way I said it. Maybe I should have said you'll sleep with someone's wife. I wasn't implying that you had to be married yourself."

Well that was something at least. In the middle of the problems I was facing, the thought of getting married was the last thing on my mind.

Little did I know that marriage was closer than I thought.

CHAPTER 5

THE ROAD SOUTH

I had left behind in Bangor my girlfriend of some three years Hilary McCowen. She and I had met through the local Methodist Church youth group in Bangor known for its coffee bar meeting place for many teenagers and the regular camping and youth hostelling trips undertaken through the year.

When I had left for Zambia it was on the understanding that Hilary would stay behind to complete her teacher training year after graduating from the Belfast College of Art and Design, but would come out to visit me during my first summer.

That time was rapidly approaching and Hilary was due to fly to Johannesburg on a student charter flight from where I would pick her up and drive back to Zambia. A long trip driving through the full length of Rhodesia and a large part of South Africa and particularly so now that I had no car!! I was going to have to do some rapid re thinking.

I wasn't in the financial position where I could buy another car and in fact having laid out sums of money to pay for the basics of life in my house plus my car I was pretty well skint.

I worked out fairly quickly that the best I could do was to book two tickets for Hilary and me to fly from Johannesburg to Livingstone in Zambia. I would drive down to Livingstone in my Government Land Rover leave it at our office then walk across the border and hitch a lift South.

Thinking back on it now, with the benefit of age and experience, I must have been absolutely mad but needs must when the devil drives.

As it happened it all went like clockwork. I drove down to Livingstone and having deposited my Land Rover I set off toward the border on foot, carrying my possessions in a small bag.

I had only travelled a few hundred yards when I heard a pick-up truck coming along behind me. I turned quickly and stuck my thumb up. The truck braked and I ran to the door.

"Where are you heading for?" the driver said in a Rhodesian accent. "Johannesburg" I replied. "Hop in. I'm only going as far as Bulawayo but that will get you part of the way." "Thanks" I said getting into the truck gratefully.

We set off at a rapid pace towards the border, crossing the road bridge next to the spectacular Victoria Falls.

"I'm in a bit of a rush" my driver said. I looked more closely at him. Suntanned and in typical shorts and tee shirt he was obviously an outdoor worker in the construction industry and employed by the company whose name I had noticed on the truck as it had pulled up alongside me.

"I've just punched one of my local workforce and I need to get across the border before the police get hold of me," he added quickly. "You know what it's like" he continued "they get right up your nose the lazy bastards, then you snap, give them a kick or thump them and you're in serious trouble so I thought it best to get back across the border and argue the case with my boss when I see him tomorrow."

I didn't know what it was like but I wasn't going to say anything. I was now worried that when we arrived at the border the news of the punch might have got there before us and the police would arrest us both with me being considered as an accomplice.

My fears proved unfounded. The border crossing was smooth, with little interest being paid to either of us or our passports for that matter.

Soon we were crossing the Zambezi on the wonderful bridge built in 1905 parallel to the Victoria Falls looking at two of the world's great wonders side by side. The falls, more than a mile wide and some 360 feet of sheer drop into the gorge over which the road and rail bridge ran.

Once we had crossed the border my companion became noticeably relaxed and chatted amiably about his life in Rhodesia and Zambia. I explained who I was and the circumstances which had caused me to be on the road to Bulawayo.

Thus we trundled happily along at a steady fifty miles per hour. I would have wished for a more rapid progression but my companion was in no great hurry, bearing in mind that he would have to face the wrath of his boss the following morning when he would have to confess his indiscretion.

The scenery along the road was much the same as that in Zambia. A vast swathe of scrubby bush with occasional fencing and gateways marking the boundaries of the many farms or ranches along the way. There was little sign of any animal life although we passed numerous Africans along the roadside some of whom gave a smile or even a friendly wave.

The afternoon light began to fade into a purple sunset and then we were enveloped in the velvety dark of the African night. A vast panoply of stars was visible around us but late into the evening I became aware of a bright silvery glow appearing across the sky ahead of us. "What's that?" I asked naively. "That's Bulawayo."

The light which infused the sky crept towards us incredibly slowly it seemed to me. The truck hadn't been designed for driving such distances in any sort of comfort and my back was feeling the strain. I longed for the city to arrive more quickly.

Eventually we hit the suburbs of what appeared to be a reasonable sized town and headed towards the city centre.

"Where are you staying?"

"I've no idea" I replied "I didn't know how quickly I would get anywhere so I haven't booked." "Have you any money?" "Yes" "OK then we'll head for the centre and I'll drop you at a hotel".

And so I arrived in Bulawayo, the first leg of my journey completed. I was grateful for my lift and watched the pickup as it drove off.

Next morning, refreshed after a nights' sleep in a comfortable bed and fortified by a good breakfast I set off again. I asked at the hotel desk for directions to the road South and having walked for a short distance picked up my first lift.

I explained where I was headed for and was glad of a ride to the suburbs. There I quickly picked up a second lift which carried me out of the city and left me on the side of the main road when the farmer turned off onto the track which led to his home.

Rather than sit at the roadside I started to walk briskly in the direction of Johannesburg, knowing that I still had some eight hundred and seventy kilometres to go. Several vehicles passed me in the next fifteen minutes and I was beginning to feel the effects of the sun beating down on me when I heard the next car approaching.

I turned to face it and saw a white Chevrolet Impala bearing down on me. I stuck my thumb up and smiled at the driver. The car braked to a stop and the young blonde woman driver stuck her head out of the window and said "Throw your bag in the boot and hop in."

I didn't need a second invitation and got swiftly into the car to find to my surprise that I was in the company of four women all about the same age as me.

"Where are you heading for?" asked the driver smiling at me in the rear view mirror. "Johannesburg" "That's where we're going too" came her reply. I couldn't believe my luck.

Of all the places that they might have been going I didn't expect that they would be travelling all the way to Jo'Burg.

The day passed all too quickly as the car hummed its way through Africa, passing from the bush land of Rhodesia into the high veldt of South Africa. I was transfixed by the changing scenery, the people along the roadside and the rolling grassland as we swept South.

The conversation in the car ranged across numerous subjects. The girls had little previous exposure to anyone from Europe so I had to explain who I was, where I had come from, why I was in Zambia and why I was going to Johannesburg. It all made for an interesting ride.

We stopped for lunch at a restaurant along the way but by evening we had covered the distance and I was in Johannesburg.

Once again I had to find a hotel but guided by the girls I was dropped off in Hillbrow, near the city centre and booked myself into the Cumberland hotel for a few nights.

Next morning opening the bedroom curtains I found that Hillbrow was exactly what it said, the top of the hill and I was looking out over the sprawl that was the city centre.

My first job was to contact David. Hilary's cousin, he had left his native Dublin about the same time that I had left Northern Ireland and had joined Leyland trucks as an engineer in South Africa. We had met on several occasions back home and I had written to him to say that I was coming down to pick up Hilary.

"How was the trip" he asked when I called. I explained that I had hitched my way down as I didn't have a car. "Very impressive" he exclaimed when I gave him the details. "Trust you to get fixed up with four women."

We agreed to meet later in the day after work and have a drink and a meal. David explained that he didn't have a car either. This posed a bit of a problem as we had no transport to get to the airport the following evening to meet Hilary's aircraft. "Not to worry" said David. "I know a girl I've met through the local Methodist church. She has a car and I'm sure if I ask she will give us a lift out."

And so it transpired the following night that David turned up with a girl called Jean and we drove to Jan Smuts airport. A fateful evening for David, although he wasn't to know it at the time, but it was to transform his life as he and Jean went on to marry a couple of years later.

We waited in the airport Terminal for Hilary who duly arrived in an ancient Constellation aircraft, the likes of which I'd never seen before and which proudly announced its arrival some couple of hours late in a cacophony of noise.

After a day or so in Johannesburg for Hilary to spend a little time with David we headed back to the airport and flew North to Livingstone.

Hilary's holiday with me in Mazabuka was all too short. She enjoyed every minute of it, travelling with me in the Land Rover watching me vaccinating children or dealing with mosquitoes or bilharzial snails.

She met the people of Mazabuka and happily mucked in with whatever was going on, enjoying my new friends and the lifestyle.

I particularly enjoyed her relationship with my houseboy. A former chef in a hotel in Rhodesia he was a good cook but was also a diplomat.

When Hilary arrived and insisted in doing things in the kitchen he would stand quietly behind her, watching her efforts and only when it became too much for him would he step forward and gently say "Excuse me madam, let me show you" and then help her to resurrect whatever she was making. It was a good working relationship and we all got on well.

CHAPTER 6

DELIVERY SERVICES

During my first couple of months in Mazabuka I had developed a somewhat tenuous relationship with the two churches in the town, one Anglican and one Roman Catholic, not because I had any strong relationship with the church, despite my upbringing in the Methodist church in Northern Ireland but more because each of the churches possessed an organ and I had a passion for playing the keyboards.

To be honest the Roman Catholic church didn't have an organ when I arrived but they had been saving money to buy themselves one for a number of years. Their efforts duly came to fruition one morning with the delivery from England of an electric organ in a large crate.

I was approached by John Whitehead, an expatriate working in the Government Public Works Department. "What do you know about these things?" he asked me, having popped into my office. "I believe you've been heard playing the organ in the Anglican church?"

He looked questioningly at me. "Yes, but that's about as much as I know about them." "Well would you like to give me a hand to put this one together?"

How could I refuse? So a short while later the two of us, along with a number of Zambian helpers, were sweating to get the components out of the crate and assemble them into a working organ.

As it turned out it wasn't too difficult as much of the organ was ready assembled and only needed to be put together like a jigsaw puzzle and plugged in and before long I was sitting at the keyboard.

The Catholic priest, a Belgian, was delighted. Very proud of his new musical instrument he delighted the congregation at its inauguration by thanking the many Presbyterians in Mazabuka for their generosity, without which there would be no organ and thanking an Ulster Protestant for helping to put it together and for playing it.

The Anglican church was typical of many to be seen in villages throughout the UK. Presided over by Canon Mudford it also had an organ which I would sometimes play for my own pleasure in my spare time.

At this point I must stress that I am not in any way a trained organist. Far from it. As a child I was sent to piano lessons by my mother but after a relatively short time I was removed through lack of effort in practising on my part.

"You'll regret it." I can still hear my mother's voice echoing through my ears. How right she was.

We always had a piano in the house and in my early teens I began to sit down at it and play with the keys.

To my amazement I found that I had a natural ability to play and could, without any real effort play any tune that I could hum.

This had developed over time so that when I reached Zambia I was confident enough to sit down at any keyboard and play a recognizable tune. I could even, with a bit of effort, read the music but usually found it easier just to play by ear.

Given this ability Canon Mudford persuaded me, on a few occasions against my better judgement to play the organ for the Sunday service. This was fine when I knew the hymns but could be a struggle if they were new to me and not out of the Methodist hymnal with which I had grown up.

I also had difficulty in keeping count of how many verses I had actually played in those hymns which ran to more than five. I got round this by asking one of the younger female members of the congregation, Janet, who regularly sat in the front row, to give me a nod when we got to the last verse.

Canon Mudford often said that I played with great verve but I was never sure whether this was meant as a compliment.

Although I had this connection with the church Hilary was nonetheless somewhat startled early in her stay to be invited to morning coffee at the rectory. Canon Mudford's wife had invited a number of ladies of the parish plus her sister visiting from the UK.

In the midst of the conversation the Canon's sister asked Hilary about her mother. When told that she was a staunch member of the Mother's Union in Armagh the visitor immediately responded that she had met Hilary's mum and knew many of her friends as well. What a small world.

Hilary's only worry was that the story of the meeting might get back to her mother who as far as Hilary was concerned wasn't aware that she was actually living with me during her stay.

I wasn't so sure that mother wasn't just turning a blind eye but coming from the era of strict Northern Ireland attitudes. (I always maintain that the swinging sixties didn't get to Northern Ireland until about 1988) Hilary was more than a bit worried but her mother never alluded to it on her return home.

A couple of weeks later Hilary and I were invited to Sunday lunch at the home of the Tate & Lyle Sugar Company Doctor and his wife who were from England. They had also invited Lye Akerele the Doctor at the hospital, and his wife.

It was a pleasant affair and we had just finished dessert when the phone rang. It was a call from the sugar plantation to say that a Doctor was needed urgently as one of the cane cutters had accidentally slashed his leg whilst working in the fields.

This was a relatively common occurrence as cane cutting was done by hand with a machete, wielded normally with some skill to cut the high growing cane at the top and bottom with two rapid sweeping movements.

In doing so it was important to keep the free arm and both legs out of the path of the machete. Within minutes our host was on his way to the plantation.

The rest of us had barely settled down when the phone rang again. This time it was for Lye. As the duty Doctor from the hospital he also was on call. An African patient in the hospital was having a heart attack and they needed Lye urgently.

"A heart attack?" Lye said into the phone. "Are you sure?" he questioned. It was very rare for an African to suffer heart disease probably as a result of their diet.

"OK, I'm on my way" Lye turned and looked at the women. "I'm sorry, I'll have to go, but I'll be back shortly. This shouldn't take too long."

He looked at me. "You may as well come with me Mike. There's no point in you staying with the women."

We ran out of the house and leaping quickly into Lye's car set off for the hospital which was only five minutes away. As we arrived I noticed one of the ambulances turning in to the entrance but didn't pay much attention to it.

Lye parked the car and we hurried through the front doors where the nurse on duty was waiting anxiously to whisk him into the ward to see the patient.

It was quiet and since it was Sunday the Irish Sisters of Charity who made up the bulk of the professional nursing staff were having their day off. I stayed outside talking to some of the orderlies who were there. Meanwhile the ambulance that I had noticed as we arrived, was discharging its patient.

Suddenly Lye appeared again, this time walking rapidly in the direction taken by the ambulance crew and their patient.

I continued to wait in the lobby whilst Lye went about his work as I wasn't medically trained and had no business going into a medical ward.

Suddenly Lye appeared alongside me. "Come with me quickly, I need your help." I followed him down the corridor and into a room.

It was very spartan. The main object in the room was a simple metal bed on which was lying a young African girl. There were no covers on the bed and she was as naked as the day she was born and obviously in the throes of giving birth.

A table to the right of the bed held a set of scales and a box of medical equipment.

"Roll your sleeves up" Lye said brusquely. I did as I was told, more than a bit surprised and wondering what was coming next.

"This girl has just arrived. She's been in labour for about 24 hours and I've no idea what they've been doing with her or giving her in the village before she was brought in but it hasn't worked. You're going to have to deliver her since the guy with the heart attack has apparently just decided to have another one."

All this information was given to me in seconds. I couldn't quite believe what Lye had just said.

I looked around for help. There was no one else.

Lye continued quickly. "I've given her a shot of anaesthetic" he said pointing at the girl's lower regions. "Just to make sure she doesn't tear she may have to be opened up slightly. If you need to do it, make a small incision here. It's mostly fatty tissue so shouldn't give you any problems."

He pointed to the spot.

"This is a vacuum pump" he continued, placing a strange looking piece of equipment into my hands. "It works like this" he demonstrated, "but don't apply it too hard otherwise the baby's head may come out egg shaped. I'll be back in a couple of minutes." At which he disappeared at a gallop out of the room, heading back to his heart attack victim.

"This can't be happening", I thought. I looked around again and yes, I was still totally on my own.

I approached the girl. She looked up and smiled at me. Her knuckles were nearly white as she gripped the metal bed head as tightly as she could.

The look on her face was one of relief and I realized that as I was the only European that she had seen since her arrival, she thought that I was the Doctor and that as far as she was concerned the cavalry had just arrived and all was well.

"How little do you know" I thought as I bent down to start my task. I could see the crown of the baby's head so I applied the vacuum pump as I had been told. The girl pushed hard but nothing moved and it seemed even to my untrained eye, that something was likely to give way if I wasn't careful.

I took the scalpel which Lye had given me and took a deep breath. I applied it gently where I had been shown. The girl didn't flinch. Thank God for the anaesthetic. I then picked up the pump again and re-applied it to the baby's head. The girl braced herself and pushed again. This time the baby moved and I turned the pump gently to the right gradually manoeuvering the head and shoulders clear.

Then with what appeared to be a sudden rush, the baby was there.

I looked incredulously at this miracle of life now sprawled on the waterproof cover on the bottom of the bed.

Picking it up gently I cleaned its face and it burst into a lusty cry. "Well at least it appears to be OK" was my first thought.

I continued to clean its face and mouth and noted that it was a boy, somewhat multicoloured by the efforts of his arrival into the world. I then wrapped him in a cloth to keep him warm pending the arrival of some assistance.

Help wasn't long coming as Lye made a breathless appearance at my side. He cast a professional eye over the scene. "Well done. It all looks good" he said. "You haven't done this before by any chance?" he grinned at me.

"No, never, I've only read about it"

A moment later the duty nurse arrived and proceeded to deal with the umbilical cord and release the baby from his maternal tie.

Lye looked at my work with the scalpel. "Excellent" he commented "now we'll have to sew her up again". He picked out a ready prepared needle and started to stitch. Then he swore. "What's happened?"

"You won't believe it but the damned needle has broken" he showed me what was left in his hand. "Well we've got one chance at finding it in here" he said delving into the fatty tissue at his fingertips "otherwise it will need an x ray"

Then he broke into a smile "Got it" His triumphant smile was a joy to behold.

We tidied up quickly and with a few words to the mother and some instructions to the duty nurse we made our way back to the car and thence back to the coffee which would be waiting for us.

As I walked into the lounge on return to our host's home Hilary looked at me. "What's wrong with you, you're as white as a sheet?" "He's just delivered a baby" Lye said with a broad grin. "He's what?" Hilary said incredulously.

Lye confirmed it and then we had to go over the detail of what had actually happened.

I'm not sure that Hilary believed the story and to be honest even today I can't believe what I actually did. It probably took only a few minutes although at the time it seemed like hours and it was so bizarre as to be unbelievable. Nonetheless a high point in my life and one never to be forgotten.

CHAPTER 7

IT'S NOT WHAT YOU KNOW
IT'S WHO YOU KNOW

All too soon Hilary's holiday was over and we set out in my newly returned car to drive back to Johannesburg.

The route allowed us to stop for a couple of days at Livingstone on the Zambian side of the Victoria Falls where, as it was coming towards the end of the dry season, the water coming over the top of the mile wide falls was reduced to a mere trickle when compared to the millions of tons which cascade over the edge at the end of the wet season. The comparison is truly awesome.

Staying overnight in a small game lodge close to the falls and with the noise of the rushing water in our ears we stood under a full moon and contemplated the magnificence of the scene. In such a romantic setting I should have taken the opportunity to propose to Hilary but to my never ending regret I didn't work up the nerve to do it. That was to come later.

We drove South through Rhodesia and the Transvaal to Johannesburg, savouring every mile of rolling scenery and having reached the city checked in again at the Cumberland hotel and contacted David.

We agreed to meet and were delighted to see that when he arrived he had Jean with him. They both wanted to hear all about Hilary's holiday and at the end of the evening Jean invited us to dinner to meet her parents.

It transpired that her father was the Chairman of the Standard Bank of South Africa. The son of English immigrants he claimed to have started life in the bank as the tea boy and had made his way to the top.

Jean's parents were a lovely couple and her brother, an up and coming paediatrician, was also home for dinner. The family lived in Houghton, an upmarket suburb of Johannesburg and they couldn't have been more welcoming.

Being South African and never having been North into Zambia they were intrigued and full of questions as to how we lived up there. They found it hard to believe that we lived in relative comfort, in fully equipped and furnished modern bungalow and that many things in Mazabuka were little different from in Johannesburg.

Having a connection within the Standard Bank was to prove a godsend a day or two later. When Hilary contacted the company with whom she was to fly back to the UK she found to her consternation that the flight was delayed by two days!

Whilst we were both happy to stay together for a little longer and to enjoy the sights and sounds of Johannesburg, I had a limited amount of money with me.

This was in a time long before credit and debit cards had been invented so getting money out of the "hole in the wall" wasn't an option.

To add to the difficulty, Zambia had a strict currency control regime to ensure that the country's finances were not depleted by too much currency being moved out of the country.

"Not to worry" Jean said when she learned of the problem. "I'm sure that dad can sort something out. Come up to the house and speak to him."

I approached her father in some trepidation but I needn't have worried. He was friendly and straight to the point. "Have you got your cheque book with you? "Yes" I replied. "Well just write me a cheque for however much you think you will need and I will cash it for you."

"But what about the exchange controls? Will you get your money back?" I asked. I didn't want him to lose out, particularly when they had been so kind to us.

"Don't worry about it. Just leave it to me" and that was that.

I had forgotten all about the cheque until some six weeks later, whilst standing at the bar at the golf club after work, I heard a friendly Ulster accent beside me.

"It must be nice to have friends in high places." I turned to see the Deputy Manager from the local branch of the Standard Bank standing beside me with a questioning look on his face.

A fellow Ulsterman, I knew him well.

"What are you on about?" I had a puzzled look on my face.

"Friends in high places who can cash cheques for you" he replied with a grin. The penny dropped.

"I've never seen a cheque made out to and countersigned by the Chairman of the bank and I'm never likely to see another" he continued.

"How do you know him?" His emphasis was strongly on the "him."

"Ah well" I said, tapping the side of my nose with one finger, "that's for me to know and for you to guess at." I kept him wondering for weeks before I told him the whole story and he laughed. "Luck of the Irish I suppose" were his final words.

Back in Jo'burg Hilary and I were saying our goodbyes at the airport. The aircraft had duly arrived two days late and now deep into the evening was preparing to board the passengers.

The day before I had finally taken the plunge and asked Hilary to marry me. To my surprise she had agreed but I would have to do things properly and write to her father to ask for his permission which in due course I did.

Meanwhile David and Jean had delivered us to the airport and were standing quietly in the background whilst Hilary and I parted. It was to be more than a year later and only two weeks before our wedding before we would meet again and a lot of water was to pass under bridges before then

For Hilary it was a long trek back home and for me a long drive back to life in Zambia.

Home in Mazabuka, life was not without its excitement and unusual moments. I previously mentioned the railway line which ran through the town. Part of Cecil Rhodes original idea to link Capetown to Cairo the line ran all the way from South Africa through Rhodesia, into Zambia and North to the Zambia copper mines which were the backbone of the economy at that time.

The recent unilateral declaration of independence by Ian Smith in Rhodesia in the face of British proposals for independence on the basis of majority rule posed major problems for Zambia.

Smith's declaration was followed by embargoes placed on the shipment of goods or services to and from Rhodesia by the International community. Zambia however is completely landlocked and its only connection to the outside world was by road, air or the rail connection South into Rhodesia.

As a result, for many years the coal used to fire the copper smelters in the mines in the Copperbelt as the production area was known was provided from the Hwange coal mines in Rhodesia and shipped North by train. The trains on their return journey carried copper.

Despite the International embargo, and Zambia's continual denouncement of the illegal Smith regime, this had to continue, but no-one was supposed to know.

It was with some amusement, therefore that the expatriate population in Mazabuka, watched the huge freight trains regularly rolling slowly through the town, normally headed by at least a couple of enormous GE Diesel locomotives.

The chain of wagons carrying coal or copper stretched for upwards of half a mile and were loaded in such a way that their contents weren't visible from the trackside.

Some would pass through during the day but often they could be heard rumbling through the night when the mournful sound of the train horn could be heard across many mile of bush, long before the train was anywhere near Mazabuka station. A sound which is etched in my memory and which I later came to hear in the USA from similar locomotives operating trains across the vast American plains.

Additionally, we had two passenger trains a day, one in each direction where the excitement generated by their arrival at indiscriminate times each day, (they weren't renowned for any semblance of time keeping), was palpable.

Crowds thronged the station. Food and drink sellers vied with each other to tempt the passengers with their wares, carried precariously on their heads. Fruit, vegetables, bread, cakes, the list was interminable.

Passengers fought to get themselves and their baggage on or off the train before, with a waving of flags and blowing of whistles, it would eventually creep into movement and lumber slowly down the track.

The track was a single line operation with passing points at various stations and locations along the way. Such operations on any railroad are dangerous if not strictly controlled and one night whilst I was in bed I was suddenly awoken by an enormous explosion.

At least that was what I thought it was. I couldn't be sure that I had heard anything but dogs were barking across the town. On looking out the window I could see nothing, so went back to bed somewhat bemused.

Next morning the town was abuzz with what had happened the night before.

"Have you heard what happened last night?" my Senior Assistant said as I came into the office. "No" I said "But something woke me."

"Oh there has been a terrible train crash. One of the freight trains traveling North ran into the back of a second train which was waiting to pass a South bound train "I was told.

The crash had happened some distance North in an area which was remote from the main road and therefore difficult to get to. Rumour abounded all day but when news eventually got back from the site it appeared that one of the trains involved had been carrying explosives for the copper mines which detonated in the accident.

The result was a crater some quarter of a mile across, one locomotive standing on end in the bush and the death of the train crews involved. The daily paper, the Times of Zambia tended to confirm the rumours in a report the following day.

"That's what comes of letting the locals run the railway" was the disparaging remark made by one of the regulars in the golf club that evening. "They couldn't run a piss up in a brewery" he added.

From time to time other strange rumblings were heard or perhaps it would be more appropriate to say felt.

Standing in one of the external offices at the hospital one morning, I heard a heavy rumble and felt the building shaking as if a very large lorry was driving past. Turning round I suddenly realized that I was alone. Walking out of the door I found my Zambian colleagues convulsed with laughter to the point of almost falling on the ground.

I couldn't see what was so funny until I realized that I was the centre of their amusement. "What's going on" I said. "It is an earthquake Bwana" One of the lads eventually managed to get the words out between his giggles.

They thought that it was hilarious that I had not realised that there was an earthquakes happening and had stayed inside the building! It hadn't crossed their minds that someone should perhaps have warned me?

This was my first experience of such an event but wasn't to be the last. They happened from time to time and many of the locals put them down to the building of the Kariba dam saying that the weight of water building in the lake formed by the dam was causing earth settlement on a very large scale.

Being no expert on the subject I'm not able to comment on whether this was right or wrong but it did provide for some interesting discussion amongst the expats.

When, in Northern Ireland, I had first contemplated going to Zambia I had been told of two former residents of Bangor who now lived there.

The first was the daughter of the sexton at our local Methodist church. A few years older than me she had gone to Zambia as a telephone operator and had subsequently met and married a South African mining engineer. They lived in Luanshya, a garden town in the Copperbelt near the city of Ndola.

I knew Margaret by sight but she wasn't a close friend as such. However, on hearing that I was flying out to Zambia her father contacted me and said that Margaret was looking forward to meeting me when I got there and would I do her a favour and take with me the one thing that she couldn't buy in Luanshya. A loaf of good Irish wheaten brown bread.

"Certainly." So when my plane touched down in Ndola, en route to its final stop at Lusaka, Margaret was standing by the fence just a few yards from the aircraft when it came to a halt outside the small terminal building.

Unfortunately, as the stop was very short and in order to let disembarking passengers leave quickly, the passengers in transit to Lusaka were told to stay on board, so I had a slight dilemma.

I was sitting in my seat clutching a brown paper parcel in which reposed the wheaten bread. Eventually I plucked up courage and rang the call bell. A stewardess appeared almost immediately to enquire as to what I wanted. I sheepishly told her that I had a parcel for the lady whom we could see standing by the fence, waving at me as I peered through the window.

The stewardess looked at me suspiciously. "And what's in the parcel?" she enquired. "Some brown bread" I said, feeling myself reddening in embarrassment. "Apparently they can't get it here" I went on. "That's OK. Give it to me and I'll take it over" which she promptly did. I could see her explaining to Margaret, who took the parcel and looking towards the aircraft waved. I was to catch up with her later

The other contact I was given before leaving for Zambia was Graham

Wallace and his wife Anne. Graham like me was an Environmental Health officer who had in his student days, some years prior to me, trained in the same office in Bangor as me.

He had then gone to Kenya to work but many were the tales I had heard about him, particularly about his swimming prowess, some of which was practised when as a student he should have been working.

My mentor in my student days, Bertie, used to recall the days when he had to drive down to the Pickie swimming pool on Bangor seafront and yell over the wall to get Graham to come out.

Graham and Anne lived in Lusaka with their three children. Graham was the Senior lecturer in Environmental Health at the Evelyn Hone College, training staff for the Zambian Health Service and they were to become a home from home for me over my months in Mazabuka, which was a relatively short drive to Lusaka.

They had a lovely house with very productive gardens filled with fruit and vegetables. Graham had a wonderful dry sense of humour and I enjoyed many hours talking with him on the veranda of their bungalow, glass of beer in hand, putting the world to rights.

Their friendship and support of a young and very green Ulsterman was much appreciated and continues to this day although they have chosen to make their home in Zambia and so we see them only rarely.

CHAPTER 8

LIVINGSTONE

Quite soon after my arrival, my stay in Mazbuka was interrupted by the need to go to Livingstone and deputise for John Muirden who was going on six weeks leave. I was to stay with David, a friend of John, as his wife was also away on leave.

Livingstone was a nice town. A few miles from the Victoria Falls it was a pleasure to be able to drive out to the falls after a day in the office and just sit beside them watching the water plunging down the 360 feet sheer drop into the gorge beneath. I never tired of it.

The wording on a sign at the adjacent car park commemorated the "finding" of the falls by David Livingstone. Not that he actually found them. After all they had been there for millions of years so it would have been more truthful to say that he was possibly the first European to see them.

What surprised me was the realization that his finding had taken place marginally more than one hundred years previously, almost within living memory for some people and far removed from my idea of history as it had been taught to me.

My first few days in Livingstone were actually spent at the airport hotel where I got to know some of the bush pilots who flew for Zambia Airways into the far flung hinterland to places further up the Zambezi valley such as Mongu.

The airport itself was a reasonable size and had daily direct services to Lusaka operated by modern BAC1-11 jets.

The flights into the bush were a different kettle of fish altogether. They were operated by De Havilland Beaver aircraft, a rugged Canadian designed plane fitted with a single Pratt and Whitney radial engine and six passenger seats.

Ideal for flying in and out of dirt airstrips in Zambia they provided the only sensible means of transport to some of the more remote mission stations and several times I watched as two or three nuns strapped themselves into their seats, crossed themselves and said a prayer for their safe deliverance before roaring noisily down the runway.

At night I sat and drank beer with the Beaver pilots, many of whom had chequered careers, often starting in military service and then running the gamut of numerous small airlines in different parts of the world, most of them destined to become bankrupt at some stage thus causing the pilots to move on.

They were gypsies in the world of aviation and were more interesting because of that.

Work in the office consisted mainly of administration duties as I didn't know John's district and wasn't expected to do much more than keep things ticking over whilst he was away and for the first couple of days he and I worked together as a handover.

My short spell in Livingstone had one sour point. I had moved from the hotel and was sharing a house with David, a friend of John's, whose wife was on leave.

One evening I decided to go to the cinema. As David didn't want to come I drove down using John's wife's Morris Minor car which they had left for my use. I parked immediately outside the cinema in the main street and went in to watch. Imagine my horror when on coming out a couple of hours later, the Morris had gone.

I looked up and down the street frantically but there was no sign of it. I questioned myself as to where I had left it and yes I was sure that I had parked right outside.

I then thought "Has David come down and picked it up for some reason?" I really didn't want to believe that it had been stolen.

I walked back through the dark streets into the suburbs and up to the house. Turning into the driveway my heart sank. The car wasn't there.

I went inside and asked David if he had moved the car. The answer was negative. The police were advised and that was that, or so it seemed.

I was due to go back to Mazabuka, a few days later and I left with a heavy heart as I didn't know what I was going to say to John when next I saw him or worse still what I would say to his wife to whom the car belonged.

I had only been back for two days when I got a message from David. "I've found the car" he said. "It was in Choma."

Choma was a town some 100 miles North on the main road from Livingstone heading towards Lusaka.

"I just heard a rumour that the car was there so I went up to see and there it was. It has a bit of damage but I can get that fixed. If you just send me 100 Kwatcha (the equivalent of £50) I'll get it sorted out."

I was so relieved that I sent a cheque in the post that afternoon. It wasn't until some considerable time later that I began to think about it. How would he have heard that the car was in Choma? Why would he have gone to the trouble of driving to Choma to look for it?

How, having got to Choma would he have known where to go to find it? Choma was a relatively large town and it was unlikely that had a local Zambian stolen it that it would have been parked in the main street or for that matter, given that some days had passed since its disappearance, would it necessarily be the original colour.

The more I thought the more I wondered. I knew that David had money problems and £50 was a lot of money in the late sixties which I could ill afford but I will never know and I may well be misjudging the man.

CHAPTER 9

FROG'S LEGS?

Back in Mazabuka after my short spell in Livingstone life was fun for a young single male.

Hilary having gone back to the UK I was one of the lads again and life returned to working, interspersed with evenings in the golf club where I was rapidly introduced to games such as liar dice, best played after everyone has had a few pints.

There were regular dinner parties and barbecues amongst the expatriates who were always happy to invite the single people along.

I was still somewhat naïve, which became obvious to me one evening when at a garden party I was approached by a young female who proceeded to engage me in conversation, firstly asking whether or not I was enjoying the food and particularly the frog's legs on crackers which I was eating.

Coming from Northern Ireland my familiarity with frog's legs was limited to the fact that I believed that the French were reputedly very fond of them. However, I couldn't be outdone so agreed that they were very pleasant.

The young lady was tall, very poised, well-spoken and sure of herself. She told me that she was the daughter of one of the newly arrived families but that they had lived abroad for some time.

"You're on your own?" she asked. "Yes." "You're not married?" I wasn't quite sure where this conversation was going but I had my suspicions.

Just at that moment one of the guys from the Bank came up. "Can I have a word?" he said to me. "Excuse us for just a minute" he said over his shoulder to my companion as he walked me away.

"She's only thirteen" he whispered in my ear. "She's what?" I said in amazement. I looked back at her, now in serious conversation with another woman.

"You're joking." "I'm not" he said laughing at me.

"I have to admit she looks a good eighteen or nineteen and you're not the only one that she's fooled." "How do you know?" I asked.

"The family was in Mufulira before coming here and that was my last posting as well so I've known them for a while."

"Thanks for the warning" was all I could say, grateful for the intervention as I realized what a fool I could have made of myself.

It wasn't the only surprise I had however. Sunday was the day off for my house servant or houseboy as they were normally called. This meant that I had to fend for myself, which was no great hardship.

One Sunday night as I was sitting reading on my sofa I heard a knock at the door. I opened it to find to my surprise a young woman outside. It was Janet, the pretty, teenaged daughter of one of the senior nursing staff at the hospital. The family were British by origin but long term residents in Zambia. I knew and liked her mother a lot.

"Hello" she said. "Come in, what can I do for you?" She smiled. "Well I know that this is your houseboy's day off so I just came round to see if you need any help and if there is anything that I can do for you?"

She smiled beguilingly at me again. "That's nice of you but no I'm fine thanks." "You won't mind if I stay and chat will you? This is such a boring town and there's nothing to do on Sunday night." It was hard to refuse and over the next few Sundays Janet became a regular feature.

I even took her out to dinner one night. By then I had found out from the other lads that if you wanted to take a girl out it was possible to drive to Lusaka in around an hour and a half, have dinner and be home again by midnight so I thought that I would give it a try with Janet.

We drove up in my Rover, had a meal and a bottle of wine in the Chinese restaurant on Cairo Road, the main street in the city, and spent our time happily chatting.

It was a pleasant evening until, on the way back, as I was driving along the darkened highway, I suddenly realized that Janet wasn't very well.

The car screeched to a halt as I braked hard, leapt out of my door, dashed round to her side, dragged her rapidly out and held her hair back from her face as she discharged the Chinese meal all over the roadside.

Somewhat shaken, embarrassed and abashed, she eventually got back into the car and I got her home.

The next day her mother caught me in the hospital. "What happened last night?" she asked me. I didn't quite know what to say.

I didn't feel that I had done anything wrong and Janet had only drunk a couple of glasses of wine when we had set off for home. "I don't really know" was my answer. "I know that Janet wasn't very well but I don't know why"

"Nor does she" replied her mum. "She didn't drink too much according to her" she carried on, looking questioningly at me.

"I don't think so" and I explained what we had had.

"I only knew she was ill when I found her handbag floating in the bath this morning" her mother continued. "I don't understand?" I said looking at her.

"Didn't you know? She didn't want to make a mess in your car so when she started to be sick she threw up into her handbag" said mum.

"What a girl" I thought. How many others would have been so thoughtful and quick thinking?

Our friendship was to prove short lived however. One evening whilst swimming with friends in their pool in the garden, I casually mentioned to Janet that she was putting on a few ounces. She stared at me coldly, but then what did I expect from being so tactless with a woman.

Nothing more was said for a couple of weeks when suddenly one Sunday evening when we were sitting on the sofa together she suddenly turned to me and said "I'm pregnant."

I looked at her unbelievingly then said stupidly "How?" "How do you think" she said before bursting into tears.

"I've ruined everything" Eventually she calmed down and told me that the culprit was Chusky, he with the fondness for snakes.

It appeared that I wasn't the only male in town with whom Janet had been friendly and with some obviously more friendly than others!!

CHAPTER 10

IT'S BETTER TO TRAVEL WELL THAN TO ARRIVE?

Given the size of my district I had of necessity to spend long periods of time driving, mostly in a short wheel based Land Rover. Some of this time was on the main road tarmac road leading either North or South from Mazabuka but long periods were also on the laterite dirt roads leading into the more remote areas.

Normally there was very little traffic on any of the roads and meeting another driver was such a rarity that it normally gave cause for a friendly wave. One morning, returning to Mazabuka along the main road from Livingstone, I had just passed the town of Monze and was happily trundling along a very straight stretch of road, some seven miles visible ahead of me as it undulated into the distance.

I was vaguely aware of a truck some distance in front heading in the same direction but paid no attention to it and given the undulating road it was only briefly in view. A few minutes later, having covered some three miles or so I came out of a dip in the road to see a large road tanker lying on its side a few hundred feet off the road on the left, its wheels still revolving slowly.

An African girl was standing beside the truck waving frantically. I screeched to a halt and leapt from the Land Rover. Running towards her I took in the picture at a glance.

The truck had been carrying a consignment of local Chibuku beer, which was pouring out and flooding the surrounding area. "Ugh" I thought as I waded into the stinking liquid.

The truck driver had been ejected from the vehicle as it had overturned and was lying on the ground. I bent over him. He was unconscious and a closer examination showed me that he was dead.

The girl was screaming hysterically. Although she had a bleeding gash on her right lower leg she didn't appear to be hurt but was obviously shocked. She wouldn't stop screaming until I was forced to slap her.

I walked her across to my Land Rover, bundled her in and drove as fast as I could back to Monze where I knew there was a District hospital. It took about ten minutes and having delivered her to the emergency arrival area I ran to the hospital Matron's office to advise her about the accident and activate an ambulance to go to the scene.

Given the fact that the girl was well dressed in European style I could only assume that she had been picked up along the route by the driver who subsequently became distracted by her presence and drove off the road.

After checking that the girl was being looked after I climbed back into my vehicle and set off again for home, following the ambulance back along the road.

I now stank of Chibuku!! There's never a dull moment I thought!!

Driving into the rural areas could sometimes prove problematical as I was to find out when a few days later I was on my way to a remote school some miles from Mazabuka.

Having turned off the main road I was happily driving along the dirt track when I heard a bump, bump, bump from the rear of the Land Rover.

Coming to a halt in a cloud of red dust and jumping down onto the road I was faced with a flat rear tyre.

"Just my luck" I thought. However, it shouldn't take too long to fix.

Dropping the tail board, I climbed into the back to get the spare wheel. Looking at the space where the wheel should have been, I thought, "I don't believe it. I'll kill him when I get back."

I was thinking of the motor transport manager at the hospital who was responsible for maintaining all the trucks.

I jumped back onto the road and settled down in the shade under a tree, waiting for someone to come along. "This could be a long wait" I thought. I also realized at that moment that being a relative newcomer to the country I had forgotten the one requirement for travelling. Water, without which I could rapidly dehydrate.

Luckily my wait wasn't too long. Some 30 minutes later I heard the unmistakable sound of a Land Rover approaching and as it drew alongside me I recognized the driver as one of the local farmers.

"You OK Mike?" I explained the situation and without too much ado he offloaded his spare wheel to replace my flat and soon I was following him back to the hospital where I replaced the wheel.

I was less than best pleased at having lost my afternoon's work and rapidly let the motor transport manager have the benefit of my thoughts. He stood looking very abashed and apologized profusely. "I'm sorry Bwana, it won't happen again" he said, with his staff looking on somewhat shamefacedly knowing that they were probably going to cop some of his anger once I had left.

Two days later I was back on the road again in a different Land Rover, heading out along another dirt road. Suddenly I heard the all too familiar sound, bump, bump, bump again. "I don't believe it" I thought to myself. "Twice in two trips!"

I halted in a cloud of red dust and having jumped out was faced with another flat rear tyre. "Damn!!"

I dropped the tailboard and looked into the back and heaved a sigh of relief as I saw the spare wheel.

I jumped in, unfastened it and dropped it out onto the road.

I turned to pick up the wheel jack and wheel brace without which I couldn't remove the wheel. They weren't there!!

"I'll have his guts for garters this time" I ranted out loud as I jumped back onto the road and kicked the flat tyre. I just couldn't believe it after all I had said the last time.

Again I sat down in the shade and waited before eventually another vehicle came along and I was rescued again.

My words to the motor transport manager when I got back to the hospital are not repeatable but I saw some of my team grinning from ear to ear as they heard me lambast him

CHAPTER 11

EAST TO CHIPATA

At the end of my first year I was surprised to get a message from Head Office advising me that I was being transferred to Eastern Province to join Charlie Mardy the Senior Health officer who was on his own up there.

And so I packed up what belongings I had, said goodbye to the friends I had made in Mazabuka and set off to drive the 393 miles up the Great East Road from Lusaka to Chipata, the most Easterly Provincial capital in Zambia.

Leaving Lusaka on a bright morning driving through the suburbs, I passed the Parliament building on my left, crowned by the square copper Parliament chamber as an expression of the copper wealth on which the country was founded.

Adjacent to it was the newly constructed conference centre built to host a meeting of the Organisation of African Unity. The building had been done very rapidly within a matter of a few weeks and not only had it used up all available building materials in the country at the time but had raised some bets amongst the expatriate community as to how long it was likely to remain standing!

Travelling East I passed a construction team building the new tarred road before eventually joining the familiar dirt surface. As with all dirt roads it rapidly became ridged into ripples, particularly on corners and could provide a rough ride if it hadn't been "graded" recently by one of the oft seen road machines which drove along levelling the surface.

Chipata to which I was headed had previously been called Fort Jameson and was one of the early settlements in Northern Rhodesia.

It is the Provincial capital of Eastern province which in part forms Zambia's border with Mozambique and Malawi and is linked to the capital Lusaka via the single main road along which I was driving.

Along the route the road crosses the Luangwa river, a major tributary of the Zambesi, and which for much of its journey forms the Western boundary of the province. Arriving at the river I was faced by a modern high level suspension bridge, constructed, according to the commemoration plaque by a well-known British engineering company.

I know nothing much about bridge engineering but enough to recognize that there had been a problem with this bridge. The sag in the middle was patently obvious and the sign at the entrance stated "One vehicle at a time and slow speed". I crossed it very gingerly!!

The road then climbed tortuously upwards towards Nyimba some 3,000 feet up on the top of the Central African plateau. The scenery was magnificent. Rolling hilltops interspersed with tracts of dense scrubby bush.

It was very easy to imagine that if you had an accident and disappeared off the road here that you would never be found.

Similarly, if you drove a short way off the road and got out of your vehicle it would be very likely that no-one in the history of the World would ever have stood on that particular piece of the earth before. A fascinating thought.

About 50 miles short of Chipata I passed another road construction team, this one working West to meet their colleagues coming the other way.

I knew that I was getting close to my destination when I reached a sign on the road, pointing the way to Chipata airport up a road to the left. From here into the town, a distance of a few miles, the road was tarred. I was to learn later that this had been done some years earlier when the area had been visited by the Queen Mother.

The visit resulted in the only piece of tarred road in the entire area, specially laid for the occasion from the airport to the town centre!

Chipata was situated about halfway up Eastern province. It was a busy, bustling town of some 32,000 people with the centre being on a crossroads dominated by Barclays bank on one corner and a petrol filling station on the other.

My new boss Charlie Mardy was pleased to see me and welcomed me into the Health office. He was a short, rotund, bespectacled Northerner from Manchester who was on his second contract in Zambia and knew his way around.

We immediately hit it off well and in a very short time were to become not only good working companions but good friends as well.

The office was much bigger than that which I had in Mazabuka. It was actually a suite of offices, ideally positioned facing the local library across the street and immediately adjacent to the Golf Club.

Not only did Charlie and I have an office each but we also had offices at the rear for our Health team and the local LEPRA representative who was responsible for leprosy care and control in the area.

"I'm afraid you're going to have to live in the Government hostel for the moment" Charlie told me. "It's just up the road so I'll go up with you, introduce you and let you get your things unpacked." "Sounds good to me."

We drove up the road running alongside the Golf course and within a couple of minutes arrived at the door of the hostel.

The building turned out to be more of a small hotel than a hostel and was occupied by most of the unmarried expatriate staff working in and around Chipata. The individual rooms were comfortably furnished with each room sharing a bathroom with one other room.

The dining room and lounge areas were spacious and Charlie told me that the food was good. What more could I have wished for? I quickly unpacked and settled in.

CHAPTER 12

THIS SPORTING LIFE

The community in Chipata was very different from that which I had left in Mazabuka. Whilst there was some farming carried out in the area around the town it wasn't as extensive as it had been in Southern province, or at least that's how it seemed to me.

The lifestyle however was similar although at first glance there seemed to be more expatriate contract staff and fewer local farmers or town residents.

I quickly found that as in Mazabuka, the sports club was the centre of the social life in the town. It was a relic of the old Colonial era with a long and chequered history.

Built in the very early days of the twentieth century when the first European explorers and settlers were venturing into the depths of Africa it delighted in its name, "The Victoria Memorial Institute" or "the VMI" as it was colloquially known.

Originally designed to provide a sporting club with bedrooms and meals available for those farmers and travellers who lived some distance from town and needed accommodation on their rare visits to collect supplies, it was now only a shadow of its former self.

A bust of Queen Victoria with the plaque reminding readers that the building was constructed "to the immortal memory of her Majesty" was still in its niche in the wall by the library but the building was slowly being eaten by termites and has probably now long since disappeared.

However, the bar was still in good working order, staffed by a number of uniformed and respectful staff and the badminton, tennis and cricket facilities were functioning well.

A short distance down the road, beyond the crossroads was the Golf Club. An off shoot of the VMI it was well patronised, particularly in the evening after work, when many of the expats would gather for a sundowner on the veranda prior to going home for dinner.

Fortunately for Charlie and me the Golf Club was right beside our office and reaching the veranda took just three minutes as we could step over the very low boundary wall and walk across the car park.

The expatriate population probably numbered around one hundred. Although the majority lived in or around the town, there were several who had been posted to schools or agricultural establishments some distance away but who were able to come to town at weekends and were generally happy to sleep in someone's spare room or grab a bit of floor space.

I was rapidly assimilated into the group. On my first evening Charlie took me across the car park and into the bar. "This is Mike" he said, introducing me to a number of interested faces.

He then rapidly ran a number of names past me as he introduced the eight or ten people who were sitting on the veranda each with a glass of something alcoholic in their hand. "Hi Mike" came the response, almost in unison.

"Where are you from?" "Is this your first station in Zambia?" "How long have you been here?" "What do you do?" The questions came thick and fast.

Charlie put a gin and tonic in my hand and I started to answer. Within minutes it seemed as though I had been there forever and that I had known these people for a long time.

They made me feel instantly welcome and within a few minutes I was amazed to find that several of them came from Northern Ireland and that one couple came from Newtownards, a town only a short distance from my family home.

Many of the group were teachers. Some from the local primary school, some from the secondary school situated just out of town and one or two were lecturers in the local teacher training academy.

There was also a sprinkling of bank staff from Barclays' bank on the corner. They lived in the bank mess provided for the junior staff although George, the manager, and his wife lived in a local house.

Most of the teachers lived in housing provided at their school whilst many of the rest of us were in the Government rest house which was also my home for the present.

The golf course was like nothing I had ever seen before. Carved out of the bush it had only nine holes.

Its major difference from any other club I had ever played at was that the putting greens didn't have any grass. Instead the putting surface was made from sand. I watched transfixed as a group of players approached the last "green" situated just in front of the veranda.

The group carried with them a piece of wood shaped like a garden rake and different only in so far as the blade was a solid piece of wood.

Charlie looked at me and could see that I was wondering what was happening.

"Local rules apply" he said with a laugh. "Watch."

I watched as the players took it in turn to mark their ball then, using the "rake" they levelled the sand by drawing a straight line, about a foot wide, from their ball to the hole and back again.

"You're only allowed one rake in each direction" Charlie remarked. I watched as the players took their turn to level the sand and make their put.

"We haven't enough water to water the greens and keep grass on them all year" Charlie explained, although by this time I had worked it out for myself.

"Doesn't it make it easy?" I asked. "Not as easy as you would think. The sand is relatively hard so although the ball doesn't run anything like as fast as on a proper green it can still be difficult to judge." I was soon to find out for myself.

We sat on the veranda and chatted over drinks as the sun set rapidly behind the hills. It was to become a regular nightly ritual and given the amount of alcohol consumed I'm surprised that my liver is still intact.

I settled in fairly quickly and soon found out that the expats were a very gregarious group. Everyone played sport in some form or other. Most people played golf and apart from games after work, there were regular weekend and monthly competitions. The course was relatively tough.

Given that the Zambia climate had two distinct seasons, dry from April to October and wet for the other six months, the course could be either baked hard where your ball would fly off the surface and could cover prodigious distances, mostly into the rough in my case, or alternatively was soggily wet when the ball would plug into the mud and preferred lies had to be used on the fairways.

For the non-golfers reading this, that means that you could dig your ball out of the mud and set it up on a small tee of mud or grass so that it could be hit relatively cleanly.

To add to this the rough was in many places almost impenetrable. During the wet season the grass could grow to several feet in height and a ball driven into it would test the best of the young Zambian caddies who accompanied us whilst carrying our clubs.

Undeterred by the fact that the grass might be hiding all manner of wildlife the caddy would plunge into it with a suitable iron in his hand. Wielding this he would disappear often for several minutes.

"Caddy!" The shout was usually followed by a cry of "Here bwana" and a club would be seen waving out of the long grass. "Have you found it?" "Yes bwana" "Is it playable?" "No bwana" "Then bring it out."

Many a happy hour was spent on the course and not a few balls were lost in that time.

Whilst both tennis and badminton were played at the main club house the male contingent also played cricket, football and rugby. The cricket and football were local games played against local town teams and although I wasn't much of a cricketer I got roped in on one of my first weekends to play for the expatriate side in a game against the "Retailers".

Turning up for the game I recognized the opposition as being comprised of members of the local Indian community, most of whom were retailers in what was known as the first class trading area.

A hark back to the colonial days this was the shopping area which had originally been used mainly by the "white" population although, following independence was now used by everyone.

Some of the Indian lads were sons of traders who had walked through the bush into Chipata some fifty years previously to set up their businesses. The match was played in good spirit and thoroughly enjoyed.

The following week I turned out again to play a match against the "Wholesalers" Looking at the opposition I was surprised to see the same players that I had seen the previous week.

"But it's the same team that we played last week" I said to our captain. "Yes" he said with a smile. "We only have a limited number of players so they just change the name of the team." I had to laugh.

Football was very different. The VMI team played in the local league which was comprised of Zambian teams, ours being the only team which contained a majority of Europeans.

The games were fast and furious. Played on pitches of variable quality and with referees of similar variable quality.

Both the crowd and the referee could get very excited and on some occasions the referee played to the crowd by performing all manner of pantomime tricks whilst running around the pitch, each waggle of his rear end gaining rapturous shouts and applause from the crowd.

Needless to say the game was often weighted heavily against the VMI team, as the opposition and the crowd loved nothing better than to see the Europeans being beaten.

Having said that, they were always played in good humour and whilst the odd dubious penalty kick or free kick would go against us there was never any malice involved.

I marvelled at the fact that some of the African lads played in bare feet against teams in football boots, yet never seemed to suffer any serious injury. They must have had feet like iron.

The VMI team was made up of players of varying standard. Some like me could kick a ball about with great enthusiasm but precious little skill, but from time to time we were augmented by players of considerably higher standard who just happened to be working in the area for a short time.

In one match we fielded two Greek "B" international players who unfortunately were only in Chipata for a couple of weeks, working for a contractor. On another occasion, being reasonably fleet of foot and able to cross the ball very well, I was playing on the right wing.

Playing behind me, in what in those days was called right half, was a young Zambian mixed race lad who by chance had just come home after working in Northern Ireland in James Mackie's Foundry in Belfast.

Whilst there he had been playing football for one of the City's biggest football teams called Glentoran and only the previous week we were led to believe, he had been playing in a European Cup match.

Now Glentoran may not be a Manchester United or Chelsea but they are still somewhat better than a knock about football team in Zambia. Shortly after the game started it became very obvious that this lad was a more than accomplished footballer and more importantly he was very fit.

Picking up the ball in our half and evading a couple of tackles he gave me a slide rule pass. Aimed inside the fullback who was marking me, the ball was angled towards the corner flag and I was expected to get to it before it crossed the dead ball line.

I sprinted flat out for all I was worth and catching up with it just as it was getting to the line I flung my right leg at it and lofted the ball into the centre of the goal where our centre forward, a lad from Everton in Liverpool (not Everton football team!) connected with it and it flew into the net.

Congratulations all round as I attempted to get my breath back.

Not three minutes later I found myself in the same situation, sprinting after another slide rule pass and just managing to get my cross in before the ball went dead.

Again we scored but this time I went back to our right half. "Great passes" I said to him through my wheezing as I tried to get my breath back again "but would you remember that I wasn't playing in the European Cup last week and you're killing me."

He laughed. "Sorry mate" he replied "but you've done really well."

"I won't get to the next one however" I said "so could you just hang on to the ball yourself for a bit longer and give me a slower pass otherwise I'm likely to corpse before the end of the game."

Needless to say we won that match but unfortunately the lad was on his way back to Belfast a couple of weeks later, never to be seen again during my stay in Chipata. Such was life in Zambia.

CHAPTER 13

THE AWAY GAME

Our rugby team was somewhat different. Comprised almost exclusively of expatriates, mostly from Europe but with a sprinkling of Australians, South Africans and even an American player we had a full size rugby pitch in the town centre.

However, given our geographical location in Zambia, we had no local opposition, with the nearest team in Zambia being nearly four hundred miles away. In order to play competitively we therefore played in the Malawi league.

Malawi was the next door country, with the border crossing a scant seventeen miles from Chipata. Like Zambia, Malawi also had a large expatriate population at that time and a thriving Rugby Union league.

The nearest major town to us was Lilongwe, some ninety-three miles away along a dirt road. Lilongwe at that time was bigger than Chipata, being a relatively large commercial centre and in later years was to become the Capital city of Malawi.

Lilongwe had a sports club and this was designated as our "home" pitch. It sounds mad when I think about it now, but during the rugby season our team and supporters, mainly wives and girlfriends, would set off in the early hours of Sunday morning to drive to Lilongwe.

A convoy of cars and Landrovers would cross the border at around seven in the morning and set off along the rough dirt road which, once inside Malawi, would skirt along the edge of Mozambique, whose border met both Zambia and Malawi at several points along the way.

At one such place, an hour or so into our journey, we would stop our vehicles and having got out would walk through a gap in the vegetation at the edge of the road, at which moment we apparently entered Mozambique.

Sitting just off the edge of the road was a Portuguese style "pub" run by an expatriate Portuguese and his wife.

Having been happily greeted as old friends and offered coffee we would then negotiate a dinner to be ready for us on our homeward journey later in the day. Not that there was much negotiating to do as the menu was always the same thing. Chicken peri peri and chips.

Dinner arranged we got back into our cars and headed on towards Lilongwe. The road was often badly rutted and as the rugby was played in the wet season it could also be deep in mud in some places, making the driving somewhat hazardous to say the least.

Our game at Lilongwe was scheduled for a ten o'clock start and despite the conditions we usually managed to get there on time.

The welcome from the Lilongwe sports club members was always warm and there were a number of old friends to meet for those of our team who had been playing there for years.

Generally speaking, we should always have had an advantage in these "home" games. As Lilongwe was the most Northerly team in the Malawi league with most of the others being based in and around Blantyre in the South of the country, the arrangement was that the Southern teams would travel North either on Friday evening or Saturday morning and would play the Lilongwe team on Saturday afternoon.

After the match the players would all retire to the bar and proceed to have a large number of drinks followed by a braaivleis, the South African or Africaans word for a barbecue, usually shortened to braai, pronounced bri. This was naturally accompanied by more beer.

The result generally was that when we turned up to play on Sunday, we were met on the pitch by opponents who often looked much the worse for wear from the party the night before and who sported numerous bruises and occasionally even a black eye from the game the previous afternoon.

The matches were hard but sporting. Playing on a pitch with a wonderful grass surface and in warm conditions meant that on return to the freezing cold of a British winter, few of us were likely to play rugby again.

We had a number of good players not least of all our Captain Billy Blair who was a solid forward. In the backs we had a good Australian scrum half and our centre, Peter Cooper, was one of those guys that every average man loves to hate. Well built, good looking, athletic, able to play rugby, golf, cricket and tennis at representative level not to mention his footballing skills which had apparently given him a trial at Manchester United a year or two previously if his story was to be believed.

A great man's man he was also a favourite amongst the girls, needless to say. But more of Peter later.

Despite a number of good players, the opposition were equally talented and despite their self-inflicted injuries from the day before we were as likely to lose as to win, but the games were well contested and good fun.

At the end of my first match I was introduced to a new drink as our team cooled down in the changing room. "Have one of these" Billy our captain said as he passed me a pint glass full of a cloudy looking liquid.

"What is it" I questioned, looking at it somewhat suspiciously. "It's ok it won't hurt you" he laughed, "It's a masharooba."

"A what?" "It's a mixture of ginger ale, lemonade and angostura bitters" he explained. "It's a really good thirst quencher." And it was.

Once we had cooled down and showered it was into the club bar to meet with our opponents and share numerous beers. Meanwhile the wives and girlfriends were entertaining themselves in the adjacent lounge, also over a few drinks.

Being typical of any rugby club bar the beer drinking generally led to raucous singing of the many disreputable songs which every rugby player knows, most of which are not suitable for the ears of the women although it wasn't unknown for some of them to join us in the choruses from time to time.

The beer drinking was followed by a continuation of the braai from the night before and so the afternoon passed happily but all too swiftly.

Eventually it was time to head for home. The sun had long since set and we were now driving back along the muddy, rutted dirt road with all of its attendant dangers. We travelled in convoy to ensure safety as each vehicle kept an eye on those in front and behind.

One night I was in the last but one vehicle. Travelling in the last car was a Scottish married couple, he being a senior immigration officer at our border control and she being the daughter of another Scot whom I had had the pleasure to meet and work with in Mazabuka a few months before.

We were chatting and singing in our car and it was a few minutes before we realized that we had lost the tail end Charlie. "There's no-one behind us" our driver suddenly said. "What do you mean?" said Peter. "Chris and Margaret were behind us and they're not there now" said Frank looking in his rear view mirror.

By this time we had stopped at the side of the road. "We'll give them a couple of minutes." We sat and waited. Nothing came along the road.

After about five minutes the decision was made. "We'd better go back and see where they are."

Frank turned the car round in the slushy muddy road and we drove back. We had covered about half a mile when on turning a corner our headlights illuminated a surprising sight.

Chris's car had slid off the side of the road in the mud and Margaret was vainly pushing it from behind whilst Chris gunned the engine and tried to rock it free. What was surprising was that Margaret was stark naked!!

I don't know who was the more surprised, Margaret or our car full of rugby players.

We pulled up beside her with a rousing cheer and all of us hopped out quickly to give her a hand. She was covered in mud from head to toe as a result of the spinning rear wheels, hence why she had taken her clothes off. Being an old hand at getting vehicles out of muddy ditches, Margaret knew that when she stood behind it to push she was likely to get covered in mud so as it was pitch black and she was well fortified with alcohol, she had decided to take her clothes off.

It took just a few minutes for us to get the car back on the road and we all fell about laughing at Margaret's expense as she stood on the other side of the car, cleaning off the mud as best she could and trying to get her clothes back on.

A few minutes later we heard another vehicle coming and we were all bathed in the lights of our friends from the front of our convoy who had also noticed eventually that some of us were missing and had come back to investigate. "What are you all laughing at?" It took several minutes before we had gained enough breath to explain and Margaret's embarrassment was doubled.

Onward to the Portuguese pub. Three-quarters of the way home we pulled in at the side of the road, climbed out and walked back into Mozambique. It seemed like a very long time, much more than the actual twelve hours, since we had stopped there on our way through to Lilongwe.

The landlord was delighted to see us again. "Wine?" he questioned "Yes of course" we chorused in unison. Large demijohns of Vinho Verde appeared along with glasses for the women. Beer was the order of the day for many of the men and soon the atmosphere was lively.

Despite having ordered dinner on our way through in the morning there was no sign of it appearing with any speed and given the noise of people and chickens in the back yard it was likely that our dinner was in process of being captured and put in the pot as we quaffed the ale.

The only difference from the morning was the appearance on seats around the walls of a number of young Portuguese soldiers.

These were conscripts the landlord told us. Mozambique was still a colony in the hands of the Portuguese and was under threat from FRELIMO guerrillas who were attempting to gain independence by force. Stationed a few hundred metres down the hill from the pub they were away from home for up to two years. Paid very little they looked pretty miserable as they watched us drinking.

Realizing the situation after speaking with the landlord, Frank turned to the rest of us. "Do you realize that these fellows are stuck here for about two years and have barely got the price of a beer between them?"

"So what?" said Jim. "Well how would you fancy it?" Frank looked at him accusingly "Let's buy them a drink. Sure it won't break us if we all chip in" he continued in his lovely South Armagh Northern Irish brogue.

"Ah why not?" said Brian, another Ulster man "Sure it'll cost us nothing." We all agreed and quickly delved into our pockets to chip in.

Within minutes another large demijohn of wine was produced and Billy took it across to the Portuguese lads. At first they were a bit dubious. They couldn't quite believe what we were doing. When the penny dropped, or perhaps I should have said escudo, they were delighted. Although they could speak little or no English their senior member made a speech of thanks which the landlord happily translated.

And so a new entente was created and was to last over several weeks as the rugby season progressed. Each time we stopped for dinner we provided wine for the conscripts.

On several evenings, after enough drink was consumed and the road running chicken had been eaten along with quantities of chips, music was provided via an old but workable record player on the bar and we took to the dance floor.

The first time this happened the soldiers looked on. The second week one of the young soldiers plucked up courage and walked across to Brian. He spoke rapidly in Portuguese. Brian looked baffled "What's he saying?" Brian looked to the landlord for help.

At first the landlord seemed reluctant to translate but Brian persisted. The landlord looked down at the bar. "He would like to dance with your wife" he said.

Brian laughed "Is that all. I thought it was something serious" he joked. "Of course he can. It means that I won't be expected to do it thank God."

Pat his wife didn't look too displeased as the young man wasn't bad looking. She stepped towards him and put her arms out "Come on" she said with a smile. He grinned and off they went.

Soon all the wives were on the dance floor as we blokes continued to down our beer.

Later in the evening we got back into our cars and set off on the last miles back to Chipata. Arriving at the border we found no sign of life in the immigration control office. The first half dozen of us to arrive were crowding into the office.

"Hello" yelled Jim whilst banging on the outside of the counter with his feet. "Hello" he yelled again at the top of his voice. "Wake up!!"

Suddenly a form appeared from below the counter. A very sleepy looking immigration officer appeared from beneath the counter where he had obviously been sleeping on the floor.

"Bwana, you are making too much noise" the officer said looking at us through his red sleepy eyes. "Why are you here?" He looked upset at having been woken.

"We're coming home" said Jim in a loud voice. "You must stamp our passports" "We are from Chipata."

"Yes" said the officer "I recognize him" He pointed at Richard. "He works in the bank" he said triumphantly.

"Hoorah" we shouted raucously as our passports were looked at with a minimum of accuracy then stamped with the entry visa. It had all gone remarkably well.

Next morning, around 11.00am Charlie and I were sitting chatting in the office when a Government Land Rover pulled into the car park. Out jumped Chris, the Senior Immigration Officer.

He strode purposefully into our office and throwing open the door said accusingly "OK, very funny, who's got it?" He glared at Charlie and me.

"Who's got what?" Charlie looked questioningly. "The bloody immigration stamp. Some bastard stole it from the immigration office as we passed through last night."

Charlie and I creased up laughing. "You're joking" I said. "I wish I was" Chris answered. "It's no joke" he went on. "We've got a queue of vehicles waiting to get into the country and none of them can move until we get the entry stamp back. So where is it?"

Charlie and I continued to laugh but Chris just couldn't see anything funny in the situation. Eventually Charlie managed to get a few words out. "Well don't look at us, we've not got it, have we Mike?" he looked suspiciously at me. "No" I responded quickly. "I certainly don't have it."

"I would try Peter Cooper or our Australian friend" Charlie shrugged his shoulders. Chris snorted turned on his heels and walked out, slamming the door behind him.

"Do you think he might have a bit of a hangover" I grinned at Charlie. "More than a bit" was the reply.

Fortunately for the immigration post the rugby season was short so they didn't suffer such indignities for too long.

Our stops at the Portuguese pub proved a great diversion for the young soldiers over the few weekends that we travelled to Lilongwe

Sad to say, a few years later, at the height of the FRELIMO freedom campaign to free Mozambique from its Portuguese past, the army detachment and the pub were attacked by guerillas with the pub being destroyed and severe loss of life amongst all concerned.

CHAPTER 14

THE DAILY GRIND

Day to day work was very different to that in Mazabuka. It usually started with me arriving at the office around 7.30am. The office staff were already there and the messenger, an official title dating back to the Colonial era, a tall Zambian named Mvula was ready with my first cup of coffee within minutes.

Charlie would usually arrive a few minutes later and sit down at the desk across the room from me. "My arse is twittering" he would exclaim particularly if he had been involved in a heavy drinking session the night before.

"Mvula" he would yell. "Where's my coffee" "Coming bwana" and Mvula would appear almost miraculously, steaming cup in hand.

Eastern Province is marginally more than 69,000 square kilometres (26,641 sq miles) in size so we were responsible for a large area, much of which was sparsely populated and quite remote. As in Mazabuka, our primary objective was to run the World Health Organisation smallpox eradication programme. This entailed vaccinating one third of the province every year. The job was carried out by lay vaccinators on bicycles who travelled in teams through the remote districts carrying their supply of vaccine and equipment in a container on the rear of their bikes.

We ensured that they were correctly trained and supervised by the Senior Assistant and were supplied with food and tents to sleep in when in difficult areas and that the vaccine was regularly delivered to them.

One day a World Health Organisation supervisor arrived in our office from Lusaka. He wanted to talk to our vaccinators and the trained assistants about the work that they carried out and how it was done. As with all such WHO staff the supervisor was from another country, in this case one from the Asian Sub Continent and had little, if any, experience of working in Africa.

Notwithstanding this Charlie was happy to let him get on with doing whatever it was that he needed to do. A lot of chattering and laughing came from the office next door as the supervisor went about his work. Late in the afternoon he came into our office.

"Have you got all the information you need?" Charlie asked. "Yes thank you" was the reply. "You've been very helpful" he said as he left the office.

Nothing more was heard for some three to four weeks, then late one afternoon as Charlie and I were sitting in the office suddenly there appeared in our car park a truck towing a very large caravan, some twenty-eight feet long.

We gazed in amazement. "What the heck's going on" Charlie said looking at me. "I haven't got a clue" I replied. We walked out to the car park just as the beaming face of the WHO supervisor appeared from inside the truck.

"Hello" he said, leaping out. "It's nice to see you again" He shook hands with Charlie. "What the hell is that?" Charlie pointed at the caravan.

"It's a caravan" was the immediate reply. "I can see that but what's it doing here?" said Charlie.

"It's for your vaccinators" beamed the supervisor. By this time all the office staff had gathered in the carpark and were gazing admiringly at the van and chattering away amongst themselves.

"For the vaccinators?" Charlie could barely get the words out. I thought he was going apoplectic. "Yes" replied the supervisor "It's for when they travel into the valley (the Luangwa he was referring to) "they will have somewhere comfortable to sleep. They told me when I was here last that it was sometimes very hard to sleep in their tents when away from home."

Charlie's face was a picture. "Have you any idea of the sort of area into which they are travelling?" He looked accusingly at the supervisor. Without waiting for an answer he carried on "They don't have any roads, there are barely bicycle tracks, they go in and out of rivers and through thick bush."

He stopped for breath and then continued "Why do you think they are riding bicycles? If there were roads, they would use a Land Rover. So how the hell do you think they are going to get that contraption into the areas where they are working? I can't believe that you listened to everything they told you and didn't work it out. Anyway there's no way that a caravan is going to be of any use to them so just hitch it up again to your truck and get the hell out of here."

The supervisor looked completely deflated and without another word to Charlie or me he got his driver to hitch up the van and within a couple of minutes they were heading out of the car park with the caravan in tow.

Charlie and I watched from the office window. "That's the trouble with these do-gooder operations like WHO" Charlie said to me. "They have to be staffed with a ratio of people from every Nation which subscribes to the Organisation, for example two people from each country. So no matter what their background they turn up in remote areas to try to sort out the problems. In reality, however good their intentions are they often make a complete cock up of it, just like now."

The sun was setting over the caravan heading forlornly back down the road towards Lusaka. "Come on it's time for a sundowner" Charlie muttered. We left the office, stepped over the wall into the golf club car park and within a couple of minutes were on the veranda with a beer in our hands.

Some of our expatriate colleagues were already there and within minutes Charlie had them in stitches laughing as he regaled them with the story of the WHO caravan. It kept him in drinks all night as he had to repeat the tale to everyone as they came in.

Work was interesting and although Charlie and I had a number of basic areas to cover, such as the smallpox campaign and the construction of new Health Centres there were also some unusual distractions.

Charlie and I weren't responsible for the Environmental Health provisions in Chipata, this being the remit of the town council which at some time in the past had probably been run by an expatriate. However, in recent years this post hadn't been filled and the local authority relied on Charlie and me to give them back up when needed.

Amongst other things this included carrying out meat inspection at the local abattoir which Charlie and I were qualified to do and took in turns.

Unfortunately, the abattoir didn't operate on preset days but worked more on the basis of need so on occasions when Charlie and I were busy working elsewhere the meat would often be left hanging in the abattoir, unrefrigerated waiting for inspection.

When this happened, inspection later in the day could prove to be a bit overpowering due to the smell of rapidly maturing meat.

This didn't seem to create any problems for the local people who were happy to wait until I had given the all clear for the meat before rapidly dismantling the entire carcase which was then carried away by the hordes waiting outside the door.

Everything was used, and I used to chuckle at the sight of a cow's head being carried away balanced safely on top of the head of the woman carrying it. An incongruous sight.

In the rural areas cattle were slaughtered at the roadside and the animal was sold literally off its own hide as it was butchered amongst the dust and dirt.

The slaughtering was very basic. The cow was tied on the end of a long piece of rope and a small boy took one end of the rope and ran one way round a tree whilst the butcher drove the cow round the tree in the opposite direction until shortage of rope brought it to a halt at which point its throat was cut with a very sharp knife and it fell to the ground.

Much as it was a chore, I benefited from this meat inspection as the animals were more likely to be suffering from diseases or conditions which I had only previously read about in my text books prior to my final exams in the UK.

Work was not without its humorous moments either. The drinking water supply in Chipata came from artesian wells below the town from which the water was pumped into a large circular concrete storage tank, about the size of a very large swimming pool.

This storage tank, just outside the town centre, contained the entire town water supply and was treated with chlorine to ensure the safety of the water. The chlorination system was very basic.

It consisted of a large galvanised metal dustbin balanced on a tripod stand above the water. A tap had been drilled into the side of the bin. Each morning the Town Foreman filled the dustbin with water to which he added a measure of chlorine powder, of the type normally used to treat swimming pools. He then opened the tap on the side of the bin to allow the chlorinated water to drip slowly into the main water tank. Simple but effective.

One morning as Charlie and I were sitting in the office a Land Rover raced into our car park and pulled up in a cloud of red dust.

The Town Foreman jumped out and ran into our office.

"Bwana, bwana" he almost shouted at Charlie. "What's wrong?" Charlie said.

It must be something really serious I thought, given the state that the Foreman was in.

"Bwana, the water supply she is buggered." "What?" said Charlie. "The water supply she is buggered" came the reply.

"What's happened to it?" Charlie asked, thinking the worst.

"The bottom has fallen out of the dustbin" came the immediate response.

Charlie and I looked at each other, then burst out laughing. The Foreman looked quite crestfallen. He had expected a more measured response I'm sure.

We were relieved that it wasn't something much more serious. Nature had taken its toll and the dustbin had rotted with age but it was easily replaced and within an hour a new sparkling water treatment system had been replaced on the tripod stand and the water supply was safe once again.

CHAPTER 15

THE MUSIC MAN

On my first visit to the Golf Club in Chipata, I had noticed a piano in the corner. On my second visit, it was quiet with few people in the bar, so I lifted the piano lid and played a few notes. Surprisingly, given the humid conditions, it was in tune so I sat down and played a few bars.

As I've said before, I wasn't a trained pianist although I had gone to piano lessons as a child but not being keen on all the practice necessary I had given up the lessons after a year or so.

Later in my teenage years I began to twiddle the keys on the piano which stood in our front room at home. To my surprise I found that I could play virtually any tune that I knew, without having to have any music. I could play by ear as the saying goes.

Now, sitting down at the piano in the Golf Club I began to idly play a few of the more recent pop tunes with which I was familiar. Beatles, Rolling Stones etc.

Suddenly I realised that the few people in the bar were listening and that one or two who had been on the veranda had come to the door to see who was playing.

I stopped. Peter Cooper strolled across from the bar, beer in hand. "You can play a bit then" he said. "I only knock about on it" I replied. "I'm not a proper pianist."

"It sounded alright to me" he replied. "I have a drum set at home, maybe I should bring it in?" He looked at me questioningly.

"Why not" I replied and at that point a new band was formed or perhaps it would be more correct to say a new duo.

Next day when I came into the bar after work, there, next to the piano, sat a full drum kit with a grinning Peter sitting on a bar stool waiting for me. Within a few minutes we were playing and thereafter we became the resident band in the bar and for all functions in town.

Many happy nights were spent with Peter and me hammering out the pop tunes of the day to a receptive audience who were happy to take to the dance floor at a moments notice. One of the wives also turned out to have a great blues singing voice and after a few glasses of wine would often join us for slow soulful songs late into the night.

We weren't paid for anything we did except by alcohol. People would come across to the piano and put a glass of gin and tonic on the top as payment for my efforts and Peter was similarly rewarded.

Often, particularly when the road construction guys who were building the new main road through the Province from Lusaka, were in town, they being a hard drinking crowd, my piano would have a line of drinks sitting on the top and Peter and I would eventually succumb to the alcohol with the performance coming to an end as Peter slid off his drum stool into the drums.

However, this didn't usually happen until the wee small hours of the morning.

Sometimes, when asked to play at more formal functions such as the New Year's Eve dinner I would "borrow" the electric organ from the Anglican Church.

This was a modest but modern electric keyboard which made a pleasant noise when suitably amplified.

The vicar was a young single Englishman and was happy to allow the organ to be borrowed so long as it was returned in good order and in time for the Sunday morning service. In fact, on several occasions he was present at the function and it was a case of returning both the vicar and the organ to the church.

It must have been a strange sight to any locals watching in the early hours of Sunday morning to see a couple of Land Rovers turn up outside the church and a bevy of men in dinner suits get out.

Then amongst much noise and occasional swearing, struggle to get an organ out of the back of one Land Rover and a vicar out of the other and attempt to get both of them into their respective buildings in good order, the vicarage being next to the church, with all concerned generally being slightly the worse for wear due to the alcohol consumed.

The weekend parties often ran through the night and on at least one occasion I drove off the first tee at the Golf Club on Sunday morning whilst still dressed in my dinner suit and not having been home from the night before.

Similarly, cricket matches would commence with members of the team looking decidedly sleepy and hoping that we would win the toss and decide to bat which might give some of us the chance to get some sleep on the sidelines whilst awaiting our turn. Happy days.

CHAPTER 16

THE LUANGWA VALLEY – TALES OF INTREPID ADVENTURERS

Whilst our social lives in Chipata revolved around the sporting facilities we were also blessed by having one of the World's best game reserves virtually on our doorstep.

The Luangwa reserve was designated as a National park as early as 1932 and covers more than 9000 square kilometres which makes it just less than half the size of Wales!

The valley through which the river Luangwa flows is at the Southern end of the Great Rift Valley providing a lush riverine vegetation feeding a vast range of animal and bird life. Situated, only some eighty miles or so from Chipata, it offered an unbeatable opportunity to see elephant, hippos, lions, leopard, cheetah, and a vast number of antelope, giraffe etc. in their natural surroundings.

I was introduced to it fairly soon after my arrival in Chipata. It appeared that a number of the blokes had taken to camping in the valley at weekends during the dry season. The leader of the group was Clive Kelly, no relation of mine but a schoolteacher who had read about the Luangwa whilst in his native North West of England and had been so taken with it that he had determined to see for himself and to do so had got a job as Head teacher in a school in Chipata.

My first visit to the valley was a revelation. Setting off after work on Friday evening three cars full of men equipped with the basics for the weekend, sleeping bags, food and several crates of beer drove the eighty or so miles down the dirt road fairly rapidly.

The scenery changed as we neared the river. The scrubby bushland typical of the Zambian hinterland gave way to the palm trees and lush vegetation of the river flood plain.

Our campsite was outside the designated National Park and game reserve, some miles up river from Mfuwe, the main game lodge and the site of the dirt airstrip into which the National Airline, Zambia Airways operated a regular air service.

We arrived in a cloud of dust just as the sun was setting. A cleared space sitting on the edge of the Luangwa river, with a drop of some ten feet into the water.

I stepped out and gazed in awe at a very large river some fifty yards wide and flowing swiftly, still swollen by the recent rainy season.

It was incredible. Looking up river I could see a pod of hippo, several of which were making the characteristic grunting noises with which I was to become familiar over the following months.

On the opposite side of the water there was a small sandy area on which a number of crocodiles were lying, totally oblivious of the fact that a somewhat noisy party had arrived in their area.

I was transfixed until a voice behind me brought me back to life. "Are you going to stand their all evening?" I swung round. Billy pointed to the back of Clive's Land Rover. "Would you give a hand to get the beer out."

I pitched in with the rest and we rapidly assembled our food stocks, beer and sleeping gear. A number of African lads had appeared on our arrival and it soon became apparent to me that these were semi-permanent staff who had been expecting us and who were there to help with our domestic arrangements.

The camp that we had arrived at consisted of a number of thatched rondavels, the round houses built by the Zambians and comprised of wooden struts and grass walls. These provided storage facilities for the food and drink and sleeping accommodation for the Africans.

I also became aware of an elderly man who had appeared from one of the rondavels and was talking animatedly with Clive.

Clive beckoned me over. "Bert, this is Mike, the latest addition to our workforce in Chipata. Mike meet Bert Schultz." I shook hands with the man.

"Bert lives in Port Elizabeth in South Africa but used to live and work here in the Luangwa and comes back every year to stay through the dry season" Clive explained in a voice which suggested that this was a fairly normal thing for anyone to do.

At that moment I didn't realise that I had just met one of the most fascinating characters who had ever lived in the Luangwa valley and whose stories of his early life were to be a source of much entertainment to all of us around the camp fire on many an evening.

Bert had arrived early in the dry season and the camp was set up for him. He had his own rondavel, the African lads had theirs and there was a latrine toilet positioned in a grass hut some distance away where it wouldn't be a nuisance.

Part of the job of the guys from Chipata was to replenish the stores for Bert and in particular to bring his supply of beer.

As the evening wore on, we sat round a blazing fire, beer in hand, listening to the sounds of the African night. Hippos snorted in the river, from whence there also came occasional splashes as both they and the crocodiles moved around. Animals grunted in the bush, the noise travelling considerable distances in the still air.

At that stage I couldn't distinguish one noise from another but Bert was an expert and happily expounded on each noise when questioned. "That's an elephant, he's quite close by. That's a lion roaring, but he's quite a long way off." And so it went on. I was spellbound.

I was to learn Bert's story over a number of nights. He was a great raconteur, particularly after a few beers and was only too happy to tell his stories of a lifestyle and time which had now passed.

Many of his tales sounded bizarre and in some cases far-fetched but we were hearing of life in the early stages of European progress into the depths of Africa. Those things which I had heard of at school and read about in many books, of daring exploits, which I had devoured as an eager young reader. Here they were sitting in front of me, in the flesh.

I can still picture the scene vividly and recall some of the stories and I retell them here, knowing that some have previously been published by Norman Carr, a contemporary of Bert and a well known conservationist and author, who spent a lot of his life in the Luangwa valley. His books such as "The White Impala" documented his life in the Luangwa and I was privileged to meet him a little later.

Bert and Norman were the first game rangers appointed to the Luangwa National Park back in 1939.

Bert had grown up in Africa and was a teenager at the outbreak of the First World War in 1914. Greatly taken by tales of the King's African Rifles in the early days of the Great War, he had set off to join them in their attempt to dislodge the Germans from German East Africa, the country now known as Tanzania.

Despite being under age, Bert joined the Regiment and proceeded to cover a large swathe of East Africa on foot as the Rifles vainly tried to catch up with the Germans who according to him were burning the local crops as they went, thus depriving the Rifles of supplies.

As they marched the column was headed by their Colonel, mounted somewhat incongruously on a donkey. After several weeks the British troops were getting somewhat desperate and with little respite in sight began to hungrily eye the donkey. The donkey was the Colonel's pride and joy, but hunger was overtaking the men and one night they decided that they would draw lots and the loser would have to despatch the donkey.

Needless to say Bert drew the short straw and during the night he was forced to creep out and ensure that the donkey met its maker. Next morning all hell broke loose. The Colonel was distraught at the loss of the donkey and was determined to find out who the culprit was. However, Bert's pals stood together and despite much questioning the perpetrator wasn't to be found.

Once the Colonel had calmed down he was also persuaded that there was no point in leaving the donkey as it was, since it could provide a good source of food for the men. Take the story as you wish. It may or may not be true but it made for a good tale.

Worse was to come however. At one point the Regiment arrived at a small village where they were to camp for the night. Sentries had to be positioned to avoid a surprise attack by the enemy and Bert was instructed to position himself on top of a nearby hill and was told to "stay up there until you are relieved."

Bert did as he was told and stayed on top of the hill all night. The following morning, he was surprised to see the Regiment packing up and marching out but as he hadn't been relieved he did what he had been ordered and stayed where he was.

The local villagers foraging later in the day were somewhat surprised to find him there but were happy to share what little they had with him. A night or two later Bert was awakened by the noise of shouting and yelling from the village below. He ran down from the hill to be confronted by the sight of an elephant rampaging through the villager's small fields of vegetables and fruit, rapidly destroying their livelihood.

The elephant was very obviously maddened and was making his way towards the village houses with intent to destroy them as well.

Given that there were women and small children in the elephant's path and their lives were likely to be in danger Bert felt that he had no option than to shoot the elephant.

He had never shot an elephant before but trying not to feel too overawed and realizing that shooting it in the head would probably be somewhat futile, he aimed into the shoulder to a point where he thought that its heart might be. It dropped and Bert instantly became a hero in the eyes of the villagers. It later transpired that this elephant had been a serious problem for a long time and its dispatch had been overdue.

Bert was able to milk his bravery for several days, being feted by the villagers with food and drinks. However, he hadn't forgotten his duties and continued to maintain his position as sentry on top of the hill.

One morning, a week or so later, he watched as another battalion of the Rifles arrived at the village, flags flying and drums beating. Bert decided that it was time to relinquish his post and made his way down the hill to confront the officer in charge. The officer looked at him in amazement. "Who are you and what are you doing here?" he asked. Bert gave him his name, rank and number and told him "I was told to take up post on top of that hill and remain there until I was relieved." he said.

"Well consider yourself relieved" the officer retorted smartly.

Bert was pleased as his little adventure on the hill had become somewhat boring and he was missing his army mates but he wasn't going to be let off quite so lightly. The officer questioned him as to what he had been doing in the days since his Regiment had marched out and left him behind and Bert had to tell him about the saga of the elephant.

The officer wasn't best pleased by the fact that Bert had expended some of His Majesty's ammunition without permission to shoot an elephant and he was put on a charge and suitably punished.

Notwithstanding all of this Bert survived the war and when the conflict had ended he determined to return North from his home in South Africa and make a life in Northern Rhodesia.

He settled in the area around Fort Jameson, now Chipata, which was very much an outpost in the bush.

Teeming with wild life, particularly along the Luangwa valley the area was a Mecca for hunters, both legal and illegal and was also being opened up to farms, producing tobacco, maize and cotton in areas where there was a suitable water supply.

Life was tough, but so were the people. Travel was difficult and mostly on horseback or foot as roads were virtually non-existent. The nearest town of any size was Salisbury in Southern Rhodesia which was reached via a long walk across country. Lusaka, now the capital of Zambia was still only a dream in someone's mind.

Once a year the farmers had to take their crops of maize and tobacco to market and this was done, according to Bert, using a long line of Africans, each of whom carried bales of the crop on their head.

The walk to Salisbury would take up to six weeks and after a short rest the team would return, carrying on their heads the provisions and equipment to keep the farm going through the rest of the year. Vitally important on the return trip however was that the sixth porter in each team carried a case of whiskey!!

Bert's tales kept us entranced on many a night by the fire and although we often heard them repeated we never tired of them.

Most of the people about whom he spoke were long gone as he was telling tales from the 1920s and 30s but some of their descendants were still alive and well in the newly formed Zambia.

Many of the early adventurers had been "Remittance men" the term used to describe those sons of wealthy English families who had blackened the family reputation in some way or other and as a result had been banished to the Colonies, never to darken the family doorstep again. To keep them away from home they were paid a quarterly allowance paid by the family lawyers as a "remittance", hence the name.

Those living in the Luangwa area would come into Fort Jameson to collect their money via the rudimentary banking service, often staying for a day or two in town at the VMI, then in its heyday. Many remittance men were hard working and became good citizens of the developing country but others were eccentric to say the least.

One such, according to Bert, was "rope soled Jones" who each quarter would arrive in Fort Jameson in some style to collect his allowance.

Immaculately dressed in a white suit, wearing the rope soled shoes which gave him his name and riding on a donkey, he was preceded on foot by an African male servant, carrying a silver salver on which was a bottle of whiskey and a glass, to provide sustenance along the way.

The story goes that rope soled Jones collected his money and then binged the lot at the VMI over a couple of days. He was then often seen leaving the town, draped over his donkey, led by the African, his suit somewhat dirty and dishevelled, with the whole performance to be repeated three months later.

Fort Jameson being the provincial Capital also contained the Judiciary and had a hangman. This post was part time and the incumbent was paid the sum of 30 shillings per head. One such man, hangman Smith, it was said, had such an abiding hatred of missionaries that he offered to hang missionaries for free!

Our evenings around the campfire weren't entirely without incident. After a few beers it was all too easy to forget that we were in the middle of Africa, in the pitch black and surrounded by wild animals. On one such evening, Brian got up from the fireside to go and relieve himself of some of the beer.

No-one paid much attention when a few moments later we heard a large splash. It wasn't unusual as hippos and crocodiles were plentiful along the river.

It wasn't until a voice yelled "help" that we were awakened to the fact that in the darkness, coming out of the light of the fire, Brian had walked a step too far and fallen some eight or ten feet into the river.

Fortunately, he had surfaced rapidly, turned into the current and had managed to make it to the bank. However, at that point the bank was very steep, the very reason for our camp site being positioned there. A fire in front of us and a steep river bank behind made it less likely that an animal would come at us from either the front or the rear.

Billy switched on our powerful searchlight and shone it down the bank. There stood Brian, up to his knees in water and dripping. He was laughing like a drain however, as were we, and for a few minutes was unaware of the danger. As a rope was quickly produced and dropped to Brian, Charlie said, "I think you ought to get out of there fairly sharpish" Brian looked a little confused "Why?"

Billy shone the light around and the semicircle of red eyes in the water became readily apparent. "Shit" said Brian and I've never seen a man move so quickly up a rope. Crocodiles can move very fast to snatch a meal as many a man has been unfortunate enough to find out.

Sitting in the baking afternoon sunshine we would often watch numerous crocodiles lying on the sandbank on the opposite side of the river. Mouths slightly open, they lay totally motionless for hours on end waiting for the unsuspecting small buck or even large bird to wander down to the water's edge. Then, in a split second blur of rapid movement, they would launch themselves and their jaws would slam shut on their prey.

It was mesmerising to watch and we could only look aghast at natures in-built cruelty.

Our weekends in the valley were memorable for the wildlife that we were able to see. In those days, prior to poaching, there were more than 23,000 elephants in the Reserve living in large herds. Antelope of all sizes and breeds were widespread along with giraffe, herds of Cape buffalo, rhino, lions and leopards.

We quickly became adept at identifying everything that we saw and I took to carrying my camera with me on every occasion when my work took me down to the valley so that I could photograph anything unusual that I came across.

CHAPTER 17

TALES OF THE UNEXPECTED

One day whilst driving along a dirt track in the game reserve I approached a Land Rover which was obviously empty. I stopped and looked around.

It was very unusual to find an empty vehicle and I didn't recognize it as belonging to anyone I knew. I thought that the driver probably wasn't too far away. The vehicle was parked on a corner and as I edged my Land Rover round the bend I was horrified to see a man, standing at the side of the road with his camera at the ready, gently lobbing stones at a lion lying some fifty feet away in the grass.

I pushed my foot down hard on the accelerator and gunned the Land Rover alongside him. "What the hell do you think you're doing?" I shouted at him. "Get in quickly."

He looked at me with a puzzled expression as if to say what's all this about. "Get in" I yelled at him again. The lion stirred, probably in anger at his sleep being broken. The man moved slowly around the Land Rover then reluctantly got in.

Looking at him I realized that he was wearing a clerical collar and was a man of the cloth. He was also new to the country, given his somewhat sunburned appearance.

"What do you think you were doing?" I asked. "I just wanted the lion to stand up so that I could take his picture" came the almost unbelievable reply.

"Where do you think you are? This isn't a zoo and that lion isn't behind bars" I said accusingly. "I'm sorry. I suppose I just wasn't thinking" came the reply. "I'm only here on a short holiday, visiting a friend." "It might have been shorter than you would think" I retorted.

I backed the short distance to his Land Rover and made sure he was safely inside it before driving on. "Don't forget that everything here is dangerous" I said before leaving him.

I drove off thinking "there's one born every minute" yet I too was to do something equally stupid some months later.

My biggest challenge was yet to come however. One morning Charlie came into the office from a meeting at the hospital. "We've lost the Doc." he said. "Pardon?" I replied, not quite sure of what he was talking about. "Our daft Doctor "he said, referring to one of the permanent medical team at the hospital, "went off four days ago to investigate an outbreak of measles up North and hasn't been heard from since. You'd better go and look for him to make sure that he hasn't got himself into any trouble"

"Me?" I enquired incredulously. "Why me?" "Well I can't think of anyone sensible from the hospital that we would want to send" was Charlie's brisk reply. "It won't take you long. He can't have got that far" he continued. "Just head North up through Lundazi then take the track towards the Mpika plateau. Apparently that's the way he was heading."

It took me about an hour to get kitted up and fill the Land Rover with the necessary supplies and bits of equipment that Charlie thought that I might need, although to be honest I wasn't quite sure why I was carrying a couple of folding tables! However, Charlie knew best. After all it was his third contract out there and he therefore had a lot more experience than me.

Off I went, heading North up the main road which lead to Lundazi, a town some one hundred miles away.

I never tired of seeing Lundazi. It was an unbelievable fairytale in the middle of the African bush. It had a castle. Not just any old castle but a German style castle complete with its rounded towers and castellated battlements and with the "serfs" cottages standing on stone pillars outside the walls.

Although I had been warned as to what to expect I was still flabbergasted when I first saw it. Reputedly the product of a British Government District Commissioner, Erroll Button, charged with building a rest house in this bush station in the late 1940s as accommodation for travelling Government Officers, he had let his imagination run riot and instead of building a basic hostelry had come up with this somewhat bizarre fantasy.

It was still a rest house but I had never had cause to stay in it and on this occasion I drove rapidly past it heading on in search of my vanishing Doctor.

Lundazi marked the end of the main road, which, for all that it was a dirt road, was at least a reasonable width and regularly had the surface levelled using one of the many road graders, which were a regular sight on the dirt roads in Zambia.

Now I was on dirt tracks, designed more for bicycles than for road vehicles and I was glad of the excellent four-wheel drive capabilities of the Land Rover. On I went, in all honesty not really sure where I was heading for and certainly with no knowledge of anything that might lie ahead.

The road gradually narrowed and soon I was driving through grass which was at least six feet high and brushing tightly along the side of my vehicle. This had unintended consequences. Given that the truck didn't have air conditioning I had the windows open to provide ventilation. The wet season was just beginning and the weather was very muggy.

Suddenly I became aware that I was no longer alone in the Land Rover. I was being besieged by caterpillars in all shades of green which were being brushed off the grass by the side of my vehicle passing through and were dropping happily on to my clothes and arms.

Not knowing which, if any, were dangerous in that the hairs on their bodies might have caused an allergic reaction, I braked hard, shuddered to a stop and rapidly jumping down onto the track, swiftly brushed off the offending caterpillars. I had no fear of them but just wanted to make sure that I didn't suffer any ill effects.

Suddenly the rain came on. The short bursts of torrential water were the opening salvos of the wet season to come. I was now driving with my windows closed, suffocating in the steamy heat and from time to time having to clear the condensation from the windscreen in order to see where I was going.

I was still enjoying myself, however the driving was getting more difficult as the track traversed a number of small ravines formed by the rivers which although dry at the time would soon become raging torrents. It was a bit of a switchback ride with me fighting the steering wheel as the vehicle bucked up and down along the track.

In the middle of all this I was caught in the heaviest downpour yet. The rain was lashing down in monsoon style when suddenly it happened. It was my own fault. I couldn't see much through the windscreen with the combination of torrential rain, and the steaming up of the windows and was probably doing around twenty miles an hour when suddenly I felt the vehicle taking off. It soared for a few feet and landed with a crash and an enormous a splash in the bottom of a river. I realised immediately that I had driven straight off a bank and was now in about a foot and a half of water.

The river was flowing strongly but as yet wasn't very deep. I looked at the bank facing me. It was about five to six feet high and steep but there was an obvious track leading up it and out the other side. The engine was still running and I didn't appear to have suffered any damage so I positioned the truck, put it into four-wheel drive, revved the engine and in the few feet available in the width of the river headed for the bank.

The Land Rover laboured onto the bank, the wheels trying to get some grip and I was just about to congratulate myself on getting out when, with a crash, the bank collapsed and I fell backwards into the river again.

I took another look, backed the vehicle as far as I could across the river and then made another run at it. Once again the front wheels dragged themselves out and the rear wheels also began to get some grip on the wet earth beneath then just as suddenly as before, the bank collapsed and I fell back into the river. This time however I heard a sharp cracking noise. "Oh, Oh" I thought. "What was that?"

I was soon to find out. Trying to position myself towards a piece of river bank which was so far undamaged by my efforts, I realized that my four-wheel drive was no more. The crack which I had heard had probably been a half shaft breaking and I now only had drive via my front wheels.

"Well that at least would be better than having drive only on my rear wheels" I thought hopefully, since it would be easier for the truck to drag itself out than push itself.

However, my confidence was severely misplaced. An hour and several more attempts later I was forced to admit that I was stuck. I got out of the Land Rover to take stock of my situation. It wasn't good I had to admit.

The river though relatively shallow was flowing quite quickly and was silting up around the wheels of the truck as I watched. I would have to keep the truck moving if it wasn't going to sink up to its axles. To add to that, I was only too aware that it had been raining and although the rain had dissipated and the sun was now shining I had no idea as to whether or not this river was being fed by larger amounts of water flowing down from the escarpment beyond me and to which I had been heading.

I weighed up my options and decided that it would be best to stay with the vehicle where I had more than adequate supplies of food and water rather than leaving it and walking back down the road from whence I had come. Someone was bound to come along eventually, although I had to admit to myself that I hadn't seen anyone for a very long time.

Ah well, I thought, just another of life's little experiences as I settled down for what might be a long wait.

And a long wait it proved to be. There were two major problems for me. Firstly I had to keep moving the truck as the water coming down the river was continuing to silt up the wheels and I wanted to be able to get the thing out of the water at some stage. There was no way I could go back to the office and tell Charlie that I had lost a complete Land Rover.

This meant that I had to stay awake through the night. Secondly I had no idea as to what wildlife might be inhabiting the area. This was a remote part of Zambia as far as I was concerned and there could be lion, leopards and snakes amongst other undesirable elements in the immediate vicinity. Fortunately, I reckoned that the river water was too shallow to have any crocodiles in it but I kept a wary eye open none the less.

It was a long night. Dawn broke, the sun rose and I continued my efforts to keep the Land Rover in one piece. It must have been mid-morning when I heard the voices.

Suddenly out of nowhere a group of men appeared. One of them incongruously wearing a pair of blue overalls bearing the name "Nakambala Sugar Estate" the sugar estate at Mazabuka in Southern province several hundred miles away, on which I had worked the previous year. I was overjoyed.

The men looked at me in surprise then started asking questions. "What are you doing there?" "Where are you going?" "Why are you staying in the river?" "Do you want to get out?"

Some of the questions seemed bizarre given my circumstances but I could understand why they were being asked.

The guy from Nakambala spoke good English and I quickly explained what had happened. He and the others had a chat about what to do then two of them disappeared to get help.

Within minutes a host of men appeared from what must have been a fairly nearby village. They didn't have any vehicles so I was at a loss to see what they were going to do. I needn't have worried. Within minutes two very sturdy and long tree trunks appeared. The men started to unload my vehicle to reduce the weight. The man from Nambala said" Which way would you like to go?" "Back the way I came" I replied, pointing back towards Lundazi. There was no way in which I could continue without four-wheel drive.

"OK." The equipment having been removed from the Land Rover and positioned on the bank the men got into the water and pushed each tree trunk under the vehicle, one at either end, allowing a substantial length to protrude at either side.

A large group of them then positioned themselves at the tree trunks on either side and at a word of command from the leader, he in the blue overalls, they lifted the vehicle bodily.

I watched in amazement. I didn't think that it would have been possible had I not seen it for myself. The team work took a little while to become established but amongst much shouting and heaving the Land Rover began to inch its way towards the bank.

It wasn't a flowing movement and at one stage amongst some concern the team at the rear started to lose their footing as they took the main weight when the angle of the vehicle tilted upwards towards the bank.

Their feet were disappearing into the silt. The blue overalls carried out a rapid assessment and decided that some better footing was required. He cast his eyes along the bank for something which would help support the team.

His eyes lit on one of the Government tables and with a sharp word to one of his colleagues it was dragged from its resting place and delivered into the water. There it was placed over the silt to provide a flat surface. Thank god for Charlie's foresight in persuading me to take the table!!

The heaving and struggling commenced again and the truck inched out of the water and upwards on to the bank. With a triumphant shout all four wheels were placed on the upslope and I was invited to get in and start the engine.

I jumped in and revved the engine. "Go bwana, Go!!" I let the clutch out and the vehicle began to slither, not forward and upward but sideways and backwards.

I had a horrible feeling that I was going to end up back where I had started. But no. With another shout the entire team gathered behind the vehicle and as I kept my foot gently on the accelerator, they heaved and shoved and the Land Rover lurched up the bank, over the crest on to the track.

A huge cheer erupted and then the entire group broke into a fit of laughter and giggles, with much hand slapping and back patting.

"Thanks" I said. It seemed a very feeble response to what had been a very sticky predicament.

They helped me reload my gear into the back of the truck and soon I was on my way again, retracing the route which I had taken only yesterday. It seemed such a long time ago. I was several miles down the road when I remembered the table. In the relief at getting back onto dry land I had forgotten all about it and it had probably disappeared into the silt of the river bed by now.

Arriving back at my office late into the evening I was met by Charlie. "Did you find him?" I had forgotten all about the missing Doctor. "No" I replied and began to relate my tale of woe.

Charlie listened carefully but didn't seem too bothered either about the fact that I had spent a night in a river or had failed miserably to find the missing Doctor.

"Let's have a drink" he said, pointing across the car park to the Golf Club. We sauntered over and I spent the rest of the evening telling my tale to the assembled expatriates.

As for the Doctor? Well he turned up safe and well a couple of days later having reached his destination and dealt with the outbreak but having lost his communication whilst on his way.

Despite the experience I was disappointed at having to give up on the trip since it was taking me into a part of the country which was very remote. My breakdown had also robbed me of the opportunity to stand face to face with the Doctor in the remote African bush and utter the famous words "Doctor Livingstone I presume?"

CHAPTER 18

ANIMAL MAGIC

Thinking back over the years I have to marvel at the fact that I and many other of my fellow expatriates survived the experience of a contract in Zambia without too much damage.

The thought of sleeping outside a game reserve on a camp bed with no protection other than a mosquito net and a camp fire in an area in which lions, leopard, cheetah and hippos roamed freely doesn't really bear thinking about and I would probably have been horrified much later in life had my son or daughter suggested such a thing when they were a similar age.

Despite the fire that we built both to keep ourselves warm in the cold nights during the dry season and to deter the wild life from coming too close, some were not easily persuaded to stay away.

Elephants in particular are creatures of habit when it comes to the paths which they travel and if we had chosen to build our camp across their right of way then that was a problem for us and not for them. On more than one occasion an elephant either walked through the Luangwa camp site or very close by during the night.

On Hilary's very first visit to the camp she and I had a relatively close encounter with one. Late in the evening as everyone was getting ready to crash out and get some sleep, Hilary whispered in my ear "I need to go to the toilet." "Well off you go then" I whispered back unsympathetically. "I don't want to walk all the way to the toilet on my own."

The toilet was a pit latrine which for obvious reasons was a reasonable distance from the camp site. I wasn't keen to walk too far in the dark so I said quietly. "Pick up the spade and we can walk a little way into the bush."

Hilary lifted a spade and we walked into the dark. "This will be far enough." We were only a hundred yards or so away from our friends but although we could see the lights and hear the voices, they couldn't see or hear us.

"Get on with it" I said and Hilary squatted down in the dark. Why do women have to be so awkward about it all I was thinking when suddenly from the darkness a few yards away came an enormous explosive rumbling fart which seemed to go on forever followed by the unmistakable sound of an elephant's digestive system working overtime.

If Hilary had been in any need of encouragement for what she was doing, she certainly didn't need it now. She was out of the crouch position, knickers back up and running all in one movement and was twenty yards away before I caught up.

"What was that?" She panted. "An elephant which just happened to be doing the same as you on the other side of the bush that you chose." We looked behind but in the dark there was no sign of anything.

"Sounds like an elephant nearby" Charlie grunted as we walked back into the firelight at the camp. "No it was only Hilary" I replied grinning, and earned myself a kick on the shins for my trouble. Hilary was only new to the group and hadn't yet got to know people well enough not to get embarrassed.

Next morning, we were up early, wakened by the morning sounds of Africa, the grunting of the hippos, and the trill of the myriad birds. Hilary and I walked towards the edge of the river and were just in time to catch sight of a female elephant wading across from our side back into the reserve on the other. She saw us and waved her trunk in the air as a warning for us not to get too close. Reaching the opposite bank, she clambered out using one knee to lever her weight over the top, much in the same way as an elderly lady might have done. A fascinating sight.

"That was probably your friend from last night" I smiled at Hilary who was watching spellbound.

Later in the year one of the other wives was to have an even closer encounter with a local resident.

One quiet afternoon Dave Sayer's wife was sitting on the toilet set within a small straw hut to provide some privacy, when to her horror she saw, through a small gap in the straw wall, a rhinoceros ambling slowly towards her. For a moment she didn't know what to do but quickly realized that screaming for help might not be a great idea. She could only hope that the rhino would walk straight past.

No such luck. The rhino is a large animal and as it wandered by it collided with the makeshift toilet causing the hut to topple over on to its side leaving the occupant sprawling somewhat embarrassingly on the ground with her knickers round her ankles.

The rhino seemed not to notice anything and continued on its way. Dave's wife waited for a few minutes before picking herself up and making her way back to the camp where on telling her story the rest of us fell about laughing.

Charlie and I were to have a very similar experience some time later. It was early in the year and we had driven North to a remote area to see whether or not the Luangwa river had subsided sufficiently after the rainy season to enable us to get supplies into the local health centre.

The ground was still very wet and we had decided to leave the Land Rover and walk along a narrow bicycle track which made its way through an area of standing water and bush.

Suddenly ahead of us there appeared from round a corner a rhinoceros heading down the path towards us. Charlie and I looked at each other. "This way" Charlie said and I followed him as he squelched his way as quickly and as quietly as possible to a small sapling tree growing about twenty yards from the track.

"They're very poorly sighted so hopefully he won't see us." Charlie whispered as we shinned up the tree. The rhino snuffled his way along the path but just as he came level with us the sapling decided that the weight was too much and very slowly but surely uprooted itself depositing Charlie and me on our backs into the water with a splash.

The rhino looked across and you could almost see it thinking "What are those two silly fools doing?" before continuing on his way.

Despite these occasional close encounters, we all survived to tell the tales.

CHAPTER 19

PLANE FUN

The Great East road to Lusaka was the only major road link between Eastern Province and the remainder of Zambia but this link was to prove very tenuous.

One night a group of FRELIMO guerillas in their war to free Mazambique from its colonial rule by Portugal, blew up the bridge at the Luangwa river crossing some one hundred miles South of Chipata, the sagging bridge which I had crossed on my original road journey to Chipata.

Whether they did it by accident, not realising that it was in Zambia, or deliberately in order to publicise their cause we will never know but the end result was that we were effectively cut off from the rest of the country until such time as the bridge could be repaired.

Since much of the food supply and all of the basic comestibles were supplied by road, this caused something of a problem. Not so much for the expatriate community who were able to drive across the border into Malawi and bring back necessities but for the local population who had no such ability.

After a few weeks, when Government realized the situation, they agreed to send a Hercules C130 transport aircraft from Lusaka with relief supplies. Although Chipata airport had a regular scheduled airline service to and from Lusaka operated by Zambia Airways with a Hawker Siddley (British Aerospace) 748 aircraft, it was still a dirt runway mainly used by small privately operated planes. A Hercules was going to be the largest aircraft to land on the strip and the airport manager, Wally, wanted to ensure that there would be no problems.

He therefore asked the Chipata town fire brigade to come up to the airport on the due day to assist his small airport team in providing fire cover in the unlikely event of an accident.

The local fire unit consisted of a red painted Land Rover equipped with a set of small ladders, there being no high rise buildings in Chipata, and some basic pumping equipment augmented by the ubiquitous stirrup pumps.

Led by Albert, a stalwart long term expatriate from the North of England, the fire crew were told by Wally to position themselves at the top end of the runway, which sloped gradually away from them, then follow the aircraft along the runway after it touched down, so as to be in position behind it should anything untoward happen.

This was the biggest event to have happened in Chipata for many years so most of the expatriate community turned up at the airport to watch events as they unfolded and to help unload the aircraft.

Albert and his crew sat and waited with growing anticipation as the dark shape of the Hercules made its appearance overhead the airfield then turned away to make its approach. This was the most excitement that they'd had in a long time.

The giant aircraft came in low and smooth and as it flashed over the runway threshold Albert shouted "Follow the plane." The Zambian driver yelled "Yes Bwana" and floored the accelerator.

The Land Rover lurched forward and started to career down the runway behind the aircraft. At the same moment the aircraft wheels connected with the runway and the pilot reversed the pitch of the four large propellers in order to slow the landing run as quickly as possible.

Immediately the fire engine was enveloped in a huge cloud of red dirt blown backwards from the surface of the runway by the force of the propellers and as it rapidly disappeared from the view of the large crowd gathered to witness this momentous arrival we erupted in a gale of laughter.

Albert wasn't best pleased as he appeared a few minutes later with his crew coughing, spluttering and wiping the dirt from their eyes. The fire engine drove across to where several of us were preparing to help unload the cargo. "I suppose you lot thought that was funny?" He looked at all of us accusingly. We all averted our eyes whilst trying to keep straight faces. "It was a very important job we had to do" he muttered as he stomped away. We burst out laughing again.

This wasn't to be the only incident of note at the airport. One Sunday afternoon at the beginning of the wet season, as a number of us were sitting on the terrace at the golf club having just finished our games, news came through the grapevine to say that the Sunday air service from Lusaka was delayed. This in itself wasn't unusual.

The flight to Chipata stopped first at the Mfuwe game lodge in the Luangwa Park where it discharged passengers bound for the game viewing and hunting resorts.

Chipata was the next stop before it continued to Lilongwe in Malawi in order to provide a service not only to the town but also to Lake Malawi which was a holiday resort. The aircraft then returned to Lusaka following the same route in reverse.

On this particular Sunday the flight was operating very late. Darkness was approaching which made things somewhat complicated. The aircraft Captain, realising that on the return flight to Lusaka he would be unable to land at the game reserve in the dark, took a decision to pick up the passengers who would have boarded the return flight from Mfuwe to Lusaka and take them on the outbound flight towards Chipata.

He would then overfly Chipata and go direct to Lilongwe carrying the Mfuwe joiners along with those passengers who were due to disembark at Chipata.

On the return flight from Lilongwe the aircraft would land at Chipata in the dark and disembark the passengers originally bound for Chipata, who had been forced to make a return journey into Malawi. He could then pick up the Lusaka bound passengers from Chipata who would join the passengers from the game park who had also made an unexpected trip into Malawi and the aircraft would fly directly back to the Capital. Complicated?

All this was communicated by radio to the airports concerned so that everyone was aware as to what was going to happen.

Chipata wasn't a well-equipped airport and although it had a relatively long runway there were no fixed night landing facilities.

News of what was going to happen filtered down from the airport to the town. The landing threatened to be fun, so a large party absented themselves from sundowner drinks at the golf club and piling into a collection of vehicles raced up to the airport to what was happening.

We arrived in time to see Wally and his team working their way along the runway setting out a series of paraffin flares on either side of the dirt strip. As they burned they cast a strange oily yellow glow, which seemed somewhat inadequate but obviously did enough to indicate the landing area to the pilot.

Meanwhile a Land Rover was parked at each end of the runway, headlights on full beam facing down the landing run, to give the pilot some indication of where he was to touch down.

It seemed an eternity before the aircraft appeared, firstly flying overhead to get a view of what was on offer. Some of our party thought that he was overflying and would just carry on to Lusaka, but just as we were about to walk back to our vehicles, someone shouted "He's turning!!"

We all looked up into the darkness and sure enough the aircraft was definitely turning. Again it made a slow pass at height over the field then flew away towards the horizon before turning again. "He's coming in" someone said "I don't believe it" said another voice. "He must be mad" said a third. I think that most of us thought the same thing.

The aircraft headlights came on and seemed to glare straight at us as they cut powerfully through the darkness although the aircraft was still some distance away and its approach seemed to take forever. It crawled towards us as we stood holding our breath. We none of us could see the aircraft, but the bright headlight beam transfixed us.

The aircraft touched down light as a feather and a giant exhalation was heard as we all breathed again. All of us had feared the worst.

Leaving the runway, it taxied to a halt by the fence, the door opened and the passengers disembarked. We all stood waiting to see the pilot. This man who had the ability to land a forty eight seat aircraft on to a dirt strip in the African bush in the dark.

Eventually he appeared. The archetypal British pilot with handlebar moustache who walked with a pronounced limp as he made his way into the building to be greeted by Wally. We just looked on in awe.

Later Wally told us that the aircraft headlights shone straight at us because the aircraft was actually pointed at an angle to the runway for some time due to the fact that the smoke produced by the paraffin flares, blowing on the breeze down the runway towards the incoming aircraft was actually obscuring the pilots' view of the landing point.

This just confirmed our original thoughts that the pilot was mad to attempt the landing.

CHAPTER 20

THE ROAD TO
THE COPPERBELT

My next experience with the airfield was somewhat more personal. One of the Barclays' Bank staff, known to all of us as Kid Miller because of his youthfulness had decided to visit his parents in Luanshya on the Copperbelt for a weekend.

Despite the distance involved, some six hundred miles, he was going to drive there and Hilary and I took up an offer to go with him to visit our friend Margaret and her husband. Another bank employee, John, also joined us for the trip.

Late in the evening, driving through the darkness, some three hundred miles down the road en route to Lusaka, Hilary and I were snoozing in the back of the Ford Cortina whilst the two guys sat in the front with Kid driving.

Suddenly Kid let out a yell "Look out!!" The car swerved and there was an almighty crunch as we hit something very hard. The windscreen caved in around us in a maelstrom of flying glass. Kid fought with the steering wheel and the car screeched to a halt.

"What happened?" We were all stunned. "It was a cow I think" said Kid. "A big black cow in the middle of the black road on a black night. Is everybody OK?"

We all got out of the car and looked at each other. "I think so" I said. We were all shaking glass off our clothes and out of our hair but surprisingly none of us had suffered any damage, not even a scratch.

"That was lucky" said John "but what about the car?" Kid was walking around it looking very distraught. The left wing was buckled, the left windscreen upright was mangled and the glass was totally shattered.

In the background we could hear the sound of a cow making a lot of noise and voices indicating that there were some people nearby.

"Get in quickly" Kid said suddenly. "Get in" he shouted to us. The three of us jumped swiftly into the car. Kid started the engine, slammed it into gear and took off down the road. "What's going on" John asked "What are you doing?"

"The villagers can get very upset if you kill something" was the response "they will demand money and can get very threatening."

Kid was a local having been born and bred in the Country so I reckoned that he probably knew more about it than I did and I wasn't prepared to argue.

We stopped about a mile down the road. "This is far enough" Kid got out and walked around the car. "It's not too bad considering that we were travelling at about 60 when I saw it."

"What are we going to do now?" John looked at the three of us. "Well it's still drivable so I vote we just carry on. We can clear the worst of the glass out of the inside so that we can sit comfortably. There's no point in sitting here all night." Kid was right and it was his car. We cleared out some of the mess, got in and restarted our trip.

It was at this point that we realised why the windscreen was important. Not that the African night was cold but it was full of flying insects. We were peppered with them. Kid wasn't too bad as he wore glasses whilst driving but John, Hilary and I had to hide behind a screen of towels to cover our faces and in that way we travelled through the city centre of Lusaka where we must have made a very peculiar sight to anyone in the street. We then had a further two hundred miles to travel up the Great North road.

We eventually arrived at Luanshya, much to our friend Margaret's relief. She had been worried about us when we hadn't arrived as early as she had expected. "What happened?" she said looking at the car in horror as we sat in the road outside her house. "A coming together with a cow." I explained.

"Are you alright?" Margaret fussed around. "Come in and have a drink, you must be foundered" reverting to a good old fashioned Northern Irish word.

"We're fine, don't worry. Do you know our friends?" I introduced them to Margaret and her husband Gordon.

We got our bags out of the car. "I'll contact you tomorrow" Kid said as he got back into the car with John. "I'll arrange something to get us home." were his last words as he drove off down the street.

After a good nights' sleep we awoke to a typical sunny day and throwing off any worries about how we were to get home, made the best of Margaret and Gordon's excellent hospitality.

A trip to the town centre reminded Hilary and me as to just how basic Chipata was. Luanshya was a garden town, designed specifically to support the local copper mine and provided with all the mod cons that we were used to back home in the UK. Not only that but the food stores were filled with items which we could only dream about in Chipata.

I made Margaret laugh when I told her that when I told her that on my first visit to the Government food shop in Chipata I had been amazed to find that there were only a very few basic food items available. Many of the shelves were empty but those covering the rear wall of the shop were filled with bottles of Premier Cru Chablis.

How or why it had got there no-one knew but it was incredibly cheap and whilst I wasn't able to buy soap or anything other than very basic food the wine supply was better than anything I had known back home in Northern Ireland.

As good as his word Kid Miller contacted us late in the morning. "How's the car?" I asked. "It's OK" he responded brightly. "It will take a few weeks to sort it out. They have to get spare parts and they aren't easily come by even in a well-organized place like this but my father can keep an eye on it".

I'd forgotten that Kid was at home and that his father was well connected in the town. "I've also organised our return trip" he carried on. "How's that?" I queried. "Have you found another car?"

"Better than that" he grinned at me. "I've got an aeroplane."

"You've what? You're kidding. What do you mean you've got an aeroplane?"

"Well" he said "they have a flying club here and one of my friends is hoping to become an airline pilot. He has a licence but needs to get more hours up, so he says he will fly us back on Sunday afternoon if we share the cost of the fuel."

I couldn't believe it and neither could Hilary when I told her. "Does he have a licence, can he fly, is it going to be safe?" All these questions poured out as Hilary took it all in. "I don't know" I said, "You'll have to ask Kid but it all seems to be ok."

Thus it was that on Sunday after lunch we found ourselves strapping into a six seater aircraft and preparing to take off. The pilot had introduced himself, explained the aircraft safety issues and told us that he would have to fly first to Ndola international airport to fuel the aircraft as there wasn't any fuel available at Luanshya. We took off and made the short hop to Ndola where to my inexperienced eye the runway looked huge as we touched down.

Refuelling was quick and twenty minutes later we were airborne again heading into a cloud filled sky and a two hour flight across country to Chipata. Breaking through the cloud we were soon enjoying a smooth flight in sunny clear air.

Hilary and I were in the back two seats and I was enjoying the experience until I began to get the uncomfortable feeling that all was not well with my bladder, notwithstanding the fact that I had visited the toilet immediately prior to take off at Luanshya.

I was well known for my lack of capacity. I looked around. There wasn't a toilet on such a small aircraft, not that I had really expected to find one. I turned to Hilary and explained my predicament. She wasn't very sympathetic.

"Why didn't you go before we took off?" she snorted at me. "I did but you know me. It always happens at the worst possible time."

"Well what are you going to do?" She looked at me accusingly. "I don't know but I'm getting desperate" I replied with an anguished look.

Hilary looked around her seat then delved into her bag. "Use this" She handed me a polythene bag. "Will it be all right?" "Well it hasn't got a hole in it, I've checked." I took the bag and proceeded to fill it quietly and in great relief.

"Lucky it was me sitting beside you and not one of the other women who might have been travelling." Hilary grinned, just trying to embarrass me as much as possible. "They would just have to have averted their eyes." I replied.

"What are you going to do with the bag?" "I'll just have to take it off with me when we land." That was the least of my worries I thought. At least I could now enjoy the remainder of the flight.

About half an hour later the aircraft went into a tight left turn. "We've arrived" announced the pilot. "By my reckoning the airfield should be directly below us."

The aircraft spiralled down through the cloud and as we broke through the cloud base I got a view of the green bush beneath. "Recognize anything?" the pilot asked.

We all peered beneath us. Nobody replied. The aircraft continued to turn in a tight circle and I was very aware that there were numerous hills in the vicinity of the airfield, any of which would have spelled disaster were we to accidentally fly into one.

Suddenly I spotted something. "We've just passed over the airport road. Go round again." The pilot continued to turn.

"There it is" I could see the tarmacadam surface beneath us. "So which way is the airfield?" The pilot looked round at us. "I don't know from up here. You'll have to fly a short way along it to see which way we are facing." It seems ridiculous now in thinking about it that we couldn't just have looked at a map and identified the aircraft direction.

We flew for a short distance. "We're going the wrong way" I shouted at the pilot, having just recognized where we were.

"OK". He turned the aircraft and we headed back along the road. A few minutes later and the airfield came into view. I breathed a sigh of relief. We probably hadn't ever been in any danger but not being an experienced flier in small aircraft I wasn't sure.

We touched down on the wet dirt runway and taxied to the buildings. Wally greeted us with a large smile as he walked towards the aircraft. "I didn't know it was you" he said with a grin "I didn't know who would be flying in from Ndola in a private aircraft" he added.

We offloaded our bags quickly as Kid began to tell the whole story to Wally. The pilot walked in with us and we sat with him whilst he had a coffee. "Thanks for that, but I'll have to be going. I want to get back before it gets dark if possible."

We all shook his hand and watched as a few minutes later the aircraft climbed away. As there were no other aircraft due to land that evening Wally offered us a lift into town. We were well into the drive when Hilary whispered urgently to me "What did you do with the bag?" I looked at her with a grin "That's for me to know and you to guess at" I said, touching the side of my nose with my finger conspiratorially. And so it was.

CHAPTER 21

YOUTHFUL ANTICS

Kid Miller was to feature again in the next few months. During the dry season we tended to vacate Chipata at the weekend and head for the Luangwa valley on Friday evening after work. What had originally been the preserve of the males had now been extended to encompass a number of women who had arrived in town either as wives, such as Hilary or as newly recruited nursing staff or teachers.

When I had arrived in town the female expatriate population could have been numbered in single figures and there had been great excitement earlier in the year amongst the unattached males when two new nurses arrived at the hospital.

They duly turned up at the bar in the Golf Club on their second evening. A pair of scousers from Liverpool they were an instant hit with the lads as sitting on their barstools they began to match the guys drink for drink and were still there in the small hours of the morning when many of the men had given up.

At last they decided that enough was enough and Charlie being a gentleman offered them a lift back to their quarters about half a mile away. Much giggling and laughter ensued as Charlie and the girls climbed into his Land Rover. Then with a cloud of smoke and some grating of gears they set off only for Charlie to drive straight into a small grove of bamboo which stood in the middle of the car park.

That was it. The girls exited the vehicle and decided that it would be much safer to walk. Charlie, to his credit, decided the same and left his Land Rover parked in the bamboo overnight.

Anyway, back to Kid Miller. A number of us were on our way home one Sunday evening having spent an enjoyable weekend sleeping under the stars and game viewing during the day. Prior to driving back Kid had decided that he would play a joke on his Bank manager and had loaded a sack full of elephant droppings into the boot of his car.

His intention was to place the droppings on the steps of the bank overnight so that in the morning it would appear that an elephant had been in town and had walked up the steps to the door, leaving a trail of elephant dung all the way up.

Five of us were in the car as we drove out of the valley on the dirt road. Rounding a corner, we were confronted by a group of half a dozen armed men, one of whom was flagging us down. They were dressed in army camouflage and we instantly recognized them as a tsetse fly and anti-poaching unit.

Kid braked and wound his window down. We came to a halt in the usual cloud of red dust. The senior team member approached and politely spoke to Kid.

"Good evening Bwana." He looked into the car and we all smiled happily at him."

Are you carrying anything in the car?" "Nothing" kid replied.

"Open the boot please" Kid got out and swung the boot lid open. Inside were a couple of small bags carrying our assorted minimal clothes and the sack.

"What is in the sack?" the officer asked with a questioning look. "Elephant shit" responded Kid. "No Bwana, what is in the sack?" the officer asked again, this time in a slightly harder tone. "Elephant dung" Kid replied looking straight at him.

"You should not joke with me Bwana." The tone was getting harder. "I'm not." was the reply.

The officer had heard enough. He barked an order to one of his team and a young man stepped forward. He thrust his hand into the sack.

"What is in it?" demanded the officer.

The young man's face was a picture as he turned to his boss, and with one hand still in the top of the sack said "Elephant shit!"

We could barely keep our faces straight. All of us in the car knew that to laugh would be deemed inappropriate and could cause the army team to turn angry. They wouldn't want to lose face. Kid tried to explain to the officer why he had the elephant dung in the car but the joke which he was planning for the Bank appeared to fall on stony ground. The Zambians couldn't understand why anyone would want to do it.

Nevertheless, we weren't carrying anything illegal and if we wanted to carry elephant dung in the car that was OK with them.

Kid climbed back in and the car was duly sprayed with insecticide being applied liberally to the boot, underside and wheel wells where the tsetse flies, the carriers of sleeping sickness, may have hidden themselves.

Having completed their job, the soldiers stood back and waved us on our way, and as I looked out of the rear window I could see them shaking their heads in disbelief at these very odd expatriates who drove around the country with elephant dung in their car. But more was to follow.

Having arrived back in Chipata, Kid was told by his fellow inmates in the Bank house, that there was no way in which he was to bring the sack of elephant droppings into the house. So Kid left the sack outside, by the fence.

After dinner he went out to pick it up and take it to the steps at the Bank only to find that it was gone. "OK" he said striding back into the house. "Very funny. Who's got it?" His colleagues looked blank.

"Who's moved the sack" Kid demanded, now getting a bit annoyed. Being the youngest of the Bank team he was used to being the butt of their practical jokes.

"No-one has touched it" John replied quietly. Everyone else nodded. "Well where has it gone"?

"Probably someone has stolen it" came the reply from one of his mates. "That's more than likely. One of the local lads has seen an opportunity, grabbed the sack and run."

The thought of it suddenly convulsed everyone into fits of laughter. "Can you just see his face when he opened the sack?" said John with tears running down his face. "All that effort to steal a sack, only to find that it was full of elephant dung." The room convulsed again.

Life moved on apace. Days spent at work in the office with Charlie, joined often in the morning by Pat, the librarian from the public library across the road from our office.

Pat and her husband Brian, a schoolteacher, came from Belfast and were on an expatriate contract like Charlie and me. Mid-morning, she would come across the road and Mvula the messenger would be dispatched to Cooper's coffee bar round the corner to buy three toasted cheese and tomato sandwiches which the three of us would devour along with a cup of coffee whilst discussing what had happened the night before or what was coming up later in the day or week.

The community had to make its own entertainment and there was no shortage of skills. A play was put on at the VMI in which a number of us strode the boards, some for the first time. I had been on the stage some years previously appearing as part of a Youth Club drama group in a typical Irish kitchen comedy. Well it certainly was a comedy by the time we had finished with it!!

Here in Africa we were presenting "Arms and the Man" by George Bernard Shaw where I played the Chocolate Cream Soldier.

It was a difficult play to produce on the small stage and difficult for the audience as well but less so than Charlie's first thought which had been "Waiting for Godot." Anyway it was a distraction and everyone seemed to enjoy it even if the audience didn't necessarily understand it.

Our next production was much more simple. Two of our expatriate teacher friends were graduates of Cambridge University, famed for its "Footlights Revue" which spawned many a great comedian and scriptwriter over the years, the most famous of which were the stars of That Was The Week That Was and Monty Python's Flying Circus.

We were not destined to be quite so famous, however the two performances of our home made revue brought the house down. Set as it was around our individual and collective experiences of being recruited to work in Zambia and our working life to date, it was instantly recognizable to all the audience.

It was also great fun to produce. I was the pianist and musical director. Sketches and songs were written by a group of us who sat around an office and ran ideas past each other. We probably got as much fun out of the writing as the show.

Looking back at it some of it was probably very silly, then so was Monty Python, but put a bunch of guys together along with a few beers, to write about their experiences in being recruited and then working in Zambia and we were bound to get some fun.

The problem was in sorting out those ideas which would be funny to an audience as distinct from those that made us roll around almost crying with laughter as we tried to write a suitable script.

One of the more serious difficulties was that however bizarre and funny the stories might have been, we couldn't afford to upset our employers, the Government and people of Zambia, by being in any way disrespectful of them or their country. It was after all providing all of us with a very good living.

Sitting in my office one afternoon the door opened and there was David. "What do you think of this?" He began to hum a simple melody. Then he began to add words in the style of rhyming couplets.

"Hang on, hang on, repeat that first line. Hum it again." I was desperately trying to get a grasp of the musical strands that were being aimed at me.

"OK I think I've got it. Let's just run across to the Golf Club and I'll try it on the piano." So both of us dashed across the car park, over the small wall and in a few minutes I was running my fingers over the keys and trying to replicate the melody.

"That's it" David shouted triumphantly and so another song was added to the repertoire. I tried to jot down a few notes on a sheet of paper just to remind myself as to the basic nature of the tune.

This was to happen several times over a couple of weeks as we progressed slowly but surely towards our performance. The tunes stuck in my mind, so much so that I can still remember a couple of them years later.

The show went well and was talked about for months afterwards with many of the audience repeating the jokes and even trying to sing some of the more memorable tunes. It was all great fun

CHAPTER 22

BACK TO THE WILDERNESS

A short while later Charlie asked me if I would like to make a trip up to the Northern part of our District to check on some construction work going on in the building of new Health Centres. "OK" I said somewhat reluctantly bearing in mind my experience in the river with the Land Rover which was still fresh in my mind. I certainly didn't fancy a repeat performance.

"Why don't you take Hilary?" He looked at me. "She would enjoy a trip into a more remote area I'm sure."

Back at the house that evening I mentioned it. Hilary jumped at the opportunity and said that it would fit neatly into some time off that she was about to have from her teaching role at the Teacher Training College. We began to make plans.

A day or two later Charlie approached me again. "You're going to have company" he said. "Dick from Public Works Department is going to go with you as he needs to have a look at the buildings as well and he can take his wife Denise." Dick and Denise were a recent addition to our community having arrived from Essex.

"I'm also going to send our Senior Health assistant and a couple of his team with you as part of a familiarisation for them."

A few days later we set off in two Land Rovers, each fully loaded with equipment in the back and on roof racks bolted on top of each vehicle, retracing the steps of my ill-fated river adventure.

Firstly, to Lundazi and its famous castle. Dick, Denise and Hilary were spellbound by it. "I'd heard about it" Dick said looking in awe, "But I didn't believe it. I thought that I was being wound up by my mates in the office. You know how it is? When you're the new boy they try anything to catch you out. Left handed screwdrivers, striped paint etc. but this place is just something else."

We spent some time taking pictures before continuing. Some miles further on we went through the river which had been my demise a few months earlier. Almost totally dry now it posed no challenge.

"Was that it?" Hilary looked at me. "It wasn't very big." She had obviously expected a raging torrent. "Don't forget that this is the dry season and it's very different in the rains." I don't think that she believed me.

We trekked on with my Zambian team leading the way, eventually arriving at the village where I was to look at the construction work of a new Health Centre just before darkness descended on us. A horde of children came rushing to meet us, followed by their mothers and a few of the village men. We decanted ourselves stiffly from the vehicles. The children backed off and stood giggling and pointing.

My team leader came across "They haven't seen white people before" he explained. I looked at him incredulously." How come?" "You're the first Government Officer who has been this far North in eight years" he replied quietly.

I was stunned. I knew that it was a very large country and there were only a few Europeans working there but I hadn't expected to be the first visitor in such a long time.

The women approached shyly, offering their two hands, placed together, in the normal form of greeting, bringing small pots of steaming maize, the staple diet.

We were being treated as honoured guests and I felt quite overcome by this display of friendship. These people had very little in material wealth yet were prepared to offer what little they had to strangers arriving unannounced as visitors.

We each took a small portion of the maize being offered as it would have been rude not to have done so but we were careful not to take too much as it could have seriously depleted their food stock.

Whilst Dick, Hilary and I were objects of curiosity to the children, Denise was very special. She was the archetypal English blonde with blue eyes and was very obviously the first such woman who had visited the village in a considerable time if not the only one.

Not only were the children transfixed by her long blonde hair but the village women and many of the men were staring in disbelief.

Gradually some of them began to overcome their shyness and before long several of them were touching her blonde tresses. Denise was happy to go along with this, after all it was part of the great experience of being in Africa.

Later in the evening we sat by the fireside eating our meal and discussing the events of the day. It had been quite enthralling for all of us.

"I'd heard about African people who hadn't seen blonde hair before but I didn't think that it still applied nowadays, I thought that was only part of history." Denise mused.

"Did it scare you?" Hilary asked. "No" Denise replied. "They were obviously only very curious and it just felt strange to be making history myself."

We all thought about how great an experience the day had been and what Africa was giving to us. Surprisingly, as Dick said, not all the expatriates working in Zambia felt the same way.

Some were unhappy about being in an under developed country away from what they considered to be the home comforts of life. "You wouldn't believe it "I said "but when Hilary and I were in Luanshya on the Copperbelt recently we met a couple from Middlesbrough who were complaining that it wasn't like home as there wasn't a fish and chip shop!"

Given that Luanshya was much better provided for than we were in the bush in Chipata, Hilary and I were quite flabbergasted"

Dick laughed. "Well personally I could think of a lot of places that I would rather be in than Middlesbrough."

"I've never been there so I can't comment" I added. "However when I was in Mazabuka I met some people who were just completing their contract and although they had been there for three years had never visited the Victoria Falls, which were only a days' drive away and they had never been to a game reserve."

"Only here for the money" Dick replied. "What a waste. Such a wonderful country and such a lot to see" added Denise. "Why wouldn't you want to broaden your experience after all we may never get another chance to see some of the world's great wonders?"

We all agreed as we began to settle down for the night.

Rather than sleep in the open we had decided to pitch our camp beds and mosquito nets inside the partly constructed Health Centre. The walls were in place and although there was no roof and there were no doors, it would be preferable to sleeping in the open in the village square.

Hilary and I chose one room whilst Dick and Denise settled in another. Each of us had positioned a large piece of wood to act as a door and we climbed gratefully into our sleeping bags and crashed out almost immediately.

I don't know what it was that woke me, perhaps it was a slight breeze wafting across me, but as I glanced up I saw something black and menacing soaring through the starlit night sky straight for me.

I let out a yell and put up my arms just as the blackness enveloped me with a crash. At the same moment Hilary awoke with a scream. We fought our way out of our sleeping bag with some difficulty.

"What was it?" Hilary almost screamed as I picked myself gingerly round the bed. Suddenly I realised what had happened. "It was the door" I said, picking up the woodwork from where it now lay half on the bed and half on the floor. "I saw it coming but had no idea what it was" I explained.

"Are you all right?" questioning voices came from just outside the gap where the door had stood. "Yes, we're fine" I replied. "The door fell in." Denise convulsed into giggles and Dick and I followed, all of us recognizing the silliness of the situation. Hilary wasn't so easily mollified. "She doesn't like being woken in the middle of the night" I explained but gradually even she saw the funny side.

I placed the door back into the aperture but this time ensured that it was very firmly in place and we all went back to sleep.

Next morning we arose early as we had much further to go. Dick and I carried out our inspection of the building to satisfy ourselves that the construction was up to standard and would be completed before the next rainy season. Then we packed up our equipment, loaded ourselves back into the two Land Rovers and with thanks and waves to all the villagers and children set off along the track.

Many of the children ran alongside us for the first few hundred yards keeping pace with us, waving and laughing until we picked up speed and gradually left them behind.

It was stinking hot and soon we were all drenched in sweat. The bush got thicker and thicker until we were fighting our way down a very narrow track through an almost impenetrable tunnel with the scrubby trees having grown completely overhead and meshed to provide a roof through which even the searing African sun couldn't reach.

I fought with the wheel of the Land Rover as I followed my team leader ahead in the first truck. The track seemed to peter out from time to time but we followed a series of slashes visible on a number of the trees along the way which appeared to show the way.

The vehicle pitched and lurched its way along and my passengers were hanging on for dear life on more than one occasion.

Suddenly the vehicle seemed to be dragged almost to a halt and simultaneously there was a loud crash. "We've lost the roof rack" Dick yelled. The rack loaded with all the gear and equipment destined for the outstation had been swept off the vehicle by the tangle of bushes encompassing the trail.

I braked hard and sounded my horn to alert the Land Rover in front. The driver braked quickly and we jumped out into a cloud of dust swirling in the gloom.

"What happened Bwana" "Ah, you've lost the roof rack." A few rapid instructions and the team got to work to rescue the roof rack from beneath the pile of equipment under which it was buried. Within a remarkably short time it was all back on top of my truck and we were ready to roll again.

The break had been useful as we had all been able to stretch our legs and have a quick drink of coffee.

"How do you know where you are going?" I asked the team leader. "I'm following the marks on the trees" he replied quickly. "Who put them there?" I was puzzled as to who had been here before us. "The mining company" he replied quickly. "De Beers I think they are called. They came from South Africa I think." he continued.

"Yes" I confirmed. It was quite likely as there were numerous minerals in Zambia but most undiscovered as yet.

Diamonds were already being mined in the nearby Congo and I had previously experienced a knock on my door one night and on opening it was confronted by an African speaking French and holding out what appeared to be a handful of uncut diamonds which he wanted me to buy.

Diamonds they may or may not have been, but even if I had been tempted to buy them what would I have done with them. I could hardly have walked into my local jewellers in Bangor and asked him to cut and polish some rough diamonds!

We were soon underway again and continued to plough through the thick undergrowth. Eventually, late in the afternoon the bush began to thin out and we found ourselves on the edge of a river. It was about forty yards across and looked to be fairly shallow although it was difficult to tell in the declining sunshine.

"It must be a tributary of the Luangwa." Dick said. "How deep do you think it is?" "I've no idea." I looked around for some indications.

"The track doesn't appear to go straight across. There's a piece of wood standing upright in the water a bit further to our left." I looked again. "And another about ten yards beyond the first one. It looks as if the track veers across the river in a semicircle to our left. What do you think?"

Dick and the girls had a look and all seemed to agree. "It looks fairly shallow" Hilary said. "Yes but maybe there is a deeper channel in the middle which we can't see from here."

I thought that there must be a reason why the track didn't just take a straight line across the river from where it had arrived at the bank.

"Someone had better walk across and check the depth before we drive into it. I wouldn't want to lose the Land Rover or get it stuck here as we are a long way from anywhere."

Thinking back, I don't know why I just didn't ask my team leader to send one of the lads across but turning to Hilary and Denise I said "Why don't the two of you paddle across and I'll drive slowly into the river but some distance behind so that I can see how deep it's getting?"

"OK" said Denise and without another word she slipped off her flip flops and carrying them in her hand stepped into the water. "Oh it's lovely and cool."

"Is it?" Hilary, not to be outdone stepped into the water and the two of them began to paddle carefully across, walking up stream towards the first of the two wooden markers that we had spotted.

I jumped back into the Land Rover and revving the engine carefully put it into four wheel drive and edged into the river behind the girls.

The river bed appeared to be composed mainly of rocks, mostly small but with some which were larger and caused the truck to rock and skid slightly as I tried to keep it going in a reasonably straight line.

The water rose up the legs of Hilary and Denise as they moved into the middle of the river then gradually started to edge further up their thighs. "I hope it's not going to get any deeper" I heard Hilary over the sound of the engine.

"Just watch your feet and try not to fall over" I shouted to them over the noise. "I think you're past the middle so it should shallow again fairly quickly."

I was right. The girls had now circumnavigated the second wooden marker and the waterline on their legs was falling.

"That's it" Hilary shouted to me "It's beginning to shallow." She and Denise picked up a bit of speed as the stones beneath their feet began to become visible again in the shallowing water and with a shout of success they walked to the edge of the river at the other bank.

I pressed a bit harder on the accelerator, safe in the knowledge that the water wasn't going to get any deeper, and quickly followed the course that they had taken. Pulling the Land Rover onto the sandy beach on the other side I jumped out and yelled back to Dick and the team. "Come on. There's no problem."

Within minutes we were all standing on the opposite bank, looking back at the track down which we had just driven and admiring the view downstream. "It's very different on this side. Strange how it changes so rapidly." We were looking at an area of much lighter bush and the track ahead of us was well defined, wider and seemingly easier to drive along.

Hilary and Denise were still wandering around the edge of the river. "Be careful down there," I shouted to them, "there may be crocodiles or hippo in the river."

"Crocodiles!!" Hilary shrieked at me. "Crocodiles! You mean you just made me walk across a river which has crocodiles in it?"

She and Denise looked around them and quickly moved up the beach. "You mean you put both of us into the water knowing that there were crocodiles in it?"

I could see that I was in trouble. "No of course not. Don't be silly. We would have seen the crocodiles if there had been any. Anyway the water is too shallow at this point for them to be lying in it." I hoped that I sounded convincing. "In any case you volunteered to walk across."

"That's no excuse" Hilary retorted. I wasn't going to get away that easily. "You should have warned us."

"It was safe enough, nobody got hurt and none of us have seen anything. Anyway the amount of noise that you are making would have scared anything away."

Hilary snorted. Dick just grinned.

It was to prove an interesting evening. We piled back into the vehicles and set off again along the track, now making good time. We were beginning to look for a suitable place to pitch camp before the sun sank when suddenly and without warning we drove round a bend and found ourselves driving into a campsite.

A number of thatched rondavels were set out, alongside which several Land Rovers were parked.

We came to a halt in the usual cloud of dust and as I stepped down on to the dirt I recognized a face striding towards us. "Hi, what are you doing here?"

It was one of Norman Carr's big game hunters whom I had met briefly once or twice in the past. He had recognized me and shaking me by the hand invited us to come across and meet the clients that he was escorting. An American husband and wife stepped forward and I made the introductions. They seemed quite amazed to find a group such as our driving through the bush.

I explained who we were and what my job entailed and they were obviously quite fascinated. "You'll stay here overnight of course?" the hunter said. "Are you sure? We wouldn't want to get in the way?" I looked questioningly at him.

"Not at all, we'd be delighted to have your company. We've been out here for ten days already and I think that my wife's probably getting a bit bored with me. Your boys can pitch camp with my team over there"

He waved his arm in the general direction of the working end of the camp where his own team were busy preparing the evening meal.

"You'll join us for dinner?" the quietly spoken American looked at the girls. Hilary looked at me. "We'd be delighted" I responded.

The evening turned into one of the most interesting that any of us ever had. The American turned out to be John D MacDonald, a well-known author of thrillers, who had brought his wife along on his hunting trip. She wasn't a hunter and had been spending most of the days reading quietly whilst her husband went out early morning and evening in search of his game targets. She was certainly delighted to meet a couple of women with whom she could chat and both of them were intrigued to meet a bunch of British people in the depths of the African bush.

Sundowner drinks were followed by an excellent meal with chilled wine. The conversation flowed as we sat under the canopy of brilliant stars visible in the clear night sky, listening to the hippos grunting in a nearby pool and the occasional sounds of hyenas and even a lion some distance away. Being in the company of a professional hunter who was able to identify all the sounds made it all the more special. A magical night which has remained in my memory.

All too soon it was over and early next morning we were back in the Land Rovers heading on to the next Health Centre before taking a more circuitous route back home.

CHAPTER 23

LIONS TO LIGHTNING

Back in Chipata things had been happening. First morning back in the office after reporting events to Charlie he suddenly turned to me. "How are you with a gun?" "Pardon?" I asked. "Have you ever hunted or been clay pigeon shooting?"

"No but why are you asking?" I was somewhat mystified. "Apparently Dickie Donkin has got a problem lion on his farm" Charlie looked at me. "He's organizing a group of us to go up to the farm tomorrow evening and stake out the area to see if we can shoot the lion"

"You're joking?" "No I'm perfectly serious." "Well who else is involved then?" "Most of the rugby team." was the reply. I stood in the office thinking "You can't be serious."

Most of the rugby team, like me, would never have had a gun in their hand let alone know what to do with it.

Notwithstanding all this, the following evening saw a motley crew of male expatriates arriving at Dickie's farm just before sundown. "I've been having a problem with this bloody lion for weeks" he said. "It's had several of my animals and I can't take any more of it. It has to go. I've got enough guns to go round I think." He pointed at a collection of weapons piled on a table in the yard. "Help yourselves and I'll show you what to do."

I don't think that he had thought for one minute that most of us had never held a gun in our hands before. Nothing daunted, we all lined up and took it in turns to pick up a gun from the pile. Mine turned out to be a heavy shotgun.

I was pleased to see that Billy our rugby team captain and doughty solid player, was handling his weapon very gingerly. "Have you ever used one of these things before?" "No" I replied. "I just about know which end is which." We both laughed somewhat self-consciously.

Dickie stood in front of us. "This is what we are going to do. I'll show you how to load up and you'll have some spare ammunition, then we'll make our way out to the back where I've staked out a young goat in the hope that it will attract the lion."

The next ten minutes was spent giving all of us the rudiments as to how our assorted rifles and shotguns worked then we set off into the fields at the rear. We had all of us been told to bring a fold up chair and we must have looked a pretty strange sight as we trooped along.

Dickie had tied his young goat to a wooden stake and it stood there bleating and looking pitifully at us as if it already knew its fate. "I'll position you around the goat in a very large circle right round the field." Dickie sounded as if he knew what he was doing. "It will be dark soon and I need you all to be totally quiet. The nearest person to each of you will probably be at least twenty yards away so you won't be able to see or talk to each other."

I was positioned between Charlie and Billy and nightfall saw me sitting in my fold up picnic chair, shotgun across my lap and ankle deep in lush grass which began to get wet as the chill air of the evening set in.

It was a bizarre operation and if not bound to fail would otherwise have been extremely dangerous. It rapidly became dark, the pitch blackness that comes in an African night where there is no artificial lighting to pollute it.

I sat there, gradually getting very cold despite my wearing a heavy jacket. The only sounds were the piteous bleating of the goat and the whine of the multitude of mosquitoes which were now attacking the hunters.

I couldn't see a soul. Every whisper of breeze or slight noise made me edgy. Was it the lion? Would I see it? When should I fire? Thinking about it in retrospect we had to be totally mad.

Picture the situation. A dozen or more blokes, sitting around in a large circle in the pitch black, armed with a motley collection of weapons and with little or no experience of shooting but prepared to face a lion if it turned up.

Firstly, had the lion arrived it would have had to pass through our circle to get to the goat. It was unlikely to have been brave enough to do that, or if it were that brave, it was more likely to have attacked one of us from behind as we would have made an easy target.

Alternatively, if the lion had got to the goat and attacked it would we have been able to see enough of it to be able to shoot at it? Dickie had said that he had a light with him and would illuminate the goat if it were attacked but would this happen.

Worst of all, as we were in a circle, what were the chances that we would shoot each other? I mused over some of this as I sat there. I had no way of telling what the time was but we seemed to have been there for a very long time.

I had tucked my trouser legs into my socks to help keep out the cold but the damp and the mosquitoes were taking their toll.

Suddenly a voice whispered in my ear. I jumped about a foot in the air as I hadn't heard anyone approaching.

"Dickie says we're to give up as it doesn't look like it's coming tonight." It was Billy passing the word around.

"OK" I stumbled to my feet and tried to work out which way I should be going. I could hear voices in the dark. Suddenly Dickie's light cut a swathe through blackness "Over here." he called and we all headed back towards the farm.

Assembling in the yard to pick up our transport there was a palpable air of relief amongst us. We had been tested in so far as we were prepared to face up to a lion but fortunately the lion had failed to show, much to the great relief of most of us if the truth were to be told.

Damp and cold had pervaded all of us and the only winners appeared to be the goat and the mosquitoes.

I couldn't believe how badly I had been bitten. Getting home I counted fifty-two bites on one ankle and lower leg and forty-eight on the other. It took a long number of days before I could forget the great lion hunt.

Although it was talked about for a long time afterwards, the lion apparently had been scared off as it didn't make a return appearance, much to Dickie's relief.

Charlie had another singular funny experience indirectly involving a lion so to speak. For some reason, probably because he liked them, Charlie had acquired a large Great Dane dog. Brindle in colour or perhaps better described as tawny, she was an amiable big dog, more likely to lick you to death than cause a problem. However it had to be said that she was very big.

Most of the time she spent in Charlie's house, looked after by the house servant through the day. On one occasion however Charlie decided to take the dog into town and had her jump into the back of his Land Rover, which was one of the smaller, short wheel base variety. On his way into the office, he decided to pull into the garage to fill up with fuel. As he stopped and got out of the vehicle, the dog casually jumped out of the back, onto the garage forecourt.

Instant panic ensued. "It's a lion" cried one of the garage staff. People ran in all directions, one of the lads even tried to climb the pole holding up the advertising hoarding.

Charlie looked somewhat bewildered for a moment until, turning round he saw what was causing the commotion. "Get into the truck!" he bellowed and the dog obediently jumped back inside.

"It's only a dog" Charlie said loudly to everyone and no one in particular. A lot of embarrassed giggles and laughter broke out as the Zambians realized their mistake and began sheepishly to make their way back.

An easy mistake for them to have made since most of them had never seen a lion. It was a misconception amongst expatriates to think that the local people were in close contact with the animal population. This was far from true which I realized on one occasion when I had to take our office storekeeper with me on a working trip into the Luangwa valley. He was fascinated when he saw the animals, the majority of them for the first time and it was a delight for me to watch his face as we stood by the Luangwa looking at a pod of hippo and listening to their grunting and splashing.

That was just one of the many joys of living and working in such a glorious environment. One of the others was the climate.

The six month dry season was guaranteed each year from April through to October so it was possible to plan in advance any outing or event which involved being outside. Totally unlike the UK where it would be difficult to plan anything more than a few days in advance as our weather can be so unpredictable. However, the constant sunshine and the heat could become somewhat wearing particularly as the wet season approached and the humidity began to rise. Not for nothing was October called the suicide month as the heat and humidity gradually became unbearable.

The arrival of the wet season was welcomed although the timing usually in early November couldn't be predicted with total certainty.

Sitting on the Golf Club veranda one Sunday evening Pat suddenly said "I can smell the rain. It's coming."

Some of the others looked at her as if she was mad but sniffing the air, I agreed. "I think you're right. I can smell it too."

A strange thing but I can remember it as if it was only yesterday. The sky had become grey through the day and although there was no immediate sign of a deluge there was no doubt that we could smell the rain. Twenty minutes later we suddenly heard it.

"I can hear it" shouted Duncan over his pint. We all listened intently and then suddenly we could all hear it. Despite the fact that it was still some miles away, the rain was travelling towards us coming up the valley which carried the road to Lusaka.

The noise of the heavy rain pouring in torrents on to the dry bush beneath was audible for miles ahead of the oncoming storm.

We watched and waited for some ten minutes and then it was upon us. As with much of the rain early in the wet season it was torrential, yet we were so glad to see it that many of the group were out on the grass dancing and jumping around like lunatics as they got totally soaked.

Surprisingly the first of the rain wasn't accompanied by the usual thunder and lightning but twenty minutes later the first lightning flash and almost instantaneous thunder crash had several people jumping off their chairs and those still outside decided that they would be better off in the clubhouse!

Nowhere else have I ever experienced thunderstorms such as those which we regularly suffered in Zambia. The beginning of the wet season was accompanied by hours of torrential rain with the storms usually building up through the day and setting off the light and sound show around four in the afternoon. Sometimes however the rain would arrive earlier in the day and could last through twenty-four hours or longer. Some old hands said that the intensity of the electrical storms was caused by the attraction of the copper ore which was the mainstay of the Zambian economy. Others said that it was because we were on top of the Central African plateau and therefore above 3,000 feet.

Whatever it was it provided some intense storms. One morning, Charlie and I were sitting in the office and were forced to put the lights on as an approaching storm was so intense that the natural daylight virtually disappeared.

Suddenly there was a blinding flash of lightning followed instantaneously by an enormous crash of thunder from directly above us. It was so loud that it was deafening.

Neither Charlie nor I had been prepared for it as there had been no previous lightning and both of us shot out of our chairs. "Shit, what the hell was that? "Charlie exploded. The lights had gone out and we were in the semi darkness caused by the extremely low cloud. There was a lot of noise and confusion coming from the other offices and Charlie stepped into the corridor.

"What's going on?" he yelled "Stop making all that racket." He glared at the senior staff members, all looking sheepishly at each other and the remainder of the team who had all congregated for whatever reason in the corridor. "It's only a thunderstorm" continued Charlie. "Get back to work."

They all started to troop back into their workplaces. Just at that moment the front door of the office burst open and Pat the librarian dashed in, absolutely soaked through, despite having just dashed across the road.

"I couldn't stay on my own over there." she explained breathlessly. "That was horrendous. It hit the road right between your office and mine" she continued. "I saw it. It must have been right overhead as the thunder was so close. I nearly wet myself."

"No one would have noticed" I said laughing. "Look at you, you're soaked right through to your knickers. You look like you've fallen into the swimming pool. Anyway did you not think that it might have been dangerous to come outside with all that lightning about?"

"I didn't think" Pat looked a bit guilty "It just scared me to death." "I didn't see it but I heard it coming" I added. "We all heard it" Charlie said, "the thunder was deafening."

"No, I meant that I heard the lightning coming. It sounded just like someone ripping a sheet of paper."

Charlie looked at me somewhat incredulously. "You're joking?" "No I'm serious. I didn't recognize it for what it was, but on thinking after Pat said that she saw it, I realized what it was that I'd heard in the split second before it hit."

Thunder was still rumbling in the background but nothing quite so close to home.

We still had no electricity as it appeared that the lightning had caused some sort of circuit break in the main supply so we couldn't even have a cup of coffee but we stayed talking about it for some little time until it gradually moved away still rumbling and crashing into the distance.

Loss of electricity wasn't unusual since the town supply was provided by a set of Perkins diesel generators which we were lead to believe were the product of the nineteen thirties and were somewhat unreliable due to their advanced years.

However, our colleagues in the Public Works Department who maintained the generators were masters of their trade and we weren't surprised therefore when the supply returned about an hour later.

The lightning strike was the talk of the clubhouse later in the day when a number of us collected over our usual evening drinks.

"You realize that the lightning melted the road outside the office where it hit." Pat said to the assembled group.

"Did it?" I said "Just as well it didn't hit you as you dashed across the road in your panic." "Stop winding me up" she said. "You didn't have to tell everybody." I laughed "Why not? It'll give them a laugh as well."

My working days never ceased to amaze me as there was always something new turning up, often things which I had heard of but certainly would never have met had I stayed in the UK to work in Local Government.

One such thing was rabies, a disease associated with mad dogs in my mind as a result of anything I had ever read back home and a disease which I certainly wouldn't have been likely to meet in my native Ulster.

"We've got a rabies problem" Charlie announced as he walked into the office one morning. "What?" I looked up at him from my desk.

"Rabies" he said again "You know what it is, you must have heard of it?" he looked at me questioningly.

"Yes of course I know what it is but what do you mean we have a problem?" I retorted.

"Mvula has just told me that they had a sick cow in one of the villages down towards Petauke and realizing that it was dying the villagers decided to kill it and eat it rather than have it possibly go to waste." "And?" I said looking at him expectantly.

"And it's likely that it was dying of rabies" Charlie continued. I looked confused "I didn't know that cows could carry rabies, I thought that it was a dog disease." I was obviously showing my ignorance.

"Didn't they teach you anything at college?" was Charlie's rapid response. "It can be carried by any mammal as far as I know" he said, "hence why humans can catch it."

"So what do we do?" Again I looked at him questioningly "It's an absolute bugger. We'll have to vaccinate the entire village and that's not going to be easy. We have to inject the vaccine into the abdomen." "That doesn't sound very pleasant" I ventured.

"Too right" Charlie replied "but the biggest problem is that we have to continue the course of treatment every day for a week. After about the third day the stomach gets a bit fed up with the injections and becomes sore and swollen and the locals aren't too keen for us to give them anymore, not that I can blame them. That means that after day two we have to vary the time that we arrive at the village and before we get too close we will have to place a team around the village to catch all those who try to run away when they hear the Land Rover coming. We can't afford to let any of them escape the vaccination in case they go down with the disease since if they get it it's generally fatal."

Charlie didn't look best pleased. "Come on" he said, "we'd better go up to the hospital and check the stock of rabies vaccinations."

"Stupid buggers" he muttered to himself as we headed towards the car park "You'd think they would know better than to eat a sick cow."

And so we spent the next few days desperately trying to save the lives of local villagers who became increasingly less keen to see our arrival as their stomachs gradually became more and more sore and swollen from the application of our life saving drugs.

CHAPTER 24

THE END IS NIGH

My time in Zambia was rapidly drawing to a close as the end of my contract approached and I had to make a decision as to whether or not I would opt to renew. I had thoroughly enjoyed my stay but in looking to my future career I realized that were I to take on another contract I would become more removed from the working life in the UK.

As Zambia was moving towards training its own people in many professional fields I would eventually have to find a job back home. If I chose to return for another three year contract I would, at the end of it, have been abroad for more than six years and might be in danger of removing myself from the UK job market due to an increasing lack of knowledge of environmental health practice in Local Government.

I could envisage being called for interview and being asked about my experience in such things as "The Caravan Sites and Control of Development Act 1960" and having to admit a total ignorance of the subject. Reluctantly therefore I decided not to renew my contract but to start applying for jobs in England.

As it happened I nearly didn't make it back to England at all since I made one of the more stupid mistakes of my short time in Zambia during my last weekend in the country. Being our last weekend, Hilary and I accompanied by two friends, Colin and Joan, decided to make a last trip into the Luangwa game reserve.

Driving my Rover 2000 car, it having been restored following my early accident, we made our way from the main tourist lodge along one of the tracks.

A lion had made a kill unusually close to the lodge and a number of visitors had been talking about it over lunchtime so we decided to see if we could find it. A short distance along the track we suddenly saw the lion. It had left its kill and wandered down to the edge of a small lagoon to get a drink. Down on all fours it was lapping at the water.

I drove the car along the track and up to the ridge bounding the lagoon in order to get a better view. Not wanting to disturb the lion I stopped short of the ridge at a point where it couldn't see the car. "Come on" I said to the others "Let's get out and have a look." "No" said Hilary, "It's not safe." "Don't be such a woose" I replied, opening the car door and getting out quietly.

Colin stepped out of the other side of the car and both of us advanced up the ridge and slowly over the top to where we could see the lion.

A magnificent young specimen he was still down on all fours lapping at the water. Suddenly he realized that he was being watched. Rising to his feet he turned slowly to look at us. Colin and I stood stock still.

As a result of killing so close to the major game lodge in the park the lion had been the object of interest of numerous people during the morning and we were probably the last straw. One minute he was looking at us, the next he was rushing towards us.

I vaguely remembered afterwards that he had given the characteristic three flicks of his black tipped tail as he started. He didn't appear to be running but was rushing across the ground just like a domestic cat, keeping his belly close to the ground as he raced towards us.

Colin and I took off. We raced back over the ridge towards the car. Fortunately, we had left the two front doors open and I bruised my ribcage as I dived over the corner of the door into the front seat.

We had only had to cover about twenty yards, and both Colin and I were fit and fast at the time, yet in the few moments that we had taken to gain sanctuary the lion had covered more than fifty yards. As I fell breathless into my seat I saw the lion crest the ridge and come to an abrupt stop as he saw the car.

He looked disdainfully at us then turning his head he strolled majestically back over the hill and out of sight. I swear I could see the grin on his face as he left. That'll teach them!

And so my life in Zambia was over.

CHAPTER 25

BACK TO REALITY?

I had decided that much as I had enjoyed my time in Zambia I had to look to the future and although my contract was likely to be extended for a further three years, staying away from the UK for that length of time would make it more difficult for me to get a job when I finally returned.

I could just picture the scene as I sat in front of the typical Local Authority interviewing panel made up of a large number of members of a local Council.

"Mr. Kelly, tell us how you think that the implementation of the latest food safety legislation might affect our Borough?"

My absence from the UK for more than the three years which I had already served might make an answer to that sort of question somewhat difficult. Not only that, but on return for a further contract I was unlikely to be posted back to Chipata. It was more probable that I would find myself sent to one of the more remote areas such as Mongu where the lifestyle might be similar but would never replace that which I had enjoyed to date.

I had therefore been applying for jobs in England which had been advertised in the professional magazine which had been sent to me from home regularly just so that I could keep in touch. I couldn't have chosen a worse time to send off applications. It was early 1971 and Britain was just moving into a prolonged postal strike. It came as no surprise therefore that prior to my leaving for home I hadn't had a single reply.

Hilary and I had decided to take a tourist trip home. The conditions of my contract allowed me to book numerous stops on the flight back so we made the most of it. Having said a tearful goodbye to our many friends in Chipata and having signed my end of contract papers and collected my gratuity we left Lusaka on a BOAC flight bound for Dar es Salaam where we spent a couple of days. From there we flew to Nairobi for a couple of days, then on to Mombassa to spend a few days on the beach. It was all new and exciting.

Finally, we left Africa for Europe arriving in Athens on a crisp, clear but cold February morning. Met by two tour representatives we were to spend some time admiring the spectacular sights which Greece has to offer.

My abiding memory was a visit to Mycenae where the ancient city ruins overlooked a valley in which a confusion of almond trees was coming into full blossom. A beautiful sight on a backcloth of a cloudless blue sky, the peace only to be shattered by a low flying Greek air force jet as it hurtled at low level down the valley. The modern world noisily usurping the ancient. Nonetheless the city with its lion gate was a sight to behold and given that it was February there were few other tourists there to spoil it.

From Athens to Rome on our tour of capital cities. Again the splendour was marvellous. The Vatican and its art galleries and museums were a first for both of us and the sheer size of St Peter's was breathtaking.

On the 15th February we arrived in London. A not to be forgotten day as our arrival coincided with the introduction of decimal coinage in the UK.

Since Zambia had used a decimal currency it wasn't a problem for Hilary or me and we switched easily into the new system without falling foul of the temptation that the general populace seemed to have of continually trying to convert the new decimal prices into "old money."

We were scheduled to spend a couple of days in London prior to flying home to Northern Ireland, not least because I needed to find out what was happening on the job front. First thing on day one therefore found me on the phone to a local authority office in a small town not far from London.

I introduced myself to the Chief Environmental Health Officer when he came on the line. "You may remember that I wrote to you about the job vacancy which you advertised?" "Ah yes" came the reply. "I didn't receive an answer from you, probably because of the postal strike so I'm calling to ask if the vacancy is still open?"

"Yes it is" came the prompt response "I take it that you are still interested in it?" "Yes indeed" I replied, giving a thumbs up signal to Hilary who was listening on the other side of the hotel bedroom.

"Can you come for an interview?" the Chief questioned. "Certainly, when would you like me there? I'm in London at the moment" I added "We've just arrived from Zambia and are spending a couple of days here before returning to Belfast."

"How about this morning then?"

I was somewhat stunned. I hadn't expected an interview quite so quickly however never one to look a gift horse in the mouth I immediately agreed.

"OK. Let's say 11.30. If you catch the 10.30 train from Marylebone station you will get here in good time."

Since it was now approaching 09.30 it was going to be a bit of a rush but 10.30 saw Hilary and me ensconced on a suburban train rattling our way out of the London suburbs heading North West.

We soon arrived in the small market town where I left Hilary in a cafe warming herself over a cup of coffee whilst I made my way to the Council offices. First impressions weren't good. The Environmental Health department was housed in a wooden temporary structure painted in a pale green colour and with linoleum covered floors. Having announced myself at the desk I sat and waited.

"Good morning. You must be Mr. Kelly" a voice said. Looking up I got my first view of the Chief Officer. "Welcome. Follow me." He shook my hand and headed off down the corridor.

"Have a seat" he said as we arrived at his office. "Cup of tea?" He looked at me questioningly. "A coffee would be great if possible." "Certainly." He opened the door and said something to the woman I glimpsed in the next office.

"Well, tell me a bit about yourself." I looked steadily at my inquisitor before commencing. I was somewhat taken aback. Dressed in grey flannel trousers and a checked green and brown sports jacket, his hair cascading onto his shoulders, he was vaguely reminiscent of pictures I remembered of Oscar Wilde the Irish writer. Not what I had expected of a Local Authority Chief Officer.

The interview commenced and I answered all the questions asked as best I could. It was obviously going well and we had even got down to discussing salaries, when from my point of view, it fell apart. I asked about buying a house in the area.

"Buy a house?" the Chief looked at me incredulously. "Buy a house?"

He asked again. "You won't be able to buy a house in this area. It's far too expensive to even think about it. Why my deputy Chief has been here for seven years and he hasn't been able to afford one. But not to worry you'll get a Council house to rent just like him."

I didn't say anything but my thoughts were that if the lack of initiative of the Deputy in his inability to get himself onto the housing market was indicative of the department as a whole then it wasn't for me.

"Well I think that's settled." We'll put a job offer in the post to you tonight" continued the Chief. "It's been nice to meet you" he led me to the door and we shook hands as I left.

I walked briskly down the street to the cafe where I found Hilary still with a coffee. "Well?" She looked enquiringly.

I sat down ordered a coffee for myself. "I've got the job but it's not for me" and began to relate the events of the morning.

Things were to change a day or two later. Amongst the applications that I had submitted was one to the London Borough of Hillingdon.

Situated on the Western side of London it is the third largest London Borough, containing a mixture of built up suburban areas, manufacturing and rural districts running into the neighbouring Home Counties.

Again I rang the Chief Officer to see if my application had been received and once more was invited for interview.

Arriving at his office in Drayton Hall I found things in this Authority to be much different. A large office complex in a converted former manor house surrounded by its original gardens it lay just North of London Heathrow airport.

I was ushered into an office and introduced to the Chief Officer, a large, bluff Lancastrian who in turn introduced me to the Head of Human Resources. Both were impeccably dressed in grey business suits and I immediately realized that this was going to be a much more formal interview than my previous encounter.

Alf Makin, for that was the name of the Chief Officer, was soon grilling me on my experience in the UK prior to going to Zambia and was obviously trying to gauge whether or not I had any practical experience. The HR representative was there to tell me about Hillingdon and how it operated.

Importantly to me they emphasized that if I were successful in obtaining a post, the Council would provide me with a rental Council house for a maximum period of six months during which time I was expected to find and possibly buy my own property.

What a difference. This was a very much more forward thinking Authority and sounded like a good starting point for my career in England.

Finally, the question of salary arose. "What were you earning in your last job?" Alf asked, then looking at the application form which I had submitted he answered his own question.

"Huh!!" he snorted. "One of those inflated African affairs. Well you'll not get that much here." He looked hard at me as if to ensure that I got the point.

I wasn't surprised. My Zambian salary had been designed to get people to move to Africa, had included a bonus to cover for lack of pension rights plus a large gratuity at the completion of service.

It was possibly bigger than Alf's own salary as Head of the department.

Nonetheless a satisfactory offer was made and at the beginning of April Hilary and I moved into a small Council one bedroomed flat on an estate just ten minutes from the office and my career with Hillingdon commenced.

The flat though small was of a modern design and more than sufficient for the two of us whilst we settled into the area. It came with one drawback however. It was on the second floor and there was no lift.

This normally wouldn't have been a problem to us as we were both young and healthy but being as our accommodation in Zambia had been fully furnished by the Government, Hilary and I didn't possess a single stick of furniture.

We had returned to Northern Ireland for a few weeks whilst awaiting the result of my job interview and I made use of the time to catch up with an old friend whose brother was a sales agent for a number of furniture companies.

Notwithstanding the fact that we were going to be living in England I was able to buy the basics of a bed, dining room table and chairs and a suite of sofa and chairs for us to sit on. Purchased at a discount price they would be delivered to whatever new address we would have in England.

No problem then, I thought.

The dining room furniture and the bed were each delivered by a two-man team who had no difficulty in getting them up the stairs and into the second floor flat.

I was at home for a lunch break when the suite of sofa and chairs arrived. The doorbell rang and on answering I found a relatively elderly driver at the door. "Kelly?" he said looking at me suspiciously. "Yes" I said. "I've got some furniture for you, where's the lift?"

When I told him there wasn't one he looked at me in disbelief. "You'll have to give me a hand. I normally deliver to shops, not to houses."

I followed him down to the large truck parked outside. He jumped into the back and wheeled a large armchair to the edge. "Turn round and I'll put it on your back" he instructed.

Doing what I was told I turned my back to him where upon he dumped the very large chair straight onto my back and head. I almost collapsed under the unexpected weight but having caught my breath and got my balance, proceeded to struggle up the two flights of stairs to our front door.

The driver waited for me to return before repeating the performance with the second chair. "I'll give you a hand with the sofa as it's too big for one person" he said when I returned to the truck again. "Thanks" I said, feeling somewhat like Quasi Modo with my back numb from the weight of the two chairs.

It was a struggle to get the five seater sofa round the corners on the staircase but we made it eventually although I felt somewhat aggrieved at having to give the driver a tip for his efforts.

CHAPTER 26

HILLINGDON –
A NEW START

Working in Hillingdon provided me with unbeatable experience. The Borough had everything from large scale food manufacturing through to the housing problems associated with a large urban area.

There were London suburbs and individual towns and small villages which had survived despite being overtaken by the spread of the big city.

It had a University and a crematorium both of which contrived to provide problems, an outdoor lido and one of the world's largest airports all within its boundaries and in a short time I managed to work with all of them and to learn about the Public Health problems which they could bring.

It was to be an interesting few years.

Hillingdon was a large Borough and the work team was organised into Divisional groups with individual specialists working in areas such as housing, noise abatement etc.

In order to test me out I was initially given a series of food safety inspections at three large food processing plants situated in the South East of the Borough. All of them had nationally known brand names but hadn't been audited for some time.

My initial visit to the first factory was somewhat daunting as I hadn't up to then been involved in inspecting anything quite so big. It was a large, noisy premises built over a number of floors in an old style factory building producing a vast range of meat products for the retail trade.

I gritted my teeth and set to. It didn't take me long to find problems and following a couple of days of continuous inspection I was forced to serve an Intimation Notice requiring improvement work to be carried out.

This was normally the first step in enforcement action and if not complied with inside the time span given in the Notice the next step would have been to recommend to the Council that legal proceedings should be instigated against the company for being in breach of the law.

I hadn't realised the effect that my actions would have. The company management took the notice very seriously and the plant was closed over the weekend to allow remedial work to be carried out to ensure compliance.

I had made my mark. However not all food producers were quite so keen to comply as I was to find out later.

Alf Makin was a good boss to work for although he was a stickler for ensuring that work was carried out properly and was heavy handed with those who in his opinion didn't come up to scratch. Some of the younger inspectors and not a few of the older ones were in fear of him not least when it came to the monthly team meeting where Alf would gather all of us together in a basement room in the office building.

Having settled down in our seats Alf would take from the table in front of him a yellow complaint sheet, known to all as a yellow peril. This sheet documented a complaint and the action taken by the individual inspector to whom it had been assigned.

Alf's voice would boom out across the room as he read out the details of the complaint. He would pause for effect, then read out the actions taken by the inspector, being careful not to reveal the name of the miscreant. Pausing again he would then ask for anyone present to comment on the effectiveness or otherwise of the actions.

Those who had worked in the Department for some time knew better than to jump in with both feet and often there would be a long pause. Eventually someone would be brave enough to venture an answer and the debate would begin. Meanwhile the originator of the generally inadequate original actions taken would be shuffling uneasily in their chair trying to bite their tongue.

One or two however were unable to hold themselves back. Dave, one of the members of the team in which I worked, was often on the receiving end and couldn't resist for more than a couple of minutes before launching himself into a vain attempt to defend his actions. This of course was what Alf wanted.

Consider it sadistic if you will but whilst there was a sharp edge to some of it, and a lesson to be learnt, much of it was tongue in cheek and designed to provoke as much humour as bad will.

Needless to say, as the new boy, I was thrown in at the deep end at my second monthly meeting. Not that I had done anything wrong I would hasten to add.

A complaint had arisen regarding bed bugs in a particular property and Alf was questioning the corrective action taken. Suddenly without warning he looked at me. "Mr. Kelly, given your experience in Africa, you must have come across bedbugs?" he questioned me.

"Given this vast experience," he continued sarcastically "would you like to give the benefit of your knowledge to your colleagues and tell them how you eradicated them?"

"Yes certainly" I replied rapidly, "they were easy to deal with. We set fire to the house!" The room burst into laughter.

"They were only thatched roofed huts after all" I continued in explanation, as if any was required.

Alf had the good grace to smile. "Not necessarily the best answer in Uxbridge then" and continued to probe for the solution.

CHAPTER 27

CHICKENS, FAECES
AND FLEAS

After my success with the food production units I was positioned into a Division which dealt with complaints in the central part of the Borough, which included the town of Uxbridge plus Hayes, Harlington and West Drayton.

As with all Environmental Health work the complaints were many and varied. Some were related to food, others to general issues concerned with rodents, the activities of neighbours, waste disposal, noise etc.

Some of these have featured on television in recent years in a programme entitled" A life of Grime" which has highlighted some of the more unsavoury aspects of the job, not to mention the amusing.

One or two which I had to deal with could only be described as bizarre. One morning I was despatched to an address in a suburb of Uxbridge where a complaint had been received from a resident claiming that a neighbour was rearing chickens in what was a residential area.

I duly arrived mid-morning outside a typical large Victorian terraced house. Ringing the doorbell I took stock of what appeared to be a fairly well maintained property.

I was rehearsing in my mind what I was going to say to the occupier when the door opened. In front of me stood a well-dressed, clean and tidy looking housewife in her early forties I would have guessed. Behind her, to my amazement the hallway and visible staircase were covered with white chickens. Several dozen were immediately visible, all very much alive and healthy looking.

"I've come about the chickens" I began. "Come inside" she said affably. "We've had a complaint" I continued as we walked down the hallway.

139

There were chickens everywhere. I couldn't believe it. We walked through to the back and the garden was full of them. There wasn't a blade of grass to be seen as the free range birds pecked their way noisily backwards and forwards across the yard.

"It's a long story" the woman began. "We didn't intend to have so many and they are all scheduled to be gone by the end of the week."

I listened to what she had to tell me and it appeared that she and her husband had made a genuine mistake but were in the process of rectifying it. I advised her that it wasn't possible to keep so many chickens in such a small space without causing a nuisance to the neighbours and that they would have to go. Keeping a small number of them in the back garden might be appropriate so long as they didn't cause any unacceptable smells or noise.

She confirmed again that they would all be gone by the end of the week and I agreed to return to ensure that this was the case.

Walking back to my car I was smiling to myself. People do the funniest things and I'm sure that when I recount the tale no one will believe the story. However, she was as good as her word and on my return later the birds had flown.

Some of the incidents that I had to investigate were not always either so easy to rectify or were somewhat more unsavoury.

Called to another house in Uxbridge to investigate a smell reported by neighbours I was standing outside a beautiful Regency style terraced house.

The door opened and I was faced by a young woman. At the same moment a strong smell of ammonia hit me and nearly made my eyes water. A dog barked inside which gave me a clue as to what might be happening.

"I'm from the Environmental Health Department." I introduced myself whilst proffering my photo identity card to prove my validity. "The neighbours have complained about the smell" I continued. "It's the dog, isn't it?"

The strong smell of ammonia got worse as she invited me to step inside. "Don't you let it out?" "I'm agoraphobic." The girl looked down at the floor. "I can't take him out and I daren't let him out on his own as he would get killed on the main road so he does everything he has to downstairs in the basement."

I was horrified, not only because of the smell which was so totally overpowering but also for the damage that it was doing to an otherwise beautiful house.

"It can't go on like this" I said. "You're causing a nuisance to the neighbourhood and I'm going to have to serve you with a warning notice to require that you cease." Her eyes welled up with tears. "What will I do? I don't want to lose my dog."

"Well you can't keep him in conditions like this. In any case it's unfair for the dog to be kept indoors and never let out."

At that moment the dog appeared, a well fed and good looking boxer, full of life. "I'm sorry but I can't advise you as to what is best but I suggest you contact the RSPCA and see what they can do to help."

It was all that I could do. I took her details and subsequently served the necessary notice requiring her to abate the nuisance. As I left I couldn't close my ears to her crying as she pondered the situation that she had got herself into.

Sometimes however the sob stories that we were given as enforcement officers were far from genuine and I learnt quickly that it wasn't always a good idea to lend a sympathetic ear.

Some however turned out to be amusing as well as bizarre. One in particular stands out. It concerned a house in multiple occupation, again in Uxbridge, in fact not far from the infamous chickens.

A house in multiple occupation is not a building which has been divided into self-contained flats or apartments but one which has been subdivided into separate rooms each occupied by different people forming more than one household and sharing facilities such as bathrooms and kitchens.

Houses in multiple occupation have to be registered with the Local Authority and are inspected with regard to their size, facilities and safety and are issued with a limit on the number of people who could occupy the premises.

It was known however that unscrupulous landlords would try to cram as many people as possible into their properties regardless of the law. It was therefore necessary for enforcement officers to make unannounced visits to premises where they suspected that the law was being flaunted.

Hence one damp miserable dark winter's night Dave and I were outside a large terraced house, rain dripping down our collars and wishing that we could be anywhere else.

"You go to the front door, announce yourself and make an entry whilst

I go round the back to make sure that no-one escapes out the back door," Dave said and moments later he disappeared into the dark.

I walked to the front and rang the bell loudly. I saw the curtains on one of the upstairs windows move slightly as someone took a quick look at who was calling then I could hear movement inside, running feet and someone calling something.

I was just about to ring the bell again when the door opened and the owner of the house appeared. Recognising me from previous visits he smiled unctuously at me and said "Yes?" I announced myself formally and proffered my identity card stating that I was entering the house under the provisions of the relevant legislation in order to inspect the premises and identify all the people currently resident there.

"But it's nine thirty at night" he replied. "You can't come in."

"Yes I can, the law gives me the authority and if you don't allow me to enter I will ensure that you are prosecuted for obstructing an officer in the course of his duty."

The penny dropped and the door opened fully. Entering the property, I was aware that there were a number of people standing in the hallway looking curiously at me.

"I need you to identify all these people by name and tell me which room or rooms they are occupying."

There then began a litany of make believe as to who everyone was and where they belonged. In order to challenge the stories, I needed evidence so had to proceed room by room identifying people from photographs conveniently left on tables or from the names on addressed envelopes also conveniently on display.

As I went from room to room I was told stories of family members occupying the rooms. Very convenient since family members don't necessarily constitute a house in multiple occupation. However this didn't tally with the photos I was looking at nor the names on the mail I could see lying on the top of a table, which very obviously indicated that the occupants of the room were of a very different ethnic background.

But where was Dave? I had expected him to follow me into the house, albeit possibly from the rear garden. I was a long way through my inspection when his familiar voice suddenly came to me. "How are you getting on then?"

"About as well as you would expect" I replied. "I'm trying to work my way through a wall of lies at the moment" continuing to sift through some envelopes as I spoke.

"Well look what I've found." I turned around. Dave was standing in the doorway, holding on to a very wet and miserable looking man who was dressed in what were some very damp pyjamas.

"He was in the back garden." Dave grinned. "According to him he's a neighbour who was just coming across the garden from next door when he bumped into me. What do you think?"

"Well, "I said. "Unless he's an Olympic high jumper I wouldn't rate his chances of getting over that six foot high fence outside without damaging himself."

"That's what I thought" Dave said continuing to grin. "I've kept him outside for a while just to see if he would change his story. He's pretty miserable now."

We got to the end of it eventually and successfully brought a prosecution against the owner for failure to comply with the legislation. It was an entertaining night though.

Some of my other visits to homes in the Borough were also entertaining but in a very different way. One thing that struck me after a very short time in my job was the apparent willingness with which I was invited into homes by women who had not asked me to identify myself before asking me to come in.

A dangerous state of affairs I would have thought and I along with all my colleagues had photographic identity cards which we were only too happy to show.

One morning around 11.30 I arrived at a house in Hayes following up an infectious disease notification related to a food handler. The person concerned had been identified as suffering from a bacterial infection which could be passed on via food. As such they were required to stay away from food handling duties and would have to submit a series of faecal specimens for microbiological examination.

Hence I was standing outside the door, armed with a collection of forms which needed to be filled in and a set of small sample jars or stool pots as they were known which would need to be filled and sent to the laboratory by the patient.

This in itself could prove difficult to explain to some people. The words faeces and stool didn't mean anything to many of the population so an explanation of what was required sometimes had to revert to using the basic English word shit.

A look of incredulity would then often follow. "But how am I supposed to get it into that little glass pot?" would be the next question and I would then have to go into some detail as to why the little wooden spoon was included in the kit.

Well here I was again on a cold dreary damp day ringing another doorbell.

Suddenly the door opened and there stood a young woman dressed in nothing more than a diaphanous negligee. I quickly told her who I was and why I was there and she confirmed that she was the patient and was a manager of a food production unit.

Looking at her standing in the cold I immediately offered to come back later. "No, come in" she said immediately. I was somewhat reluctant as she appeared to be alone in the house and one of the last things our lecturer at college had warned us about prior to us being sent into the big bad world as newly qualified officers, was the danger of being caught alone in a house with a determined woman, particularly if they felt that there was any way by which they could coerce you into providing a good reason as to why they should qualify for a Council house or be moved further up the housing waiting list.

As this was a private house and some distance from the office I didn't really want to have to drive all the way back later in the day so I stepped inside and was ushered into the front room.

"Sit down" the young woman said. "What do you have to do?" she questioned.

"Well firstly let me prove who I am" I quickly showed her my ID card, thinking that it was definitely best to do so under the circumstances. "I have to fill in these forms to confirm your details and then explain what happens next."

"OK, would you like a cup of coffee?" I was a bit nonplussed. Given the state of dress or should I say undress that the woman was in I was feeling less than comfortable.

"I'll just put the kettle on and I'll be back in a minute." She left the room and I heard the kettle being filled in the kitchen. I then heard her going up the stairs, probably to get dressed I thought.

Time passed and the kettle boiled. I heard her come back down the stairs and she called from the kitchen "Tea or coffee?" "Coffee" I replied adding "Black with sugar." "Fine" came the reply.

A few minutes later she entered the room carrying two cups of coffee. Her time upstairs had been well spent. Her hair was brushed and pinned back, her makeup had been skilfully applied but she was still wearing only her see through negligee and it was very evident that there was nothing beneath it.

My eyes didn't move from the forms that I was filling in and I've never completed a set more rapidly. As I was leaving the house she smiled sweetly at me and said "You will be back won't you?"

I beat a hasty retreat and spent some time pondering just what it had all been about.

A similar problem occurred a few months later. A call had come into the office from the occupants of a rented property who were complaining that the house was infested with fleas. The house was let to a group of nurses and as I lived close to the hospital I decided to call in around 12.30 as I was going home to grab some lunch.

It was a smart looking detached property and as I rang the doorbell I wasn't sure what I was going to find. The door opened and there stood a young woman in her nightdress.

"I'm from the Environmental Health Department, come to see about the fleas that you've reported, but I can come back again later" I added quickly, bearing in mind that I was only a quarter of a mile from my own house.

"Oh no, come in" she replied stepping backwards. I entered the house and she shut the door. "I'm glad you've come so quickly. We're absolutely infested. I'm bitten all over, look" and without further ado she whipped her nightdress up over her head exposing her naked body to me.

She had certainly been badly bitten. "No, no," I said quickly whilst looking away. "Cover yourself up, I don't need to see the bites, I'll take your word for it." She dropped her nightdress and I could only wonder at what had possessed her to do such a thing.

As a nurse she had presumably seen more than her fair share of naked people and possibly the word "Health" in my job title had confused her into thinking that I was also well used to seeing naked people as part of my job. Suffice to say that in all my years of work I learned never to be surprised at the things people did.

CHAPTER 28

THE BODY OF PROOF

Other aspects of the job were in many cases very sad. One day I was called to a house in Uxbridge which had been occupied by an elderly man. He hadn't been seen for some time before the neighbours began to wonder where he was and called the police. They broke in to find his body and it was very obvious that he had been dead for some time.

A clean up job was required as not only was the body in a bad state of decomposition but the man had been a recluse and a hoarder.

I and the other Council staff who attended the scene had never seen anything like it. The house in itself was reasonably clean, with no filth and dirt around nor any livestock such as fleas, unlike many other properties which we had to visit, but the owner had been an avid collector of a vast variety of things with his collection filling every available space in the house and expanding into the yard at the back.

His own living space had gradually reduced to a few square feet encompassing his bed, chair, TV and bathroom.

His collection was neatly arranged and grouped. One room was full, floor to ceiling with newspapers and magazines all neatly packaged. A second room was filled with suites of furniture, all of which had their feet or castors removed so that they could be piled one on top of the other up to the ceiling.

The back yard held a collection of timber, neatly sorted by size and stacked in what was a custom built open sided shed. Across the yard above head height was a series of wires on which were strung a large number of bicycle wheels all of them without tyres but again arranged perfectly by size.

We gradually worked our way through the house, listing the contents and deciding what could be retained for its value and what need to be disposed of to avoid any possibility of a health nuisance.

We had reached an upstairs room and I as the slimmest forced a way in through the almost impossible gap available through the door. The room was filled with sheet music and equipment.

I cleared a bit of space to allow the door to open further and the team of beefy male workers began their job of sorting through what was there. Suddenly a groaning noise came from under the piles of music and papers.

The work force as a man leapt out of their skins, two of them jumping simultaneously for the door and fled down the staircase.

"What was that?" "Is there someone under all this mess?" The noise had been brief and had stopped as quickly as it had started.

The foreman went back and started to pick through the mess with some trepidation as the rest of us watched from the doorway. Suddenly he pulled something out and started to laugh. "Here you are, here's your body under the mess."

He triumphantly held aloft his find. An old cylinder record player with a record still in place. Our movement of some of the other articles had been sufficient to release its mechanism and produce one last groan of sound.

Laughter all round as we marvelled at this genuine antique and the collection of cylinder records which we found with it.

Visits to other homes could be equally tragic. One woman lived in a flat on the outskirts of Uxbridge. Middle aged, on her own and desperately lonely, she regularly called the office with a complaint just to have someone visit to view an imaginary or very minor problem related to her rented apartment.

As she lived in my working district, it regularly fell to me to call on her and although the house couldn't be described as ideal, nor was it as clean as it might be, it wasn't posing a risk to either her health or the health of her neighbours. However, it was always in a bit of a state, as also was she, and depending on her state of mind she could be in varying states of dress no matter what time of day it was.

Entry to the property when she was fully dressed meant stepping over the clothing and other items strewn on the floor and often having to avoid stepping into the chamber pot sitting on the floor and in danger of overflowing. This notwithstanding the fact that the flat was small and the fully functioning bathroom was only a few feet away. The joys of environmental health!! At least it was never boring.

147

Environmental Health also included the legal duty of an Environmental health officer having to be present at the exhumation of any body. Although exhumations were not regular events, except on one occasion when a new road was being constructed in the town centre at Uxbridge, more of which later, it fell on me to be present at an exhumation in Hillingdon cemetery.

Apparently a body had been buried in the wrong position in the graveyard and the family members were unhappy that the grave was in an open grassed area over which the public could walk at will. They had therefore asked that the dearly departed be exhumed and reburied in another plot. Thus I found myself entering the cemetery at 6.30am one dark February morning.

It was like something out of a Hammer horror movie. It was cold, damp and fog was covering the cemetery. I could see very little. Through the darkness I could hear the clink of shovels being wielded and following the sound I made my way up the hill.

Gradually I became aware of a light ahead of me and through the mist appeared the sight of a small group of people gathered around a grave which was open and from which the coffin was about to be raised.

I joined the group, introducing myself to the officials present and the police constable alongside whom I was standing.

Slowly the coffin came up. Given that it had only been buried for a short while it was in perfect condition and gave no cause for health concerns.

Proceeded by a member of the clergy it was quickly moved to another plot in the cemetery for re interment, all of this being accomplished before the daylight grew too strong and revealed our activities to those who lived in the houses which overlooked the graveyard.

A strange activity but not quite as bizarre as the exhumations which accompanied the building of a new road to bypass Uxbridge town centre. Unfortunately, the plan called for the road to pass through the graveyard of one of the oldest churches in the town.

I wasn't involved but many of my colleagues had been, as once again an Environmental Health officer had to be present throughout the proceedings. The exhumations involved a large number of bodies and was carried out by a reputable London firm who specialised in such work.

The job turned out to be somewhat different than perhaps envisaged. The graveyard was in a low lying area of the town through which passed a local river.

As a result, the exhumations produced a number of old graves which were below the water table. This resulted in the exhumation team finding some bodies which were partly mummified and coffins which had disintegrated and left the bodies lying in water.

The job of retrieving these bodies became either an ordeal or fascinating depending upon how you viewed such things. The mummified bodies were a look at history as many were little changed from the day on which they had been buried.

For many of the exhumation workers however, some of whom had been recruited on a daily basis from the local labour exchange, the work was far too extreme and they couldn't cope with the stress raised by confronting mortality in such a direct and bizarre fashion.

The fact of having to search through the water for body parts was just too much and many didn't survive their first day at work.

I on the other hand benefited much later in my career when I was able to use this experience when writing a dissertation on the subject of stress as part of an MBA degree.

I enjoyed my time at Hillingdon and learned a lot very quickly. Having been abroad for the early part of my career and having trained in Northern Ireland I had quite a bit to learn and often got it wrong due to my lack of understanding of the "in house" systems.

As an example, one morning I had received a complaint from a local housewife that a milk bottle which had been delivered by the Hillingdon branch of a National dairy company had been contaminated.

On looking at the bottle a black dirty mark was readily visible inside the glass but the bottle was empty and had the appearance of having been washed. There was no evidence therefore that the black mark had been present in the bottle when the milk had been delivered to the customer and whilst I didn't disbelieve her, there was no way in which the complaint could have been proven in a court of law.

I therefore wrote to the complainant explaining this to her whilst simultaneously writing to the diary outlining the complaint and the action which I was taking and suggesting that although no blame could be directly laid at their door, they may wish to contact their customer in order to promote some good will.

Having signed the letters, I didn't expect to hear any more about it and was therefore very surprised to find the letters back on my desk the following day with a terse note written on them by Alf Makin, the Chief, asking "Who authorised this?"

At the time Alf had an excellent way of monitoring all out-going mail. All letters were dated two days in advance and passed to him to review before they were posted. This allowed him to retain anything which he didn't deem suitable.

The note had come all the way down the chain of command via the Deputy Chief, Divisional Chief, Section Head and eventually to me with all of them denying responsibility and initialling the page.

I looked at it and thought to myself, why does such an obvious "non-starter" as a legal complaint need to have authorisation from the top? It wasn't as if I had recommended legal action be taken. Surely anyone with half an ounce of sense would have realised that?

I thought for a moment and then scribbled across the bottom of the letter "I did" signed my name on it and sent it straight back up the line.

I waited for what I thought would be the inevitable call upstairs but it never came. Alf probably thought that it wasn't worth pursuing.

Sometime later, on one memorable afternoon, I did get a call to "come up to my office". I rapidly went upstairs and was ushered into Alf's room by his secretary with a pleasant smile.

"Sit down" came the gruff order. I sat. Alf was looking at one of my letters and I wondered what was coming. "I've been reading this" he showed me the correspondence. "Are you sure that you've used the correct piece of legislation?"

I cannot now remember exactly what my letter had been about however I do remember being bold as brass and thinking I'll bluff this out and answering "Yes."

"Don't you think you would have been better using" and Alf proceeded to quote a section from some alternative regulations. He's bluffing, I thought and quickly said "No, I didn't think that section was relevant in this particular case."

Alf would have made a good poker player. He looked me straight in the eye and said "Well let's have a look then. Reach behind you on the shelf and get the Butterworth."

Butterworth was the Public Health bible and came in a series of encyclopaedic volumes covering the vast range of Acts and Regulations in force and with comment and precedent from legal cases in which they had been used.

Heart in mouth now I turned and looking across the volumes which covered a complete shelf I chose the correct book. I lifted the heavy tome, placed it on my lap and leafed through it until I found the legislation I was looking for.

I thumbed down it to the section which Alf had specified and read it quickly. "No" I said, "it doesn't cover what is needed in this case" and I passed the book across the table with my finger pressed firmly on the correct section.

Alf read it. "Yes I think you're right" he said with a smile. "You've got it right. Now put it back and go back to your desk." I stood up, replaced the book and with a feeling of intense relief left the office.

"That was lucky" I said to myself as I walked slowly down the stairs. "I won't try that approach again. He's a bit too wily and has been around for a very long time."

I wondered thereafter if Alf had been seriously worried that I might have been using the wrong legislation or, as I thought, was it more likely that he just wanted to make sure that I had checked for myself to ensure that what I was doing was correct. Whatever it was it had certainly taught me a lesson.

Firstly, always to make sure that I had checked all alternative possibilities and secondly not to try to out bluff a master poker player since you can only be lucky once.

CHAPTER 29

FOOD SAFETY?
YOU'RE HAVING A LAUGH

Food hygiene was a favourite part of my work and I was involved with inspections of many of the restaurants within the Borough. The majority were generally of a good standard and posed little or no risk but there were always exceptions.

Some of the smaller ethnic restaurants which were springing up all over the country at that time had little food hygiene knowledge and needed a lot of work from our department to ensure that they met the required standards.

Most of the owners were keen to learn but there were always exceptions and having given one restaurant several weeks of attention and seeing no change in the scruffy and unhygienic standards in the kitchen I was forced to request that the Council instigated legal proceedings against the owner.

As a result, I made an appearance in the witness box at Uxbridge Magistrates Court one morning testifying as to the unhygienic conditions that I had witnessed over several months. The magistrates took little convincing and found the owner guilty on all charges. The owner stood looking very forlorn in the court and when fined some £500 looked shocked. His lawyer requested time to pay on the grounds that the owner had little money. I thought that this was a reasonable request but the Magistrate would have none of it.

"Call yourself a businessman" he thundered from his seat "you'll pay immediately or I'll have you consigned to prison."

At his point I must have looked shocked. The food hygiene offences had been committed and it was right that the law had to be upheld but I couldn't see the merit of a prison sentence in this instance.

This wasn't always the case. Every Summer Hillingdon Borough held a "show" in a large open area outside Uxbridge. It was a type of agricultural show similar to those which occur annually across the UK and feature all manner of equipment and displays.

Naturally within the show ground there were food stalls offering various items ranging from ice cream to burgers and chips. The Environmental Health team had been involved in the show for many years and had got their food safety control measures down to a fine art. Prior to the event the show organisers had to submit the names and addresses of all companies who would be offering food for sale at the show ground and each company was sent a letter detailing what was needed for them to comply fully with the food hygiene regulations. They were also warned that inspectors would be present at the show throughout its two day duration and that any breach of the law would be dealt with severely.

My turn to be one of the duty inspectors at the show duly arrived and I found myself wandering through the showground on a blisteringly hot summer afternoon looking at the various food stalls and assessing their standards. I would willingly have been somewhere else, not only because it was a beautiful day and there I was, having to be dressed appropriately as a Council official in shirt, tie, jacket and buckets of sweat, but there was a World Cup football match being played on TV and I could have been watching it at home with a cold beer in my hand.

Ah well, someone had to do it and I knew that one of my colleagues was working his way around the other side of the ground, feeling equally bad.

It was all going well, with the food outlets apparently having made the effort to ensure full compliance with the law, until I saw the bloke in his white food server's coat lying stretched out on the grass in the sunshine beside a burger van. I walked to the front of the queue, pulled out my identification card and announced my presence to the spotty youth serving the customers. He opened the side door to let me in.

Looking at the dirty, greasy floor and the uncooked burgers and buns piled everywhere I knew that this was going to be a problem.

"Are you in charge?" I asked. "Nah, he is." He pointed a dirty looking finger out of the van at the recumbent white coat lying on the grass.

"Oi Bill" he yelled over the noise of the show "It's public 'elf … wants to have a word with you."

The owner reluctantly picked himself up from the grass and made his way into the van. I started the inspection whilst spotty youth continued to serve the line of customers.

"Are you the owner or do you just manage it for someone else?" He looked disinterested. "Owner."

I looked around the van. Apart from being dirty and disorganised I could see no hand washing facilities and no waste bins, soap or obvious cleaning materials.

"Where are your hand wash facilities?" I asked. "Over there" he said pointing out of the van to a water standpipe in the grass some feet away from the van and provided by the Council for site wash down purposes. He grinned.

"What about your soap and towels for hand washing?" A grubby piece of cloth was produced after some searching in a filthy cupboard, but no soap. "and your waste disposal facilities?" I continued.

He laughed and pointed at the Council waste skip some 25 yards away. "There you are guv. Dead handy" was the reply and he started to laugh. He obviously didn't think it was a serious matter. "OK you're nicked." "What?" He looked incredulous.

"I'm reporting you to the Council with a view to prosecution for failure to comply with the food hygiene regulations" and continued to detail the failures. I duly submitted my report to council and a prosecution was issued.

Once again I had to appear in Uxbridge Magistrates Court but to no avail as the defendant who lived some distance away in Kent didn't make an appearance. The Magistrate queried whether or not the summons had been correctly served and as this information wasn't readily available the case was set back for a week.

One week later I was back in the courthouse but again no defendant. This time it could be shown that the summons had been correctly issued so not wishing to hear the case in the absence of the defendant the Magistrate ordered that an arrest warrant be issued. Thus a further week later I stood in Court and watched the defendant being led into the proceedings handcuffed to a police officer.

All this in respect of five relatively minor food hygiene failures. It was really quite bizarre and he didn't look quite the "jack the lad" that he had set himself out to be on the day of the show. The end result was a stiff fine for each of the offences, the fine probably having been increased by the Magistrate as a result of the inconvenience and expense that the defendant had caused by his failure to appear. A salutary lesson to him.

One entertaining facet of our work was the sampling of alcoholic beverages as served in the many pubs and hotels in the Borough. From time to time during the year the Department had to test the alcohol content of the drinks being served to customers in bars. A team of three, usually two Environmental Health officers and the laboratory scientist from our office would sally forth to check on a selected number of bars.

The process was very straightforward. The three of us would sit down in the pub and order three half pints of beer with three chasers, these being any straight alcohol such as whisky or gin. Whilst we could each chose a different beer the three chasers had to be identical i.e. three whiskies from the same bottle or three gins etc.

Once served we would drink the beer whilst the lab scientist would surreptitiously try to pour the three alcoholic chasers into a bottle which he would then take outside in order to test the alcohol content. This test would reveal whether or not the content of the drink was to the correct legal standard and carrying it out informally saved the cost of sending it for testing to the official Public Analyst.

If the test proved satisfactory we would move on to another bar. However, if the test indicated that there may be a problem with the drink, we would then repeat the order and when the three chasers were placed on the bar the lead officer would declare his or her identity to the barman and state that the drinks were being taken for formal analysis. The look on the barman's face at that moment was usually indicative as to the possible illegal water content in the alcohol.

The three drinks would then be poured into separate sample bottles, sealed and labelled. One sample would be sent to the Public Analyst, one was given to the publican for them to have examined should they see fit and the third was retained by us for presentation in court should there be an alleged discrepancy in the results.

Much of the fun in an evening of sampling was caused by our lab scientist. Knowing that he would have to pour his three original samples into a bottle and take it outside to test whilst not raising the suspicion of the bar staff he had devised a cunning method. This involved a filter funnel connected via a length of plastic tube to a bottle all of which was hidden in an inside pocket in his jacket.

Imagine the look on the face of the local heavy drinker propped up on the end of the bar as he watched our lab scientist apparently pour three straight whiskies into his inside jacket pocket!! He couldn't believe what he was seeing and whilst his eyes tried to focus on what was happening he wasn't sure enough to actually comment on it.

CHAPTER 30

FLIGHTS OF FANCY

After some four years at Hillingdon I began to realise that although I had done well there and had been promoted, I now needed some new challenges.

My next move in local Government would probably have been to aim for a post as Divisional Head in a large local authority or a Deputy Chief post in a smaller or more rural Authority but it was likely that my relative youthfulness would weigh heavily against me.

Local Authority appointments, certainly at senior level were normally made by a committee comprised of the Chief Officer, the Head of Personnel or Human Resources, and a goodly number of the elected members of the Council.

Such groups expected that applicants for a senior post and definitely for a Deputy Chief role would be suitably grey haired and show the gravitas and pallor of one who has worked his way up through the ranks over many years. I wasn't convinced that as I was still in my mid-twenties and youthful looking that I could overcome the norm and would therefore have to wait for a number of years before success might come my way. However suddenly out of the blue came a very different opportunity.

Opening the weekly copy of the Journal of my Professional Institute and turning immediately to the back pages to read the job advertisements, as all members of the profession regularly did, my eyes were transfixed by the words "British Airways" which headed a large and colourful advertisement.

It stood out immediately from all the others, not only for the name but for the style and layout which instantly differentiated it from the typical Local Authority advertisements.

British Airways Medical Services were looking for an "Assistant

Hygiene Officer" to join a small team responsible for the airline's hygiene requirements worldwide.

It was just too good to be true I thought as I read through the details. A qualified Environmental Health professional was required, preferably someone with a food safety background and experience outside Local Authority would be an advantage.

The salary being offered wasn't any better than that which I was already getting so the post wasn't a move upwards but merely sideways at best, but here was the chance to gain some experience in a blue chip company in the private sector which would stand me in good stead.

My thoughts were that if I was successful in my application I could spend a couple of years with them before moving back into Local Government in a more senior position. Little did I know what was to follow.

I wrote out my application and was delighted a week or so later to be invited for interview and even more so when having been interviewed I got a call say that I was going to be offered the job. And so my great love affair with British Airways began, an affair which in my mind would last for two years but which in the event became a career which went on for more than thirty years.

I joined the airline on 17th November 1975. The company was in the throes of the amalgamation of the two State owned airlines British European Airways (BEA) and the British Overseas Airways Corporation (BOAC). This had nominally taken place the previous year but it still had a very long way to go in the minds of those who worked in the two companies.

Both were Government owned, and although they occupied adjacent maintenance facilities at the Eastern end of Heathrow airport that was about as close as it got and it would take several more years and the privatisation of the company before the two airlines would eventually become one.

BOAC was the long haul operation designed originally to serve the far flung ends of the old British Empire whilst BEA was the domestic and European network designed to link the UK with its near neighbours. Staff who had worked for BOAC considered that they had been employed by the better airline and were not best pleased at being amalgamated with what they considered to be a lesser company. Those who had worked for BEA considered their new partners to have too high an opinion of themselves. It was to take a long number of years to work out the differences and get the two workforces to work together for the common good of the company.

Originally BEA and BOAC both had their own separate medical departments but these had been amalgamated as the Air Corporation Joint Medical Service some years prior to the combining of the two airlines, so at least Medical Services had a head start on how to make the joint venture work.

Allied to the problems of amalgamation was the fact that the state owned companies had effectively been branches of the Civil Service and were being run accordingly. Rank was everything. It denoted your position within the company, your salary, the size of your office, the number of windows you were entitled to, the floor covering, the size of desk at which you sat and even the seat that you would be entitled to when flying on one of the company aircraft.

I found myself working in a hierarchical "us and them" scenario and given that my position in the company was relatively lowly I had to quickly get used to the culture and work out how things were done. In those early days everyone in the Medical Department was addressed formally. I was always Mr Kelly, never Mike. Our Doctors were always addressed as Doctor and the secretaries were never anything less than Miss or Mrs, dependent on their marital status.

The Medical Service provided a full range of medical care to all employees from recruitment to retirement and was located in Speedbird House, the airline Head Office situated in the maintenance base at Hatton Cross at the Eastern end of Heathrow. The department was divided into three "medical" sections, Ground, Air and Overseas, with each name obviously relevant to the working location of the employees that it was looking after so my first couple of days were spent in getting to know who was who amongst the teams of Doctors, nurses and support staff.

My boss Bill Horne, like me, was a Public Health inspector by training but was in reality a frustrated pilot who, although a fully qualified glider instructor, flying regularly out of Booker airfield outside High Wycombe, had for whatever medical reason been unable to satisfy his desire to fly large aircraft.

The third member of the team was Peter Jerram, with whom I shared an office. Peter was a microbiologist who had originally been employed by BEA as a laboratory technician to carry out microbiological testing of samples of milk supplied from outstations in Europe where food and beverages were being picked up for service to passengers.

My immediate thoughts were how stilted the whole organisation was. One almost had to bow and scrape to those who were perceived to be in the hierarchy. It was much worse than local Government where at least I was able to speak face to face with my boss without having to pass a request upwards through several layers.

Bill was a plain speaking Northerner and was quick to speak his mind which probably did him no favours in the long term and eventually he was forced to leave, but more of that later.

CHAPTER 31

FROM FRYING PAN TO FIRE

My first shock came when I was taken to see the flight kitchen which provided the food and equipment for the long haul flights to destinations mainly outside Europe. Housed in Comet House, it was in the building immediately at the rear of Speedbird House so was literally only a couple of minutes' walk from my office. Having had no previous experience of a large kitchen providing meals for aircraft I didn't know what to expect so when I stepped into the building through the rear door what I found myself looking at took my breath away.

Not the size of the operation, but the cramped space and the sheer squalor in which some of the work was being carried out. Bill had accompanied me and could see the look of shock on my face. "We've got a new building under construction a couple of miles away on the South side of the airfield" he said quickly. "It's due to open next April." This to my mind didn't excuse the conditions that I was seeing.

"This is the stripping and washing section where the crockery, cutlery, glassware etc. from inbound aircraft is stripped of all waste food" Bill explained.

"It's then machine washed after which it's fed back into the food production area." The noise in the room was constant and the volume of equipment waiting to be processed seemed to my untutored eyes to be vast.

I could see immediately why a new kitchen was required. Apart from the lack of space, the old "Meccano" style bolted together metalwork supported conveyor belts, along which the equipment was passing slowly towards the washing machines, was festooned with debris and dirt, hanging like cobwebs from virtually every inch.

Whilst realising that this had no effect on the safety of the food being

161

produced in the adjacent kitchens, I was surprised by this example of a lack of effort at maintaining cleanliness in the area.

Even allowing for the difficulty in cleaning caused by the poor design of the conveyors, there was really no excuse for it being in the state that it was. Was this the accepted standard of food safety in the airline? If so I wasn't going to be happy.

Bill walked me slowly through the remainder of the building where I got some idea of the scale of the operation and the number of people involved. It was mind numbing in its size and the poor working conditions.

When a day or two later I visited the short haul kitchen, providing food for the domestic and European flights from premises on the North side of the airport I was relieved to find it in somewhat better shape. When I queried the state of the Comet House kitchen Bill was quick to defend himself.

"It's not through want of trying" he said almost wearily. "I've written page upon page of detailed improvements that are needed. I'm only surprised that the Local Authority inspectors haven't closed us down yet. I've told our Director but there doesn't seem to be any interest."

A short time later Bill called me into his office "You've seen the worst now let's go and have a look at the future and tell me what you think."

We jumped into his car and headed out along the South perimeter road. Turning left just before the Beacon roundabout we arrived at a building site where a new building which looked suspiciously like a large warehouse was going up.

"Welcome to catering centre South." Bill said as we hopped out of the car. We made our way to a security office where, having announced ourselves, we were suitably kitted out for a visit to a building site.

"Follow me" said Bill and we walked through the doorway into the building. "It's enormous" I said. Bill nodded.

Looking down the building from where we were standing I could just make out the farthest end. "180,000 square feet" said Bill, anticipating my next question. "Roughly a quarter of a mile long from front to back. It will be the largest in the world when it's finished."

A smaller man walked towards us. "Hi Willi." Bill motioned to me. "Meet Mike Kelly, he's our new Assistant Hygiene Officer. This is Willi Kraus our Executive Chef." he said turning back to me.

Willi stuck out his hand and smiled. "Welcome to the madhouse.

162

What do you think of this place?" he said with a slight German accent. "It's enormous" I found myself saying again.

"Yes, it's a great improvement on where we are now don't you think? Come on and I'll show you round. Be careful. It's still a building site and a long way from being finished."

Willi led the way and we toured the site with me trying to get a grip on where everything was and how the building would operate when it opened.

At that stage and despite my short visits to the existing catering units, my knowledge of flight catering was virtually nil and it would take a while before I understood how the processes and systems had to work to ensure that each aircraft departure was properly catered. Little did I know then that some years in the future I would be responsible for those self-same operations.

Leaving the building an hour or so later Bill turned to me "Well what's wrong with it?" he asked looking at me expectantly. "It's a spectacular building" I answered. "That's not what I asked," was his immediate reply. "OK, OK. Given that I'm not experienced enough to know whether or not it will work as a building my main problem with it would be the wall surfaces."

I could almost hear Bill sigh with relief. "And" he said. "Go on."

"Well" I continued "the walls in the food handling areas are only tiled up to six feet above the floor. Above that they are only painted blockwork which will be very difficult to keep clean."

"I've been telling them that for months now, until I'm almost blue in the face but can I get them to change it? Originally it was all going to be tiled but the recent recession that the business has been going through has called for cost cuts and this is one of them." He went on "I've tried getting the local authority guys to work at improving the specification but they won't get involved."

This lack of tiling was to become the source of much trouble for Bill over the following year. To be fair he was trying to make a professional stand and getting little or no support from anyone in the Medical department.

Whether or not it was his persistence in arguing the case and not being prepared to give in gracefully which led to his subsequent resignation I don't know. It may well have been as much to do with his display as a rear gunner in a Lancaster bomber enacted in the office with Bill sitting on a chair whilst operating another chair between his arms as the guns. He was happily spraying his office with non-existent bullets whilst making the appropriate noises when the door opened without warning and Bill found himself spraying the Medical Director and an accompanying visitor. The look on the Director's face was a picture.

I'll never know, but this was probably the last straw. Bill left about a year after I had joined. His departure left a gap which Medical Services chose not to fill, thus leaving Peter and me to run the operation much as we pleased. Eventually, a year later, it was decided that on the basis of his long service, Peter should become Head of Department, and we would recruit a third team member, Malcolm (Mack) Puryer, a former colleague of mine at Hillingdon and an ex Naval man with vast experience.

Peter turned out to be a difficult man to work with, although it has to be said that I was more than difficult to manage, being very strong willed and not happy necessarily to accept the status quo as being the right way to make progress. Peter's management style was one of deference to senior managers and a desire not to upset any of them by rocking the boat.

I in turn felt somewhat aggrieved that the senior job had gone to a microbiologist rather than an Environmental Health specialist. This was based on the fact that the job content covered a great deal more than food safety and I and my new colleague had the broad based qualifications and knowledge to cover all these aspects whilst to my mind Peter didn't. It meant that Mack and I would have to cover the gaps in his knowledge but not get paid for it.

Malcolm made a great colleague. He was good at the job and could be very laid back on occasions in the office. Our office was situated on a corridor which ran through to the changing rooms for all our nursing and dental staff. This meant that in the late afternoon, at shift change, a number of the nurses would walk past our office. If Malcolm was in the mood, the work was done and Peter was away on a trip, he would pop his head around the door and invite them into our office for what he called "a happening."

At some stage in his first few days with us he had acquired a very large glass laboratory flask. This had been sterilised to remove any prior contamination and Malcolm now filled it with a potent punch made up from a variety of juices and alcohol. Only he knew what the mixture was.

The "happenings" would often turn into a serious party with a dozen or more people enjoying a libation and on more than one occasion some people chose to leave their car in the office car park and get themselves home on the bus. Whilst these get-togethers would have been seriously frowned on by the senior management had they known of them, they fostered a great deal of team building amongst the staff and are still fondly remembered many years later.

Apart from the old flight kitchen, a further surprise to me on arrival was the apparent lack of connection between the Hygiene Branch and the Catering Division. It seemed important to me that if the hygiene team were to make any progress in improving and maintaining good standards of food hygiene then we must have a good relationship with the guys who were organising the supply of food worldwide.

I have to admit that in the first instance I had found the catering team by accident. They were on the same floor level as Medical Services but on the opposite side of the building. Speedbird House was a square building built around a hollow centre with entrances on two sides as well as through the main front reception area. As a new boy I found myself one day accidentally walking through the wrong corridor entrance and straight into the Catering Division offices. I obviously must have looked a bit lost as one of the men sitting at his desk looked up and said "Looking for someone?" I explained who I was and he introduced himself.

"I'm George Perry, I'm one of the Route Catering Superintendents." He smiled and asked me a bit more as to which section I was part of in Medical Services. From his questions it became obvious that he hadn't much more than a passing knowledge of who worked in the Hygiene team and what they might be doing. I was surprised.

George pointed me in the right direction for my office and I left with an invitation to come back and visit when I had settled in. When I got back to my office I mentioned to Bill that I'd been in the Catering offices.

He looked at me quizzically "Where are they?" he asked. "Just round the corner on the South West side of the building." He didn't reply and we left it there.

My visit to the Catering team was the start of something new and over a relatively short period of time the Hygiene and Catering teams got to know each other very well, with each developing an understanding as to how the other worked and what the end result was supposed to be.

The catering operation was divided into three geographical areas of the world, each headed by a Superintendent who in turn had a team of Route Catering officers. George Perry headed up the Europe and Africa Team with his colleague Hugh Martindale in charge of Middle East and Asia and Len Cupitt heading up the Americas.

At that time the teams were predominantly male, many of them trained chefs with extensive experience and great food knowledge. I quickly learned that the three Superintendents were legends in their own lifetime and had careers which dated back to the early days after the war and aeroplanes with propellers which had to stop overnight and whose passengers were accommodated in places such as the Karachi guest house or Wadi Halfa in the desert in Northern Sudan.

Many were the interesting tales which they could tell and which I was privileged to hear. Over the years to come I would get to know many of the team very well and build friendships which have lasted to this day.

It was a golden age in air travel. The Boeing 747 "Jumbo" jet was in the early years of service and the Vickers VC 10 and the Boeing 707 were still the mainstay of the long haul routes whilst the Trident in its many guises was opening up jet services into the European and domestic network gradually replacing the long serving and much loved propeller driven Vickers Viscount and Vanguard aircraft.

In those days the aircraft were divided into only two classes. Most passengers travelled in Economy which made up the middle and rear sections of the aircraft, whilst a small minority travelled in luxury in the First Class cabin in the front of the plane.

The problems involved in putting food on to aircraft at the many stations across the world were immense. Long haul services were forced to make many stops en route to the furthest ends of the World as the aircraft didn't have the long range associated with today's flights.

Now, in the twenty first century, we take it for granted that we can fly from the UK to Australia making only one stop to refuel, usually at Singapore, Bangkok, Dubai or Hong Kong.

In the early days of my aviation career a flight to Australia stopped at least twice and sometimes three or more times dependent on the aircraft being used. This meant that food and beverages had to be picked up at each stop, many of which were in areas of the world where the availability of the food and the standards and quality of its production could be very suspect. My first overseas visit was to prove just that.

CHAPTER 32

FROM EMPEROR TO RULER

Having spent a few weeks settling in I was working in the office one morning when Bill gave me a call. "Can you come into my office Mike?" It was an order rather than a question. Bill looked up at me from behind his desk. "I want you to go down to Addis Ababa" he said. "The flight goes on Monday and I want you to go and have a look at the flight kitchen."

"Has anyone been down there before?" I asked, hoping that there would be some information available from a previous inspection. "No, we haven't actually done much overseas work in recent years" came the admission.

"OK, what do I need to do?" Bill had obviously thought it through as he rapidly explained that Ann, the departmental secretary, would organise my tickets and would contact the BA Station manager at Addis Ababa to ask him to book me accommodation in whichever hotel the crew were staying at. And so the following Monday night I was in a seat towards the rear of a VC10 aircraft heading to Addis.

The flight was overnight and on arrival in Addis the next morning I was met by the local BA Station Manager as I came down the steps into the bright African sunshine. "Good morning, welcome to Addis, did you have a good flight?"

The pleasantries exchanged I was escorted through the terminal and put in a taxi to the local Hilton hotel where I was to get a couple of hours sleep before being picked up later in the day to start my inspections. I was grateful for the opportunity to get my head down for a couple of hours, since the flight had been less than comfortable, partly due to my mixture of excitement and trepidation at this my first overseas assignment and secondly due to the lack of practice in sleeping on an aircraft, a skill which I was to pick up fairly rapidly.

The alarm beside the bed rang all too quickly and I awoke groggily, taking a little time to work out exactly where I was. Then just enough time to have a quick coffee before setting off back to the airport. Finding the BA office, I re-introduced myself and the manager made a quick phone call to the kitchen.

A few minutes later the door opened and a slightly scruffy figure entered the office. "Hello Kurt" the manager stood up and immediately introduced me.

"This is Mike, from our hygiene team in London, he's come to have a look at what you do in your kitchen." Kurt looked at me suspiciously.

I held out my hand. "Hello, pleased to meet you." I explained what I was expecting to do and with little further ceremony Kurt said "Come with me" and we set off out onto the tarmac on the aircraft handling side of the terminal building. A uniformed soldier blocked our progress for a few seconds, but then recognising Kurt waved us through.

The flight kitchen was at the edge of the airport terminal area and we reached it fairly quickly. I put my document bag down in Kurt's office, put on my white protective coat and followed Kurt into the kitchen.

"We've had a bit of a problem" Kurt said looking round at me, "the oil fired oven blew up last week." I looked at the scene of devastation in front of me. It was obvious where the oven had stood since the wrecked brickwork and tiling stood as a testament to it.

"It was almost brand new" Kurt continued "but they obviously didn't put it together properly." "Did anyone get hurt?" I asked. Kurt grinned. "Fortunately not, there wasn't anyone working here when it happened."

I looked around and wondered where I should start my inspection since nothing in my previous career had prepared me for this. My first thought was that there was no way in which food should have been prepared in conditions such as this since there was every chance that it would be contaminated by the lack of even the most basic food safety standards.

The preparation areas were dirty and there was a serious risk of cross contamination since there was little or no separation between the raw food items and the cooked food with food handling staff being involved in handling both at the same time.

Kurt knew that the standards were bad and knew also that my final report would be damning, and so it was. At the end of the inspection I gave him a list of improvements needed and said that I would return in a couple of weeks to see what had been done.

On my return to London a day later, I walked into Bill's office. "Well what was it like?" he asked. "Absolutely awful" I said and began to give him a breakdown of the problems.

He listened intently and then said "I think we ought to go next door and talk to George." With that he got to his feet and marched forcefully into the Catering Division office with me hot on his heels.

"Hello lads, what's the problem?" George could see that Bill was on a mission. "Mike's just got back from Addis and he says that the conditions in the kitchen are terrible. Go on Mike tell him." "I know" said George before I had the chance to open my mouth, "but we don't have any alternative. There's no other kitchen on the airfield or anywhere near which would have the capability." He continued to explain as we listened.

Eventually Bill stopped him. "Well we have to think of something. It can't go on like this otherwise we'll kill someone. We'll have to change the menu to make it safer. Take off the high risk food items such as the cold meats and salads and replace them with hot freshly cooked items." I could see George's face change colour as Bill spoke. The ramifications of such changes were enormous. They would require changes in equipment such as crockery and cutlery plus the need to be able to find storage space on board the aircraft to accommodate the change from cold to hot meals.

It became obvious that this was the first time that such a proposal had been made to catering and it wasn't going down well. There followed an almighty argument as to what could be done and what couldn't. Words such as "How dare you tell me what I must do out of my overseas stations!" rang through the air.

Eventually Bill said "Well that's my professional opinion, take it or leave it. The problem is yours but don't blame me if someone goes down with food poisoning" and turning on his heel he marched out. I followed sheepishly.

Two weeks late I was on my way back to Addis to assess the improvements made since my last visit. This time my visit would be memorable for a different reason.

Going into the kitchen I could see that some effort had been made to improve things although there was still a long way to go. However, in an effort to keep the progress going I complimented Kurt on the efforts which he had made and he looked suitably pleased.

This time the inspection had been carried out in the morning, immediately on my arrival on the aircraft from London, and by lunchtime we were finished so Kurt said that he would take me back to my hotel.

Getting into his car we drove a short way down the road towards the city. "Would you like a beer?" Kurt looked at me. "Why not. I've finished for the day" I replied and with that Kurt steered the car into the car park of a roadside cafe/bar.

Inside it was cool and modern with polished wooden bar surfaces. After a couple of bottles of beer Kurt relaxed and began to tell me a little about himself. A Swiss national and a trained chef he claimed to have originally come to Ethiopia as a Chef to the Emperor Haile Selassie who had been overthrown just a year or two previously. Married with a Swiss wife and two children back home in Switzerland he had been in Addis Ababa for so long that he had become "localised" and now had an African wife and numerous children. The story was intriguing.

After finishing our beer, we got back in the car and set off again towards the city. Reaching the centre and within sight of the Hilton hotel where I was staying, Kurt drew the car to a halt again and looking at me said "Let's have another beer."

I wasn't keen but loathe to argue with him I followed him out of the car. There was no restaurant or bar in view. In fact, we were parked on the edge of the main road beside a fence made from sheets of corrugated iron. Kurt walked along the fence for a short distance then coming to a loose piece of the metal work he pushed it aside and holding it open motioned me through.

I stepped through the gap and found myself looking at a piece of waste ground on the edge of which stood a corrugated iron building about the size of a small garden shed in England. A number of men were standing outside it all with beers in their hands while on the ground a group of women were cooking something over an open wood fire.

Kurt spoke to the men as we walked up to the group and from their laughter and comments they obviously knew him. Inside the shed was a bar where a young woman was serving a couple of men and three or four girls who were the only customers.

Looking around I realised that the place was obviously a shebeen and

171

the girls were probably of dubious reputation. Having said that everyone was very friendly. There was lots of laughter fuelled no doubt by the beer and it appeared that Kurt was a regular customer or at least was well known to the group. "They're mostly from the airport" he confided to me "and have just finished their shift."

By now the beer was beginning to have its effect on me. I had started the day straight off the aircraft and was suffering from a lack of sleep. I suggested to Kurt that I really ought to get back to my hotel.

"I'll take you back in just a minute." He was enjoying the banter with the lads. Suddenly he turned to me "You've not had the local dish have you?" I looked around, unsure of exactly what he meant. He wasn't expecting me to take one of the local girls with me was he? I hoped not. "Injera wat" he said. "What?" I repeated. "Yes, wat" Kurt said "it's the local food".

Without another word to me Kurt spoke quickly to the girl behind the bar and all was arranged. A few minute later one of the old women that I had seen squatting on the ground outside came in and proffered a tray to me.

I looked at it aghast. It was a circular metal tray advertising a well-known brand of English biscuits. On the tray was a large piece of what appeared to be a spongy grey flannel blanket but which was in fact a form of bread. On one corner of the bread was a conical heap of minced raw meat. On the opposite corner was a heap of chilli pepper. "You take a piece of the bread, use it to pick up some of the meat, dip it in the chilli then eat it" Kurt demonstrated as he spoke.

I looked at it. My mind was in a turmoil as my food inspection training came to the fore. All those diseases that raw meat carried, not least tapeworm, never mind Salmonella rushed through my head. However, thinking that I can't be rude and decline the food as it might not be appreciated and I was a visitor and representing British Airways, I tore off a piece of the bread, wrapped up a small portion of the raw meat, added some chilli and put it into my mouth.

Forcing myself not to gag, I swallowed it. This was followed by a second piece. My actions went down well as the locals applauded my efforts. "You can have it cooked if you would prefer?" Kurt's voice came to me through the general hubbub. I thought of the women cooking outside and decided that it probably wouldn't be any better.

"No thanks, I'll just finish this bit and then I really must go." Twenty minutes later I was in my hotel bathroom on my knees, bringing it all back. My professional training told me that it was far too quick for this reaction to have been food poisoning but my stomach combining with the thoughts going through my brain had conspired to get rid of it all.

The following morning, I was woken suddenly at 6.30am. The phone beside my bed was clamouring in my ear.

"Hello." "Mr Kelly?" "Yes". "This is British Airways at the airport. There's a Mr Followell here, just arrived from London. He's from BA Catering and would like to see you here immediately." "OK, I'll be there as soon as I can."

I leapt out of bed and dashed to the shower. Mr Followell from Catering, who was he? I hadn't heard of him. How important is he? What's he here for and why didn't anyone tell me he was coming? The thoughts rushed through my head as quickly as I was getting myself dressed and into a taxi to the airport.

Arriving at the terminal I looked around. The BA flight from London was long gone as were the passengers and the airport staff. I looked out at the aircraft apron. There, sitting on his suitcase, was someone whom I had never seen before but who must be Mr Followell.

I walked outside. "Mr Followell?" he got up and put his hand out. "Mike Kelly?" he questioned. "Yes" and at that point started a friendship which has lasted to this day.

Peter, as he introduced himself, began to explain why he was there. "Haven't you heard?" he looked at me. "Heard what?" "The food poisoning" he continued "When did you get here?"

"Yesterday morning." "Well the flight that you got off had a problem after it left here en route to Nairobi. Apparently when the Captain was eating his soup he found worms in it and immediately declared himself ill and unfit to continue the flight. Stirred up quite a storm I believe."

Peter continued "That's why I'm here. When the news reached London, Clivas (John Clivas was Head of Catering at the time) called me into his office and told me that I was on the next flight down here."

"Worms in his soup? Well I know what that was." I had spotted the problem the previous day when inspecting the dry stores in the kitchen. I explained to Peter. "They're using packets of dried soup mix in

173

the kitchen rather than making fresh soup. When I was in the dry stores yesterday I found some of them infested with meal worms probably from flour beetles that had got into the packets. We disposed of them but nobody told me that they had just made soup for the outgoing flight. No doubt some of the worms from the infestation were in the flask of soup provided for the Captain."

Peter grinned. "Well that's that then. They're not likely to have caused him any permanent damage are they?" He looked at me for the answer.

"No. Not pleasant to come across in the bottom of your soup plate but not harmful in any way. Actually they probably gave the soup a bit of body." I couldn't help myself.

"That's terrible" Peter said accusingly then burst out laughing. "Nothing more for me to do then" "Well you can come with me and have a look at the kitchen after we've taken Kurt, the Manager, to task over causing such a problem."

I led the way to the kitchen and having spent some more time auditing the facilities we left Kurt with no uncertainty about what we thought of his catering.

Later that evening having been out together for a meal in a restaurant a short distance from our hotel Peter gave me some more amusement. We were walking way back along the footpath leading to the hotel when a man approached us and whispered something to me.

"What does he want?" Peter looked at me. "The usual" I replied. "He just offered us his sister."

"Well that's an improvement" said Peter "They normally offer me their mother!!" We both laughed.

I was to do one or two more trips with Peter on future occasions but for the moment I settled into what became a working routine for the three of us in the Hygiene team.

Each month was broken into one week on a long haul audit of two stations, flying out on Monday and home on Saturday followed by one week in the office writing up reports. Then one week on a short haul trip either in Europe or perhaps a UK domestic station and the fourth week being a mixture of whatever was needed. As a team we revolved around each other with one of us in the office whilst the other two were travelling.

The long haul stations continued to be a revelation. In the mid nineteen seventies, the Middle East stations were extremely busy and growing the volume of business which they were handling.

Aircraft flying to the Far East and Australasia had to refuel and this, accompanied by the growth of countries such as Dubai, Abu Dhabi and Oman, meant a serious increase in the number of aircraft flying through the area every night.

The increase in size of aircraft caused by the introduction of the Boeing 747 jumbo jet had greatly increased the problems of catering and ground handling. These aircraft in an instant had increased the passenger load per plane from 150 on a VC10 or Boeing 707 to nearly 500 people.

The problems which this brought came home to me on my first visit to Abu Dhabi, the next door neighbour of Dubai and one of the United Arab Emirates.

I arrived to inspect the catering facilities and the BA station manager introduced me to Peter Bressler the manager of the flight kitchen.

We walked from the BA office along the front of the terminal building to the kitchen which was immediately next door. Going inside we climbed the stairs to what was a very busy production unit operating in a very small space.

Although it was still fairly early in the morning the meal production was well advanced. A large number of chefs and cooks milled around, some preparing the raw food, some carrying out the cooking and others filling meal dishes. There was little space to move. Peter, the manager apologised. "I'm sorry about the mess, but we haven't got much space." "I can see that" I replied looking around. I was visually trying to assess what food safety risks there were amongst the organised chaos that I was looking at.

"That's not the only problem" Peter continued. "This wasn't designed as a flight kitchen. We are actually in the old airport terminal building and this is the original airport restaurant kitchen. It was never designed for all this. Worse still we don't own the property, it still belongs to the airport authority and as such we're not allowed to make any changes to it." He took a deep breath. It seemed like he was trying to get all his frustrations off his chest in one go. "You'll see what I mean in a minute."

I started my inspection. Given the shortage of space and the numbers of people involved they appeared to be doing reasonably well. As I walked around I could see the preparation of the meals but I couldn't see where the aircraft trolleys were coming into the building nor for that matter could I see any refrigeration other than a couple of small stand-alone refrigerator units against one wall.

"Where do the inbound aircraft trolleys arrive off the flights"? I turned to Peter. "Come and see" and he walked towards the door.

We went outside onto a balcony which ran along one side of the building. I stood looking amazed at what was happening in front of me. Backed up against the balcony was a catering highloader, the truck used to load and unload the catering equipment from the aircraft at each stop. These trucks had a hydraulic lifting mechanism which allowed the covered rear of the vehicle to be raised to the level of the aircraft door, a considerable height when talking about a jumbo jet.

Normally when the equipment was offloaded from the aircraft and brought back to the flight kitchen the truck would reverse against a custom built loading dock at ground level which enabled the equipment to be wheeled off the lorry into the kitchen.

Here in Abu Dhabi however we were at first floor level and the trucks were raised to full height and were being off loaded directly onto the balcony. Well directly wasn't quite right. The balcony had a standard height balcony rail running its full length to stop people falling off. As a result, the loaders on the truck were having to physically lift each aircraft trolley and manually pass it over the rail to colleagues standing on the balcony.

"We don't have an elevator in the building and the airport authority won't allow us to cut a piece out of the balcony rail to make things easier." Peter explained. "It makes things very difficult."

That was an understatement. Each trolley when loaded could weigh up to 250lbs and given that many of them contained breakable items such as glassware and crockery they had to be kept level.

This would be compounded on trolleys being despatched to outgoing aircraft as many of them would contain the plated up cold meals for service on board, which wouldn't take kindly to being thrown around. I just shook my head.

"OK, where's your refrigerated storage?" I asked. "Just along here" Peter pointed along the balcony. There at the end stood a large walk in cold room. I walked along to it, and glancing at the temperature gauge on the outside to see what it was reading, stepped inside.

Another shock awaited me. Standing inside was a very tall Pakistani pastry chef, fully wrapped in what appeared to be a heavy woollen army greatcoat and busily rolling out a large quantity of dough destined for a pastry product.

Despite the greatcoat the Pakistani was visibly shivering. "What's going on?" I turned to Peter. He looked apologetic. "The kitchen doesn't have much air conditioning and is too warm to prepare pastry. This is the only cold room that we have so we have to do it in here."

"It's not exactly hygienic is it? That greatcoat isn't very clean and although there won't be any problem with the pastry as it is going to be cooked there is a lot of cold ready to eat items in here which could accidently become contaminated."

I looked around and made notes as to what was in the cold room whilst monitoring the temperatures with my thermometer. "Is this the only cold room you have?"

"Yes and we really need a couple more." "How many flights are you handling"? I could only imagine what the logistical problems might be.

"Well apart from yourselves we have Lufthansa, KLM, Swiss, Gulf Air" The litany continued as Peter reeled off a number of others. "And do each of these have two flights?" I was alluding to the fact that aircraft going one way had a reciprocal flight going in the return direction thus you had at least two aircraft to handle for each airline with two sets of equipment and two different sets of meals.

"Yes." Peter nodded his head. "And how many are jumbos?" "Only half at present but KLM and Swiss are introducing theirs in the next few months. But we are getting a new kitchen. It's being built already and will be finished in six months." "Thank goodness for that" I responded adding" but why did you leave it so late and you have all these problems?"

"Well you know how it is"? Being relatively new to the airline business I didn't know, otherwise I wouldn't have asked the question, I thought to myself but I wasn't going to be rude as Peter very obviously had enough problems without me being sarcastic.

"The kitchen was just about big enough to deal with all our business before they started to introduce the 747. We knew that it would take some time for all the airlines to buy them and get them into service and the airport authority wasn't prepared to build a bigger kitchen on the off chance that we would get 747s through here. They could have gone to

177

other stations in the Gulf area. As it happened we didn't have any until late last year but then three of our major customers introduced them simultaneously and we've been a bit overwhelmed."

I could understand it. In my short career to date with BA I had already come across the rumour machine on a number of occasions so I could imagine what would have happened. "Did you hear that BA (or any other airline you care to name) are going to be bringing a jumbo in here in October?" One person within the airport may have heard a snippet of information somewhere which may or may not have been correct and so the rumour would begin to spread around the airport.

The information more often than not was incorrect and such was the nature of things that no-one in their right mind was going to spend vast sums of money on building a new facility on the back of a rumour. Usually it became a "let's wait and see" situation. "We'll build a new kitchen when we get the business."

And so the catering unit manager was forced to work in conditions that were difficult at best and at worst could be dangerous from a food safety point of view.

I made more notes as we walked back into the kitchen. "Where's your tray set up area?" I asked and Peter pointed towards a door at the other end of the kitchen. "Follow me."

Through the door we went and as I surveyed the tray preparation area where each customer tray was being loaded with the crockery, glassware and cold food components before being placed in the aircraft trolley for transportation to the plane I didn't know whether to laugh or cry.

The room had previously been the airport first class restaurant and despite its change of use it remained exactly as it had always been. The carpeted floors and low over table chandelier lighting were still there, but now the tables were laid in lines with a team of tray setters dodging under the low lights whilst trying to load equipment and food onto the trays.

Carpeted floors are not the best surfaces for a food preparation area as they suffer badly from items that are dropped and they can't readily be kept clean. The marks and stains from dropped food items were readily visible.

"The airport authority?" I looked questioningly at Peter." Yes" he said, "No changes in here either." I looked at it in resignation, wondering just where I should start with my report.

Business in the Middle East was booming at that time and within a couple of years, new kitchens had been built in all of the major destinations. Dubai was growing so fast that in the midst of the building bonanza it was almost impossible to get a hotel room unless you had booked months ahead. Stories abounded of businessmen arriving at the airport, hiring a taxi and paying the driver to park it somewhere quiet overnight so that the traveller could sleep in the cab as there were no hotel rooms available at any price.

This was to continue for many years whilst the city mushroomed from a small town situated on the mouth of a creek in which the dhows which traded across the ocean to India anchored to offload their cargo, to a major metropolis of world beating high rise buildings each trying to outdo their neighbour in scale. Similar changes were taking place in all the Emirates, Gulf States and Oman.

Visiting Dubai in more recent years it was almost impossible to reconcile today's city with that which I knew in the late 1970s. The Arab dhows were still anchoring in the creek to offload and load their motley cargoes ranging from electrical white goods and carpets to food, all of which were piled on the roadside awaiting transportation.

Seamen can still be seen relieving themselves in the rickety wooden structures attached to the stern of the ship, the toilet being little more than a wooden box suspended precariously over the sea and the discharge going straight into the water beneath. All very well when out at sea but none too pleasant when happening at the quayside in a creek with little water movement, but the dhows provide the only real connection with the past.

The high rise buildings and six lane motorways which now define the city are a far cry from the early days.

Doha the capital city of Qatar was also a revelation in more ways than one. The flight kitchen was similar to that in Abu Dhabi in that it was somewhat basic by modern standards. The Manager Sammi Hassan was somewhat distant in his approach to food safety and wandered around behind me as I inspected the facility, dressed immaculately in a gleaming white Italian suit which seemed somewhat incongruous in the somewhat murky conditions that I was looking at. Even more so when after lunch he appeared in a different suit, but no less impressive.

I was less impressed however by the food hygiene standards or lack of them that I was listing in my report, one of which included the lack of proper hand washing facilities in the food preparation area. This I had noted when in turning on the taps to ensure that there was a hot water supply I immediately had a deluge of water cascading over my feet. Looking beneath the basin I realised that it wasn't connected to a waste pipe! My own fault for not recognising this before turning on the tap.

This visit was to provide another surprise. My station audit included an inspection of the hotel being used to accommodate our crew.

Given that BA had in excess of 12000 crew at that time and on any night of the week upwards of fifty percent of them would be staying in a hotel somewhere in the world, the crew hotels were an important facet of our job. The safety of the crew is of paramount importance not just because of the Health & Safety at Work legislation but also because any illness or injury which prevents a crew member from operating will have a knock on effect on the operation of their next flight and any delay or cancellation of a flight has serious financial and customer relations implications.

The standards of food hygiene and health and safety in hotels across the World were variable and often found to be wanting, even in those hotels with very recognisable four and five star names.

My first visit to Doha was an example when my inspection showed that the hotel which BA was using was less than perfect. As a result, I had raised issues with the manager and was providing a list of improvements needed to ensure compliance with internationally recognised standards.

A return visit was made a few weeks later to assess improvement. There had been little change so I was forced to reiterate my concerns and suggest that unless improvements were made I would be recommending that British Airways moved the crew to an alternative hotel.

Having finished my work, I was in my bedroom in the hotel, around 4.00pm, packing my suitcase ready for departure to London that night when I heard a knock at the door. Opening it I found a man standing outside.

He introduced himself in a strong English accent. "I'm the hotel owner's Chief of Staff, do you mind if I come in?" I was somewhat puzzled but stepped back to let him enter the room.

"Certainly. What can I do for you?" "I have come to offer you the Sheikh's personal thanks for your visit and as a memento of your visit and token of his respect for you, he would like you to accept this gift."

He proffered a large brown envelope and held it towards me, looking somewhat abashed.

It took me but a few seconds to recognise what was happening and to compose my reply. "Thank you very much but I can't accept it. Please express my thanks to the Sheikh for his kindness but tell him that within my contract of employment with British Airways I'm expressly forbidden to accept gifts of any kind." It was all very formal but I was very well aware that in my refusal I had to be careful not to cause offence to the Sheikh.

"Are you absolutely sure?" he queried. "Absolutely" was my immediate reply. In no way would I accept a gift, which given the size and shape of the envelope being proffered, seemed likely to contain something of considerable value.

It was a mantra which I maintained throughout my career. I was not bribeable. My ethics were such that this was something that I would not do under any circumstances. It was anathema to me and although I was going to come across it again, in different forms, my view wouldn't change.

He relaxed immediately. "All right, can you accept a coffee?" he asked. "Yes of course" I replied and we set off downstairs to the restaurant where we proceeded to spend an interesting half hour in conversation.

Later that evening, as I was leaving the hotel for my flight home I was called into the manager's office. "I just wanted to thank you for your visit and to wish you a pleasant trip" the Egyptian manager said in excellent English as I sat in his office.

"I would also like you to accept this small token of our affection and thanks" he pushed a red box across the table towards me. "Not again" I thought to myself. "They don't give up easily."

I hadn't opened the envelope during my afternoon encounter but this time I thought I'll open it just to see what they think I'm worth. I lifted the lid.

The box contained a gold cigarette case and lighter accompanied by a gold pen. Inside the lid was the name Cartier. I shut it quickly and slid it back across the table.

"That's very kind of you but under the terms of my contract with British Airways I am unable to accept gifts of any kind and I hope that you will understand that I must decline your kind offer"

He looked disappointed. "If you are sure?" he looked hopefully at me. "I'm sure thanks" I pushed my chair away from the table, got up and proceeded to make the customary handshakes as I headed for the hotel door.

I knew in my mind that the manager must have known that I had turned down the earlier offer but they had been prepared to try again just to make sure. My view was that it would have been easier for them just to have carried out the remedial work that was necessary in order to make the hotel acceptable.

Some people may have thought that I was mad not to accept but ethically I knew I was right and I couldn't live with myself if I thought that people believed that I could be bribed and that my reports could therefore be manipulated.

Not all of my visits to the Middle East were to provide problems and some had unexpected amusement attached. Visiting Bahrain on one occasion and having finished work in the late afternoon my colleague the Hygiene Officer for Gulf Air who was escorting me around the kitchen asked if I would like to have a quick look at Bahrain before it got too late.

"Yes I'd be delighted. One of the problems with the job is that although you visit a lot of places you don't often have time to see much of them." I explained. "In my first few months working at BA I went to Frankfurt three times but didn't get away from the airport until the third visit" I continued.

He laughed. "Yes I can imagine. Let's jump in the car and I'll take you for a quick drive around.

So off we went on a whistle stop tour around the city. After about fifteen minute he said "We'll take a look at the Summer palace whilst we're here. This is an alternative to the main residence of the Emir and it's open to Europeans and particularly the women to come down and use the beach."

We pulled up outside an imposing building and walked through towards the beach where a number of women were lying sunbathing.

Just as we got there a small Arab gentleman appeared, walking slowly along admiring the view and tolling a set of beads in his hands.

"It's the Ruler!" my companion whispered to me. "Sheikh Isa the Ruler of Bahrain. Some of the expats call him little Jimmy" he explained quietly.

Just at that moment the Ruler turned and seeing us walked over.

"Good afternoon Sir" my companion nodded his head. "Good afternoon" the Emir replied. "You work for Gulf Air?" It wasn't so much a question as a statement since my colleague was dressed in Gulf Air uniform. "Yes Sir" he replied and quickly introduced me. "This is Mike Kelly from British Airways. He is here to audit our facilities".

The Emir looked at me with sharp eyes. "You are enjoying your visit?" "Yes very much Sir." I answered, not really sure as to the form of address that one should use when speaking to a Ruler.

"Are you from London?" he asked looking at me with interest. "Yes I am" I replied. "Ah" he said, "I used to visit London quite a lot but I tend to go to Singapore to shop now."

"Why is that?" I responded.

"Too many foreigners in London these days," he replied with a grin on his face and a twinkle in his eyes.

We all laughed.

CHAPTER 33

OPULENCE

Those early days in the Gulf area, whilst challenging from a food safety point of view were often very entertaining and interesting.

On one visit to Dammam in Saudi Arabia, a city on the mainland just a short distance from the island of Bahrain, I along with my colleague David Randon, the London based BA Catering Manager for the Middle East region at the time, was invited to dinner at the home of the then owner of the flight catering facility at the airport. The owner, a Sheikh in his own right, wished to discuss the terms of his contract with the airline in the comfort of his own home.

At the appointed hour a limousine arrived at our hotel to collect us and we drove through the dusty streets to the outskirts of the city. Arriving at a very large walled and gated villa we were ushered into the expansive hallway where the Sheikh was waiting to greet us. He shook hands and welcomed us in Arabic which was translated by an interpreter.

"The Sheikh is very pleased to meet you and to welcome you to Dammam." We returned the greeting and more handshaking took place before we were invited to enter a room on our right.

I walked through the doorway into an opulently furnished lounge. My feet almost sank into the cream coloured deep pile carpet, so much so that I felt guilty that I was walking on it wearing my shoes which were dusty from the desert sand which coated the driveway outside the front door.

"Have a seat" the interpreter said. "Would you like a drink, a Scotch maybe?" He rapidly translated as his boss opened a very large corner wall unit. My eyes opened in surprise. I was aware that Saudi Arabia was a dry country and that alcohol was forbidden but there in front of me was the largest collection of single malt Whisky (or Whiskey if you are Irish) that I had ever seen outside a specialist Whisky retailer's shop.

"Go ahead, have what you like" the interpreter translated as the Sheikh smiled benignly at us and encouraged us by waving his arms towards the bottles.

Although I wasn't a whisky drinker it would have been rude not to accept and after a few moments we were comfortably ensconced in deep armchairs whilst beginning the discussion of the catering agreement.

It didn't take long for me to suspect that the need for an interpreter was in reality a ploy by the Sheikh to give him more time to think through the points which were being made to him in relation to the deal. Whilst the interpreter was supposedly translating what we said to the Sheik, he in turn was rapidly thinking through what his reply was going to be. I could read it in his eyes which occasionally narrowed as David was speaking and therefore gave away the fact that the Sheikh fully understood what was being said before it had been translated. A neat move I thought, as I listened to the bargaining.

One thing that had struck me when we entered the room were two very large televisions sitting side by side at one end. David had also seen them and being curious he asked why.

"There are many TV stations available here not only from Saudi but from other nearby countries" the interpreter said, "too many for one television so we need two in order to have all the stations available." In today's world of digital television this wouldn't be necessary but in the nineteen seventies this was opulence beyond belief and David and I were suitably impressed.

More was to come however. After our discussions had come to a satisfactory conclusion the Sheikh stood up and invited us to eat. We walked through to an elegantly furnished dining room where the table was set in beautiful glass and china and where to my surprise a woman was waiting for us.

"This is my number four wife" the Sheikh introduced us. "She is Egyptian and can speak a little English." The woman smiled and walked forward.

I knew better than to extend my hand to shake hers, which would have been a serious mistake but smiled at her and acknowledged her greeting.

We sat down to a sumptuous meal the centre piece of which was an individual large leg of lamb placed before each of us. Enough meat to feed a family back home I though as I looked at it.

As an additional favour we had each been provided with a set of cutlery with which to carve our lamb, the Sheikh being aware that it wasn't customary to eat with one's fingers in England.

I was fortunate to be seated next to the Sheikh's wife who made a very pleasant companion over dinner and conversed well in English. A truly magnificent meal and a memorable night.

CHAPTER 34

CREW TRAINING – TAPE WORMS TO ORGASMS!!

The work of the Hygiene Branch didn't just cover food safety but included all facets of Environmental Health with the exception of the legal enforcement duties.

British Airways was an enormous company when I joined, employing in excess of 60,000 people. Almost every profession and craft that you could think of was represented in the airline, from Doctors through lawyers to painters, decorators and carpet fitters. The Airline even owned its own housing estate on which many of the workforce lived, all of which was the product of Government ownership and the building of two airlines immediately before and after the 1939-45 war.

As a result, our department was involved in problems related to all parts of the company. Apart from food safety we audited the supply of drinking water to the aircraft at airports worldwide, the management of waste disposal from aircraft, the eradication of rodents and other unwanted animals and insects on aircraft, the cleaning and sanitising processes on board and for many years we were heavily involved in Cabin Crew training, along with the assessment of crew hotel accommodation.

To add to all of this, I often maintained that anything out of the ordinary, which was a problem to whomsoever had received it initially and which might be remotely related to "health or hygiene" in the widest sense of the terms, would arrive on our desks.

This proved to be the case in later years as the airline expanded and our expertise got us involved in diverse areas such as infectious disease control, design of aircraft toilets for use by disabled passengers and even cosmetic products supplied in washbags.

What the job provided more than anything else was a variety of work which was unrivalled anywhere else in the Environmental Health field and so long as you didn't mind the extensive travelling and periods away from home it was very fulfilling.

Cabin Crew training was a whole new world to me and somewhat daunting to start with since I had no experience of public speaking or lecturing. My induction into the training arena was to be short and sweet.

I accompanied Bill to the crew training centre at Cranebank, a large building, a few minutes' drive from our office, and a custom built facility for the training of crew.

In it were the simulators on which pilots were trained to deal with all possible incidents that they might face when flying, and aircraft mock ups in which cabin crew were trained in safety and evacuation procedures as well as how to serve meals and drinks on board and how to deal with disruptive passengers.

Several cohorts of crew would be passing through the college in any week and in my early days their training courses would last up to six weeks. Over the years this would gradually be reduced and our role in training would be handed over to others.

I sat in on the lecture which Bill was giving to the latest intake of new cabin crew. It was scheduled to last for some two hours in the afternoon and was split into two halves. The first dealt with personal health and safety when abroad and the second was purely concerned with food hygiene on board the aircraft.

Personal health and safety was important to the young people sitting expectantly in the lecture theatre in front of us. Recruited from all areas of the UK and in some cases from much further afield they had little experience of overseas travel. This was the mid nineteen seventies so many of them would not have experienced travel outside the UK before.

It was important therefore to give them some understanding of the diseases and illnesses that they might expose themselves to if they weren't careful.

To make it all more interesting we had a gruesome collection of specimens to illustrate our talks.

I was as fascinated as the students on that first day as Bill worked his way through the lecture pulling what appeared to be a never ending collection of bottles and jars from his bag. These contained amongst other things some roundworms and a large portion of a tapeworm, both preserved in jars of formaldehyde and reputedly recovered from the intestines of crew. These inevitably drew gasps of horror and sometimes revulsion but were good proof as to why you should be careful when eating food in strange countries.

Added to these were a variety of insects including fleas, bedbugs and lice and to top them all was a glass box containing the largest spider I have ever seen, easily the size of my hand. The following day Bill popped into my office. "Here you are" he said handing me the collection of specimens. "It's your turn today." And that was it. I was in at the deep end.

After my first couple of attempts I gradually became confident, recognising very early that the crew were keen to learn and that the job of the lecturer was 80% theatre and 20% fact. In other words, I had to entertain my audience in order to be able teach them. The lectures became good fun and I hope that the majority of my students enjoyed them as much as I enjoyed giving them.

Whilst the basics were the same for each class the audience was always different and although I had heard it all before, it was new to them and I had to keep it fresh and fun. Often the classes provided their own humour sometimes through interesting questions and sometimes by mistake.

The red faced blushing girl who meant to ask me a question about bacteria but mixed up her organisms with her orgasms brought the class to a giggling halt as her colleagues fell about laughing. It was a classic.

Knowing that some people have a serious aversion to spiders I always warned each class before producing our enormous specimen but despite this on one occasion one of the male trainees went from his front seat to the fifth row of the banked seating in the auditorium climbing over his friends in a mad rush to get away when the spider appeared.

He was genuinely afraid and took some calming down but like the others had to be aware that such things existed in the big outside world.

The training often put a large strain on our small section particularly when crew recruiting was at its height and we were forced to do daily lectures.

Nevertheless, I was disappointed when after quite a long number of years the training regime was moved away from us and reduced in length at the same time. I've often thought that our crew were less well prepared in later years but then I suppose that the world had changed and they weren't necessarily visiting such remote areas as their predecessors.

CHAPTER 35

A NEW KITCHEN

The new British Airways catering unit at London Heathrow opened in a blaze of publicity in April 1976. It was a world first in terms of size and production methods but like all such openings it wasn't without its hitches.

From a food hygiene point of view, it should have been a vast improvement on its predecessor with improved hygiene standards but the sheer size of the building and scale of the operation meant that it brought its own particular problems. One of the first difficulties was to try to ensure that the staff moving from the old decrepit site didn't bring with them the reduced levels of hygiene that had been allowed to grow up in that building. To cope with this a series of training programmes had to be carried out followed by supervision of work in progress.

Most people outside the airline catering industry have no concept of the scale of the operation needed to provide food on international services across the world. The kitchen was capable of producing in excess of 25,000 meals per day, ranging from tea and biscuits at the bottom end of the scale to full First Class five course dinners which would have graced the table of any decent restaurant.

The jewel in the crown was of course Concorde which had to have a specially designed meal service to cope with the short length of flight involved due to the speed at which it travelled.

The menus included many high class cold items designed to tempt the palate of the jaded First Class traveller but which required a great deal of manipulation during preparation and placing on the plate prior to service on the aircraft, all of which brought food safety issues.

The wall surfaces which Bill had railed about the previous year fell into a minor category when we were faced with other more serious concerns.

Once again the stripping and wash up areas were to be at the forefront of our problems. The building had been designed with one of the largest wash up areas in the world. Capable of washing 85 tons of equipment daily on five parallel washing lines it was equipped with the very latest in five tank industrial dishwashers.

Each was a long metal monster through which passed cutlery, china, glassware and the trolleys in which the food was carried on to the aircraft and from which the customer meals were served as the trolleys passed down the aisles.

Before washing the dirty dishes, all the food waste had to be manually scraped off the incoming plates and a rushing water flume carried the waste food down a metal trough into a disposal system comprised of a large circular tank set beneath the floor into which the food waste was deposited and was then macerated. The water which had carried the waste discharged through a sieve like revolving inner jacket which removed the solid materials, as the water passed into the main drainage system. The recovered macerated waste was then piped out into large containers for transportation to land fill disposal sites.

Following the official opening, I was to spend long periods of time in the new kitchen watching the operations and commenting on the hygiene standards. Within a couple of days, the new waste disposal system began to cause problems. The macerators weren't working correctly in the tanks and as a result the waste wasn't being transferred correctly into the disposal pipes.

Failure of the waste system was a disaster. It was imperative to the whole operation that the washing of equipment was carried out efficiently and on time. Outgoing meals for departing aircraft were dependent on clean equipment being available on which the meals could be set.

As the waste processors ground to a halt the stripping area had to be provided with plastic sacks into which the plates etc. were scraped before being put into the washing machines.

Within hours we were feet deep in plastic sacks full of waste food since our manning levels weren't designed for a replacement process.

To add to all this, the loading dock at the rear of the building, at which the trucks offloaded trolleys full of waste food and dirty equipment from the incoming aircraft was open to the elements and rapidly became a magnet for birds attracted to the inevitable occasional food spill.

Within a short period, the birds became adept at pecking at the plastic bags of waste in order to free a food supply for themselves but in the process spilling quantities of waste onto the dock.

Large swing doors were provided to separate the external environment from the inside of the building but it didn't take long before the more wily birds worked out that if they timed it perfectly, they could gain access to the interior of the building by skipping nimbly through the doors as they swung slowly closed.

Much as we tried to keep the birds out the more they tried to get in. All sorts of remedies were suggested but when the birds began to find their way into the food handling areas desperate measures were needed.

"I've found the answer" the Unit Manager said to me as I walked into his office one morning.

"What's that then?" I queried. "Ultra sound" he replied quickly. "Look." He proffered an advertisement from a Trade magazine.

I looked at it. I had seen it before and wasn't convinced. The picture showed a sound box supposedly giving out a high pitched noise which was inaudible to the human ear but which birds could hear. The pitch was supposed to be at a level which would upset the birds and drive them away. I didn't want to sound too sceptical but in my mind I didn't really think that it would work. "Well anything's worth a try. Let's see if it will work."

A couple of days later I was back in the wash up area with the manager who introduced me to a young woman who was the sales representative of the manufacturing company. Very attractive looking she obviously had the manager entranced by her sales pitch.

"Where would you like me to set it up?" she looked around the work floor. "How about over there?" he suggested looking at a space between the first stripping belt and the wall.

"That's fine" I replied and without further ado the speaker was positioned and plugged into a nearby electrical socket. There was no perceptible noise from the box and the only indication that it was working was a small light glowing. The three of us then walked a short distance away to watch the results. The staff working in the area watched with that look on their faces which said "They're all mad!"

It wasn't long before a couple of sparrows were spotted flying across the room. They gave no indication that the presence of the acoustic

192

deterrent was bothering them in any way. I pointed this out to the sales girl and got a withering look in response. "Give it a few minutes" she said. "I may need to increase the volume a bit to overcome the background noise."

To be fair the noise in the equipment strip and wash area was always somewhat overpowering. It was an industrial site with large volumes of equipment being moved. Hundreds of trolleys were being manhandled through the area and the crashing of metal containers intermingled with the incessant noise of mechanical conveyor systems and the clinking of glasses and china passing into the machines, not to mention the sounds generated by the washing machines themselves.

She walked across to the sound box and twiddled with a couple of small knobs. There was no apparent change but then if the sales blurb was correct we shouldn't be able to hear anything since the sound being transmitted was at a range too high for the human ear to hear. The sparrows continued their flight around the building, occasionally dropping to the floor to pick up the odd piece of food which had fallen.

"I don't think it's working" I said again after some five minutes of bird watching. The girl turned to remonstrate with me again. "Give it some more time" she said.

"I'm sorry but I don't need any more time to consider it. Look for yourself." She turned back towards the box as did the manager.

A horrified look crossed her face as she saw that one of the sparrows had alighted on the top of the sound box!

Whatever noise was coming from the box it certainly wasn't a deterrent for the birds. We had to think again.

Eventually it was decided that the strip and wash area would be separated from the food production areas by the introduction of electrically operated glass sliding doors operated by an electronic eye. This only allowed the doors to open when they were approached by a person.

Keeping the birds contained within the "dirty" area of the building reduced the food safety hazards to a minimum and also allowed our pest control contractor to concentrate his efforts in one area

Shortly after the electric doors separating the wash up from the kitchen had been installed a different method of bird catching was suggested. Apparently one of the employees was the proud owner of a sparrow hawk and he suggested to the manager that he would be happy to bring the hawk into the building at a relatively quiet time of the day and with all the doors closed, release it in the strip and wash area.

The hawk would then rapidly despatch any sparrows that were unfortunate enough to be in the building at the time. The manager, at his wits' end as to how to get rid of the bird problem reluctantly agreed and on the appointed day the sparrow hawk was brought into the building.

It had been decided to carry out the work when the staff were on a meal break and the area was therefore relatively quiet and free from people who not only might get in the way but who might also object to the culling. There were therefore very few people around to watch events as they unfolded.

The sparrow hawk was in an enclosed box and was brought out into the light very carefully. His owner was obviously very proud of it and the bird was certainly very beautiful. All the equipment had been switched off so that it wouldn't be distracted. The hawk sat on the owner's wrist for a few moments quietly blinking in the light then launched itself into the air.

Almost immediately it spotted a sparrow and spiralled rapidly into the chase. The sparrow showed a great turn of speed as it realised that its life was in the balance. Hurtling across the large expanse of the wash up area it was heading straight for the kitchen with the hawk closing rapidly for the kill. But this was where local knowledge gained supremacy. The sparrow knew the building whilst the hawk didn't.

Arriving at the closed glass doors the sparrow made an abrupt right angled turn. The result was inevitable. The hawk didn't see the glass and with a loud thump flew straight into it at high speed landing on the ground in a heap of feathers. I's neck was broken and the bird was dead. The owner was distraught as were those who had witnessed the event. A very unhappy end to what had seemed to be a good idea at the time.

The electrical opening glass doors were to provide other problems as well. They surrounded the complete kitchen area, keeping it free from outsiders walking through the food preparation areas thus keeping the food safe from extraneous contamination.

Chefs entering the hot kitchen where the raw food was cooked had to wash and sanitise their hands before going in. To facilitate this, wash hand basins were provided outside each entrance with hot and cold water, soap and an alcohol based hand sanitiser which the chefs had to apply to their hands once they were washed and dried.

One morning, one of the Chefs called David Gaff (an unfortunate name given what was about to happen) thought that it would be a funny idea if he surprised his colleagues by walking into the kitchen carrying some of the sanitiser in his hands then throwing it on to the hot stove causing a small explosion of fire as the alcohol in the sanitiser burst into flames.

This he did, forgetting that the sanitiser was covering his hands. He caused a surprise all right. As he threw the liquid contents of his hands on to the stove it burst into flames which instantly ran backwards setting his hands and Chef's white uniform alight. His colleagues fell about laughing as he leapt frantically around the kitchen, arms flailing, beating himself to put the flames out.

Happily, no serious damage was done but it was a lesson to the others not to play around in the workplace.

CHAPTER 36

DOWN ROUTE OPERATIONS

My understanding of the practices and processes in the food production area grew over time and I never ceased to marvel at the culinary skills shown by the Chefs in their handling and preparation of some of the best food that I've had the privilege to see and taste.

I know that aircraft meals are often decried by the general public but given the restrictions placed on the transportation and storage of the meals on board an aircraft, the food served in those early days of my career was as good as that served in many top class restaurants.

In fact, the methods of production were generally those used in top class kitchens, from which many of the Chefs and certainly the Executive Chef had come. In time this was to prove a problem.

I also learnt a great deal about food and wine from working closely with the Route Catering team at menu presentations where meals proposed for aircraft meals would be developed and tasted before being placed on the menu.

My first presentation was a real eye opener. I was auditing a kitchen on the Asian sub-continent with my Catering colleague David Randon. Day one had gone reasonably well and although I had found a number of problems which needed improvement I was generally happy with what we had seen.

"Are you going to join me for the menu presentation tomorrow?" David asked me in the taxi on the way back to the hotel.

"Well I have some work to do on the airfield but I would be interested in seeing what you do when that's finished. What actually happens and when are you expecting to start?" I replied.

"Probably around 10.00am so if you want to join me just come across to the kitchen when you've done your checks on the airfield." And so the following morning, having started early, I walked across to the flight kitchen shortly after 10.00am.

"Welcome Mr Kelly, come in." I was ushered through the reception area and into the main Board room of the building where David had already started and acknowledged my arrival with a brief nod of the head.

The room appeared to be full of food and people. Every available surface was covered with aircraft meal dishes each filled with the food which was being proposed for future meals on board. The complete range of meals was there. First Class to Economy, breakfast through to dinner with lunch, morning coffee, afternoon tea and a variety of differing snacks making up the display. It was mind boggling.

Up to that moment it hadn't really crossed my mind as to how much work had to go into planning and presenting the passenger meals. My interest had purely been on the safety of the food.

David was slowly working his way around the dishes, looking closely at each to judge their presentational quality, then tasting them. By his shoulder stood the Executive Chef fingers twitching nervously as he awaited the verdict. Beside him was the kitchen Manager looking similarly anxious.

David was holding a sheaf of paper in his hand which I later found out was the menu specification, devised in London and sent out to the Caterer as the guide to what they were expected to produce. The caterer in turn would provide a costing which was expected to be within the price range that the airline was prepared to pay.

A line of more junior chefs and food workers was also hovering in the room. They were there to fetch and carry, taking some food items out to be re-worked and bring more and different foods into the room.

Everything was tasted even down to the bread rolls. Portion sizes were checked against the specification as were the ingredients. David looked imperious as he worked his way along the food. Nothing missed his eagle eye and being a trained chef with a long history in some of the best hotels in London prior to joining BA he knew exactly what each delicacy should look and taste like.

Whilst quick to praise those items which met the exacting standards he was equally quick to point out the deficiencies. "What's this supposed to be?" He looked accusingly at the Chef whilst prodding what seemed to be an omelette. The Executive Chef's eyes dropped. David investigated the dish further. "The filling isn't what we asked for and the omelette is over cooked."

"No Sir, that's absolutely fine. It's exactly right." One of the junior chefs had taken it upon himself to intervene.

"Wrong move" I thought as I stood watching the performance from the side lines.

I looked at David and thought that he was going to explode. The Executive Chef stood there with that look on his face which said "I'm going to kill you once these BA people have left the kitchen." David controlled himself and said quietly. "I think I'm a better judge of how good this is rather than you." The junior chef seemed prepared to argue the case but was quickly ushered away whilst still protesting.

I smiled to myself and continued watching as the presentation continued. It was amazing watching a professional at work.

I was fascinated and over the following years learned a great deal about food and drink from David and his colleagues as I was privileged to attend a number of such presentations.

One in particular sticks in my mind. Arriving by chance at a flight kitchen at London Gatwick airport one morning to carry out a hygiene audit I was told that a small menu presentation was due to be carried out for the Chief Executive of a charter airline owned at that time by BA.

I was invited to attend and being happy to do so stood in the presentation room to watch the Chief Executive walk along a line of food and give his impression.

As with all menu presentations the Executive Chef and his team had gone to a lot of trouble to prepare a good and varied selection of hot meals to be served to the passengers on flights to their Mediterranean holidays in the forthcoming summer.

Pausing at the last dish the Chief Executive asked what it was. "Beef bourguignon" the Chef replied. "Huh" said the Chief Executive in his blunt accent. "Call it what you will it looks like a stew to me."

Then turning to the airline catering manager standing next to him he said "Whatever happened to those giant sausages that we served last year with beans and chips? They'll never eat this stuff out of Manchester you know" looking back at the bourguignon.

If looks could kill, the Chief Executive was dead. I thought that the

Chef contained himself really well although I have to say that the air turned somewhat blue a few moments after the Chief Executive had left. All that work for nothing was the general consensus and it has to be said that I didn't altogether agree with the belief that passengers from Manchester wouldn't appreciate a meal other than bangers, beans and chips.

CHAPTER 37

DISASTER IN LONDON!!

By the beginning of the nineteen eighties aircraft had increased in both size and the distances that they could travel without having to stop to refuel. As a result, the numbers of meals which had to be provided from individual kitchens was increasing and the old hotel production methods were no longer able to keep pace and mass production lines slowly became the norm in flight kitchens.

On time delivery of meals to departing aircraft was also critical. Flights had to depart on time and keeping an aircraft waiting at the departure gate was considered a serious offence since the costs incurred could run to several hundreds of pounds per minute. The delay cost for a small aircraft such as the Boeing 737 was £350 per minute whilst a Concorde could cost up to £1000 per minute. In any case the food had to be maintained in perfect condition until it was served to the passengers and therefore it couldn't be left standing around.

In hotels and restaurants, it had long been the practice to coat cold canapes and cold plates of meats and fish with aspic glaze to keep the food looking at its best. Within flight catering in the early eighties this was still the case and British Airways was no exception.

All cold food items produced in the long haul kitchen were coated in aspic prior to being plated ready for service. This glazing was done manually by chefs using a ladle and a large tank of liquid aspic. The size and shape of a very large sink, the tank was made of stainless metal and had an outer jacket through which hot water was passed. This allowed the aspic in the bath to remain warm and liquid for quite long periods of time.

Items such as canapes and cuts of meat and seafood were placed on wire racks which fitted across the top of the bath. Warm glaze was ladled from one side of the tank and poured over the food items thereby giving them a coating, the unused aspic draining back through the wire rack into the tank to be re-used. The racks of glazed food were then placed on tiered trolleys to cool for a while before being placed into a cold room to await final plating.

I had watched this process on many occasions and had raised my concerns about the safety of the product. Aspic is made from animal products and in its warm state is an ideal medium on which to grow bacteria. It is therefore imperative to control the usage and temperature of the product when it's handled in the food industry.

This was well known and a set of rules had been drawn up in the use of the glazing bath. These included the need to boil the aspic when preparing it then using it for periods not exceeding twenty minutes at which point the tank should be drained and cleaned before being refilled with fresh aspic.

All very well but not really practical in the real world and although I had often watched the process, as had the Executive Chef, it was likely that when our backs were turned the control processes were conveniently forgotten.

Wednesday 14th March 1984 started like most other days. I arrived at the office at around 8.00am and was enjoying my first cup of coffee when Peter called me into his office.

"There's a bit of a problem with some crew sickness down route" he said pushing some telex messages into my hand. "I don't suppose it's very much. You know what crew are like. Eating in some greasy spoon to save their allowances no doubt. I'm off to Stavanger so I won't be back in the office until Monday morning. I don't expect you'll have any problem sorting it out." With that he was gone.

Crew sickness wasn't unheard of but usually affected only one or two people and usually was the result of eating out at some low grade restaurant down route so I wasn't alarmed by the situation. I took the telexes back into my office, sat down and started to read through them. As I read I began to realise that this wasn't a normal outbreak of illness involving one crew.

In my hand I had a number of telexes each reporting a number of operating crew who had fallen ill with symptoms of food poisoning the previous night in cities in different parts of the world including the USA, the Middle East and Africa. Something was seriously wrong.

Just at that moment my phone rang. "Hello Mike" It was Frank Preston, the Director Medical Serves. "Has Peter seen you?"

"Yes" I replied "and I've got the telexes in front of me. They don't make good reading so I'm just on my way to Catering Centre South to see Willi Kraus and try to figure out what the problem might be. I'll get back to you as quickly as I can."

"Fine" Frank said. "I'll leave it with you at the moment".

I jumped into my car and hurtled across to the flight kitchen. Running into the building I almost collided with Willi, the Executive Chef. "Have you heard the news?" Willi said. "Yes." I replied. "Come to my office."

We went into his office and I sat down. "What do you think?" he looked at me closely. "We have a problem Willi. I've got telexes showing twenty-six crew sick in five different places."

"It's more than that, I've got more than fifty crew sick." Willi showed me another group of telex messages on his desk. "I'm in process of changing the crew meals" he continued. Crew on the aircraft were supplied with their own set of meals which were different from those provided for the customers.

"Good" I said "but it may not just be the crew meals." He looked at me "Why do you say that we've not had any complaints from any passengers?"

"Yes but you know what crew are like. They consider that any meals left over in First class and Club class are a perk for them and given the choice they'll eat those rather than the crew meals provided."

"But we've not had any customer complaints." Willi said again, trying desperately to keep a lid on what was threatening to explode.

"That's not surprising, looking at the telexes. It looks like all the crew concerned were due to operate flights last night but called in sick and as a result of the numbers involved the majority of the flights have had to be cancelled due to lack of crew. Any passengers who are ill won't have had time to contact the airline yet, but if it is the customer meals it won't be long before we start to hear from them."

"It seems that all the affected crew operated out of London on Monday and went sick on Tuesday giving something like a twelve hour incubation period before the sickness started. Don't say anything to anybody yet

202

Willi. We won't know anything until we've got more information from the sick crew as to what they ate."

Willi nodded. His face looked grey at the thought of what may be happening. "I'm going back to the office to start collating all the information as we get it. I'll come back to you in an hour to see where we are. Meanwhile carry on with your menu change for the crew."

Before I left I walked round the corner into the food hygiene laboratory which Medical Services ran as part of our surveillance of food safety in the kitchen. Samples of food were taken on a daily basis and processed by our own small laboratory team under the very able guidance of Carole Burslem our food laboratory scientist.

"Hi Mike" she looked up from her workbench. "I take it you've heard? I've been trying to get Peter or you on the phone."

"Peter's just left for Stavanger so it looks like it's down to you and me" I grinned at her. "Oh thanks for that!"

We sat for a few moments going through the information that we had and I told her of my suspicions that it wasn't necessarily a crew meal to blame but could turn out to be something worse.

"I've got some samples from the Monday meal production growing as we speak and although it's a bit early I may have some indications as to what we might be dealing with by lunchtime."

"Great. I'm going back to see Frank and set up our information collating process but I'll be back in an hour."

Back to the office and a meeting with Frank and his Senior Doctors. I explained my thinking and told them what was happening re the crew meal menu change in the kitchen. "We'd better organise stool testing for all the food handlers in the kitchen" Frank looked at his team. Heads nodded. "The nursing team can sort that out."

"I'll start collating the information as it arrives." I said. "We'll use our main office as it has more space. If, as I suspect, passengers are involved then the numbers may be very high." Nods around the table again. "Who should we be talking to within the rest of the company?" asked one of the Doctors.

"I'll tell them upstairs" Frank said quickly. Upstairs was the Head Office function of Chief Executive, Legal Director, Chairman's Office and Operations.

"Don't give anyone any information other than the absolute basics" I said quickly, then felt somewhat abashed as I was talking to my Director. "I mean we don't actually have any concrete information as yet and we don't want to start any hares running."

Frank agreed and added "We'd better brief the Press Office as the news will get out somehow or other. Let's get together again at lunchtime and pool what information we've got."

We broke up and so began one of the worst weeks of my life. I went back to my office and told our secretarial team what was going on. I warned them that we might have to drop all normal work and concentrate on the food poisoning event if it became bigger.

Mid-morning found me back in the kitchen with Willi and by lunchtime we got our first break. Carole called me "Mike I think we've got a Salmonella in some of the samples we took on Monday." Great news in that we now had a decent clue as to what we were looking at but the bad news was to come. I ran round the corner from Willi's office to our laboratory. "What's it in?" I asked.

"That's the problem, it's in more than one sample and they're from different foods" Carole looked up at me from the bacterial culture plates she was studying at her bench.

"So what have they got in common? Is there one single food item present in all the samples?" "We've got all sorts of things here" Carole looked a bit perplexed "Seafood, lobster, chicken" she bent down and looked again.

"So what have they got in common?" I asked again, speaking as much to myself as to Carole.

It took us a moment looking at what was in front of us then the penny dropped. "ASPIC"

"I told them so" I said to myself. Only the previous Wednesday I had been at one of our regular quarterly meetings attended by the Head of Catering plus the Hygiene team and Director Medical Services when I had berated the catering team about the poor standards at the flight kitchen and had warned that if conditions weren't improved dramatically that it was an accident waiting to happen. It gave me no pleasure to find that my warning may have come true.

Straight into Willis office. "It's the aspic Willi" he looked stunned. "Are you sure?" "Yes as sure as we can be. Carol's found Salmonellae in the samples she took on Monday. You'll need to get all the aspic covered cold plates off the menu and any aspic coated items which are due to go out on flights today must be taken off. You'll also need to close down the cold kitchen and sanitise it thoroughly."

I went back to Medical Services and updated Frank on the laboratory findings. We now had upwards of a hundred crew sick and the administration team were up to their necks in paper, busily logging each case as it arrived. Later in the afternoon we had further confirmation that it was passenger meals that were the cause of the illness when several more clues gave this away.

On the Monday afternoon Kurt Hafner, one of the senior managers in the Catering Team had hosted a lunch in the Catering Centre board room for some visitors. It was catered using First Class products from the kitchen. On Tuesday Kurt and some of his guests had become ill with food poisoning symptoms.

Also on the Monday a Concorde aircraft had flown around the UK on a test flight. It carried a number of staff including some secretaries who had been given the privilege of flying on this very special aircraft. A scratch meal had been put on the flight for them and several of the staff had reported ill on Wednesday. One slightly amusing side issue came out of this incident when it emerged that one of the secretaries didn't eat the food on board but had taken it home in her bag and fed it to her cat. The cat subsequently developed food poisoning symptoms and jokes about the Secretary's pussy abounded for days afterwards.

By the end of the week we were dealing with more than seven hundred cases of illness making the outbreak one of the largest ever to have occurred in the UK.

Having been very fortunate in being able to identify our source by Wednesday afternoon we were quickly able to change all the menus and ensure that the on-going food product was completely safe with all affected or possibly affected items having been removed.

Reports of illness continued to come in over the next few days and into following weekend, but with the information we had by then, we were able to link all of them to flights which had departed from Heathrow on the previous Monday or Tuesday.

The case proved to be a salutary lesson not only for BA but for all major airlines and aspic disappeared off airline menus worldwide like snow melting in summer. As a result of the outbreak British Airways was obliged to pay out a vast sum of money in compensation to those passengers affected and in some cases to Companies who had lost key members of their staff.

For example, the Cunard shipping line whose replacement crew for the QE2 liner went sick after a flight to the Seychelles where they were due to join the ship on a round the world cruise. This meant that the crew on board had to continue the voyage for a few more days whilst the relief crew recovered.

For me it was a challenge. As the only member of the Hygiene team in London when it happened I was thrown in at the deep end from the start but was pleased when it was all over to know that despite the enormity of the situation I was part of a team which got the investigation right.

Although the airline had to take a lot of stick at the time and pay out compensation, the way it handled the situation with its customers got it a lot of praise.

Some years later I was having dinner with my family in a restaurant in Port Andratx in Mallorca when a large party at an adjoining table began to discuss the case, one of the party having been affected. His description of what happened and how he felt that he personally had been dealt with was very pleasing to hear. He praised the airline for how they had handled the situation and was certainly not deterred from flying with it thereafter. Handling the outbreak didn't do any damage to my reputation either and for many years afterwards I was asked to give presentations at food safety conferences worldwide to talk about the difficulties in the mass production of food and how to handle the consequences of getting it wrong.

CHAPTER 38

RATS, REPTILES AND BODIES

My early days in the airline brought a realisation that I had a lot to learn. Like most passengers I had no idea of what went on behind the scenes to keep the airline operational.

Most people when boarding a plane think little of how the food is supplied from the many places that the flight may visit, where the drinking water comes from and how the waste produced on board is dealt with. Fewer still will think about the many rodents, insects, and reptiles which may gain access to the aeroplane during stops.

Rodents are a particular problem as I was quick to find out. A rat or mouse can easily gain access to an aircraft at any airport around the world by walking down the air bridge attached to the aircraft which allow passengers to board and disembark the aircraft but may be left unattended for periods of time between flights during which time the rodents may seize their opportunity. They can also get on board via cargo or even in baggage brought by passengers.

They are a problem because once on board they will make their way into secluded areas of the plane where they have a penchant for gnawing at the miles of plastic coated cables which support the aircraft functions. They may even find themselves getting trapped inside bits of equipment which are meant to move but are prevented from doing so by the presence of the furry animal and there is nothing that a pilot hates more than an equipment failure in flight. Their presence on board is therefore considered to be an air safety problem.

Equally important is the fact that rodents have very little in the way of passenger appeal. Passengers strapped into their seats during take-off are very likely to panic if faced by the sight of a large rat wandering down the aisle as the plane leaves the runway. As a result, any sighting or suspected sighting of a rodent on an aircraft will lead to the plane being grounded until the animal is caught and catching them is not an easy task.

When I joined the airline in 1975 rodent control was carried out by fumigating infested aircraft using hydrogen cyanide. Apart from being very dangerous to the pest control operatives its use had two problems.

Firstly, hydrogen cyanide was likely to be extremely damaging to the aircraft fabric due to its acidic nature. Secondly as the product was mainly used to fumigate ships, the pest control company staff trained in its use, were based at a major sea port, some considerable distance from London's main airports which could result in lengthy delays before a team could arrive to fumigate an aircraft. This was unacceptable in terms of the cost to the airline of keeping the aircraft on the ground so we were tasked with finding a more acceptable method.

Fortunately, a new up and coming pest control Company was at hand to offer a novel idea. "How about using methyl bromide?" David, their CEO asked one afternoon in Peters' office. Peter and I looked at each other. "Tell us more."

David quickly expounded on the idea that methyl bromide which was a liquid at temperatures below 40F could be warmed up and the resultant gas used as a fumigant. "Methyl bromide is a very good fumigant effective against a large variety of targets but it has no smell so it's normal to add picrin which you will know better as tear gas and is readily detectable." David continued.

We warmed to the idea but the effects of methyl bromide on the aircraft interior had to be fully investigated before we could carry out any tests to see how effective it might be against rodents.

One of the standard rules in the airline industry is that any materials used for any reason on an aircraft must comply with a set of tests to prove that their use will not compromise the stability or safety of the aircraft in any way. This requirement came about in the light of experience over many years where the use of chemicals on board had been found to cause corrosion in the metal of aircraft.

In one of the most damaging cases a leak of chemical from a passenger toilet caused a fatal aircraft crash when over time the leaking chemical rotted the metalwork around it and caused the aircraft tail to fail.

Methyl bromide was no exception to this rule and our engineering colleagues had to give it the all clear before we could continue our research. This took some time but eventually, nearly a year later we got the go ahead. David was certain that the gas would work on an aircraft but obviously it had never been tried so what were we going to do?

"There's only one way to check and that's to get an aircraft, put some mice into it and then fumigate the plane" Peter suggested tentatively.

"How will you get one?" I looked at him across the desk. "I'll have to get the Director to ask Operations to lend us one for a day and stress that if we can get this right it will mean a serious saving of time and money for the airline." It took some time to convince everyone but a couple of months later Peter, David and I were standing beside a VC10 aircraft lent to us for the day and parked only a hundred yards from our office.

Next to the aircraft stood a mobile laboratory manned by staff from the Pest Infestation Control Laboratory, a Government organisation based in the nearby town of Slough whom Peter had persuaded to help us to monitor what was happening. The fumigation team stood ready with their bottles of gas and a heating apparatus which looked somewhat basic but was guaranteed to work David assured us.

Work commenced with the team ensuring that the aircraft was completely clear of people and then sealing up all external vents. The area around the aircraft had been cleared and cordoned off with a series of barriers and large signs stating "No entry – poisonous gas."

Peter and I stood by watching. The operation seemed to go quite smoothly considering that it was a first attempt. A bottle of gas was suspended on a set of spring scales at the bottom of the steps leading up to the aircraft door. A long flexible pipe ran up the steps and into the aircraft cabin. Inside the team had rolled out along the length of the cabin a polythene hosepipe punctuated every couple of inches by small holes through which the gas would escape into the plane.

"I think we're ready" David said quietly. His team members came out of the doorway, closing it behind them and sealing the gaps left by the hose passing through it before coming down the steps. The heater needed to heat the methyl bromide bottle to convert the liquid into gas was started up with a roar and off we went. "We measure the quantity of gas passing into the aircraft by weighing the bottle, hence the spring scales "David explained. He had forgotten that he had told us this before when we had discussed the possibility of using this novel means of fumigation.

The afternoon passed slowly as the gassing continued. It took some eight hours to complete the process. When the aircraft had been totally filled with gas the senior fumigator climbed the steps and disconnected the solid external hosepipe from the flexible polythene pipe inside the plane, then sealed the door absolutely tight. The steps were disconnected and the plane left filled with gas for four hours to enable the fumigant to work.

The team stayed with the aircraft to ensure that no-one would enter the exclusion zone and attempt to board the aircraft. When the required time had elapsed the fumigation team, wearing their gas masks replaced the steps, boarded the plane, opened all the doors and used electric fans to allow the gas to be exhausted from the plane. They then ensured that no gas remained on the aircraft before allowing us to board. The cage of mice was checked and the process was declared a success as all the mice had been killed.

Peter, David and I were very happy with what we had seen and after writing a protocol and drawing up a full set of instructions the fumigation of aircraft using methyl bromide became a standard method of ridding aircraft of rodents and other pests.

Despite the fact that our senior operations and engineering staff had the power to authorise the fumigation of an aircraft, it appeared that many of them were reluctant to ground an aircraft, due to the cost involved in doing so. As a result, we would regularly receive phone calls at our office during the day or at home at night asking for our "go ahead" to ground a plane in order to fumigate it. Through the next twenty years I was to get many such calls, some of which were funny and others quite bizarre.

One morning just before 10.00am I was sitting at my desk when the phone rang. "Operations control here, sorry to bother you but we have the New York departure (he gave me the flight number) ready to board the passengers and some of the crew claim to have seen a rat in the cabin. What should we do?"

It's pretty obvious what you should do I thought to myself. "You'll have to take it out of service and have it fumigated" I replied.

"But the passengers are in the jetty lounge ready to board and we haven't got a spare aircraft." I could hear the desperation in his voice. The lack of a spare aircraft was obviously going to make the problem bigger than it might otherwise have been. If a replacement aircraft had been available, the passengers would only have been delayed by an hour or two whilst it was readied for the flight. The absence of a replacement meant that the flight would have to be cancelled causing disruption and passenger discontent at both ends of the service.

Despite what passengers may sometimes think, most airlines don't keep spare aircraft sitting around waiting in case one breaks down and has to be replaced. It's a bit like your family car, you don't keep a spare one in the garage in case your first one breaks down, do you?

Sometimes the airline schedule is such that there may be a spare aircraft available as a replacement when an aircraft may be released early from the engineering base after some maintenance has been completed. In this case Ops Control had obviously looked at the schedule and realised that this couldn't be done.

"I'm sorry" I said. "I understand the problem that it's going to cause but International Regulations don't allow us to knowingly export a rodent into another country. Just out of interest where has the aircraft been on its last flight?" Not that it made any real difference, I thought to myself.

"It arrived from Bombay this morning" came the swift reply. "Well it definitely can't fly to New York with a rat on board, specially one which may have come from India. The Americans would throw the book at us and possibly impound the aircraft if they found out. You know what sticklers they are for playing by the rules. In any case what would the passengers think if they saw a rat on board during the flight?"

"OK" I could hear the deflation in his voice as the phone went dead. About an hour later the phone rang again. "Ops Control, sorry to bother you again. We've sorted out the New York but I just wanted to ask a question". He carried on without stopping. "Would it have been all right if we had sent the aircraft to Toronto?"

I didn't know whether to laugh or cry but having recovered my breath explained quietly that the International Regulations wouldn't permit us to send an aircraft with a rodent on board to anywhere in the world.

Whilst rodents provided the majority of our problems, followed closely by cockroaches, they weren't the only things to cause concern on our aircraft and over the years I learned to expect the unexpected.

Sitting at my desk one summer's afternoon I was startled when Ops Control called. "We have a problem" the conversation started. "Yes?" I replied expectantly. "Yes. We are the handling agents for a Middle Eastern airline, and as our team were unloading the cargo they found a body"

"A body?" I replied incredulously. "Do you mean human remains?" "Yes." "Was it listed on the cargo manifest?" "Yes" came the prompt reply.

"Well what's the problem then?" I asked, thinking why have they contacted our office? "It's not in a coffin"

"It's not in a coffin?" I replied incredulously. "No, it's loose loaded between a cargo of figs and a cargo of fish and we don't know what to do with the figs and fish."

"I'd better come down and have a look then. I'll be at the aircraft in about ten minutes." In the nineteen eighties, the Hygiene team all had airside passes not only for ourselves but also for our cars. This enabled us to drive through the security gates on to the aircraft apron at any of the Terminals at Heathrow.

Ten minutes later I drew up alongside a Boeing 727 aircraft alongside which the cargo unloading team were waiting. "It's in there, mate" their leader said to me pointing towards the rear hold. He followed me as I climbed inside. "There" he said, pointing at what appeared to be a large cardboard box.

It certainly wasn't a coffin or at least a coffin in which human remains should be transported internationally on an aircraft. In the somewhat elderly Boeing 727 aircraft the cargo wasn't loaded into containers before being put in to the aircraft but was loaded "loose" as individual items into sections of the hold separated by cargo nets to stop the cargo moving during the flight. The cardboard coffin was nestling happily between a consignment of figs and one of dried fish as I'd been advised.

I thought quickly. Although the coffin wasn't solid and didn't comply with International Regulations a quick look confirmed that there was no leakage from the box and therefore no contamination of the food products.

"OK offload it and put it in the mortuary" I told the team leader. "I'll call the cargo manager and get him to contact Kenyons to arrange for a proper coffin." Kenyons was an undertaking company which was contracted to BA to deal with such eventualities.

"What about the rest of the cargo?" the team leader looked at me and his team mates waited expectantly. "That'll be OK. Just off load it as normal and send it on its way." I drove back to my office thinking why do these things happen when I'm the only team member in the office?

In later years when I became Head of the department, it was more often than not going to be me who had to deal with the more bizarre events, but that was what made the job interesting. I never knew what each day would bring.

Of course I wasn't the only person faced with the unexpected and several tales came to my knowledge over the years none of which I could personally verify but all of which had a solid basis of truth although the story may have been embellished somewhat in the telling across the airline.

My "body" may have been something unusual but not quite so frightening as the experience of a cargo handler when, on opening the cargo door of an aircraft which had just landed, he found himself face to face with a tiger. I don't know which of them was the more surprised but I know that it's not easy to get a cargo door shut quickly. The big cat had been in transit and had somehow escaped from the container in which it was travelling.

Two of our catering handlers also got a shock when, on removing a catering container from the rear galley of a Boeing 747 just arrived from Nigeria, they came face to face with a cane rat which had obviously hitched a lift.

Now the cane rat is a very large rodent. I can vouch for this having seen one on the garden pathway in a hotel in Gambia, West Africa. It was sitting there in broad daylight and was so large that people walking along the path took a very large detour to avoid it. A rat as big as a cat would be doing it a disfavour as the cane rat can be 70cms long and weigh up to 10 kilograms in the wild.

This one in the galley of our aircraft was obviously large since the two very hefty catering loaders took one look at it, rapidly abandoned the galley and in fear of being followed, jumped off the catering truck which was parked with its raised platform some twelve feet above the ground.

The rat also abandoned ship according to the story and was last seen heading down the road tunnel which led from the central airport area to the cargo terminal. Despite the efforts of the Authorities to kill or capture the rodent, which would have posed a possible threat of introducing rabies or other transmissible diseases into the UK, it was never seen again. A tall story perhaps? I don't know for certain but I believe it to be true.

One night I was awakened by the phone ringing. My wife on whose side of the bed the phone was placed handed it to me without a word, surmising that in the early hours of the morning the call was most likely for me.

"Good morning Mr Kelly. Ops Control here. Sorry to wake you so early but we have a problem." "Go ahead" I replied, trying to get my mind to function. "We have had a message from the Captain of a flight inbound to Gatwick who says that they appear to have a snake on board. Can you speak to him? I'll page him through."

Suddenly I was wide awake. A voice came through the phone obviously via a radio link up. "Good morning. Sorry to have woken you so early." "Good morning Captain, I understand you have a snake on board" I replied.

"Yes, some of the crew claim to have seen it and we believe it's in one of the overhead stowage bins in Club Class" came the response. "Where have you come from and how far out are you?" My mind was whirring as I tried to envisage the situation and work out some sort of answer. I couldn't imagine what sort of panic might ensue on the aircraft if the snake came down on to the heads of any passengers seated beneath the bins.

"We're inbound from Denver and about two and a half hours to touchdown." I thought quickly. "How big is the snake?" "About a couple of feet long we believe." Pretty big then and coming from Denver it could be poisonous was my first thought.

"OK. Well I suggest that you turn off all the cabin heating immediately. Being a reptile the snake won't be able to move once it gets cold. All the passengers have blankets as it's an overnight flight and you probably have a few spare for anyone who gets overly cold. You can tell them it's a technical fault with the heating system if you have to. I'm assuming that the passengers haven't seen the snake?"

"Not as far as I'm aware." came the reply. "Fine. I'll have our pest control contractor at the airport waiting for you on arrival. I suggest that you get the passengers to disembark as quickly as possible but leaving all their hand baggage in the overhead bins. Once we've located and disposed of the snake we can get their baggage unloaded."

"Thanks for that. I appreciate your thinking and your help. My First Officer has just turned the heating off. No doubt we'll get plenty of complaints but at least the passengers may be a bit safer."

The captain sounded a bit relieved and I wished him a safe arrival. As he disappeared from the line the Ops Controller came back to me.

"Thanks for that Mr Kelly. I was listening in so I know what's happening. I'll contact the pest control contractor and have him standing by. Sorry again for having to wake you at three in the morning." "That's OK. It's all part of the job" I replied before hanging up. Yes, it's all part of the job and that's what makes it all the more interesting I thought as I snuggled back under the duvet and tried to get back to sleep.

Following a search of the aircraft on its arrival at Gatwick the snake was found coiled up in an overhead locker. Identified later as a harmless Californian king snake it was beautifully marked with white diamonds on a grey and black skin.

Harmless it may have been but its presence would have caused panic had it been seen by the passengers during the night.

How did it get there? A question I've been asked on numerous occasions later when telling the tale. I don't know for certain but I would guess that someone was bringing it home as a pet in their carry on baggage, this being in the era before hand baggage was searched quite as thoroughly as it is today.

And who, on suspecting that their pet snake may have escaped from its bag is going to be brave enough to press the call button and tell the flight attendant "I think that my snake may have escaped." We'll never know.

Called one grey damp winter's morning to deal with some nasty insects found in the hold of an aircraft recently arrived from Cape Town I found the area around the plane suspiciously deserted. I walked across the apron and on staring into the cavernous hold of the Boeing 747 found that the loading team who were supposed to be off loading the flight had taken shelter from the cold drizzle falling outside and were sitting on the floor playing cards.

"Where are these dangerous insects?" I asked somewhat sarcastically as I hadn't expected anyone to be inside the hold. "Over there mate" replied one of the team.

Stacked in the far corner of the cavernous hold was a large consignment of fresh cut flowers destined for the London market. I approached cautiously to find myself looking at a number of brightly coloured and different looking insects which were very obviously a collection of South African garden insects, some of which I recognised from previous encounters in the garden of my cousin in Johannesburg.

Very different in appearance and colour from their English counterparts their appearance had proven to be a good excuse for the loading team to down tools. Aware of the fact that the passengers who had arrived on the flight were still in the baggage reclaim area in the Terminal building awaiting their luggage and had been waiting for some considerable time I had to make a quick decision.

"OK lads, back to work" I looked at the team. "It's nothing to worry about, there's nothing harmful on board, just a lot of garden insects." "You sure mate?" said the leader looking at me suspiciously. "Yes and if it's any consolation I'll stay here with you as you offload."

That was enough to get them going and I stood watching whilst they got back to work, occasionally and surreptitiously moving my foot up and down, like an Irish dancer, to kill one or two of the more bizarre insects which were making their way out of the flowers and across the floor of the hold, the sight of which may have been enough for the team to down tools again.

It worked and the passengers got their bags.

CHAPTER 39

WATER, WATER EVERYWHERE
BUT NOT A DROP TO DRINK

Having joined the airline and settled into my job the auditing of the many stations that British Airways flew to across the world gradually became a routine. Each audit took at least two full days since it included the flight catering facilities, the crew hotel or hotels in some larger cities, the aircraft drinking water and toilet servicing arrangements and the airport passenger facilities including restaurants and cafes.

A flight catering audit would take at least a full day dependent on its size and in some major cities such as New York, Sydney or Hong Kong this could be extended to a day and a half or more.

Crew hotels were audited to check food safety standards in the kitchens, the quality of the drinking water supply, the standards of cleanliness in the rooms and the fire safety provisions.

Added to this were the facilities which the passengers never think about but which are important to ensure their safety. For example, the drinking water supply for the planes. All aircraft carry a large quantity of water on board to provide for hand washing in the toilets and water at the taps in the galleys where the food is stowed and the early Boeing 747s used on intercontinental flights had drinking water taps to enable passengers to serve themselves during long flights. The average passenger will probably think little, if at all, about where the water on board comes from, particularly now that bottled drinking water has become the norm to supplement that which is supplied to the galleys and toilets.

However, given that aircraft travel to a variety of destinations there was a need to ensure the safety of the drinking water uplifted and it fell to the Hygiene team to check what was happening at each airport.

I very quickly learnt that the location of the airport was not necessarily a good guide to the quality and security of the water provided to aircraft. In most airports drinking water was delivered to the aircraft via a water bowser, a small self-propelled tanker which collected the water from a supply point somewhere on the airfield. The water was then transported to the aircraft where it was pumped into on board storage tanks through an inlet valve positioned under the belly of the aircraft.

Since British Airways couldn't control the quality of the mains water supplied to the taps in the airport we had a set of written standards as to how the water must be treated before being loaded on to the aircraft.

The water bowser had to have a regular cleaning and sanitising regime. The mains water tap from which it was filled had to be protected from contamination when not in use and chlorine had to be added to each uplift to ensure water safety.

A number of other international carriers had similar standards but I was surprised to find that many others didn't and few appeared to check that the standards were being maintained.

In my naivety on my early audits it came as a surprise to find that standards weren't always being complied with. At best, there was insufficient chlorine being added to the water and at worst there was a severe risk of contamination.

The fill point from which the water was picked up could be anywhere on the airfield. Often it was nothing more than a tap on a wall, unprotected from the dust and dirt blowing around it and sometimes used for multifarious purposes including vehicle washing and even the washing of clothing in one city on the Asian sub-continent all of which was likely to allow the water to become contaminated. But even in Europe conditions weren't always perfect.

Coming down the aircraft steps on arrival one morning at a well-known European city I was met by the British Airways station engineer.

"Hi Mike" he said "Nice to see you again." I had met him on previous audits at another station.

"I thought I'd better catch you as you arrived as I think we have a major problem here." "Oh yes?" I queried thinking that it was certainly very unusual to be met by the engineer on arrival.

"Come with me" he said walking away from the aircraft, "You can check in through immigration in a couple of minutes. This won't take long."

Relaxing after work at Victoria Falls, 1968

Wet season road, 1968

On the open road, Zambia, 1968

Vaccination at a primary school, Zambia, 1968

Chusky with a python, Mazabuka, 1968

Working hazards, South Luangwa, 1969

Helpers at river crossing, Eastern Province, 1969

Health centre construction, Eastern Province, 1970

Elephants in my working district, South Luangwa, 1970

Road hazard, South Luangwa, 1970

Castle in the bush, Lundazi, 1970

Boeing 747-400 on which I flew hundreds of thousands of miles

Full catering uplift, Boeing 747, 1991

Rodent and California King snake found on aircraft after fumigation

Partial set of false teeth found in aircraft breakfast

On the ramp, Heathrow, 1994

Concorde take off. I was privileged to fly on the aircraft several times

The aircraft had been parked on what was known as an outside stand. It wasn't at the terminal building but was some distance away from it, at the edge of what appeared to be a construction site and the passengers were being transported by bus to the arrival building.

We walked a short distance from the plane towards an area where a building had obviously recently been demolished and work was going on to clear the site. "It's a shambles" the engineer said. "They're tearing the place apart to rebuild in time for the Olympics but with no real thought as to what they're doing. "What do you think of that?"

We had stopped at the edge of the concrete aircraft apron and I was looking at a tap fixed on the top of a water pipe standing upright and alone in the middle of a morass of mud. Connected to it as we watched, was a water bowser being filled, which would have been bad enough given the unprotected nature of the tap amid the surrounding mud and dirt from the construction work, however more horrifying was the fact that the mud around the tap was blue, stained by the chemical used in the servicing of aircraft toilets. The tap was very obviously being used to fill the toilet servicing vehicles as well as the drinking water bowsers.

"I don't believe it!" I was almost speechless. This was a major European city so what were the airport authority thinking about. "How long has this being going on?"

I looked at the engineer. "Well I only spotted it this morning when our aircraft was positioned on to this outside stand. We're normally on a jetty at the terminal building as you know but the terminal is about to be demolished hence where we are. I don't know when the old servicing building was demolished but it looks like it's only been a few days ago."

"OK" I replied "but we'll have to ban all drinking water uplifts from here with immediate effect. It's not as if the aircraft has flown very far so it shouldn't be a problem. London will just have to ensure that there is enough water on each aircraft for the return trip. Can you send them an immediate message and I'll back it up in writing when I get back?"

"Will do. I'll walk you into the terminal as strictly speaking as you shouldn't be out here without a valid airside pass but I thought you needed to see this."

"This place has always been a problem" I said as we walked towards the building, "but that's as bad as it can get. Last time I was here at least they had two separate taps although I wasn't convinced even then that they were being used correctly. I also had a problem with the use of their staff."

"How was that?" said my colleague. "Well as I was watching the water bowser departing to the aircraft after filling up I noticed that there was a mop and bucket on the back of it. When I asked what it was for I was told that when the driver of the water vehicle had connected his hose to the aircraft and begun filling he would then go on board the plane and clean out the toilets!!"

"You're kidding?" The engineer looked at me in disbelief. "I wish I was."

A similar story prevailed in another European capital city where the airport operators couldn't understand that a drinking water fill hose left dangling unprotected about a metre above ground level at the side of a busy road along which passed a constant stream of airport vehicles was liable to become contaminated and pose a risk to customers.

It seemed unreal to me that BA was forced to suspend water uplifts from a major European city but we had to in order to protect our customers.

CHAPTER 40

SPANISH SIESTA

When it came to flight catering I was also in for some surprises. Over the years I've often been asked "Where are the worst facilities that you've ever seen?" Most people asking the question are expecting my answer to be that the worst are in some third world country and that the best are in Europe or the USA.

In reality the best facilities are found wherever there is a good management team and conversely the worst are always where the worst management teams are working. I've seen some wonderful kitchens in the Asian sub-continent and some truly terrible premises in the USA and Europe.

Some of my audits over the years became memorable not only because our team visits were able to encourage improvement and thus gave us job satisfaction but also because of the many great people that I met along the way and some of the most beautiful places in the world which I was privileged to visit.

Many of the people involved in flight catering and the airline business were characters and became legends in their own lifetime. One of these was Joe Palmies, the owner of the flight catering unit at Barcelona in the nineteen eighties. On my first visit to Barcelona I arrived on a sunny summer's day to be met by Joe in the office of the BA station manager.

He was the picture of what I had always expected the Spanish gentleman to be. Sporting a small goatee beard and dressed in a beige camel hair coat slung casually over both shoulders with his arms hanging loose.

He shook my hand and said "Let's go for lunch."

The Spanish way of life is very different to that in the UK and a long lunch followed by a siesta is the norm. I wasn't exactly ready for lunch having had a meal on the aircraft en route to Barcelona but was forced to go along with the offer since it had been extended to the BA manager who appeared keen to accept.

We set off in Joe's car towards the nearby coast and were soon seated in the sunshine in a very busy restaurant obviously frequented by large numbers of airport staff on their lunch break. Joe was a lively companion and quickly let me know that he was a former employee of BEA a forerunner of British Airways and had been educated at Manchester Grammar school.

The meal passed fairly slowly and I began to worry about getting my audit carried out but Joe wasn't to be hurried. Eventually we finished and headed back to the airport where we parked outside a small two storey building set in an agricultural site, green and grassy with a crop of maize in evidence, but within a short walk of the airport terminal building, visible across the field.

It was somewhat surreal and certainly not what I was expecting. Joe ushered me inside and we walked up the stairs and through what was a very small production kitchen into his office. "Sit down Mike" he said as he parked himself on one side of a large and cluttered desk.

I sat down and looking around realised that the central well beneath the desk into which one would normally place one's legs was a solid mass of spider's webs. It obviously hadn't been used or cleaned for some time and didn't bode well for the rest of the building.

I quickly went through the necessary paperwork and was soon outside in the kitchen watching the small number of staff working on their next flight. Things weren't quite as bad as I had thought they might be. The unit was small and limited in its facilities but was generally clean and although old, the equipment such as refrigerators all seemed to work.

Going downstairs into the equipment wash up area was very different however. As I walked into the room I came face to face with a very large dog! "Don't worry he's very friendly" Joe said quickly.

"But he shouldn't be in the wash up area with all the clean equipment" I replied quickly. "I have to keep him here because of the threat of burglars" Joe said. "We're a bit remote from the rest of the airport and surrounded by farmland so we are an easy target."

The dog seemed friendly enough so I pushed my way past him and went further into the room. The equipment washing machine was in the middle of the room but stacked beside it was a partly dismantled motorcycle complete with a selection of spare parts amongst which were the baskets of recently washed clean equipment.

Having seen enough I walked back upstairs to Joe's office and began to explain to him in no uncertain terms what I thought about the overall situation in the kitchen. To be fair he took it very well and agreed to make immediate improvements and without further ado walked into the kitchen and calling his team together began to give a series of instructions at least that what I assumed he was doing since as I spoke no Spanish I had to trust him.

"That's it" Joe said. "Come back tomorrow and you will see a change."
"I hope so" I responded.

"I'll drive you down to your hotel" Joe added. I packed up my equipment and saying goodbye to the staff we walked out to his car. It was early evening and the drive into the city took only twenty minutes. Arriving at the hotel Joe looked at me and said "I'll wait here for you to check in then we can go out."

I was a bit taken aback and hesitated enough for Joe to say "Go on, hurry up. I'll wait for you." Having checked in showered and changed I rejoined him some twenty minutes later in the hotel bar where he had been joined by another man.

"Hey Mike, come and meet Rick" I put out my hand to the blond haired man smiling at me. "Hi Mike, I'm Rick van Digele, I own the flight kitchen at Reus along with Joe."

Joe broke in. "We have three flight kitchens. One at Barcelona, one in Reus and a third at Girona. There are three of us involved in the business but our friend at Girona can't be with us tonight. We each own seventy-five percent of our own kitchen, such as I do in mine here in Barcelona, and the other two own twenty five percent between them so we all have a share in all three kitchens. You understand?"

"Yes I think so" I replied. I soon got to understand the arrangement as I was to visit all three kitchens in the next few days.

Rick was very friendly and we soon started to chat about the business and friends we had in common in the industry. Eventually Joe said "Come on let's go." We walked out, climbed into his car and without further ado we drove off into the city, eventually arriving at another bar.

The evening passed quickly. My two companions were excellent company and the conversation flowed. Late in the evening, Spanish style, we moved to a restaurant to eat and it appeared that Joe and Rick were well known in the locality as a number of people stopped to speak as they passed our table.

After dinner I was expecting to go back to my hotel so was surprised when Joe said "Let's have a nightcap" and pulled in at another bar. Entering the dark interior I realised that we were going down market as the bar was staffed by topless girls. It wasn't what I was expecting and as it was now getting late I would have been happier to have been driven back to my hotel to get some sleep!

It was busy and I was surprised to see how many women were there along with male partners. Joe seemed to know a large number of the girls and clientele assembled around the bar and proceeded to spend the next half hour in animated conversation with a group of them, much of which went over my head due to my lack of Spanish. I wasn't sure what time it was when Joe eventually decided that it was time that he took me back to my hotel but I was grateful to climb into my bed and was fast asleep in seconds.

The following morning I woke bright and early and having audited the hotel as part of my station audit requirement, made my way back to the airport and Joe's kitchen in the early afternoon. True to his word it had been transformed overnight and the wash up area was now clean and sparkling, minus the motorcycle and dog. Years later I was to learn that on the day I arrived, Joe had actually been living in the kitchen having had a domestic upset. Subsequent visits over a number of years were to prove equally memorable for different reasons.

On one occasion, having finished the kitchen audit, Joe once again drove me down to my hotel and said "I'll wait for you in the bar" then when I joined him said "we're going out for drinks and canapes."

I followed him down the street as we walked into the centre of the city and was surprised when we turned into a car showroom. It was full of people and the champagne was flowing amongst a buzz of conversation. Looking around I rapidly realised that we were in the main Ford Motor Car dealership in Barcelona where they were launching the latest Ford Scorpio car.

We mingled with the other guests and once again Joe seemed to know a great number of people judging by those who came over to have a chat with him. As the evening progressed we were joined by two women, one of whom, judging by her accented English was French. After some chat Joe said to me "We're going out to dinner with the two ladies. The French lady is a Contessa and her husband died eighteen months ago" he whispered conspiratorially in my ear.

It was a pleasant meal. Both women spoke good English and were entertaining and as we finished the Countess invited us back to her apartment for coffee. A short walk took us to a very large and elegantly furnished apartment in a quiet residential area. As the Countess set about making the coffee I asked for directions to the guest bathroom and was directed to a room just off the entrance hallway.

Making my way in my eyes were drawn to a relatively small painting hanging on the wall. What drew my attention wasn't the painting itself so much as the signature on the bottom. Picasso.

I stood and looked at it and to me, although I'm no expert, it appeared to be a real painting and not a print. But was I right?

Having finished and washed my hands I made my way back into the lounge where the others were sitting. "I've placed your coffee over there" the Countess smiled to me and pointed to a chair beside which my cup was waiting.

Joe looked at me expectantly and I gave him a questioning look. He obviously knew what was in the bathroom and the question that was in my mind. He didn't say a word but nodded his head to indicate that I was right.

As we walked back towards my hotel later I asked him. "Joe, what's with the picture? Is it a genuine Picasso and why does she keep it in the toilet?

"It's very simple" Joe replied. "You remember I told you earlier that she was widowed about eighteen months ago? Well it was her late husband who bought the painting. However, she doesn't like it, but because it was her husband's, she doesn't want to get rid of it so she has put it in the one room which she rarely, if ever visits, the guest toilet, so she doesn't have to look at it." It's a strange world I thought.

Another visit to Barcelona some years later produced another strange dinner engagement. Following the usual routine Joe drove me to the hotel after the kitchen audit and waited whilst I checked in.

This time after a drink at the hotel we made our way into the city finishing up in a bar which I recognised from a previous visit. The topless bar.

It was busy and lively and as always Joe was talking with a number of people, one of which he introduced to me as the manageress. A heavily built woman with an expansive bosom she spoke English with a strong accent. After some time, Joe suddenly turned to me and without explanation said "Choose a girl" and pointed at the staff behind the bar.

I wasn't quite sure what he was insinuating and obviously looked a bit perplexed so he continued "We're going out for dinner and I'm bringing the manageress with us so to make up a four you choose one of the girls."

I looked at the group serving behind the bar and chose a slim girl who looked as if she could do with a good meal. "That one" I said pointing at her.

The manageress spoke quickly in Spanish. The girl I had chosen stopped what she was doing and looked a bit startled. The manageress spoke again. This time the girl quickly left her position, ran round the back and a few moments later appeared beside us having grabbed her clothes and dressed on the way. She was introduced to Joe and me and I was surprised to find that she could speak a bit of English.

Off we went to dinner which turned out to be very pleasant, with some interesting conversation in which both women were able to join. The evening was one of many which made me realise just how poor we British generally are at speaking other languages particularly in comparison with our European neighbours, many of whom are at worst bi-lingual and at best multi-lingual where we British struggle to speak our own language properly.

It was a somewhat bizarre experience made even more so when at the end of the meal we walked back to the bar. As we entered the manageress quickly said to my dinner companion "Get your clothes off and get back to work."

Without a backward glance my erstwhile smartly dressed companion took her dress off and walked back to her work station behind the bar wearing little more than a broad smile. A strange world indeed.

CHAPTER 41

NEW YORK, NEW YORK

Whilst kitchens in Europe could provide surprises, nothing had prepared me for my first visit to the USA. Like most people in the UK in the mid nineteen seventies, never previously having been to America, I had an expectation, probably built on images from cinema and television, that all things in the USA were bigger, better and more modern than those in Europe. Boy was I in for a surprise!

My first trip across the pond was to New York and I landed at John F Kennedy airport with a mixture of excitement and trepidation.

New York was the jewel in the crown and the premier destination on the BA network, being a heavily utilised business route and a major money earner. It was therefore important that our passengers were well catered for when flying into and out of the city. The route was so important that BA had its own terminal at the airport, thus marking itself out from the many other International airlines who had to share a terminal with numerous other carriers.

On arrival I duly presented myself to the BA airport manager whose office in the Terminal was a hive of activity. He seemed less than impressed by my arrival but to be fair he was probably plagued with visitors from "Head Office" in London, all of whom had a legitimate reason for being there but who nonetheless took up a lot of his time.

"What was it you said you were here to do?" he looked at me suspiciously. I explained who I was and what I was in New York to do. "I sent you a telex message" I added. "Oh yes, I remember something about it. Jane" He called loudly and a young woman appeared from the next office. "This is Mike Kelly from Medical Services in London. He's come to see the catering facilities and the honey wagons." The latter a reference to the toilet servicing trucks and a term which was used worldwide. "Hi

Mike, welcome to New York. Is this your first visit?" She held her hand out in greeting.

"Yes" I replied, shaking her hand. "Well I hope you get time to enjoy it. I've organised all your visits for you. Here's a list of times and people that are going to look after you." She passed it to me. "You start here tomorrow morning at 9.00am. If you come to the First Class desk in the Concourse someone from the flight kitchen will come across to pick you up. Meanwhile if you take a taxi down town you're booked into the crew hotel and they are expecting you to contact them this evening on arrival."

"Thanks, that's really great and I appreciate the trouble you've gone to set it all up." I really did appreciate it since I had found out already in other places that there was nothing worse than turning up in a strange airport and having to make contact myself with all the people I needed to meet. "You're welcome" came the familiar American reply and she looked as though she really meant it.

Driving into Manhattan from the airport in the heavy evening traffic I was spellbound by the views, the streets so familiar from television and movies yet so different from those at home. The traffic and bustle as we got further into the city was almost overpowering. Yellow cabs racing breakneck down the major one-way street system weaving in and out through the traffic. The steam rising from manhole covers at street corners. The thousands of people thronging the pavements and most of all the enormous skyscrapers, first viewed as the cab raced down the slope towards the tunnel which would take us under the river and on to Manhattan Island. I was transfixed.

The cab pulled up outside the Lexington Hotel and I checked in. "Mr Kelly welcome to the Lexington. The Manager is expecting you and will meet you here at 6.00pm."

The receptionist handed me my room key and I made my way up several floors in the lift, or should I say the elevator as it's known in America. Opening the door, I found myself in a small and very dated looking room. I was disappointed. I had expected a modern state of the art hotel but here I was looking at an early 1950s room at best and probably something much earlier if truth be told. Wooden sliding sash windows which were glued shut by the application of several layers of paint looked out at offices and another elderly looking brick built hotel to the rear.

The air conditioning unit attached to the window clanked ominously as it struggled to reduce the hot clammy New York temperature. A look around showed that the room was generally clean but definitely showing its age. Even the TV was ancient. "Welcome to New York" I thought to myself.

The following morning, I presented myself at the BA First Class desk as requested and was duly met by a driver who had come from the flight kitchen to pick me up. The drive to the unit took about ten minutes. It was out of the terminal area but still on the edge of the airfield with aircraft flying close to the building as they took off or landed.

Walking into the premises I was struck by the same feeling that I had when I had entered my hotel room the previous evening. "This place is old."

Although I hadn't been in my job for very long I was already used to seeing relatively modern bright and well equipped kitchens in Europe. This was none of those. It was large in the fact that it was in a large building but it appeared old, with very well used and tired looking equipment.

It was both busy and chaotic at the same time with little apparent separation between the various operating areas and with a lighting system which gave an overall picture of grey. I was to learn quickly that this kitchen was a model for hundreds of others throughout America.

The airline business in the USA was in the process of being deregulated, something which was to happen in the UK and Europe some twenty years later with the same effect. New low cost operators were beginning to challenge the older long serving airlines and as a result a price war was in operation and costs were being cut.

Profit margins were pared to the bone and the profits in the flight catering industry were minimal. There was therefore no cash available to build new state of the art kitchens or even to refurbish many of the old premises. As a result, many of the kitchens were fighting for survival. Most of them, like those in other parts of the world had been built to cater for smaller aircraft and smaller numbers of passengers. They were now struggling to cope with the modern world.

I walked around the kitchen with the manager and his team. They were well aware of the shortcomings of the building and were doing the best they could, but if I was to do my job properly I realised that this was going to be an uphill struggle and my report on the hygiene standards wasn't going to make me popular.

Even some of the basics were missing. The management team thought it was all right to walk into the kitchen without wearing any protective clothing. That is with the exception of the obligatory baseball cap!! What chance did I have therefore to persuade the rest of the team that food hygiene was important!

Over time changes were made and food safety standards gradually improved but in the following months and even years, I was to see similar kitchens, in fact identical kitchens as many owned by the same operators were built to the same plan, across the USA.

A couple of years later I was to face a major change in New York. Concorde, the world's first supersonic passenger aircraft had entered service and the British Airways Concorde service from London to New York had become the flagship operation of the airline. As such the hierarchy in London decided that a new flight kitchen was needed specifically to cater for the aircraft.

A decision was made to join forces with Forte Flight Catering later to be renamed as Alpha Flight Catering, the major UK provider of airline food and a division of the Forte hotel and catering organisation at that time.

Forte had worked with British Airways for many years in the UK and Europe so it came as no surprise when I was given the news. "They're going to start operations with only the two daily Concorde services" I was told by the Route Catering manager. "All other flights will stay with the existing caterers. How soon can you get out there and have a look at the new kitchen?"

"Probably next week if I can get the details sorted out today" I replied quickly. "That's great. I'll come with you if that's OK with you? I've not seen the place myself as yet."

And so the following week we arrived at JFK airport to be met by the manager of the new Forte flight catering unit.

"Hi Mike." Andy stuck his hand out. "Good to see you again" Andy was from London and we had met at Forte units in the UK on a number of occasions.

We jumped into the waiting car and were driven immediately to the kitchen. "I thought you would like to see it as soon as you got here, just to get an idea as to what we will be working with." Andy said.

The new kitchen was off the airport about a ten minute drive away, heading into Long Island rather than towards Manhattan. We turned off the freeway into an area of what the best American detective story writers would have called "mean streets". It was certainly a pretty run down area of town.

The car pulled up outside what was obviously a warehouse of some sort. "Well this is it." Andy looked at me for some sort of response. I said nothing, preferring to wait until I had a chance to see the interior. "It's not a great area. We're in Jamaica which is a bit of a rundown area of mixed business, warehousing and low cost housing" Andy continued, leading the way into the building. It was a large solidly built concrete floored warehouse with an open metal framed roof.

"There's a lot to be done" Andy walked slowly across the floor. "This is going to be the hot kitchen area. Raw preparation will be over there and the cold kitchen will be there."

He pointed at the relevant areas but it was a lot to take in given that the floor was covered in builder's materials and equipment not to mention the numerous workers hammering, drilling and installing fixtures and fittings. By the time we had finished our walk around and looked at the plans I could envisage what the place might look like. It wouldn't be a state of the art facility but it would suffice and over the following years I was to get to know the building very well. Starting as a kitchen to supply only the Concorde services in due course over a number of years it expanded to cater for all the BA flights from Kennedy airport.

The expansion process was fraught with difficulties. The original building was a warehouse, part of a collection of buildings which formed a square block.

Forte's first expansion was to take a lease on the property next door. Unfortunately, the floor level next door was eight feet lower than their existing property. This meant that a very long ramp had to be constructed to allow the aircraft trolleys and equipment to be wheeled from one area into the other.

To add to this the building was open metal framed and had to be fire protected. This had been done by spraying the metal beams with a cement type fire retardant which, whilst satisfying the needs of the fire authority, didn't come anywhere near to providing a smooth readily cleansable surface. However, I reconciled my food safety thoughts with the fact that since we were looking at high level steel beams, there was little likelihood of the food coming into contact with them and being contaminated.

Over the next couple of years expansion along the block and round the corner continued but more problems were to emerge. Arriving one morning on one of my regular site audits Andy greeted me by saying "We've taken a lease on the next warehouse round the back. It's given us more space but we've got a problem." "How come?" I asked.

"It backs on to a ready mix concrete site. You know, one of those places that makes concrete and delivers it to building sites in a special truck?" "So what's the problem?"

"The wall separating the building from the concrete site. Come and look." I was intrigued as to what I was going to see as we weaved our way through the building into the newly acquired premises which were as yet unused.

One look at the rear wall was enough. It appeared to be little more than a sheet of half inch thick plasterboard which certainly wasn't strong enough to withstand the pressure of the tons of aggregate stones used in cement manufacture on the site behind, with the result that a large proportion of them was spilling in a tidy heap into the new kitchen extension. "Well at least you've got the aggregate on site ready for your new concrete floor" I laughed at Andy.

"It's all right for you to laugh but I was hoping to have this place up and running before the end of next month." "Why don't you offer to buy them out" I questioned. "We've tried but they aren't willing to move. They're playing hard ball just to get us to increase the offer as they know that we desperately want the entire site. As it stands at the moment we have all of it apart from their concrete manufacturing yard which we've now surrounded on three sides."

"Mind you it's not our only problem" Andy continued. "We had an armed raid into the building last Tuesday." "What?" I exclaimed in horror. We were making our way back to Andy's office past the receiving dock where deliveries took place. "Yes" he said. "Just here. They came in through the delivery bay when the doors were open to take a food delivery. I don't know what they were after but our guys raised such a racket and the alarms were triggered which frightened them and they made a fast get away."

Walking into Andy's office I looked at a small round hole in the window behind his desk. It hadn't been there on my last visit. "Is that what I think it is?" Andy grinned. "I think so. We aren't sure where the bullet came from or when or why it was fired at our building but luckily I wasn't here at the time. The police think that it was probably an accident and wasn't aimed at us."

"It comes with the territory" Andy continued. "It's a pretty rough area." Looking out of his window he said "Come and have a look at this." He motioned me over. "See the girl standing on the street corner?" I looked out and saw a young woman dressed in jeans and heavy jacket standing nonchalantly at the crossroads junction about one hundred yards away. "I don't know what she's selling although I could hazard a guess, but she'll be working on our late shift this evening. Surprisingly enough she's one of my better girls so as long as she works well and doesn't cause any problems I don't have to worry about it."

I could see Andy's point. Getting good staff in that area must be difficult I thought. This was a long way from the relative peace and quiet of our catering unit at London.

Despite all the problems and the fact that the building had never been designed to be a kitchen it generally worked well and although I had many a good natured battle with the management team over the maintenance of food safety they always tried to maintain the highest possible standards and this was to continue through their change of name to Alpha and then the eventual sale of the business to Flying Foods Group with whom I was to continue the relationship.

Apart from the work, my visits often provided some unexpected entertainment. One night, having finished work, Andy invited me to go to dinner with him and some of his management team. We hopped into a couple of cars and drove to Queens, one of the five New York City Boroughs.

Pulling up outside an Italian restaurant we were soon seated round a table in what was a very local family run business. We were just in the middle of our starter when the door behind us burst open and two large men dressed in heavy overcoats and wearing soft hats stood either side of the door looking around the restaurant.

After a few seconds giving all of us the once over they were satisfied with what they had seen and giving a sign through the doorway they stood aside to let three elderly gentleman walk in. The owner and his family

233

greeted the new arrivals deferentially but also as old friends and they were ushered to a table and were soon chatting.

The whole performance had only taken two minutes and all that had been missing was the violin cases I thought. I looked at Andy. "Don't ask" he said "and yes it's what you think it is."

"I had a little problem in my first few weeks here" he continued. "I wasn't happy with the garbage collection from the kitchen so I put it out to tender and appointed a new company. A week later, when the contract had supposedly changed I looked out the window when I heard the garbage trucks arrive and was amazed to see the original contractors turn up. I raced down to the garbage area and was about to remonstrate with them when one of my team stopped me. "Don't get involved" he said. "It won't change anything. That company has the contract for all the garbage handling around here and no matter who you choose, these guys will still pick it up."

"It was an early lesson as to how things are done around here and despite what I might think or want I don't get paid enough to be found in an alleyway some night after having had an accident."

There was general laughter around the table and as we carried on with the excellent meal I pondered over the differences between New York and London.

New York city in my early years of visiting was a hotbed of sleaze. Like most tourists on a first visit, I was looking forward to seeing the sights for which the city was famous. Everything from the Empire State building through Times Square and Broadway with the Rockefeller Centre, Bloomingdales, Macy's and Wall Street thrown in for good measure.

Whilst most of the buildings lived up to their publicity and I was mesmerised by the vast array of skyscrapers allied with the noise and bustle in the streets, no-one had warned me as to how low life had sunk in the city centre.

On my first visit, after work, walking through Broadway to Times Square and 42nd Street I was appalled to find that the streets were lined with sex shops and live sex shows.

Not just one or two discreetly offering their wares amongst the theatres, but a constant barrage of shops and shows, each with staff outside the doors brazenly trying to entice customers inside, calling out their wares in loud raucous voices in language which would have had them arrested in London for a breach of the peace and common decency. Added to this were numerous girls plying their trade and soliciting any man walking down the street.

Amongst all of this was a constant stream of tourists and visitors, some trying to find their way to theatres, some looking for restaurants and many like me just there to look at the sights and the famous lights. The greater majority were more than a bit overwhelmed by all that was going on and were desperately trying to ignore the indecency all around them.

Whilst I was able to cope with it, I felt bad for those visitors who had brought children with them to show them the bright lights of this world famous city but were having to come to terms with the depths of depravity into which it had sunk.

Fortunately, in later years a new Mayor was to take over the running of the city and one of his first jobs was to clean up the city centre and drive the sleaze out of town.

New York was also to throw me a few surprises in the food safety arena. Given the large number of daily flights which BA was operating into New York and therefore the number of hotel rooms required each night to accommodate the crew, the airline decided to buy a hotel in down town Manhattan.

A suitable property was acquired and the Fitzpatrick Hotel group was appointed to run it. It was relatively small with only four rooms on each floor and rising some forty floors it was something of a shoebox standing on its end and slotted between the skyscrapers around it.

The rooms were of reasonable size and well-furnished but although there was a breakfast facility there wasn't a restaurant. This was partly down to the small size and lack of space but also because the hotel was surrounded by restaurants and it was thought highly unlikely that crew could be persuaded to eat in the hotel and a restaurant would therefore lose money. However, after a days' work not all crew would wish to go outside, particularly in the winter when the weather could be very cold.

To cope with this eventuality, it was decided that a number of local restaurants would be approached and asked if they would be willing to provide a delivery service. Menus would be placed in the crew bedrooms and meals would be ordered via the hotel reception desk who in turn would receive the meals on delivery and advise the crew member to come down to reception to pick them up.

All very well and good but my worry was that as these restaurants had not been checked for their food hygiene standards and by inference, since British Airways was recommending them to the crew, should there be an outbreak of food poisoning, the airline might have a serious responsibility problem.

It was decided with my boss that I should go to New York, meet with the manager of Fitzpatrick Hotels and carry out an inspection of the restaurants concerned.

On the appointed day I met Sean, the Fitzpatrick manager of the BA contract. A fellow Irishman he was happy to meet me and explained that all the restaurants had been advised that I was coming and that I was to be escorted through the day by Noreen, one of his duty managers at the hotel.

He handed me a menu. "This is what the crew have in their rooms." It was a compilation of foods from four different premises, one delicatessen, a Chinese restaurant, an Indian restaurant and a Pizza house. Pretty standard fare for crew I thought.

"If you're ready we'll make a start" said Noreen and suiting her actions to her words she strode off towards the door with me rushing to catch up with her. "We don't have far to go. It's only over there" Noreen pointed across the four-way road junction.

We crossed at the lights and made our way into what was a typical New York deli. Opening off the street it had a central service island with a cold buffet counter back to back with a hot food unit. It looked clean and smart and was well populated with locals.

I was introduced to the manager who although he had been warned that I was coming was looking at me very suspiciously. I took my electronic thermometer out of my bag and quickly scanned the temperatures of both the cold and hot foods on opposite sides of the stainless steel display unit.

There wasn't much difference between them. The foods were tepid and therefore there was an immediate worry about food safety.

"Where is the food made" I asked. The manager pointed toward a staircase in the middle of the floor. "Down there". "May I have a look?" "Sure help yourself."

I walked to the staircase and descended into the depths. The stairs were steep and half way down I caught a brief glimpse of what appeared to be a toilet set into the wall. At the bottom I was confronted with a basement room which was obviously under the street above.

It was small given the size of the restaurant and was cramped for space. Staff working in it were almost falling over each other. Food safety standards were basic. Protective clothing was minimal and food was scattered indiscriminately across a variety of working surfaces. The ceiling was low and a large metal sewer pipe was suspended beneath it, running across the room. Sitting on top of the pipe was a large rat trap.

"This is the chiller" the manager opened a heavy door to my left and I stepped inside. It was an old style cold room, small with a separate freezer unit built in at the end. I walked across and opened the freezer. Inside was a jumble of food items mixed together with some of them frozen to each other showing that at some time they had been defrosted and then had refrozen.

As I stood inside I realised that it didn't feel particularly cold and a quick check of the temperature showed me that the freezer was having problems staying below freezing point. The refrigerator or chiller as the manager had called it was also a mixture of foods piled together in no particular order, raw vegetables and raw meats mixed with cooked meats with a very obvious risk of cross contamination.

"This is the only one you have?" I already knew the answer but thought I should confirm it any way. "Yup" came the reply. "It's not very cold" I looked at my thermometer. "It gets pretty hot here in the city in the summer" came the answer.

I looked around the room. All the food preparation was done here. There appeared to be only one sink. It was in the corner and was very obviously used for everything. Dish washing, food washing, hand washing all at the same time by the look of the piles of food, and dishes sitting around.

Looking above my head I spotted the only sign of a food safety policy in the premises. A piece of cardboard was hung from the ceiling on two bits of string.

On it was written "No spitting in the food preparation area"!!

Noreen and I walked out having thanked the manager for his time. "Phew" she said. "That wasn't too great was it?"

A bit of an understatement I thought. "Hope they get a bit better."

We strolled across the street and into a Pizza restaurant. Basically a take away it had a carpeted floor running at a slight slope towards the service counter. My heart sank as I felt my shoes sticking to the carpet as we walked towards the front. Noreen asked for the manager and a young woman appeared.

"Hi" She was obviously a working, serving manager, dressed as she was in the company uniform with a somewhat dirty looking apron on her front. Her lank, greasy looking hair hung down her back in an uncontrolled swathe with no protective hair covering.

"What do you guys want to see?" "A quick look at your back of house preparation area and storage facilities if that's OK?" I answered. "Yea, come on round the back." She pointed towards the end of the service counter and Noreen and I made our way in.

It was untidy and scruffy with little attention having been paid to cleaning detail, however the cold rooms worked well and as most of the products were bought in ready-made and came in jars or packets the risks were fairly low.

"How much training in food hygiene do your staff have?" "We've all been trained" she said with a smile whilst pushing her greasy hair back from her face with her hand. I wondered just how often she did that through the day and when and where she would wash her hands.

The saving grace was that a pizza is generally made to order and is baked in a very hot oven so there was little chance of any bacteria surviving. There was however the possibility of a stray hair or two being dropped onto the pizza after cooking and prior to delivery to the customer. It may not cause food poisoning but it could prove to be an unpleasant find in your mouth, I thought.

Leaving the Pizza take away restaurant we walked along the block to the next major road junction. "I take it you weren't too impressed there either?" Noreen looked at me. "I didn't think it was too great. And that hair." She shuddered at the thought.

Next stop was an Indian restaurant. I was welcomed with some enthusiasm by the manager and after some pleasantries and having declined some tea we entered the kitchen. At least this place looks like a proper kitchen was my first thought. A bevy of chefs all dressed in "whites", the standard chef's uniform the world over, were hard at work. There were so many they were standing shoulder to shoulder with barely room to move.

They all smiled happily at me in almost perfect unison. "Hello Sir." The head chef was introduced to me and was at great pains to show me around.

The kitchen was well equipped and for a second or two I thought that it might not be too bad. However, a brief look showed that once again there was a distinct lack of proper cleaning with visible debris present on the floor and equipment. There were no sanitisers available for disinfecting working surfaces and there was evidence of serious cross contamination between raw and cooked food items. To add to all this there were numerous cockroaches running around. As we left I looked at Noreen. "It's not getting any better is it?" she said. I shook my head almost in despair.

Our last visit was to a Chinese restaurant. Entering the building I was struck by the up market look of the interior with its gleaming table settings. Welcomed by a very pleasant manager we progressed to the kitchens, once again in the basement. They turned out to be very well equipped and in excellent working condition. The cold rooms and freezers were large, with excellent separation between cooked and raw foods. There were wash basins, sinks and sanitisers in abundance and the staff seemed to be clean and well trained.

Noreen smiled at me. "It's good isn't it?" She was positively relieved that we appeared to have found something good. "Yes but there's one major problem." Noreen looked at me quizzically "What's that?"

"Well do you see all those little black things lying along the back edge of all the preparation tables and along the edges of the floor about a quarter of an inch deep in places?" "Yes" she replied looking at me for some guidance. "Well those aren't caraway seeds. They're mouse droppings. This place is absolutely alive with mice. They all over everything." "Ugh" Noreen said with a visible shudder "You're joking aren't you?" "I wish I was, Noreen"

I wasn't surprised. In fact, I was more surprised that I hadn't seen much evidence of rodent infestation in any of the other premises. Rodents are a major problem in cities across the world and as most of the kitchens we had looked at were underground there was a high risk of rodent infestation. Our problem was still to find somewhere safe for the crew to eat and it was to take some time.

CHAPTER 42

ASIA AND THE INDIAN SUB-CONTINENT

New York wasn't the only place to cause problems with the crew hotels. Many other places around the world had similar pest infestations and food safety problems or worse.

When British Airways decided to begin flying to Brunei in the 1980s I was sent out to audit the flight kitchen and possible crew hotel accommodation. Brunei Darussalam to give the country its proper name is a Sultanate situated on a large island shared with Borneo and Malaysia. A small but wealthy country it has a long heritage and culture and I was fascinated to see that both ancient and modern cultures existed side by side in the capital city, Bandar Seri Begawan, where many of the city population lived in wooden houses built on stilts in villages which stretched a long way out into the sea estuary.

There they continued their centuries old way of life side by side with an extravagant new city built on the mainland where the Sultan's Palace and the Sultan Omar Mosque with it's lavishly decorated concrete ceremonial barge on the lake outside, along with the modern office buildings and plethora of traffic in the streets bore witness to a new order and lifestyle far removed from that of the villages on stilts.

The city and its people were warm and friendly and I enjoyed my short stay however I was to have problems in finding a suitable crew hotel. Hotels in Brunei were in short supply. The few large International hotels were not particularly interested in accommodating airline crew so I was left with limited choice.

The two hotels that I was offered were small considering that we had to accommodate a full Boeing 747 crew which was in the region of nineteen people. Both looked small but pleasant from the outside however their looks gave no indication as to what I would find inside. In the first hotel, having been shown into a bathroom, I turned on the cold water tap to be faced with a river of extremely brown, dirty looking water which certainly wasn't of drinking quality. The second hotel proved to have equal problems when on entering a bedroom I found myself facing a wall down which water was oozing. It seemed that the wall backed on to an outside slope and was not very watertight.

Needless to say neither passed muster and we had to beg one of the larger hotels to reconsider their views on having our crew stay with them.

Other parts of the world also brought their own particular problems. My first visit to the Indian sub-continent in the late nineteen seventies was an eye opener.

Whilst I was used to Africa through my previous work there, nothing had prepared me for India so arriving in New Delhi for the first time came as something of a shock.

I wasn't expecting the vast numbers of people. African towns had been busy with bustling crowds but this was something entirely different in scale. Thousands of people were on the streets both by day and night.

The colours were vibrant in the hot dusty atmosphere and the smells were unbelievable. Spices, fruit, vegetables, animals, dirt, rotting garbage and people produced a combination which has to be experienced to be understood. The noise was incessant. The traffic in the streets was unbelievable and unfathomable in its complexity. Cars, buses, taxis, ox carts, bicycles, people manhandling large unwieldy carts of goods piled high and precariously and pedestrians swarmed across the road, taking up all available space and making progress by dint of what appeared to me to be a game of chance.

The vehicles fought for every available space as it appeared and it was nothing on the larger roads to be met by a line of traffic, six or more vehicles wide spread across the width of the road and driving straight at the taxi in which I was riding. All this accompanied by the incessant sounding of horns. I soon got used to these driving standards which prevailed throughout the sub-continent and often marvelled at the skills of my many taxi drivers.

Cars came in one of only two varieties. The first was a Morris Oxford of nineteen fifties vintage, now manufactured in India and the second was a smaller Fiat of similar age. Neither of these had any form of air conditioning. The heat was unbearable but opening the windows wasn't a good option. Firstly, it allowed the dirt and noise to get into the car and equally important it meant that on each occasion that the car was forced to stop, I would be besieged by beggars whose hands would rapidly appear through the window.

India has an enormous population and the standard of living within the country varies from the sublime to the intolerable. Begging was a way of life for a large number of the population and I quickly learned that no matter what my personal feeling might be towards those who were so badly disadvantaged there was little that I could do to help them. In fact, giving money to one person would result in dozens more appearing as if from nowhere and clamouring and fighting at the taxi window or worse still besieging me in the street if I was foolish enough to walk alone outside my hotel.

It was particularly bad in Calcutta, or Kolcatta as it is more properly known today. The crew hotel was in the city centre and I was appalled on my first visit to see disabled beggars being placed in the street early in the morning by people whom I can only assume were their relatives. There they were left through the heat of the entire day, unable to move, their begging bowls placed beside them. The most appalling of these was a poor unfortunate who could only be described as a torso. No arms or legs, incapable of movement or speech and dumped on the footpath every morning. For someone from a much more privileged life it was hard to comprehend.

The other extreme was to be seen in New Delhi where the crew hotel backed on to a beautifully tended golf course, or in Bombay, Mumbai as it's now known, where the crew hotel was on Narriman Point on the seafront of the city where in the cool of the evening the members of the Middle and Upper Classes strolled elegantly in groups along the very British style promenade enjoying the cooler air beside the sea.

This continent never seemed to sleep or at least if it did, only a small percentage was asleep at any one time. No one had warned me about the noise either. Millions of people working, travelling and living on the streets created a noise level beyond belief at times. People everywhere in all shapes and sizes and in all manner of dress. Some obviously wealthy with the women in expensive looking wonderfully coloured saris whilst at the other end of the spectrum were the dirty half naked children running along and playing in the dirt at the side of the road.

Workshops were spread in buildings along the roadside. All manner of things were being fabricated using methods and equipment which to my untrained eye appeared in some instances to belong in the age of Charles Dickens. Car repairs, metal forging, printing, clothes manufacturing, the ability and desire of people to make their way in the world was there in abundance.

The hotels which BA used in India were of the highest standard and arriving in New Delhi on my first trip I was welcomed by the hotel manager. British Airways was a very important customer to them. In those early days the flight catering was also provided by the hotel company and the flight kitchen was actually part of the hotel, at the rear of the main building.

The following morning when I began my audit I was met by the BA Catering Officer for Delhi. His was an important job as he had to oversee each aircraft uplift to ensure that all necessary standards were being met and he was to prove a mine of experience and assistance to me as I learned how things were done in India.

The kitchen proved to be a bit like the curate's egg. It was good in parts. It was far from ideal but given the location I thought that it was better than I could have anticipated. The main areas of concern were the lack of food safety knowledge and the poor standard of equipment that was available. This I learned very quickly was as a direct result of the monetary controls in place in India at the time. To keep their currency in good shape the Indian Government had banned the purchase of any item manufactured outside India. Where possible everything had to be made in India. Thus all items of kitchen equipment from spoons to ovens and dish washing machines had to be sourced locally. This often meant that equipment was built from pictures seen in magazines and using elements of guesswork to try to understand how it should work.

Added to this were a number of things which we in the UK would have taken for granted. These included dish washing liquids, bactericidal hand wash soaps, detergents and paper towels. None of these were available locally. However, necessity is the mother of invention and following my first visit and subsequent report, the flight catering company employed an industrial chemist to begin making their own cleaning products in house.

I could not be anything other than impressed at their efforts to improve and over the following twenty years I witnessed massive changes in food safety to the point where the Indian kitchens became some of the best in the world.

Meanwhile back to the beginning. How were we to deal with the problems in front of us? Training had to be the answer and we had to start at the top. The managers of the business had to be convinced that there was a need for change, that the attitudes and standards which had applied over many years were now deemed to be unacceptable.

One problem that I faced was that of overcoming the natural reaction of managers and their workforce who seemingly agreed to what they were being asked to do, with much head nodding, smiling and murmuring of "yes sir, yes sir." It took me a while to understand that all this apparent agreement meant nothing and through my first few years of working there were to be many disappointments and often a feeling of banging my head against the wall and seeing little improvement. Changes did occur gradually and once the momentum started it was to increase rapidly year on year.

This was a long way ahead however and in my early days I was to witness some dreadful sights. The kitchens were often poorly constructed, badly lighted and with poor refrigeration. Food handling standards were often abysmal, with little or no separation between the handling of raw and cooked foods and a great risk of cross contamination.

Staff training was virtually non-existent and there was no understanding of the concept of food hygiene. Given that many of the people employed in the kitchens lived in sub-standard housing surrounding the airports, this was not surprising. They were forced to live in overcrowded housing with no running water and no proper toilet facilities. These conditions of course were not confined to the Indian sub-continent but were prevalent across the world in many of the countries into which International airlines were operating, and not only in the so called third world.

The surprise in my mind was that despite all of the problems there were relatively few recorded instances of food poisoning which had been directly related to the food served on aircraft. Standing in my first kitchen in India I didn't realise that I was looking at one of the better examples and wasn't prepared for those I was to come across later.

Often the kitchens were constructed from Kota stone which was the local equivalent of marble. It was a smooth easily cleansable surface but had a problem in that it came in large rectangular blocks which when reaching floor level provided a right angled joint which was difficult to keep clean. Labour was cheap in that part of the world so most kitchens employed a large number of cleaners whose normal method of cleaning was simply to wipe the floor with a very dirty looking cloth attached to the bottom of a long handle like a mop, with the person wielding it usually dressed in a uniform of khaki coloured shorts and shirt and often barefoot. No detergent or liquid soap was available so the level of "cleaning" was very debatable.

The floor generally had a large open drain running along it so that copious amounts of water could be swilled along it into the drain. This conveyed all the debris from the floor into the drainage system which from time to time would block, backfill and overflow back into the kitchen.

On one occasion I walked into a kitchen to be faced with two kitchen porters sitting squat legged on the floor with a set of pots between them. To my horror they had removed the metal grille from the drain and were rinsing out the pots in it. The unit manager wasn't best pleased when I pointed out that this raised a risk of contamination. "But we've always done it like this" he protested "and we've never had any problems." "There's always a first time" I replied.

This wasn't the only problem that I was to come across. Working my way through one kitchen I opened a door and looking into a small room saw an elderly woman sitting on a stool. Beside her was a collection of small butter dishes which had come off passenger meal trays from an inbound aircraft. The woman was happily removing the remains of butter in each dish by scraping it out with her finger nail and placing it on a growing pile on a plate beside her. The butter was obviously destined for re-use sometime later but for what purpose I could only guess. I was appalled and made my feelings felt very strongly.

Action had to be taken in all cases to ensure the safety of our food uplift and to this end we worked very closely with our colleagues in the flight catering team to design menus which would be safe but which would still be interesting for our passengers. Where conditions in any kitchen were found to be unacceptable we would for an alternative caterer but where none was available we would then have to look at all menu items and remove those items which would be considered "high risk" such as cold meats, shellfish, salads, creams, cold desserts etc. and substitute them with foods items which were fully cooked or with a low risk of being dangerous.

Competition between airlines has always been fierce and prior to the advent of the low cost carriers, one of the main areas in which competition flourished was that of customer service on board. To this end the airlines went to great lengths to produce and serve good quality food and in particular in First Class where our passengers were deemed to be the elite of travellers and were expecting high class service for the fares that they were paying. Taking off the cold meats and shellfish and replacing them with something like a tomato and asparagus salad with a vinaigrette dressing wasn't deemed to be haute cuisine and didn't make us popular with our menu design team and the food purists in particular, nor for that matter the customers, but as a food poisoning outbreak in 1984 was to prove, it was much more damaging and expensive to get it wrong.

Progress in improving the hygiene standards was slow but there was a great deal of job satisfaction in seeing the improvements that were being made albeit it was sometimes very frustrating. There were however some entertaining moments. One of my catering colleagues, John Shearman, whilst standing in one of the kitchens in India was amazed to see a large drain cover being raised in the middle of the floor and even more amazed to see a young and very slightly built man extricating himself from the drain. John was horrified since the man was covered in the excrement which came from the very large sewer running underneath. "What's going on?" he cried in horror. "Get him out of the kitchen." The manager looked somewhat bemused. "But he is unblocking the drain sir." came the explanation. "I don't care what he's doing" John yelled. "Just get him out of here and then clean and sanitise the entire area." Of course with labour charges being so cheap it was less expensive to put a man down the drain to clean it than to hire expensive equipment, even had it been available.

But there was progress. In some of the kitchens hand washing after using the toilet was deemed important enough to place a man permanently in the toilet accommodation to oversee the hand washing and stop people leaving the facilities without washing their hands. During a visit to one such kitchen my catering colleague Bob decided to see how effective the system was and having used the urinal walked towards the door to leave. The Indian gentleman standing by the door stepped forward and firmly said" Wash your hands" whilst pointing to the wash basins. A strong statement of intent on his part since, given the local culture at the time, many staff would not have been prepared to challenge a senior manager. Bob was suitably impressed and pleased.

Sri Lanka was a BA destination for aircraft flying both direct from London and also from Johannesburg in South Africa to the Far East via the Seychelles and Colombo. On the introduction of a Boeing 747 on to the route I flew to Colombo to ensure that the increase in aircraft size wouldn't have a deleterious effect on the food safety since upgrading from a VC10 to a jumbo was tripling the number of passengers on each flight.

Dave Moynihan, the Route Catering Officer who was tasked with ensuring the quality of the food on the flight was travelling with me. A former Chef, Dave had never been to Sri Lanka before but prior to the trip he had researched the catering facilities and I'd updated him on the food safety standards which were acceptable as long as the menu was chosen carefully.

Dave's problem was the size of the aircraft. Because of its height the 747 needed a catering truck capable of being raised to reach the doors. He had contacted the caterers and they had assured him that as another airline had recently introduced a wide bodied aircraft, they had purchased and were using a truck known as a high loader. Armed with this fact Dave was satisfied and we duly arrived at the flight kitchen. All seemed well until Dave went out to look at the high loader. It stood proudly behind the flight kitchen, gleaming in its new paint. Dave walked over to it. "How do you offload the dirty equipment?" The kitchen manager looked puzzled. "How do you offload it?" Dave said again, this time a little more anxiously. The new truck was a high loader but the floor of the truck was very obviously a couple of feet higher than the docking bay used by the existing smaller trucks to offload the dirty aircraft equipment.

"You don't have a loading dock which is as high as the floor level of the truck." This of course was long before the invention of the tail lift for trucks. "Oh that's not a problem sir," the manager beamed "we don't take the equipment off the truck, we wash it all on the lorry."

I thought that Dave was going to choke. "You what?" "We take all the equipment out of the trolleys and put containers of water on the truck and wash them by hand." The manager beamed again. Dave walked away, head in hands. "I don't believe it" he looked at me. Despite the obvious hygiene risks involved I had to stop myself laughing.

"Well they'll either have to offload the truck by hand using all available labour or they'll have to find a fork lift truck somewhere and off load each trolley individually" I ventured. "They've off loaded manually in Abu Dhabi" and I told him what I'd found there on my first visit. "OK. We'll have to work something out with them" Dave walked back towards the kitchen.

Later that day we watched the caterers as they handled the wide bodied charter aircraft from France. True to their story the truck came back from the aircraft loaded with all the trolleys of used trays, plates, crockery etc. and parked behind the kitchen. An army of men clambered on board and began the process of emptying all the passenger trays out of the trolleys, stripping off all the waste food, then washing all the plates and cutlery by hand in buckets of tepid water. Dave and I watched the process incredulously. "They certainly aren't going to be doing that with our flights" Dave muttered and I agreed.

We had to think it through with the unit management team. Eventually we convinced them that what they were doing wasn't hygienic as the equipment was being washed in lukewarm water rather than being sterilised by passing through a dish washing machine. They decided to solve the problem by building a long wooden ramp supported by uprights on the ground. Positioned at the rear of the truck, it allowed the trolleys to be walked off into the stripping and washing area. It was really amateurish in construction but it worked and would suffice until they could have their loading bay rebuilt to accommodate the new requirements.

This wasn't the only problem on that particular trip. As part of my remit I had to audit the crew hotel situated about twenty minute drive from the airport on the beach at Negombo. Dave asked if he could join me on the audit and I agreed. I already knew what the premises were like, having been there previously. It wasn't good but hotels in the area were scarce. I began my audit and all was going reasonably well until we got to the kitchens. They were very basic. Walking into the butchery there was a strong smell redolent of stale meat and blood. I could see Dave's nose wrinkle in disgust. As we moved forward I looked at the wooden chopping block centred in the room which appeared to have black cover on its top.

Dave took a step forward and the top suddenly lifted as a huge swarm of bluebottle flies took off from the surface on which they had been feeding on the drying blood and waste meat fragments. "Oh my God"

Dave spun backwards away from the scene and looked in horror at me. I shrugged my shoulders as if to say "what did you expect?" We completed the audit in relative silence but worse was to follow. As we finished, the hotel manager invited us to join him for lunch. "Do you like curry" he asked and Dave was quick to respond "Oh yes, that's a favourite of mine" this despite having seen conditions in the kitchen. "I was working on the principle that a well cooked curry would kill anything that might be in the food" he explained to me when I queried it later. "That's settled then" the manager said as he led us to a table in the dining room.

I said nothing but wondered quietly if Dave had ever had a Sri Lankan curry. The meal arrived and Dave was served a large portion of the curry. He took his fork and without ado plunged a generous fork full into his mouth. I watched with interest. It took about twenty seconds to register. This was probably the hottest curry that Dave had ever come across in his life. His face turned bright red, his eyes bulged and watered as he forced himself to swallow. I grinned as I helped myself. I like my curries very hot and having had one in the hotel on my previous visit knew what to expect.

To Dave's credit he made a reasonable job of coping with the meal but afterwards when he got me alone his comments were unrepeatable. "Why didn't you tell me you bastard?" "Well you were so keen to have a curry I thought that I shouldn't disappoint you." I said with a laugh. "You should have seen your face!!"

"And what about those flies" he added "Absolutely disgusting. I thought that it was some sort of cover on the block when I first saw it."

"So did I."

CHAPTER 43

SOLDIERS AND
STOMACH PAINS

This wasn't to be my last unusual experience in Sri Lanka. It was a troubled country at the time with freedom fighters waging war on the Government. Whilst the fighting was taking place in the North of the country there were occasional bombs planted in and around the capital city Colombo.

In this respect it was somewhat similar to my native Northern Ireland which was also experiencing what was euphemistically known as "the troubles" at the same time and with similar disastrous effects.

My next visit to check for an improvement in standards in both the flight kitchen and the crew hotel coincided with the introduction of a night time curfew in the country. "This might pose a bit of a problem" I thought to myself. The BA aircraft on which I was scheduled to depart passed through Colombo late at night. I discussed the situation with the local BA manager who tried to reassure me. "It won't be a problem. It will be very quiet coming from Negombo up to the airport and you're not likely to see anyone along the way or at least until you get close to the airport. I've never had any trouble." I wasn't convinced.

The time came to leave the hotel. I said farewell to the hotel manager who was waiting at the door with his team to see me off the premises and followed my suitcase as it was carried out to the taxi. An ancient Ford Cortina awaited me. As I climbed in to the back the diminutive driver looked over his shoulder. "The airport please" I said. "The airport?" came the question. The driver didn't look altogether happy with my choice of destination. He shook his head and said something out of the window.

A group of hotel staff gathered at the rear of the car and with a great deal of shouting they began to push it. The driver released the clutch, the car jerked severely and the engine coughed into life. We rattled off down the road. It was midnight and there wasn't much life to be seen along the Negombo road. I glimpsed an occasional cow watching us suspiciously as we trundled past. It was stifling. There was no air conditioning in the car, not that I had expected any since it wasn't common in any taxis at that time. I knew that opening the window to let some air in would also allow an influx of local insects including mosquitoes and I decided to open it only by a small crack and suffer the build-up of heat.

All was going well until we joined the main road leading from Colombo city to the airport. It was still very quiet with no other traffic. Obviously the curfew was being observed by the local population. I was watching intently through the windscreen and suddenly saw a red light. It was being waved by someone standing in the middle of the road. As we got closer I realised that the someone was a soldier. It was a road block and the man waving the red light was supported by some heavily armed companions.

My driver slammed his foot on the brakes. There was a nasty clanking and screeching sound and I realised with some horror that the brakes on the car were as functional as the starting motor had been when we set off. Looking forward I could see that we weren't going to stop before hitting the roadblock. My immediate thoughts were that if this happened in Northern Ireland a vehicle failing to stop at a roadblock would inevitably be hit by a couple of well-placed bullets. I feared the worst.

So did my driver. As the car slid relentlessly towards the soldiers he slid down in his seat to the point where he was barely visible to anyone in front of the car. At the last moment the soldier stepped away from the oncoming car and we gradually but noisily clanked to a halt a few feet past him.

A rifle barrel suddenly appeared through the driver's window. The soldier holding it was obviously not amused and had just set about the driver verbally when he spotted me in the rear seat. His demeanour very rapidly changed and he almost sprang to attention. "Sir, sorry Sir," he looked worried, as though he had committed a crime. "Sir, where are you going?" "To the airport" I replied, quickly pulling my ticket from an inside pocket. "Thank you Sir." He took it from me and glanced at it. I'm not sure that he would have been able to read English but he appeared satisfied as he handed it back.

"Thank you Sir. Go ahead please." He waved us on our way but not without a few chosen words in the local language to the driver, by which, although I didn't understand a word, he very obviously castigated him on his failure to stop when required. I breathed a sigh of relief and contemplated what might have happened.

Jet setting around the world at someone else's expense, staying in top class hotels and often being treated as a VIP would seem at first glance to be a wonderful way of life and on many occasions it was. Through most of my career with British Airways I enjoyed my job immensely, took pride in working for one of the worlds' top airlines, got a lot of job satisfaction and was very aware of the privilege which I had and the respect in which my job was held by others in my profession.

Many of my colleagues in the world of Environmental Health thought that I had the best job in the world and would have given their right arm to have had it. However as with all things there were down sides. I was travelling extensively, certainly in my early and more junior days, with the result that I missed a lot of the joy of watching my children growing up.

On the positive side the job allowed me to take my family on holidays to some of the more exotic parts of the world courtesy of the staff travel facilities available to all airline employees. This gave my children a greater understanding of the world and its cultures and differences.

Travelling regularly across the world was fraught with dangers, some more obvious than others. Despite my training in food safety and my care in choosing what to eat, particularly in the more obviously unhygienic areas, the risk of picking up a food borne illness was always present. Happily I remained relatively unscathed with only the occasional need to resort to medication to reduce the rumblings of discontent which broke out in my stomach from time to time. However on one visit to India it went disastrously wrong.

The BA crew hotel contract was out to tender and I was in New Delhi spending five days auditing a number of hotels as possibilities for the provision of crew accommodation. All of them were large four or five star properties and the week, whilst hard work in auditing two large hotels per day had gone well. Friday night arrived and I was congratulating myself on a good week's work when I began to feel some discomfort in my stomach. I had just finished a meal with my Indian BA colleague and knew from my professional training that whatever the problem was, it couldn't be the

252

result of what I had just eaten as the incubation period for any food borne illness would have been too short.

I cast my mind back over the last couple of days and nothing came immediately to mind. I hadn't been eating anywhere other than in the hotels which I had been auditing and whilst I had seen some shortcomings in one or two of them there had been nothing to suggest that I was shortly going to be in dire distress.

By this time, I was walking alone around the garden at the rear of the hotel in which I was staying, hoping beyond hope that the manifestly increasingly disturbing symptoms of severe stomach pain and distension were going to miraculously disappear, whilst knowing beyond doubt that this wasn't going to happen.

I made my way back to my bedroom and what followed I will leave to your imagination. Suffice to say, I wasn't able to leave the bathroom at any time in the next four hours and for part of that time I wished that I could die. Apart from being ill I was worried by the fact that I was due to return to London a few hours later on an early morning departure and a car and driver had been arranged to pick me up at the hotel at around five o'clock.

As the departure time approached I made the decision that however bad I felt I wasn't going to miss the flight. If I was going to die I would prefer to die at home. Not very rational thinking, I know but I wasn't really in a great state to think properly. I dragged myself into the bedroom, threw what few bits and pieces I had with me into my suitcase slowly made my way down to the reception desk and checked out.

"Good morning Mr Kelly" the receptionist greeted me with a bright smile. "Your car is outside." I smiled weakly and walked slowly out. Dawn was breaking and the driver held the car door open. "I'm not feeling very well so we may have to stop along the way." "Yes sir." He smiled at me as though this was the most normal thing that a departing guest would say.

We drove slowly into the main road and headed off to the airport. Delhi was waking to a new day but whilst there were numerous people around the traffic was quite light. Along the road I watched people going about their early morning tasks. It was slightly misty and smoke curled lazily into the air from numerous small fires burning in the fields that we were passing.

Suddenly I felt my stomach beginning to well up. "Stop please." The driver looked in his mirror and obviously saw the signs of discomfort on my face. He braked quickly and I leapt from the cab and ran to a wall which separated the road from the adjacent field. There I presented a very unedifying sight as I leant over the wall retching violently. There was nothing left in my stomach and hadn't been for some hours but my stomach was still in trauma. I walked back to the car. The driver said nothing and we drove on.

Arriving at the airport I met the BA Manager at the check in desk. I explained my plight to him and he was immediately very sympathetic. "I know exactly how you feel" he said. I'm not sure that he did but I gritted my teeth and said nothing. He meant well. "I'll check you in and then take you round to the Doctor in Port Health here in the airport."

Minutes later I was explaining the situation to a young Doctor. Without a word he reached into his cupboard, took out a large syringe and filled it from a bottle taken from a refrigerator. "Let me have your arm please. This will stop the vomiting. Drink plenty of water whilst you are on the aircraft and if the symptoms persist see your Doctor when you get home." I thanked him and made my way slowly through the departure area. Whilst happy to have help in getting rid of my symptoms I was worried as to whether or not the needle had been sanitised before being plunged into me. These were the early days of the HIV epidemic and its spread via dirty needles was well known.

I climbed wearily up the aircraft steps to be met by two bright young women. "Hello Mr Kelly. We hear that you're not feeling too good. Come with us and we'll look after you." They led me quickly into the First Class cabin. "We're very quiet up here this morning so you should be able to get to sleep." One of them handed me a blanket. "Wrap yourself up in this and if there's anything you want let us know. I don't suppose you'll feel like eating anything?"

I shook my head quickly. "Thanks for the blanket" I managed a slight smile. "Not at all" one of the girls replied with a wicked grin. "It's for our own benefit, just in case you die along the way we don't have to worry about covering you up." They both laughed and then she said "Seriously, if you need anything please let us know and we hope you'll be OK."

I lay down and almost immediately fell asleep. We were over Europe when I woke several hours later and surprisingly my symptoms had disappeared, not to return.

CHAPTER 44

JET LAG AND DUTY TRAVEL

My work was often tiring and often encroached into my personal time. The airline industry works twenty-four hours a day, three hundred and sixty five days a year and the Hygiene team was expected to react to whatever came along no matter what time of day or night. The fact that somewhere in the world it was a working day was sufficient reason for me to have to work.

After learning the ropes in my early days, travelling soon became routine and navigating my way through an airport anywhere in the World was second nature. Organising my audits was important if I was to make best use of available time, spending as few nights away from home as possible, which saved cost for the company and home life for me.

In order to complete a station audit in Europe within a two day time frame it was usually necessary to depart from London on the first flight of the day so many a Monday morning found me checking in for a flight at six o'clock, joining the hundreds of other bleary eyed business men and women queueing at the check in desks.

Flights to Paris and Amsterdam were the worst as they were the first to take off at Heathrow following the night time curfew. Scheduled to depart at 06.30 meant checking in at 05.30 which in most people's eyes was ungodly. It was so early that on some mornings in Terminal 4 at Heathrow there was a queue of passengers waiting impatiently for the roller shutters to be raised to allow them to proceed through departure and security checks. All this of course long before the disaster of 9/11 in New York which led to much more stringent security checks resulting in it taking a great deal more than ten minutes to get from check in desk to the aircraft.

Travel conditions were improved in 1986 by the introduction of

Business Class and its lounges. Business Class or "Club Class" as it was known in BA resulted from an understanding that in an aircraft where First Class or Economy was the choice, business travellers who baulked at the expense of First Class, were paying a full economy fare to allow for flexibility in their flight times whilst holiday makers were travelling on cheap excursion fares. The business travellers were felt to be getting a poor deal as they were not getting any value for the extra money they were paying. Hence the birth of Club Class and the arrival of the airport lounge all designed specifically for business travellers. A boon first thing in the morning when after checking in they could go to the lounge for a quick cup of strong black coffee to help wake up.

The one other thing which massively improved my working life on aircraft was the banning of smoking during flights. Smoking on domestic flights was stopped in 1989 but it took almost another ten years before it was banned on all BA aircraft. Prior to then smoking on board had been the norm, a hangover from earlier days when it was considered the height of sophistication to be a smoker.

Looking at it in hindsight, the whole idea of being able to smoke in flight was ludicrous. The risk of accidentally setting fire to the aircraft via a lighted cigarette being dropped into a waste bin full of paper or lost down the side of a seat must have been fairly high. Not to mention the risk to the health of those people seated in a confined space and forced to breathe in the fumes which by now were known to be dangerous.

To make life more comfortable for the growing numbers of non-smoking passengers, non-moking areas had been designated within the aircraft cabin. But how ridiculous was that? In the economy cabin towards the rear of the aircraft certain blocks of seats were designated as being the smoking section, but how could the smoke be prevented from drifting into the non-smoking areas? Passengers in the rows immediately in front of or behind the smoking section were unable to escape the cigarette smoke wafting over them whilst the effects could often permeate the whole cabin.

The situation in the First Class cabin was even more ludicrous. In most aircraft the cabin was small, seating perhaps as few as eighteen elite passengers. One ridiculous idea, which actually became the reality for a while, was that one side of the cabin would be a smoking area whilst the other side, separated by only the narrow aisle would be smoke free. How?

Similarly designating the last two rows of seats as the smoking area was an alternative which made a mockery of keeping the forward section of the cabin smoke free.

The result was that I, along with many other passengers, would disembark from a long flight feeling and smelling as though I had been kippered. Banning smoking on board aircraft was a great step forward.

Despite the many early starts to my working week, there was nothing more amazing than being seated by the window as the aircraft climbed out over the South of England, breaking through the dark grey cloud layer into a blue sky and sunshine as it turned towards Europe. Sometimes after take-off the flight would be held just above cloud level to allow space for passing inbound aircraft and no matter how often this happened I never lost the thrill of speed as the plane surfed along the surface of the layer of cloud beneath. Summer mornings were beautiful as we sped South across France towards Spain or more easterly across Germany and my geographical knowledge was greatly improved as I studied the landscape beneath.

Within Europe jetlag wasn't a problem as there was rarely more than a two hour time difference between London and the city of arrival but long haul flights could prove more of a problem. Over the years I noted that jet lag seemed to affect people in different ways. I was always aware of it and knew that after a long flight I could be irritable, a point brought home to me regularly by my wife who complained as to how bad tempered I was and would often suggest that if my behaviour couldn't improve then I shouldn't come home but should just stay away!! Looking back at it, I really don't know how she put up with me over all the years.

I also learnt that despite the fact that I might think that I was fine and that my brain was working properly there were many instances when due to jet lag this wasn't the case and I soon realised that writing reports or a letter whilst on an aircraft on the way back from a long trip or even within three days of arrival home wasn't necessarily a great idea. Thoughts which had appeared to be world changing when on the aircraft seemed at best ridiculous when re-read a few days later and at worst were downright embarrassing. Over the years many people have asked how I combated jet lag and what they should do when travelling a long distance by air. It all depends on the individual. In my case on arrival home from a long international flight, usually at a very early hour in the morning, I would have a cup of coffee, read my accumulated mail then go to bed and sleep for about four to five hours. I would then get up, have some lunch and go into the office to work through the afternoon. This tended to get my internal clock reset towards UK time.

When overseas the aim was to get as much sleep as possible which wasn't always easy. Arrival into the USA, particularly the West coast, was usually mid-afternoon which meant that my body clock was well ahead of local time where back home due to the time difference it was already late evening.

In order to function properly the following day, I found it was essential to stay awake as far into the evening as I could, otherwise if I went to bed when my body clock told me that I should, I would find myself waking at around 3.00am in my hotel bedroom having had eight hours sleep and then staying wide awake for the next four hours until time to get up. On many occasions, despite my efforts, I found myself seeing the kitchen floor rising and falling in waves in front of me whilst at work in a flight kitchen the following afternoon, a sure sign that my body was falling asleep.

My flight could often be a memorable experience. Travelling as a staff passenger I couldn't ever be sure of my seat. The Company was quite happy to sell any seat right up to the point of departure and it sometimes happened that on checking in for a flight I would be placed on standby at the desk. I then had to hang around until check in had closed and hope that there would be a no show passenger and a seat would become available.

Sometimes in my early career when this happened it had a positive effect. As a junior staff member I normally travelled towards the rear of the aircraft but when the flight was very full and I had been placed on standby, any seat available might be at the forward end of the aircraft and was therefore a bonus. Later in my career when I was privileged to be able to fly in the First Class cabin it worked in the opposite way. My expensive First Class seat would be sold and I would be downgraded to the rear of the plane. On one occasion in London, having been given a boarding card, my seat was sold in the time it took me to walk from the security check to the boarding gate!

Let's face it however, the airline is in business to make money and turning down the possibility of selling a premium seat to allow a staff passenger to fly for free doesn't make any sort of business sense. Such was life but when I had just completed a long and arduous week working on behalf of the company it sometimes felt a bit of an injustice to be stood down from a flight and have to spend another night away from home. Luckily it didn't happen too often.

However, on two occasions being offloaded caused a bit of a problem. The first happened on my first visit to Japan. The BA catering contract in Tokyo was out to tender and I was invited to travel to Tokyo with the catering team which was to have discussions with the Catering company which was the incumbent supplier.

Heading the team was Bob, the Catering Executive for the route, assisted by Peter, a Procurement Manager who would discuss the financial arrangements. I was coming along to audit the kitchen and we were to be joined in Tokyo by two of our catering representatives in the area. We agreed to meet at Heathrow airport on a Saturday evening to board an overnight flight to Tokyo, giving us some time to recover on Sunday before beginning our work in the flight kitchen on Monday morning. It was not to be.

Arriving at the check in desk, the young woman took my paperwork and having put the details into the computer looked up at me and said "Sorry Mr Kelly but all staff have been put on standby. I'll check and label your baggage but you'll have to keep it with you. Come back to me there was a pause as she looked at her watch and checked the flight details on her screen in about forty minutes."

I retrieved my paperwork and suitcase and wandered off into the terminal. I hadn't got very far when I heard a voice. "Mike, over here." Looking round I spotted Bob and Peter standing by their luggage next to a pillar. "Doesn't look too hopeful" Bob said as I walked over to them. "That bad is it?" I looked at him. "Yea. Apparently the first flight this morning was overbooked and there has been an overspill on to ours." The three of us hung around for about thirty minutes watching what appeared to be a never ending stream of passengers checking in for the Tokyo flight. Bob looked at his watch. "Come on" he said as he picked up his baggage. Peter and I followed him across to the check in desk. The girl looked up at us, recognised us and gave a faint smile. "Sorry gentlemen but the flight is totally full so you've been offloaded." We looked at each other in exasperation. "Would you like me to book you on tomorrows' flight?" She waited expectantly. "That's a bloody pain in the arse but we've got to get there" Bob growled in his broad Scottish accent. "Are you both OK to carry on tomorrow?" He looked at Peter and me. "Yes I'm all right with it" I said quickly. "Me too" added Peter. "OK we'll meet back here tomorrow but let's aim for the earlier flight which may give us a slightly better chance of getting there since if we don't make the first one we then have a chance for the second."

"Book us on the first flight." Bob looked at the check in girl without waiting for an answer from us. "OK" Her fingers typed quickly on her keyboard. "That's it done. You'd better have your paperwork back" she smiled again and passed over the papers. "I'm sorry you didn't make it." "Not your fault" I responded quickly. "It's just the way these things work. Some you win some you lose."

Forty minutes later I opened my front door and stepped into the hallway, lugging my bag with me. "What's up?" Hilary appeared from the lounge having heard the door opening. "What's happened?" she looked worried. "We got off loaded." "What all of you?" Hilary queried. "Yes, all three of us. It's a real pain but we're booked on tomorrow morning's flight so hopefully we'll get away."

The following morning it was back to the airport. It felt like deja vu. I checked in at the same desk I had been standing at just a few hours previously. "What's it looking like?" I asked the girl checking me in. "It's pretty full" she said looking at her screen to get the numbers. "Keep your fingers crossed and you may be lucky. You were off loaded last night according to this?" She looked up with a query in her eyes. "Yes" I confirmed, "along with my two colleagues." "What are you going out for?" the girl looked up again and I explained about our business meeting. "It's a bit off when you are going out on company business and they offload you" she looked sympathetically at me. "Tell me about it, but at least I got a night in my own bed at home." "Come back to me in about forty minutes"

"Where have I heard that before?" I thought as I picked up my bag and headed away from the desk. Bob joined me a few minutes later to be followed shortly by Peter. "Well?" he said. "Touch and go again" I replied. "It doesn't look great."

However, this time luck was on our side. When we walked back to the desk at the appropriate time the girls waved three boarding passes at us. "Got you on this time but only in economy. You had better be quick however as the flight's closing and they won't wait for you at the boarding gate."

The following morning, we arrived in Tokyo at 9.00am. It hadn't been a comfortable flight and none of us had got much sleep. Looking bleary eyed and somewhat unkempt the three of us walked out of the baggage retrieval hall into the main airport concourse. Bob had sent a signal on Saturday night to tell the caterers that we had been delayed but were hoping to be on the early arrival on Monday morning so there in front of us stood a reception party.

The three senior managers from the catering company bowed in unison, then straightened up to hold out their hands in greeting. "Bob San. Mike San, Peter San, welcome to Tokyo." They were accompanied by two of our BA catering staff who were based in Japan. We acknowledged the greetings appropriately.

"It's too early to go to your hotel as they won't have your rooms ready so I think we should go to the kitchen" the Chief Executive said. It wasn't exactly what any of us would have wished for but we had to go along with it. Arriving at the kitchen we got straight to work and I was soon absorbed in auditing the facilities whilst my colleagues began the discussions about the contract.

After a short break for lunch I continued working. As the afternoon wore on it became more difficult to concentrate as tiredness set in so I was glad to get to the end of my work at about 5.00pm. I walked into the conference room where the discussions were taking place.

"Ah Mike. We were wondering how you were getting on" Bob grinned. "Finished?" "Yes I've done all I need to do today although I've got a few things that I need to complete tomorrow. How about you?" "Yes we're just about there at the moment. The Chief Exec has just ordered a car for us to take us to the hotel."

Great I thought to myself. I'm just about dropping. "We're going to check in and have a shower and change and then they'll pick us up at six thirty to go for a meal" Bob continued. My heart sank. The last thing in the world that I needed at that moment was a meal.

CHAPTER 45

RAW FISH AND KARAOKE

Checking in at the hotel Bob turned to Peter and me "I'll see you here at 6.25. Don't be late, they're punctilious time keepers." And they were. At 6.30 on the dot the limousine pulled up outside the door to transport us into town.

On arrival at the restaurant we were ushered inside to be met by the Chief Executive and his team. Much bowing and handshaking then took place in the time honoured Japanese manner. The restaurant was an authentic Japanese venue. Our group of some twelve people were led into a private dining room by a beautiful Japanese girl in full traditional costume and we were quickly seated squat legged on the floor around the low tables.

It was difficult to stay comfortable in such a position but earthenware cups of sake were passed around the table and the conversation began to flow so our minds were quickly taken away from our somewhat cramped seating position. The meal was my first experience of Japanese cuisine and I didn't know quite what to expect. Much of the food that appeared was totally unknown to me and to my BA colleagues and explanation of what the dishes were was difficult for our Japanese hosts as whilst their working English was good they weren't able to translate the ingredients on each plate so the three of us from London were eating blind so to speak.

Many of the dishes were composed of raw food items, some of which were easily digestible but others were more difficult for the European palate to swallow. However, I was conscious that we had to make the effort as not to do so would have led to a loss of face for our Japanese hosts and we were aware that this wouldn't be a good thing. Once again I found myself thinking "The things I do for British Airways!!"

Two things stood out during the meal. One of the dishes out of some twenty plus which comprised the menu, was delivered in a lidded box, reminiscent of the airline economy meal boxes which were being used at that time on some of our European flights. Inside the box, along with the food, was a flower. The serving girl when presenting me with my box apparently got it wrong and gave me the box the wrong way round so that the flower was pointing in the wrong direction. At least that's what I was told later.

Next moment the Chief Executive roared at the girl, apparently chastising her for her mistake. As a result, the poor girl was forced to back out of the room in abject apology, on her knees, facing me with her nose pressed to the floor. I was appalled although I didn't show it as this was part of Japanese culture and we were guests. The positioning of the flower had made no difference to me since I knew nothing of the culture but it obviously meant a lot to others.

Later in the meal I was presented with a large glass in which was a yellow coloured food with a consistency similar to a mousse but which apparently contained raw egg. Being a food safety specialist the thought of eating a raw egg wasn't very appealing and was made less so when one of my hosts said "Be careful as you eat it. Try not to get too much on your lips as it will burn your skin." "Burn my skin!" I thought. "If it burns my skin what will it do to my innards!"

After what was an entertaining meal with some excellent light hearted conversation we finished and got up to leave. Having had a cold shower in the hotel I had overcome much of my early tiredness and the application of several cups of sake as it had been enthusiastically passed round the table had helped but I was now beginning to feel it and was looking forward to getting into my bed. It seemed to have been a very long time since I had last gone to bed at home on Saturday night.

We climbed into two limousines and sped through the town. Expecting to be heading towards the airport I was shocked when the cars drew up in a side street and we were ushered into a building and up a flight of stairs. Doors opened and I found myself inside a night club. A long table ran down the room with seats positioned on each side. A number of bottles of Scotch were placed along the centre of the table and a line of young Japanese girls was waiting to welcome us with broad smiles.

"What have we been brought to?" I asked myself as the girl who had been appointed to me led me to my seat. She sat down beside me and filled my glass with Scotch. "Drink?" she smiled at me. I looked around to see that my companions were getting the same treatment. At what point will this become an embarrassment and what else are the girls expected to provide? I feared the worst.

My fears were not to be realised however. This was not some sort of brothel but instead was a karaoke bar. At the time the Japanese were very much into karaoke and this bar was only one of many which provided an outlet for Japanese business men to indulge themselves. Although the club had been very empty when we arrived it wasn't long before it filled up completely with tables of raucous men swilling drinks and competing as to who could sing best.

I have to admit that I found it difficult to keep my face straight when watching a normally very formal Japanese businessman sitting in his pin striped suit, singing the old Sinatra favourite "my way" in Japanese but I had to endure a few more hours before we eventually persuaded our hosts that we really did need to get to bed and were able to make our way back to the hotel where exhausted I crashed into bed. It had been a night to remember.

Some years later when I was Head of Environmental Health at BA I returned to Tokyo and once again came face to face with Japanese cuisine. On this occasion, having audited the hotel being used to accommodate the BA crew, I was invited to join the hotel Director of Sales and the General Manager for a meal in the evening. Once again I found myself being escorted into an authentic Japanese restaurant. The surroundings were beautiful with the restaurant positioned in the hotel garden.

The three of us were in a private room with its typical bamboo framework and paper thin decorated walls. We were being looked after by a waitress in a beautiful kimono and as I had expected were squatting at a low table, the centrepiece of which was a very large silver salver covered in an amazing array of seafood.

The lobster in the middle of the salver looked beautiful to me, not only because of its size and presentation but because it was the only item on the plate which was cooked. Everything else was raw!!

The sales Director spoke good English and immediately encouraged me to help myself. The General Manager didn't speak English but was making encouraging noises. I didn't quite know where to start but began to make an effort at the thinly sliced and more attractive looking pieces. To be fair they were generally very tasty once I got used to the cold texture. One or two items I definitely didn't like the look of but gradually as we worked our way through the platter I realised that I was going to have to bite the bullet and taste everything.

The king prawn was definitely one which I wasn't looking forward to. It looked exactly as it would have done on the fish counter at our local supermarket. Grey and cold on a bed of ice. Picking it up with my chopsticks was a feat in itself but putting it in my mouth and chewing it was something else. I shuddered.

To be honest, once I had got over the cold feeling of it the taste wasn't too bad. Slightly sweet and chewy however I wouldn't be too keen to repeat the experience.

There were a couple of other items on the table which had caught my eye earlier. Eventually I plucked up courage to ask the question "What are these?" I pointed at two small portions placed in individual silver ramekin dishes not much bigger than large egg cups.

"That one is fish liver and the other is fugu fish" the Sales Director smiled at me happily. "They are both famous delicacies here in Japan" he continued "Go ahead and try them." Worse than the prawn I thought to myself whilst smiling back at him. The thought of eating raw liver was less than appealing and fugu fish!! The name lingered in my memory for a few seconds and then it came to me.

The fugu fish is poisonous if not filleted and treated properly by the chef. It contains several poisonous organs including the liver and the skin which produce tetrodotoxin which is 1200 times more toxic than cyanide and has no antidote! At that moment I realised that my knowledge of food safety was not an advantage. I would probably have been better not knowing anything about the fugu fish. Yes, it is a famous delicacy in Japan and is loved by numerous Japanese but many of them have died as a result of eating it.

I smiled weakly and placed two small portions on my plate. Taking a deep breath, I slid the raw liver into my mouth and swallowed it all in one movement. As it slid down my throat I wondered if the translation of my original question had been correct and if not, was the liver actually part of the fugu fish or was the fugu the next piece which I was about to eat? Whichever it was I'll never know but at least I'm here to tell the tale.

Having cleared the salver of fish I thought that we were finished, but no. The waitress appeared with some equipment which she placed on the table. Next came a plate of finely sliced meat followed by a plate of sliced green vegetable looking similar to a cabbage.

All was explained to me by the Sales Director as he put together the equipment which turned out to be a water bath with a heating mechanism attached. "This is the famous Kobe beef" he explained. "It comes from Wagyu cattle." He held some up for me to look at. The beef was so thinly sliced that I could almost see through it but I could also see that it was very heavily laced with fat. It looked almost like a lace curtain.

The water heater was started and soon the sliced vegetables were being cooked on the table in front of me. Then the beef was added for a few minutes, just enough to get a colour change in the meat before it was put on my plate. "How do you like that? Very good isn't it?"

I was too polite to do anything other than nod my head enthusiastically but I haven't raced to my nearest Japanese restaurant in London to try it again. I'm not a great lover of fat on meat and although the slices were extremely thin I didn't really get a lot of flavour from them and would have preferred a good filet mignon if I were being honest. Nonetheless it was another cultural culinary experience which I enjoyed because it was all new to me and the setting and the people were wonderful but somehow I don't think that Japanese cuisine is really for me.

CHAPTER 46

IDI AMIN DECLARES WAR!

Following my earlier career in Zambia, Africa held a particular love and fascination for me and continues to do so to this day. It's a fascinating continent full of extremes. Stretching from the Mediterranean in the North to the South Atlantic and Indian oceans in Southern Africa it has a vast range of differing countries and people.

Providing safe food for our passengers from some of the countries to which BA flew was challenging. On many occasions my colleagues and I had to be strong willed with our Catering Department friends who were often put into almost impossible positions by having to cater flights from new destinations where the available facilities were either non-existent or basic at best. Despite these problems the catering team were expected to provide the standards of culinary excellence normally expected by BA passengers.

One case in point was in Tanzania. British Airways had served Tanzania with flights to Dar es Salaam for many years but in the late nineteen seventies the Marketing Department saw an opportunity to serve the growing tourist market in the country and decided that flights from London to and from Dar es Salaam would land at Arusha, a growing city in the Northern part of the country, close to some of the main tourist attractions.

This decision having been made, some of my catering colleagues were sent to Arusha to assess the possibilities of catering the flights although they weren't very optimistic, given that the existing kitchen in Dar es Salaam was already known to pose considerable problems.

The day after they got back I met them in their office to hear the worst. "Well?" I looked at Graham. "What's it like?" He shrugged his shoulders. "There's absolutely nothing at the airport so we're going to have to cater it from a hotel." "You've found a half decent hotel then?" I looked at him again. "Oh yes" he replied. "You don't look overly pleased about it?" I could sense that something wasn't quite right.

Some of his team were grinning. "Tell him Graham." Graham looked at me. "Well we tried everywhere but couldn't find anything in Arusha so we've had to go up the road a bit to find a decent hotel which is capable of doing what we need." "How far up the road?" I had the feeling that I wasn't going to like the answer. "About thirty miles" he replied. "It was the only place we could find and we looked everywhere didn't we?" He looked at his team for support

"And?" I waited for some more explanation. "Well it's a five-star hotel (he named a well-known hotel chain) up in the hills towards the National park. We'll have to give them some training and we'll get a couple of highloader trucks shipped to them." He made it sound so easy but I knew that it wouldn't be.

And so the operation got underway. My boss Peter had been assured that all was well so it was some time later that I found myself delegated to visit the hotel and check the facilities. It was to be an interesting trip. I had scheduled my audit to tie in with another station so on a hot afternoon I found myself boarding a twin-engined Fokker F27 aircraft operated by a local carrier to fly up to Arusha from Dar es Salaam.

Being aware of the problems that often happen with small regional carriers I had been at the front of the queue at the departure gate and was sitting in the front row of seats, immediately behind the forward cargo space and the cockpit.

As I sat there I heard a bit of noise from behind me. There was an altercation going on between the crew and a boarding passenger and from what I could hear we appeared to have one more passenger than we had seats. This was why I had chosen to be quick out of the starting blocks when the flight boarding had been announced. At least I had a seat.

A few moments later the flight attendant walked up the aisle past me and went on to the flight deck. Next thing I heard raised voices again. This time it appeared to be the Captain who was annoyed. "Bloody stupid idiots. They couldn't organise a piss up in a brewery! They're forever getting the figures wrong." He continued to rant in a loud voice about the inadequacies of the local population in general. Given that I was the only non-African on the flight I felt a bit uncomfortable about what I and the rest of the cabin were listening to so I kept my head down and was studiously looking at the safety card which I had taken from the seat pocket in front of me.

Suddenly I heard a quiet voice. "Mr Kelly?" I looked up to find the flight attendant questioning me. "Yes" I smiled at her. "You work for British Airways?" Again the questioning look. "Yes" I confirmed. The girl looked relieved. "Captain's compliments, Sir, and would you like to join him on the flight deck?" I realised that this was their way out of an awkward situation in having more passengers than seats. "Certainly, I'll be delighted" and immediately began to move. I walked through the forward cargo space and entered the flight deck.

"Good afternoon Captain." The Captain, a very young looking European, turned in his seat and stuck out his hand. "Thanks Mr Kelly you've got us out of a tight spot. This is my First Officer." He pointed to the right hand seat where a young Tanzanian officer put out his hand in greeting. I was surprised. Given the abusive tirade against local people that I had just heard from my seat in the cabin I hadn't expected to find a Tanzanian First Officer up front and wondered what those comments had done for the relationship between the two pilots. Happily all went calmly through the flight and the pair seemed to work amicably together as we made our very bumpy flight to Arusha.

Graham, my catering colleague, was at the airport to meet me and we were quickly on our way to the hotel which was providing the flight catering. It was a nice property, situated in the hills some distance from the airport and my audit of the kitchens quickly showed that the catering facilities were more than adequate for the job in hand.

After work I was settling down to a quiet meal with my colleague when the hotel manager, a Swiss, ran into the dining room in a state of panic. "Ladies and Gentlemen I have to advise you that Idi Amin, the President of Uganda, has just announced that he is declaring war against Tanzania and will attack the country. We will therefore have to protect the hotel since he may bomb us!"

Graham and I couldn't believe what we were hearing. "I think he's lost his marbles" I said quietly. "What, Idi Amin?" "No the manager" I replied. "We know that Amin has lost his but we're a long way from Uganda and even if he had an aircraft capable of flying here why would he want to attack a hotel?"

The manager continued to fuss around, coming to each table in turn to speak with the guests. Eventually he reached ours. "What do you think?" he said, looking at us carefully. He was obviously seeking some form of reassurance.

"Personally I think that it's highly unlikely that the hotel will be attacked." I replied. "It's typical Amin bluster and even if he had the resources it's a long way from Uganda to here and why would he wish to attack a hotel? He's more likely to attack a military position close to the border". "You think so?" The manager looked at me carefully. "I was thinking that we should black out the hotel by having all non-essential lights turned off." He continued "What do you think?" "Well if it makes you feel better go ahead." At that he rushed off and we settled down to finish our meal.

Shortly afterwards a few of the house lights dimmed and when I went to my room I found a message on the phone asking that all guests keep the bedroom curtains drawn and avoid allowing any unnecessary light to escape through the windows. I grinned to myself.

A few moments later, having dimmed all the bedroom lights I stepped out onto the balcony to enjoy a few moments in the warm African night air. Much to my amusement, on looking down towards the garden I was amazed to see the swimming pool bathed in light from its underwater lighting system proudly proclaiming the logo of the hotel, colour printed in the tiles on the floor of the pool. A beacon to any wandering Ugandan air force plane I thought as I retired to bed with little worry of any attack during the night.

The following morning I had a very early start. It was still dark but our aircraft from London en route to Dar would arrive at Arusha at 10.00am and the meals had to be at the airport on time. I entered the kitchen to find my colleague already there amid a sea of activity. "Why so much food?" I asked. I knew that the hotel was catering the flight to and from Dar es Salaam, but this was only a snack in both directions as the flight time was very short. However, looking around I could see that the main meals for the return flight to London that evening were also being prepared and packed. "Surely they don't need to be in such a hurry to get the London sector meals ready. It doesn't depart until late this evening?" "Yes they do" Graham replied. "They have to take it with them this morning." "What??" I was aghast.

"Yes" he continued "because the journey to the airport is so long and takes so much time with the slow moving trucks they take all the food with them in the morning and then wait at the airport all day for the return flight."

I took a moment or two to let it all sink in. "But surely you can't leave it sitting on the trucks in the heat all day? It would be inedible by the time it was served on board?" This was the first that I had been told about the handling at the airport and I was seriously worried. "Stop worrying" Graham grinned "I've got it all under control." "We've leased space in a large cold room at the airport and the return meals are loaded into that for the day." "Does it work?" I had previous experience of airport cold rooms which were often less than reliable.

"Yes, it's probably the only thing in the airport kitchen that does work but we've checked it thoroughly and it works well. You'll see for yourself when we get there." I wasn't convinced. "What will happen if it breaks down?" "We'll worry about that when it happens" came the less than reassuring reply.

I monitored the kitchen operation then watched as the meals were carefully loaded onto the trucks which set off for the airport. "Right" said Graham "let's get some breakfast" I followed him into the restaurant with the realisation that I felt very hungry.

We caught up with the trucks later in the morning just before they arrived at the airfield. It had been a long slow journey down from the hills for them. Showing our BA passes to the armed guard at the gate we went through the fence which separated the landside Terminal building area from the airside of the airfield where our Land Rover drew up alongside a fairly decrepit looking building.

"The flight kitchen." Graham said. "You can see why we weren't keen to use it." "Is it as bad inside as it looks from here?" "Absolutely. It was probably all right when it was built but it hasn't had much business over recent years and has been allowed to run down. The only good thing it has is a brand new cold room which is where we'll hold the catering for the return flight. Come on let's go in and you can see what I mean."

We went inside and a look at the cold room proved what I had been told. It was an oasis in a desert and so long as it continued to work it would suit our purpose.

The L1011 Tristar resplendent in its British Airways colours arrived spot on time, creating a flurry of activity on the airfield as the support services swung into action. I watched as the catering team loaded the food uplift and took a moment of pride a little later as the aircraft climbed away from Arusha on its way to Dar es Salaam.

Little do the passengers know what it takes just to provide them with a sandwich en route to Dar, I thought as I climbed back into the Land Rover.

CHAPTER 47

AN EARLY START
IN KHARTOUM

The problem that I had on my flight to Arusha was similar to an experience when travelling from Khartoum to Nairobi.

Having completed an audit in Khartoum in Sudan I had decided that to make the best use of time I would fly to Nairobi in Kenya to carry out an audit there.

My flight from Khartoum was scheduled to depart at 7.00am so once again I was travelling to an airport in the early hours of the morning. It was still dark when the taxi was stopped by an armed guard at the entrance to the airport.

"Passport please. Where are you going?" The guard looked closely into the car. "Nairobi" I replied as I put my passport back into my travel wallet. "Domestic Terminal" the soldier grunted.

"International, I'm going to Kenya" I replied. "Domestic Terminal" he grunted again and pointed at a darkened building to the right. I decided that it wouldn't be sensible to argue. "Thank you."

The taxi drove a few yards and came to a stop outside the building which the soldier had indicated. I paid the driver, picked up my bag and walked into the building. Inside was turmoil. The electric lighting wasn't working and the Terminal was in complete darkness in which a large number of prospective passengers were milling around. Two airline employees were standing behind a desk, lit only by a single Tilley oil lamp. They were being besieged by a host of people all clamouring simultaneously for their attention. I slowly and carefully worked my way through the crowd until I reached the desk. Eventually one of the check in staff, for that was what the two men apparently were, recognised the fact that I was there. "Yes?" he said looking at me. "Nairobi?" I queried. "Yes" came the prompt reply. The soldier had been correct. I now felt embarrassed that I had thought anything else. "Can I check in?" I looked hopefully across the desk. "At seven o'clock," came the prompt reply.

"Seven o'clock but that's the departure time?" I queried, hoping that he was wrong. It was only 5.30am so I had a long time to wait. "It's delayed" came the words that I hadn't wanted to hear. "Where do I check in?" I asked. "Here" came the instant response.

"OK." I stepped one pace sideways, turned and leaned back against the desk. I wasn't going to move away, lose my place then have to fight my way back through the melee to get to the front again.

There was nothing for it but to wait and watch. Shortly however I was joined a by a couple more Europeans. "Do you know where the Nairobi flight is checking in?" "Right here but not until 7.00am." They joined me standing in front of the desk.

The light gradually improved as the sun rose slowly over the airfield. Seven o'clock approached. By now there was a small group of Europeans standing around me. Suddenly the check in agent, who had been steadfastly ignoring my presence at the desk turned and with a large smile said "Nairobi, Sir?" I handed my paperwork to him and within minutes I was through security, boarding pass in hand.

The departure area was no less chaotic than the check in area had been. It rapidly became obvious that the departure board system wasn't working and there were no flight departure announcements being made. Some aircraft were leaving but information appeared to be by word of mouth or rumour, the latter causing groups of people to suddenly rise from their seats and rush madly towards a departure gate, only to be told in some instances to go away and sit down.

I carefully watched what was happening on the tarmac outside the windows. Most of the aircraft that were leaving were small turbo props which I assumed were bound for local destinations up country. Suddenly I noticed a Boeing 737 being towed on to a stand a short distance from the building. "That looks more like something which would be flying to Nairobi" I thought to myself and kept a wary eye on it. Eight o'clock came and went and still there was no indication as to when we would leave but the 737 was being loaded so things still looked hopeful.

Suddenly I noticed the agent who had checked me in walking purposefully towards a departure door. I rose quickly and walked over to him. "Nairobi?" I said holding out my boarding card. "Yes, Sir, we are ready to board."

I was on my way. Boarding the aircraft, I found my seat by a window half way down on the left side. I had a great view of what was happening outside. A red carpet was being rolled out from the front door of the plane. We obviously had a VIP joining the flight. As I watched, two army trucks pulled up alongside and a bevy of soldiers leapt out. Much shouting and gesticulating went on as an officer attempted to get them to line up in two rows just short of the aircraft.

They were barely in place before a large black limousine drew up and a smartly suited Ugandan stepped out. The officer saluted, the VIP acknowledged and climbed the steps into the aircraft with barely a glance at the two lines of soldiers drawn up as a guard of honour. The doors closed and we were underway. The Chief Stewardess, who, complete with reddish coloured wig, bore more than a passing resemblance to the British comedian, Les Dawson when he was in drag, carried out the safety demonstration as we taxied to the runway.

The engines were opened to full power and we raced along the tarmac. As we hit the take off point I heard the wheels come up and for a few seconds we were hurtling along just feet above the runway before the nose suddenly went up and the aircraft roared skywards at a very steep angle. "Well that's a different way to take off" I thought to myself. "Why the steep angle when there isn't a hill of any size within miles of the airport?" Then it dawned on me. The pilot was showing off to the VIP that he had on board.

Our pre-flight safety announcement had revealed why the flight had departed from the domestic terminal. We weren't flying direct to Nairobi but first were going to make a stop at Juba, then a city in Sudan but now the capital of the Republic of South Sudan. As we landed at Juba those of us travelling to Nairobi were told that we would have to leave the aircraft, pass through immigration control, identify our hold baggage and re-board.

I walked down the steps on to a very wet tarmac. Although the sun was shining it had been raining heavily before we had landed. I looked around. It was a small airport with very limited facilities. A large number of soldiers, recently arrived on a Hercules transport aircraft were wandering around amongst the puddles. At the edge of the tarmac stood the control tower. Not very tall, it leaned decidedly towards the aircraft somewhat like a strange leaning tower of Pisa. There appeared to be no glass in the windows and a controller or at least I assumed that was what he was, was hanging out of the top floor window, shouting instructions to people beneath. Bizarre.

I followed the crowd into the small building to look for my luggage. The bags arrived in a heap, thrown casually through a hole in the wall. I looked for mine but after a few minutes realised that it wasn't there. I had seen it being loaded in Khartoum as I sat by the aircraft window so where was it? I spoke to one of the airline staff standing close by me. "It's probably with the domestic baggage" he said. "Go through there and collect it." He pointed out of the building towards a gate in the airport perimeter fence. I was walking quickly towards it when a call came from an armed guard sitting somewhat incongruously in an old chair on the edge of the tarmac, his rifle across his knees.

He was indicating that I should go back to the terminal. I went across to him to explain that my bag was missing. It was difficult as he didn't speak English but he eventually seemed to understand and waved me through. I went out through the gate and joined a group of Ugandans who seemingly were waiting for their baggage. Time passed and I was beginning to worry that my flight would depart without me when a large high sided truck rolled slowly round a corner towards us. It pulled up alongside then suddenly without any warning, suitcases were flying through the air, being thrown over the sides of the lorry by unseen hands inside.

There was much hilarity from the crowd around me and as I watched I saw my bag sailing through the air to land with a crash on the wet ground. Grabbing it, I raced back through the gate towards the terminal building. Rushing inside I proffered my passport to the immigration officer who stamped it without a word and pointed to the door.

I ran across the apron to the aircraft and placed my bag in the hold before breathlessly climbing the aircraft steps. The door closed behind me. It had been a close call.

Arriving at Nairobi I was surprised that there was no-one at the arrival gate to meet me. I had expected Bob Ferguson, our BA Catering Executive to have been there as he was a friend and knew that I was coming.

I walked through an almost deserted International arrivals building to the British Airways office and knocking on the door stepped inside. "Hi Mike" Bob was there along with the airport manager and one or two other staff. "Where did you come from?" he asked, looking surprised. "Khartoum, did you not get my message?" "Yes I did but when I asked Sudan Airways about their flight from Khartoum they said that it wasn't coming. In fact they said that they haven't had one for a couple of weeks." "Shows how little they know." "How was the flight?" Bob looked at me. "Have you got all day?" I said. "It was an experience is the only way I can put it. I think the piece of thick string in the middle of my breakfast roll just about summed it up."

CHAPTER 48

MUCK AND BULLETS
IN BEIRUT

The threat of bombing in Tanzania may have been a long way from reality but in Beirut it was only too real as I found out on my one and only visit to that divided city in the early nineteen eighties. I didn't know what to expect on arrival. The full scale war hadn't yet broken out and British Airways was still flying into the city so an audit of the flight kitchen was needed and I had drawn the short straw in the office.

My arrival was expected and having met the BA manager and discussed what I needed to do I was introduced to the catering manager and taken directly to the flight kitchen. Nothing had prepared me for what I found. It was old, rambling, and dirty. Cleaning was not something which was a priority and there were accumulations of dirt and food debris lying beneath equipment and along the coving between floor and walls.

Some of the equipment appeared not to have been cleaned in a very long time which was proven by my worst find. In the bakery was a large dough mixer positioned in a niche in the wall. The mixer was surrounded by an accumulation of dirt and old flour which was so large that it reached from the floor to the top of the revolving mixing bowl, a height of some three feet, providing a solid overcoat of dirt within which the bowl was turning. It was disgusting and having finished my inspection I promised to return in the morning to see what improvements they would make during the night as a result of my unhappy comments.

Back at the BA office one of the local team was waiting to drive me to my hotel. We drove out of the airport in a BA liveried van, heading towards the city and within minutes were faced with a road block. A gang of very unsavoury looking and heavily armed men waved us to a stop and demanded to see our identification. There were no pleasantries, just a few grunts followed by a wave of the head signifying that we could proceed.

Proceed we did, but not very far as the next road block was visible even as we left the first. "Who are they?" I asked my companion. "Every group is different" came the reply. "Each of the factions within the city is trying to control its own area and will only let people that they know through their barricades." We passed through at least four barricades on our way to the hotel. Each group stopped us and the ritual was much the same. ID had to be provided and was closely scrutinised before we were allowed to proceed.

The air was chilled with an atmosphere which was frightening in its intensity. Coming as I do from Northern Ireland where the "troubles" had broken out in the Autumn of 1969 I had experience of road blocks but had never before come across an atmosphere which was so inherently scary. It seemed that the slightest provocation would cause problems. As we drove through the city I could hear sporadic gunfire and from time to time could see tracer bullets glistening in the sky. I was delivered to the Bristol Hotel with a promise that I would be collected again in the morning.

Checking in I got the impression that the hotel wasn't very busy and in fact during my overnight stop I didn't see another soul apart from the staff. My room fronted on to the street and had a very large window from floor to ceiling. Looking out I watched the activity below and again could see tracer bullets arcing into the sky in various parts of the city. Later in the evening, around 10.00pm, having had a meal, I was sitting in an armchair reading a book when suddenly and without warning gunfire broke out in the street in front of me. I watched as a line of tracer passed my window from left to right followed almost immediately by some going the other way.

I dived for the floor and lay flat. Although the bullets were passing outside I didn't know who or what was being aimed at and how good the aim actually was! As I lay there I thought "How ridiculous! If I wanted to be shot at I could go home to Belfast and be shot at in comfort." The firing seemed to go on for a while but was probably only a few moments and it stopped as suddenly as it had started.

The following morning when I was picked up at the hotel my colleague asked, "Did you have a good night?" I told him what had happened. He just laughed and said "Pretty much par for the course. It happens all over the city every night."

As we talked we were driving along the corniche, the dual carriageway road running along the edge of the sea towards the airport and I suddenly realised that we were driving along the wrong carriageway, on the wrong side of the road. "I know it's a silly question but why are we driving on the wrong side of the road?" "That's easy" came the reply, "this bit of the road gets shelled sometimes by warships off the coast. The shells hit the carriageway that is closest to the sea but apparently they can't hit this side. Don't ask me why."

He carried on driving as though it was the most normal thing in the world. I didn't ask who "they" were as it seemed of little importance if a shell was going to arrive out of nowhere.

Flying home later that day I was faced with another more personal problem. Having gone back to the kitchen in the hope of being able to get some improvement in standards I was taking my leave of the Manager when he said that he wished to give me a gift. I declined politely but he continued to try to push the point.

Back at the BA office a little while later I was checked in and awaiting the aircraft arrival. "You're OK today" the duty manager said from behind his desk. "It's coming in." I obviously looked a bit blank as he continued, "The aircraft comes from Damascus and they radio ahead to check if it is safe to land. If not, they will overfly and go straight to London." I was amazed at this revelation but after the night's activities that I had witnessed I could understand the precaution.

The plane duly arrived and I was walking to the aircraft when the Manager of the flight kitchen suddenly appeared beside me. "Mike I've put a couple of boxes in the cargo hold for you. You can pick them up on arrival." Before I could say a word he was gone. I was horrified. What had he done and what was in the boxes?

Later standing at the carousel at Heathrow watching the luggage arriving I spotted my case and had just picked it off the moving belt when I saw two wooden boxes appear. I watched them go round twice. I had hoped that if they weren't labelled I could just walk away and leave them. It wasn't to be. I could see my name and details on them in large writing. I off loaded them, put them on a trolley and walked towards the exit. What do I do if I'm stopped by Customs as I exit? I haven't a clue what's in the boxes. It could be anything. My heart thumped as I walked through, trying to look calm and unconcerned. I wasn't stopped and as I walked out into the arrivals hall I breathed a sigh of relief. Getting home I explained the boxes to my wife. "You'd better open them and find out what they are." I opened them very cautiously and pulling back a sheet of covering paper I found myself looking at a consignment of large mangoes packed very carefully to avoid damage. All that worry about nothing!

I was to be the last hygiene team member to visit Beirut. Shortly afterwards the route was closed down when it became too dangerous to operate into the city. The story goes that the last flight left in rather a hurry. As gunfire and shells began to appear on the airfield the Captain was reputed to have said "I don't care who is on board and who isn't but get the doors closed now as I'm leaving." And with that he asked for push back clearance.

Life was nothing if not interesting in BA.

CHAPTER 49

INCIDENTS IN FLIGHT

Travelling to various destinations across the world could be entertaining in itself. Given the rules which governed staff travel which I've mentioned before, I could never be certain of getting on the flight on which I had been booked, let alone knowing which seat I was likely to be given. It was very much in the lap of the Gods so to speak. Whichever seat I finished up in, I often had the pleasure of being seated next to a passenger who proved to be an entertaining companion during the flight.

On one of my early trips on a full Boeing 747 I was given an aisle seat in the centre block in the economy cabin. Shortly before take-off I was joined in the seat next to me by a middle aged woman apparently travelling on her own. I said good morning to her as she settled down beside me and she smiled as she responded and then apologised for my having to get out of my seat to let her access her own.

Given the restricted space available in the area around each seat, getting in and arranging one's belongings and the items that might be needed during the flight is an art form in itself. The woman chatted to me as she positioned her belongings and once again apologised. We settled down and watched and listened whilst the crew went through the emergency escape procedures. The engines started and we moved away from the departure gate, slowly rumbling towards the take-off position at the end of the runway. I watched through the window as best I could, given that I was two seats away from it across an aisle, as we passed the various terminals and other aircraft. Through the many years of my career no matter how often I flew, I never lost the thrill of the take-off and landing.

As we made our way out I became aware that the woman beside me was becoming slightly agitated. Out of the corner of my eye I could see her body tensing and she was tightening her grip on the arm of the seat.

She was obviously not looking forward to the next few minutes. The aircraft turned on to the end of the runway and as the engines began to rev up to full throttle she suddenly said to me in a small voice. "Would you hold my hand as we take off?"

I was very surprised but reached across with my left hand and took her right hand in mine. She grasped me with an iron grip and closed her eyes as the aircraft roared down the runway. The nose lifted as we reached take off speed and the plane rose smoothly and effortlessly into flight as we climbed steadily away from the runway. The wheels came up with a thud beneath the cabin but my hand remained in the vice like grip. The aircraft engines slowed as the plane levelled off. The woman's eyes opened and she gave me a somewhat embarrassed look. "I'm sorry but I'm a terrible flier and this is the first time that I've flown anywhere without my husband." I smiled back at her. "Don't worry. Lots of people dislike flying and particularly the take-off and landing. My sister in law is exactly the same. She hates it." I gently tried to release my hand. "Oh I'm sorry" she said realising that she was still holding on to me very tightly. I laughed "Don't worry. I'll get the circulation back in my hand in a minute." I knew that my comment may have embarrassed her even more but I said it light heartedly in order to reduce her tension. It worked.

The flight passed quickly as we flew across the Atlantic and all too soon we were on the descent. As the aircraft nose went down and we were advised to fasten our seat belts she looked at me and said "Do you mind?" as she took my hand again. "Of course not." And so I descended into New York hand in hand with a female stranger. Funnily enough it wasn't to be the the last time that I would be asked to perform the same function. There are a large number of people who hate flying and need a bit of reassurance.

On one particular flight the situation was a bit different. I was flying to Belfast on the shuttle service. The shuttle service was introduced in the nineteen eighties from London Heathrow to the domestic airports served by BA at the time and replicated the services operated in the United States by Eastern Airlines from New York to Washington DC and to Boston.

At the time, British Airways operated Trident jet aircraft on routes to Manchester, Glasgow, Edinburgh and Belfast. The aircraft were relatively small, carrying around 100 passengers and often during the peak traffic periods in the morning and evening the flights would be overbooked which would cause problems when some passengers had to be left behind.

The decision was taken to improve the customer service by providing a back-up aircraft so that when the first aircraft was full any remaining passengers would be put on a back-up flight which would fly immediately after the first flight had taken off.

Given the number of back up aircraft which flew during peak traffic periods the service rapidly became known as the "shuttle", a name which stuck for a long number of years and which became synonymous with all BA European and domestic services even when they weren't actually shuttle operations. Business travellers regularly said "I'm on the shuttle to Paris tomorrow" or whatever other European destination they were heading to.

On the morning in question I was designated to travel in the back-up aircraft and duly boarded with some eight or ten others. We were liberally spread around the centre of the aircraft and I was fortunate enough to have a window seat on the left side. It was a summer morning, cloudy but bright and the take-off was smooth. The aircraft climbed through a layer of cloud and was then held just on top of the cloud level. It was exhilarating as we raced across the tops of the cloud, one of the few occasions when the passengers can appreciate the speed of the aircraft.

As we were in level flight the crew began the meal service. Two stewardesses walked the trolley down the aisle and positioned it by the row of seats immediately behind me. They locked the brakes on and had just begun to serve when without warning the aircraft dropped like a stone, going down several hundred feet in a brief second, then just as quickly it went straight back up. All hell broke loose. The two women in the seats behind me began to scream. I glanced round as the aircraft made another plunge earthwards and saw that one of the stewardesses had had the presence of mind to throw herself across the top of the trolley thus stopping it from unloading its contents. Simultaneously the bells rang and the seat belt signs illuminated. The aircraft continued to buck and plunge but not quite as ferociously as it had done a few seconds previously.

I looked across the aisle at the woman seated by the window on the far side from me. She was obviously in a panic. She looked as though she didn't know whether to scream, cry or be sick. She had grabbed a sick bag out of the seat pocket in front of her but was making no use of it as she desperately tried to hang on to her seat. Realising that she needed a bit of help I quickly undid my seat belt and breaking all the rules dived rapidly across the aisle and into the seat beside her.

"Don't panic, it's all right. We've just hit a bit of clear air turbulence. It'll calm down in a minute." She looked at me silently then nodded her head. Her face was white and her hands were gripping the arms of her seat so tightly that her knuckles were turning white. The Captain's voice came across on the PA system. "Ladies and Gentlemen, Captain speaking. I'm very sorry about that sudden unexpected and severe turbulence. I hope that none of you have suffered any injury and the Purser will be going through the cabin to check with you just as soon as I can switch off the seat belt sign. Please be assured that the aircraft is designed to cope with turbulence such as this and is perfectly safe. We will be climbing to a better altitude in a few minutes which will reduce the problem."

As he was speaking the turbulence was fading and the aircraft began to climb away from the cloud layer beneath it. I turned to the woman beside me. "Are you OK?" "Yes thanks" she replied in a Northern Irish accent. She was mopping tears from her eyes. "Is it always this bad?" she questioned me. "This is the first flight I've been on. Well the second really. My son bought me a ticket to come over to England to see him so I'm on my way home."

I quickly told her that this wasn't the norm and that she had just been unlucky to hit such a bad batch of turbulence. I explained that I worked with the airline and was a very regular traveller. "Thanks for coming over to me" she continued. "I just didn't know what to do or what was happening." At that moment the aircraft gave another small lurch and she visibly jumped. "Don't worry. I'll sit here with you all the way to Belfast." "Thanks" and she gave me a weak smile. The flight continued more smoothly. The stewardesses having pacified the two ladies who had been behind me, cleared up the mess made by the falling coffee pots and restarted the service. As they got to me the senior of the two women quietly said "Thanks for your help. That was very thoughtful."

I stayed with the woman until we landed in Belfast, being able to reassure her at every noise and movement that the plane made as we approached Aldergrove airport. I don't know if she ever had the courage to fly again and I wouldn't blame her if she hadn't as it was certainly the worst bit of turbulence that I ever flew through on that route. Not one for the faint hearted.

Given the number of flights which I made in more than thirty years in numerous different types of aircraft into and out of a variety of airports ranging from the very large to the very small I was fortunate to only have suffered only a very few incidents. Most of them were minor but one or two have stuck in my mind.

One of the earliest happened on a VC10 flying into Dammam in Saudi Arabia. We were on our final approach to the airfield, not much more than a mile from touchdown. Suddenly the engines surged into full power and we began a steep climb away. I glanced out of the window beside me and thought I glimpsed a flash of grey beneath us. The aircraft levelled out as it turned to starboard and the re-assuring voice of the Captain came across the public address system.

"Sorry about that ladies and gentlemen. I can assure you that there's nothing wrong with the aircraft but we were advised of a military emergency by air traffic control. Apparently a fighter aircraft was running out of fuel as it approached the airfield and had to make an emergency landing. In fact, as we climbed away those of you beside a window on the left side may just have got a glimpse of him. We'll be making a circuit to approach the airfield again and should have you on the ground in about twenty minutes." So I had seen something beneath us after all.

A year or two later I had a slightly more personal view of things going slightly awry. I was travelling back from an audit in Malawi with my catering colleague Peter Followell. Once again I was on a VC10. We had met the Captain and crew during our stop in Blantyre as we were staying in the same hotel. Our return trip was taking us from Malawi to Dar Es Salaam in Tanzania where we would refuel and pick up more passengers before continuing to London.

Just after the dinner service had been completed the Captain came through the aircraft to speak to the passengers. He was the youngest Captain on the fleet at the time and a thoroughly nice chap. Arriving beside our seat he chatted with us for a couple of minutes and then said "If you would like to come up to the flight deck I'll be very happy to show you around." We thanked him and a few minutes later Peter made his way forward. He must have been up there for some twenty minutes or so before coming back. "Your turn" he said with a grin and made way for me.

I walked forward and waited outside the flight deck door whilst the Purser went through to ask the Captain's permission for me to enter. He came out and waved me through. Stepping inside the cockpit I was warmly welcomed by the Captain. "You know my colleagues" he waved towards the First Officer and the Engineer Officer who made up the three-man complement. They looked round and said "Hi" almost in unison.

The Captain pointed to the jump seat immediately behind his. It was one of two positioned immediately behind the seats occupied by the Captain and the First officer and was normally used to accommodate extra crew members or senior pilots carrying out routine checks on the capabilities of the crew flying the aircraft. I sat down and the Captain went through a short briefing, checking that I knew how the seat belt operated, and pointing out the emergency exits should anything go wrong. I had been on flight decks previously so was familiar with the seat belt which was very different from that worn by the passengers. It had two straps which came over the shoulders and independently clipped into a circular buckle which also held a lap strap and a strap which came up between my legs. Very similar to the straps in a baby's car seat. To release the belt, the buckle had to be turned clockwise.

The crew chatted with me about details of the flight and the about what I did in the Company and how often I flew. As we progressed I could hear the various communications coming over the radio from air traffic control through a set of headphones which I had been given. I had been taught on previous flights how to wear the headphones on one ear so that I could hear conversation on the flight deck but could also hear the commands being given over the radio.

We were approaching Dar es Salaam and the Captain turned in his seat and said "If you would like to stay up for the landing you're very welcome?" I tightened my belt and peered through the front windscreen. Dar was visible as a bright glow in the otherwise intense darkness of the African night. We passed the airport on our left side as we made what is known as the downwind leg on our approach to the landing. On the Captain's instruction I had moved my seat into its locked landing position and had a good view as we flew out over the sea and began our final left turn to line up for the runway.

"Watch your speed" I heard the Captain say. The First officer was making the landing. The runway threshold lights blazed red in front of us as we roared in. As we passed over them I thought for a brief second that surely I shouldn't be able to see them that easily from my seat behind and to the right of the Captain? I knew enough about flying to know that the aircraft should flare shortly before touchdown. The nose should rise and the aircraft should settle on its main wheels before the nose comes down and in the flared position my view would be upwards into the night sky. Just at that moment we hit the ground with an enormous thump. The aircraft seemed to shimmy from side to side as it bounced back into the air. I heard the crash of falling implements from the galley outside the door. At the same moment I thought I heard the Captain say "I have control." There was another bounce before the aircraft got all its wheels on the ground and with a roar of engines in reverse thrust we slowed towards the end of the runway.

There was an uneasy silence on the flight deck as the aircraft made its way towards the terminal building. The landing had obviously not been good but no-one was going to say anything before I left the flight deck. We came to a halt and I rapidly extricated myself from my seat. "Thanks Captain" I said with a smile as I let myself out into the aircraft cabin. "That was a bit rough" the Purser said to me as I passed him on my way back to the main cabin. "Yes just a bit" I replied.

I got to my seat and Peter looked up at me. "What was that? Did you land it?" he said jokingly. "You could probably have done it better. What happened?" "I'll tell you when we get off." I didn't want to say anything much as there were other passengers within earshot.

When we disembarked we were met on the apron by Dave, the BA Manager at Dar. We had taken a bit of time to get off as we had let other passengers go in front of us. "Hello Peter" He stuck his hand out in greeting "I saw your name on the flight list." Peter introduced me. "You may be in for a delay I'm afraid" the manager continued. "The crew are deciding as to whether or not they need to declare a heavy landing. Apparently they landed a bit nose first and the oleo leg on the front wheels is stuck where it has jammed upwards. Have a look and you can see that the plane is sitting a bit nose down."

We looked. The engineer from the aircraft had been joined by the station ground engineer and they along with the Captain were walking along the underside of the plane running their hands along the fuselage. "They're feeling for wrinkles in the metalwork" the manager confided quietly to us. "I knew it was bad but I didn't realise that it was that bad" I said.

Peter looked at Dave "Mike was on the flight deck for the landing." "I bet that was interesting after the event?" Dave grinned. "I don't know, I got off as quickly as I could after we taxied in since I thought there would be a few words exchanged that I didn't need to be part of." We walked into the terminal and awaited events.

Some while later Dave came across to us in the departure lounge. "The good news is that you're going. They've sorted out the oleo and everyone appears to be happy. The bad news is that the Captain taking you on the next leg has overloaded the fuel. You know what they're like. They always want to have more in reserve. We've worked out the fuel and I think that he has far too much and with all that weight he will have a problem getting airborne."

"You're a real Jobs' comforter." Peter said. "No I'm being serious. Speaking personally, I don't think that I'd want to be on this one on take-off." Peter looked at me. "What do you think?" "I don't know" I replied. "Surely the Captain must know what he's doing?" I knew that the flight deck crew always erred on the side of caution when it came to everything that they did and they meticulously worked out the fuel requirements for every flight they made. "I think we'll be all right."

"Well don't say that I didn't warn you" Dave grinned as he waved us towards the departure door. We climbed into our seats and settled down. The aircraft taxied slowly to the take off point at the end of the runway. As we reached it the Captain came on the public address. "We're at our take off point and have got air traffic permission to take off but we will be staying here for a few minute to burn off some excess fuel that we have on board." Peter looked at me. "Dave was right then."

To prove the point, the aircraft sat at the end of the taxiway for more than five minutes with engines running at high power before eventually turning on to the runway. Peter looked at me as we began the take-off run. He was holding his fingers crossed and I could swear that there was an audible sigh of relief from him as the nose lifted and we climbed out over the sea. Two incidents in one evening but all was well in the end.

There were to be other occasions when I was invited to sit on the flight deck, sometimes as a direct result of the flight being full and there being no alternative. Travelling on the flight deck was always a privilege and was at the discretion of the Captain. Some were happy to have a staff passenger sit with them whilst others weren't so keen. Sometimes however I was asked to assist.

On one flight we were descending through cloud into Rawalpindi airport. As we began our spiral downwards air traffic control advised us of the presence of a military transport C130 Hercules aircraft which was in the arrival pattern with us. "Can anyone see him?" the Captain asked. From my position on the jump seat I joined the other crew members in peering into the murk. "I've got him" the First officer called out. "Turning below us at about three o'clock"

At that moment we began a turn to starboard. The Captain turned quickly to me "He'll be over your side in a moment. Keep an eye on him for us and let me know if he looks like he's getting any closer."

I dutifully kept an eye on the Hercules, watching him like a hawk as he continued his descent through the cloud. A few minutes later the Captain queried where the Hercules was and I was able to confirm that it was moving away to our port side and slowly disappearing from our track. We landed without seeing him again.

Some years later on a flight to Toulouse I was again on the flight deck. This time it was on a Boeing 737 and there were only the two pilots and me. Toulouse is the home of the Airbus aircraft manufacturing company. The airfield at Blagnac has two parallel main runways. The passenger terminal is on one side of the airfield whilst the huge Airbus manufacturing site is facing it on the opposite side.

It was a clear sunny day and we had a good view of the airfield as we made our approach. I had a set of headphones on and heard the air traffic controller give us our final instructions. "Speedbird 372 clear to land runway 14 left." I watched as the runway approached. I never lost the thrill of seeing the landing from the flight deck.

As I looked at the runway lights glaring ferociously at us through the clear Summer sunshine I could see an aircraft at the holding point at the end of the runway obviously waiting for us to touch down before making its way to the take off point. Or at least that should have been the case but as I watched I saw the aircraft begin to move slowly forward, turning on to the runway directly in front of us.

"Going round" The Captain's call was clear. He pushed the throttle levers forward and the engines surged as the power was applied. We continued to descend for a few moments before the aircraft began to pick up speed then began to climb away.

"Gear up" and the wheels were retracted. Both he and the First officer were busy for a few minutes ensuring that the aircraft was correctly positioned in a circuit which took us low over the city rooftops before we could turn back onto our landing run.

"What the hell was that about?" the Captain said. "They did say 14 left didn't they?" He almost seemed to doubt himself. "That's what I heard" The First officer confirmed. "What did you hear?" The Captain looked briefly over his shoulder at me. "I heard 14 left as well" I replied.

The Captain had already spoken to air traffic control re the incident and would be talking with them again as soon as the aircraft arrived at the Terminal. Meanwhile he had to speak to the passengers to advise them as to what had happened and re-assure them that all was well. It was an incident which showed that despite all the training and safety procedures built into flying there were still opportunities for it to go wrong. A simple mistake by the Captain of one aircraft might have proven fatal had the visibility not been good.

Another more amusing incident was to happen much later in my career. A few months after the tragedy of the events on 11th September 2001 when the twin towers in New York were destroyed I was flying back from an audit in Oslo. It was a Friday night and the flight was full of business people returning to London at the end of the week.

As often happened my seat was sold and I found myself standing hopefully at the departure gate along with a Stewardess who was returning from a short holiday. I had almost given up hope of getting home when at the last minute the gate staff called both of us over. "I've got you seats. One in the cabin and one on the flight deck. As you're travelling on duty Mr Kelly you will be on the flight deck."

New rules introduced after the recent atrocities meant that only staff travelling on duty could have the flight deck seat. The stewardess was on holiday so didn't qualify. I was happy just to have a seat so made my way quickly on to the aircraft and stood outside the flight deck door until the Flight Purser had time to speak to the Captain. He then turned and waved me in. Having been introduced to the Captain I took my seat and almost immediately said to him "Thanks for letting me have the seat Captain. It's greatly appreciated." "No" the Captain replied "Thank you." The emphasis being on the "you" I obviously looked a bit puzzled. "No I'm very pleased to have you up here" he continued "because you're in charge of the door."

He looked over his shoulder at me "You know that the cockpit doors have been modified to stop intruders getting in?" I had heard that a new locking system had been very quickly designed and put into place following a serious incident on a BA flight to Nairobi when a man had entered the flight deck and attacked the crew.

"Well" he carried on, "I don't know what idiot designed it but it's effectively a vertical steel bar with a set of horizontal locking arms on it. It's hand operated by turning that lever" he pointed it out to me "and once the lever has been turned no-one can get in here from the Cabin unless we turn the handle to release the bolts. The problem is that if something goes wrong up here we're snookered. If I'm flying the plane and suddenly and unexpectedly have a heart attack and pass out over the controls, my co-pilot, can't get any help. I'm slumped over the controls, he has to try to fly the aircraft and he can't get up to open the door to get help from the rest of the crew. Hence I'm delighted to have you up here with us as it gives me a greater sense of security."

I grinned. "Well that's a first. I've never been "IC door" before. Maybe I've found my role at last." We all laughed. However, it was a serious point being made by the Captain and it wasn't too long before a more permanent and workable solution to the problem was found.

CHAPTER 50

CHANGING CAREER

Life in the Company wasn't easy through the late nineteen seventies and into the eighties. The airline business has always been very cyclical and financially difficult. Increased fuel costs raised fares and there was a decrease in traffic which in turn meant that the airline costs had to be slashed resulting in many staff were being made redundant.

The changes resulted in my job being moved and for a while I found myself in a Health and Safety Section being run by Captain Jack Jessop, a real gentleman. For a short time I carried out Health & Safety audits at some overseas stations whilst my previous boss Peter Jerram tried to run the food safety section using one or two of the laboratory staff from the pathology laboratory in Medical Services but the changes didn't work and it wasn't long before I was back in my old role.

Nineteen eighty-eight brought more change. A new corporate Head of Human Resources had been appointed and had decided that the company needed to make better use of its employees. The Master of Business Administration degree (MBA) was considered at the time to be an essential for people aiming for top positions in any company and a decision was made to introduce two MBA degree courses to be offered to selected employees.

One would be a full time course run at Lancaster University and the second a part time course to be run by the University of Bath. I applied for both courses and was delighted to be selected for the Bath University degree. This meant a change in lifestyle as the course was to be run over a two year period.

During each three term academic year, lecturers and Professors from the University would travel up from Bath to Heathrow every Wednesday and Thursday evening to deliver lectures to the class after the students had finished their normal days' work. Classes started at 5.30pm and finished at 9.00pm making it a very long day.

Two topics would be dealt with in each term and we would be expected to do the normal reading and write case studies etc. in the same way as full time University students whilst at the same time continuing to carry out our existing jobs.

In addition, weekend residential courses would be held at the University during holiday periods such as Easter when we would be expected to travel to the University on Friday afternoon and stay in the student halls of residence for a couple of nights whilst attending lectures through the day.

The course contained 52 people drawn from all areas across the airline, with a couple of outsiders from the BAA which was the company which owned and operated Heathrow airport. We were an eclectic mix ranging in age from mid-twenties to early forties but it didn't take long for us to settle down into a mutually supportive group.

Having to attend lectures every Wednesday and Thursday evening meant that I had to change my working week. Instead of scheduling my trips to be away from Monday to Saturday I now had to schedule myself to be away Friday to Wednesday so that Wednesday and Thursday effectively became my weekend. Fortunately, my colleagues in the Hygiene Branch were very considerate and helped as far as possible by allowing me to do many of the European short trips and fewer of the long haul audits which were more difficult to fit into the time available.

Coming towards the end of the course I had to decide on the subject matter for my final dissertation on which my degree would depend. I looked at all the subjects we had covered and decided that operational management was the area which appealed most. This was partly because the subject lecturer had been an operations manager outside academia and therefore had a much better understanding of the real world than those of his colleagues who had spent a life in academia who, whilst understanding the theory, had little working understanding of the difficulties in the actual practice.

Secondly it gave me the opportunity to use the operating practices in Catering Centre South, our major catering base in London as the core of my work, based on the fact that it was a hugely complex operation and therefore worthy of some examination. It was also unlikely that my lecturer who would have to oversee, read and mark my dissertation or his colleague at Warwick University who would also read and mark it, would have any knowledge whatsoever of a major catering operation and would therefore have to accept a lot of what I said as being correct.

After much thought I decided that the subject of my dissertation would be titled "The introduction of manufacturing practices into the making of aircraft meals." This was based on the fact that making aircraft meals using the principles of producing food in a hotel or restaurant kitchen was no longer valid in a market where more than 25,000 meals were being produced out of one kitchen on an average day.

The introduction of production lines and moving conveyor belts was essential if the required time scales were to be met but this had to be tempered by the need to retain quality in the final product.

My dissertation wasn't a definitive masterpiece when finished but it was good enough to get me through. As part of the exercise my lecturer paid a visit to the flight kitchen to have a look at what I was doing. He watched the production in amazement and finally commented "You could write the Encyclopaedia Britannica about what's going on in this place." Shortly after I had completed my Degree and before the graduation ceremony had taken place, I got a phone call late one afternoon from Renu, the secretary to Mike Street, the Head of Catering. "Mike would like to see you in his office at 10.00am tomorrow if that's OK?" It wasn't so much a question as a statement of fact.

"Yes that's fine. Have you any idea as to what it's about?" I queried. Renu was the soul of discretion so I was none the wiser when I entered Mike's office at the appointed time.

"Hi Mike, thanks for coming." I knew Mike well having worked with him over the last couple of years. "Can I introduce you to Maurice Decarteret" I shook hands with the other occupant of the office. "Maurice is moving from his job in Motor Transport to take over as the new manager at Catering Centre South." "OK" I replied. "I would like you to join Maurice as the Senior Operations Manager. What do you think?"

I was flabbergasted. This was straight out of the blue and totally unexpected. My mind raced through all the problems that this would bring me. It was probably the last place in the world that I would want to work but this was a senior management position. A serious step up from the existing management position that I held.

"What would the job entail?" I needed to know a bit more and gain time whilst I thought. Mike went through the two positions detailing the responsibilities that we would each have. Maurice would be in overall charge whilst I would run the food production and the supply operation.

Mike outlined a salary to me and asked "What do you think?" "I think that I need a bit of time to think it over. Would you mind if I have some thoughts, discuss it with my wife and let you know tomorrow?" "Yes that's fine."

It was a no brainer really. I went home to talk it over with Hilary. "I don't like the idea of the job but it's a Senior Management position and it's being offered to me on a plate. When am I ever going to get a better opportunity to move up? And what if I turn it down? Am I ever likely to be considered for a senior post again?" We agreed and the following morning I phoned Mike and accepted the job.

CHAPTER 51

IN AT THE DEEP END

The following month saw me installed as the new Senior Operations Manager at the flight kitchen. It was to prove the most difficult two years of work that I ever experienced. I had two immediate problems. Firstly, I had no experience of working at this level and secondly everyone in the kitchen already knew me but in my previous incarnation. I therefore had a problem in convincing them that I now had a new position and wasn't just there as some sort of extension of my old job.

The task which Maurice and I had been given had a single focus. Reduce costs. My first target was to cut the cost of the annual food budget from some £22m to £20m whilst improving the quality and Maurice had to cut the manpower from 1750 to 1250 or below.

He was experienced in people management having previously worked in an industrial setting in the Company whereas I was coming from a very sheltered background in Medical Services where although I had heard of some of the industrial goings on I had never been part of them. It was going to be difficult.

Cutting the food budget proved to be somewhat easier than I had at first thought. A close scrutiny of the passenger load figures for each flight, over a couple of weeks showed a number of discrepancies. The load figures showed two totals. These were the number of passengers booked to fly on each service and the number who actually flew on the day. There is always a difference because not everyone booked to fly will actually turn up on the day and on many services, particularly within Europe, the difference could be 10% or higher. This meant that if we catered each flight to the booked figures we would often be putting more meals on board than would actually be needed. This would be both wasteful and costly.

This had been known for a very long time and to cope with it, all flights were initially catered to a figure which was a percentage below the actual booked number of passengers. The percentage used was based on computer generated historical knowledge as to which flights had most "no shows" as the missing passengers were known.

Meals for some aircraft would therefore be loaded to a figure 5% below the number of passengers who had booked to fly whilst other flights might be under catered by 12%. However, statistics are not infallible so to ensure that we didn't get it wrong and leave some poor passenger without a meal a last minute top up system had been devised.

The numbers of passengers checking in for each flight was monitored and when critical numbers were reached and extra meals were deemed to be necessary, these were delivered to the flight by a truck filled with a selection of meals, strategically positioned on the airfield and able to reach any aircraft within a few minutes.

I realised that any such system can be open to abuse and there was a distinct possibility that some of the meals ostensibly provided for passengers never made it to an aircraft but provided good quality lunches etc. for any number of airport workers. Controls needed to be strengthened if we were to save costs. A close look at the figures also showed me that at the weekend we seemed to produce more joints of meat for First Class service than we needed for the number of flights we were serving.

At the time First Class passengers were offered a table side trolley service which presented a full joint of roast meat from which they could choose the cut or slices that they preferred. To be able to do this the aircraft was supplied with a number of joints part cooked in the flight kitchen then finished off in the oven in the aircraft galley.

A look at the figures indicated that the volume of joints of beef passing through the butchery at the weekend was greater than the number actually required for all the departing flights. Somewhere along the way we were losing up to sixty joints and the suspicion in my mind was that we were supplying a number of homes in the Heathrow area with their weekend family roast!

I asked a number of questions but didn't get any satisfactory answers as I tried to figure out how the meat was disappearing out of the building. We had security systems in place but like all security there is always a way of getting around it if you are clever and try hard enough. I appeared to be getting nowhere until one afternoon whilst I was walking through the kitchen having a look at what was happening, I was approached quietly by one of the women. "I hear you're looking for some meat" she said softly. "How do you know that?" I looked at her. "You know what it's like in this place. Word gets around. If I were you I'd look at the trolleys coming out of the cold kitchen." She walked away.

The cold kitchen or larder as it was sometimes called was the large chilled production area in which all cold food such as cold meats and salads was prepared and loaded into the trolleys destined for the aircraft. No raw food was allowed into that section due to the risk of cross contamination so there should be no reason to find any raw meat there.

To date my investigation had been based around the hot kitchen where all the meat was cooked as that seemed to be the most likely place to start looking for the missing joints. However, I hadn't anticipated the clever thinking of those involved in the meat scam. Everyone in the building knew that there were security cameras positioned in a number of strategic areas monitoring the movement of people, food, equipment and stores throughout the building and recording what was happening. Filled trolleys coming out of both the hot kitchen and the cold kitchen en route to the despatch bays for loading on to the trucks and hence to the aircraft were constantly under surveillance.

A look at the pictures of trolleys leaving the cold kitchen seemed to show nothing untoward but a count of the number being loaded on to some trucks told me that we were loading one or two more than the designated number for the flights in question. I advised our Security team and we planned our tactics.

A surreptitious check of trolleys being held in a cold room in the cold kitchen on a Saturday morning revealed two which were fully loaded with joints of raw beef. We marked them in an unobtrusive manner so as not to look different and then tracked them as they were transferred through the building and on to a truck which left the building on its way to deliver a catering load to an outbound flight.

The truck passed out of sight of the main building and was followed a few minutes later by a Security team. A short distance down the road they came upon the truck, stopped with a van parked close behind it and the two trolleys of meat in process of being transferred. Game over!

The clever part of the operation was to have ensured that the raw meat didn't follow the normal route from the butchery to the kitchen for cooking. Instead it was loaded into a trolley and transported a short distance down a back corridor which connected to a number of areas including the rear entrance to the cold kitchen. This corridor for some reason wasn't covered by a security camera. So whilst we were looking for cooked joints of meat being stolen, the thieves were actually stealing the raw product.

This was a small step in the saving of costs but larger savings were needed. Again it was one of the staff who came up with the answer. One of the constant complaints which the management team were faced with was that of staff saying "The managers never come down to see what is happening. You never see a manager on the floor." This I knew to be patently untrue as both Maurice and I regularly tried to make time to walk around the building and talk to the team although it was often difficult to find the time.

I always enjoyed walking through the building, watching what was happening and talking to the workforce. It was the only way by which I could learn what was going on in the production areas and also to gain the confidence of the workforce. Chatting with a couple of Chefs one morning one of them said "I don't understand why we don't have any yield controls in here. It's standard in most hotel kitchens."

"You'll have to explain that to me I'm afraid, since I'm not a Chef." "Well," he continued "It's pretty simple. When you are making up meals you need to know how many portions or items you get out of a box or packet or jar so that you know how many you need to order for a particular menu." I asked him to give me an example.

"Take a box of 6F size tomatoes. Each box should contain 100 tomatoes but you then need to know how many of those tomatoes will be usable. So you check a number of boxes over a period of time and count how many tomatoes there are in each and how many may be damaged. Say four are damaged on average so you finish up with 96 usable ones, then 96 is your yield on a box of 6F tomatoes. That means that if you are preparing a cold plate for the Club class menu and each plate has a half tomato on it, one box of tomatoes will provide enough for 192 plates."

It all seemed very clear. "So what happens at the moment?" "Well each Chef just tends to go to the stores and collect whatever he wants. That can lead to a lot of waste. He might only need a dozen tomatoes so he goes and collects a box and whatever is left over gets put in the cold room and may be used later or may just get forgotten about and go to waste."

There was no doubt that this needed to change so a team of trainee Chefs was put together under the leadership of one of the Senior Chefs and they began to work out the yields of everything that we used. It took weeks of concentrated work checking everything and anything.

Once the work had been completed the stores were placed under the control of an ordering and issuing team and were closed to the vagaries of Chefs who now had to order correct quantities for their menus. It worked well and the cost of waste dropped dramatically.

Another area of waste which I came across related to the purchase of "sundries." I was working through the accounts for the past year when I found an item labelled "sundries" which totalled £10,000. I called one of the Chefs into my office. "What are sundries?" He looked at me as if I were mad. "Well they're all the small things." "Such as?" I pursued the question. "Well things like paper hats, stirring spoons, knives... those sorts of things." I was stunned. "You mean we can spend £10,000 a year on Chef's paper hats and wooden spoons!! Who signs for them?" "Anybody" came the reply. "Anybody?" I was incredulous. "Yes, just about. All the Chefs can sign for whatever they want." Another hole down which money was being poured was quickly closed.

Saving money was one thing but keeping up or improving the quality of the food was something else. I hadn't been in the job for very long before I was faced with a number of complaints about the quality, or lack of quality, to be more correct of the soup provided on some of our First Class menus. Customers were complaining that it was too salty.

The soup was prepared daily in the flight kitchen and sent chilled to the aircraft in waxed cardboard cartons. It was then heated and served on board. Following up on the complaint I went down to the hot kitchen in the afternoon to discuss it with Peter Gray, one of our Senior Chefs, or Tubby as he was affectionately known to all his colleagues. "Just take me through the procedure Peter."

"It's very simple" he said. "We make the soup fresh every morning and then it's put into this large heated storage container from which it's dispensed into cartons as it's needed for each flight. It then goes to the despatch cold holding room where the flight is made up for despatch to the aircraft."

"Let me get this right." I went through the procedure again. "So the soup basically is made up in the morning and then stays heated through the day until used. There's nothing added during the day?" "No" came the quick reply. "We only need to make one batch each day"

"Does anybody taste it?" "Oh yes. Whoever makes it up in the morning will taste it before it is put into the heated holding container."

"And what about the rest of the day?" Peter looked a bit nonplussed. "I'm not with you?" "Well surely if it's in a heated container all day it will be reduced by evaporation, not to mention the fact that it's also being reduced in quantity by being portioned out to flights. Surely that will increase the salt level in it through the day? That means that all the later departures will have a much higher salt content in their soup."

"I see what you mean." Tubby looked a bit disappointed. "I don't know why we've never had complaints before since we've always done it this way." "Time for a change though" I said.

The incident raised a question in my mind as to how much of the food was being checked before it left the building. I queried it and found out that it was a bit erratic. Some Chefs tasted products as they were made whilst others just accepted that it would be all right if they were following the recipe. A recipe for disaster I thought to myself.

Given that the kitchen produced more than 25,000 meals per day it was effectively a factory. The quantities of food used weekly were enormous. For example, we used eleven tons of salmon in our various menus each week. The fact that the job was very routine every day for each of the workers made it more difficult to maintain the high levels of quality expected by the customer.

It's difficult when looking at eleven tons of salmon in a week to remember that this is someone's meal that you are producing. Even more so when you think that the type of food being produced was not that which would normally be eaten by many of the employees.

Having seen the need, I decided to introduce a tasting panel which would meet on a weekly basis to taste at random some of the products which we were making. I didn't want a panel made up of professional Chefs so I introduced a number of people from various areas in the building. People such as storekeepers, despatch staff and secretaries. People who weren't working directly with the food and had no professional food knowledge.

Our first meeting was held in an office on a Friday morning. A selection of food items both hot and cold and from all cabins on the aircraft was brought in to sample. Each taster had a sheet of paper and was asked to comment on the visual appearance of the food, its taste and texture, marking each section out of a possible ten points with ten being excellent and one being bad.

I realised that I had got it wrong when we came to a breakfast which had been produced for the Concorde service to New York. All of the food had been brought to the table in the dishes in which it was being served on the aircraft. This immediately made it easy to identify whether it was an Economy meal, a Club Class meal etc.

My tasters tried a Concorde breakfast. "What do you think?" I asked. "Very nice" came the less than convincing reply. I looked at them. "Are you sure?" They looked at each other. "Let me put it another way. If you had spent £10,000 on buying your ticket and you were presented with this as your breakfast would you be impressed? Let's be honest about this."

There was a bit of uncomfortable looking away from me for a minute and then one of the girls spoke up. "It's pretty grim." "Thanks, would you like to explain why you think that?" She began to get her confidence. "Yes, the colour is all wrong. The scrambled egg looks greyish green to me" and suddenly the serious discussion began. "You were influenced by the fact that as it was on a Concorde dish it should be good?" "Yes" was the answer from all of them.

At the next tasting session all of the dishes were decanted on to unmarked plates so that there was no telling which class they were destined for on the aircraft. The discussions became quite animated and once the Chefs realised that the sessions weren't aimed at picking on them, they also began to contribute very positively to the meetings and so became very productive.

Areas outside the food production also gave me problems. The equipment washing area at the rear of the building had always been difficult as I've mentioned previously. It was one of the largest washing units in the world containing five parallel washing lines each equipped with a huge "five tank" washing machine so named because they contained five major washing, rinsing and drying areas.

All the food handling equipment from the aircraft was washed, including the trolleys in which the trays of food were stored on board the aircraft and some eighty-five tons of cutlery, crockery, containers etc. passed through the unit every day. It was an industrial work site of the very worst imaginable.

The waste food being stripped off the incoming passenger trays produced a smell and the noise was incessant. I could never understand how people were happy to work in the area but many of them were long term residents. Those working on the stripping belts were faced with a ton of waste food to be scraped off the plates every day. Others had a day of hard labour, pushing and pulling the heavy trolleys around.

Many of the staff were from the Indian community and as a result the waste food water disposal flume was sometimes referred to by the workers as "the river Ganges." This wasn't meant as a derogatory term but as a joke between colleagues.

Any problem within the equipment wash section had knock on consequences. As fast as equipment was being washed at one end of the building, clean equipment was being filled with food and despatched at the other end. Although there were storage areas in which some excess equipment could be stored, the basic principle was to keep a balance between what came in and what was required to go out on the daily services.

To ensure that the outstations which had to cater the return flight always had the correct amount of equipment, each aircraft had to depart with a full set, even when the out bound plane wasn't full of passengers. For example, an outbound 747 aircraft to Miami with only 275 passengers on board still had to have a full set of equipment as the return flight may have 358 booked passengers and so on. As a result, all the crockery, cutlery etc. had to be counted and packed into units for the outbound services. It was the bane of our lives.

Not only was food supplied to the aircraft but there were also trolleys full of drinks, plus sundry items such as bottles of sauce, baby foods, mustard, rubber gloves, washing up liquid for use by crew on board, tea towels etc. The list was endless. Given the numbers involved it wasn't surprising when sometimes items were missed but any lack of equipment would result in a complaint being received from an irate crew member.

I was sitting in my office early one morning when the door flew open and the girl responsible for the dry stores packing area stormed in. She was waving a yellow sheet of paper indicating that this was a crew complaint. "I've had enough of these bloody people." She was virtually screaming at me. "Let's have a look." I held out my hand and took the sheet from her. It was a typical complaint.

"Once again we have no oven gloves in First Class. When will those idiots in catering get it right? This is the second flight out of London this month that I've had to work with no gloves. It's not good enough!!" The crew member had obviously been as irate when she wrote the complaint as the young woman standing in front of me was.

The team leader continued "We pack 2,600 items on each flight every day and she complains when we miss one!!" "OK I understand. Sit down and let's discuss this. Would you like a coffee?" She sat down.

"I can see why you're annoyed, given the number of items that your team pack every day but look at it from the Stewardess's point of view. I don't suppose you've travelled in First Class?" She shook her head. "Well the problem with the oven gloves is this." I began to explain.

"First Class provides silver service to the customers. This means that hot food such as the meat has to be rotated through the ovens very quickly throughout the meal service so the crew are constantly reaching in and out of the hot ovens to put in and take out food. If they haven't got any oven gloves they stand a very high risk of burning their hand or arms. Do you understand?" She nodded.

"Given that the woman who wrote this had probably just burnt her arm on the door of a very hot oven you can imagine what she was thinking and feeling? Hence the vitriolic note. Bear in mind that it's unlikely that she's ever been in this building and she has no idea as to what you and your team have to do. She doesn't realise just how much work goes in to putting the flight together. It's easy to think that it's only one small mistake by your team, one item out of several thousand that you put together for each flight, but the crew member doesn't care how many other flights you got right. As far as she is concerned you got it wrong and she suffered as a result. So what should we do?"

She looked at me blankly. "Well why don't you reply to her, apologise for the missing gloves and invite her and perhaps a couple of friends to come to the flight kitchen to see what you do? She might not come but at least it's worth a try."

And so we started a series of visits to the kitchen by interested members of crew. It was successful in part. All of those who visited were impressed by the size of the operation and could understand the difficulties that we faced.

However, they were only the tip of a very large iceberg and we could only hope that they would pass on some of the information they had received to their colleagues.

CHAPTER 52

CAN I GROW IT FOR YOU?

The size of the in-flight services operation was something which even many people working in the airline didn't comprehend although some in the outside world were very aware, particularly of the opportunities that it might offer.

One afternoon my secretary Jane popped her head around the door. "I've got a man in the office who says he's from the Australian Meat Corporation and would like to speak to you. He hasn't got an appointment so would you like me to send him away?"

I looked at my diary. "I've got a spare 20 minutes or so, so you can show him in." A few minutes later a young well-dressed Australian male was standing in front of me. "Sorry for the intrusion but I was in the area and just took a chance to call in." "Have a seat" I proffered my hand and he shook it and sat down in front of my desk. "I'll get straight to the point. Do you guys use beef?" "Yes" I replied. "Well we can grow it for you" was his immediate response. "What do you need? Three months, six months, twelve months old, whatever it is we can supply it." I was surprised but intrigued. I hadn't really thought of our beef supply in terms of growing it specially for us.

He carried on to explain exactly what he did and where his company could help British Airways. Having listened to the spiel I broke in. "Sorry but I'm not the person you need to talk to. Yes, we do use beef but it's purchased via the BA Procurement Division so you'll have to talk to them." He was disappointed but felt better when I gave him the names of the people to whom he had to speak.

The Procurement Division had a massive job when it came to purchasing. They bought everything that the airline required for its operation including the major requirements of flight catering. Given the numbers of passengers carried each year the catering operation had to be run with almost military precision if all flights were to be correctly catered.

My encounter with the Australian only increased my understanding of what was needed on a daily basis and the volumes and numbers were staggering. For example, when a decision was made by our menu planners to put fillet of lamb on our business class services across the North Atlantic for one quarter in a year, it meant that since lamb fillet is very small, some 360,000 lambs had to be sacrificed to provide the quantity needed. Needless to say, our New Zealand suppliers were only too pleased to provide for us.

Before anyone gets too excited about those poor little lambs you have to consider that the provision of meat was and still is a major part of the New Zealand economy and our portion of the lamb was only a very small part, with the remainder such as leg of lamb etc. no doubt going to other companies elsewhere.

New Zealand was also the provider of some of the wine required for the airline. Once again the volumes required for service across our route network were immense. So much so that the airline had appointed a wine manager, Peter Nixson to ensure supplies a job which meant continual tasting of wines from across the world and negotiation with suppliers to get the best deals possible.

The world's airlines are major purchasers of wine, second only to the largest supermarkets and in order to provide the quality of wine expected by our discerning customers, particularly those in the premium cabins, the airline, having selected a wine, would have to purchase the entire vintage to ensure a continued supply throughout a menu cycle. This could often raise problems where smaller vineyards were concerned and some in New Zealand were typical examples.

Many years ago on an early visit to a possible new supplier in New Zealand, Peter tasted a blended Chardonnay which he thought would be ideal for British Airways' European routes but it needed to be supplied in small bottles. This posed serious difficulties. The New Zealand wine trade was still in its relatively early days and the vineyard owner explained that they couldn't supply in small bottles as these weren't available.

"That's a pity" Peter explained. "We would have liked to buy the entire vintage." "The entire vintage?" "Yes." At this, the vineyard owner's immediate response was "Leave it with me for a few days and I'll see what I can do." A couple of days later he called to confirm that he had bought a bottling plant with which he would be able to provide exactly what BA needed. This was the start of a long and happy relationship which continues to this day.

The staggering part of the story however was not that the owner of the vineyard bought a bottling plant but that the purchase of the entire vintage at that time was reputed to have been something in the region of 32% of New Zealand's wine exports to the UK for that year. It's a story which I heard from Peter and although I wasn't there myself to verify it I don't disbelieve it.

Whilst large numbers of passengers are regular business travellers, the majority of people only fly when going on holiday so have little thought as to how much food and drink has to be purchased to satisfy their needs.

When a launch event was held in London to introduce the new BA Club Class many of our regular passengers were invited. As part of the show there was a display of wines which were to be offered on the new service. Included in this were some English wines which had been added as a show piece to indicate how the quality of English wines was improving.

Samples were being offered and as I was looking at them I overheard one of our invited passengers remark to one of the team standing behind the display "It's a shame that we don't get English wine served on board. Why don't you use it?"

"Unfortunately our English vineyards are small and they don't produce enough for us to be able to use. If you take this particular one," the team member pointed to a small range of bottles on the table, "the vineyard in question would only produce sufficient wine for us to supply all aircraft out bound from London until around midday on day one of our new product."

The customer looked surprised. "They produce so little?" "Well it's a combination. They produce a limited amount and we need very large volumes."

Having said this, the airline supplies some very good wines to its customers and over the later years of my career I was privileged to be able to taste and get an understanding of many of them. Even those served in Economy Class were of decent quality whilst those in the First Class cabin on long haul flights were good by most standards. Chateaux Lynch Bages, Talbot, Leoville-Barton, Cantanac Brown, Puligny-Montrachet, Meursault etc. were only a few of the many great names which graced BA menus.

My tenure at the Flight Kitchen was to be relatively short. As a senior manager I was invited to attend the monthly meeting with Mike Street the Head of Catering where all aspects of the work were discussed and future strategy was planned.

At my first meeting one of the items on the agenda was the sale of the catering operation. This was no surprise as rumours had been circulating within the airline for some time. The history of flight catering was one of airlines being set up in their home country and in order to feed their passengers having to provide some form of catering from their home base airport. Flight kitchens owned and operated by airlines therefore sprang up across the world with each airline catering for its visiting competitors at its home base whilst relying on them for catering when away from home.

Over the years there had been some consolidation and a few companies whose main business was airline catering were slowly taking over across the world. As a result, although we were operating the largest flight kitchen in the world at that time, we were unable to compete on price with larger companies who operated more kitchens and we couldn't attract profitable business to ours as we couldn't cater other airlines over a range of destinations. And so at the very first of many regular management meetings chaired by the Head of Catering which I attended, I found myself listening to the early death throes of my job. A plan was being drawn up by which British Airways would divest itself of its flight catering. The end was going to be inevitable.

What I also realised was that I didn't want to be there when the catering unit was sold. This would be disastrous insofar as when the business was sold I would be sold along with it or made redundant!! These were the rules governing the transfer of a working business.

I can't say that I enjoyed my two years in-flight catering but it taught me a lot. It was with a sigh of relief however when I changed jobs in early 1992, shortly before the flight kitchen was sold and I found myself back in Medical Services but this time as Head of the Hygiene department.

CHAPTER 53

BACK TO THE FUTURE

Things had changed. Not only had my old boss Peter retired but there was also a new Director who had put his own stamp on things by changing Medical Services into Health Services, a title more in keeping with the departmental role in Occupational Health rather than medicine.

He and I had not met prior to my re-joining as a senior Manager, but a meeting had been arranged to decide what I was going to be doing. Up until then the Hygiene Branch had reported to the Director through one of the senior Doctors. Jim was a decent enough Scotsman and no doubt saw my return as the position remaining the same, in that I would report to him and he in turn would report to the Director. I with my two years' experience in a senior post didn't see it like that and fortunately neither did the Director. I turned up at his office to find that Jim was delayed but Mike Davies the Director, wasn't prepared to wait.

"Do you know what you're taking on?" "No I've been told very little." "OK. Well obviously the Hygiene Service is yours and you know all about that. However, that isn't enough to justify your Senior Manger status so I'm going to add the BA Travel Clinics to your remit. You know about them?" "Well I know of them and no doubt I can catch up fairly quickly" I replied.

The Travel Clinics were something which Mike Davies had brought with him as an idea when he had joined British Airways. Operating under the BA Brand and from clinics within BA offices in London they provided a travel service of advice and vaccinations for people travelling abroad.

"In addition I want you to open a BA Optician's franchise here at Heathrow. All the details have been arranged already and work is underway to get premises up and running. We have a lot of staff many of whom would benefit from having an optician close to hand. On top of that we need someone to oversee the Administration here so I want you to take that on as well." The first two sounded OK but Admin.? I really didn't like the sound of that but it wasn't worth having a discussion about it at this point.

It was a bit of a change and not all of it for the better. Trying to run all four sections proved to be a real problem. My main focus had to be on the food safety and environmental health since this affected the airline as a whole and the safety of passengers and crew was a prime responsibility. The travel clinics and the optician were the brain child of the Director so needed to be carefully nurtured since he perceived them to be a money maker which would bolster his departmental budget.

Last but not least was the administration. On the surface the women and men who provided all the administrative functions which kept the department running were a quiet, sensible bunch of people who worked hard at their jobs and in truth this was the case. Under the placid facade however lurked the myriad of petty squabbles and disagreements such as besets all work places once the surface is scratched. "I won't work with her because..." "He won't do this and why should I..." "I don't like them so why should I share an office with them?" "Why do they get paid more than I do?" etc. etc. The administration team individually were fine but put them together and all sorts of problems arose.

My hygiene team was short staffed with only three of us expected to oversee some 270 stations worldwide. To add to that one of my previous colleagues wasn't best pleased that I had been brought back to head the section when he had every expectation of getting the top job himself.

He was a great guy in many respects, was reputedly a member of MENSA, the club for those people with above average intelligence, but had a propensity to take days off work for a variety of sometimes implausible reasons. On one "sick" day off he had been seen passing through the airport terminal obviously en route to somewhere else and was apparently well enough to have been at work.

During my previous stay in the Hygiene team one of our colleagues who worked in an adjacent office had written on the noticeboard in the general office, "Twenty-two reasons why I am not at work today" which included such things as "the cat has fallen down a manhole; my car has been stolen and I have to go to the police station; my car has been found

312

and I have to go to the police station; and of course the old favourite my Granny has died."

It provided great amusement on the day, primarily because many of the reasons listed had been used. My predecessor had lived with it but I wasn't prepared to do the same so as quickly as possible I arranged a meeting in my office to discuss the situation and lay down the ground rules.

"I know that you'll be disappointed at having me back as Head of Department as I'm sure you would have hoped to have been given the job yourself but I hope that we can work well together. I have a great regard for your ability in the field work which you do and the good things that you've brought to the team since you joined."

He sat and listened quietly and I carried on. "I'm aware of your record of sick days and I'm also aware that on at least one occasion when you called in sick you were seen leaving the airport to travel somewhere else for a reason not related to your job. I'm quite prepared to start our new working relationship with a clean slate but let me make it perfectly clear that if I ever have any reason to believe that you are taking time off for anything other than valid purposes I will come down on you like a ton of bricks. I'm not prepared to lose my job because you've been up to something stupid. Do you understand? Now is there anything that you would like to say?"

He smiled at me. "No, I think you've made it very clear" "Good, so let's get on with doing a good job." Six weeks later he handed in his resignation. I was genuinely sorry to see him go because he was really good at the job when he put his mind to it and could be a great asset to the department.

The administration was also to prove problematical from day one. I had inherited two women each of whom had specific problems. The second was to come to light a year or two into the job but the first had to be dealt with right at the beginning of my tenure. A young woman who had difficulty in working with people who were not of Anglo Saxon origin and had raised an unsavoury issue when faced with a new recruit to the office. Although it had happened prior to my appointment I knew that it was an issue that I would have to deal with so I invited the woman concerned to come to my office where I laid down my ground rules in no uncertain terms.

Having listened me she began a tirade, trying to justify her actions, adding that I couldn't do this to her. I held up my hand to stop her. "Let me just remind you. In the last two years I've been dealing with a bunch of loader drivers in Catering Operations and compared to them you're a pussy cat so don't think that I'll be frightened off by your bravado. Do I make myself understood?"

She looked at me and for a moment I thought that she was going to start again however common sense took over and she nodded her head. I couldn't say that we became friends but her attitude towards me changed perceptibly and she caused me no further major problems.

The second woman was completely different. A senior secretary to one of the doctors she had worked in the department for many years and was well thought of. I had no expectation of any trouble from her and in fact I didn't realise that there were issues with her for some little while.

Given that I had to travel frequently as part of my job I had to delegate my administrative responsibilities during my absences to David, our Health Services statistician, to whom I always gave a briefing before I left and generally thought that I was leaving a reasonably stable situation and he would have no problems.

However late in the afternoon on one occasion this woman had become argumentative, loud and somewhat stroppy. I had seen no evidence of this behaviour whilst I had been in the office and in fact I was on fairly amicable terms with the woman.

A few months later when I was away again, I came back to find David very stressed as he had been unable to control the woman the previous evening when in his words he had come across her stumbling down the corridor bouncing off the walls and in his view somewhat the worse for wear through alcohol.

I had a word with her and of course she denied there being any problem. I was aware however that she and her husband had separated some little while previously and suspected that this could be at the root of any problem.

A few quiet words with some of the other secretaries raised my suspicions further as more than one of them suggested that a bottle of alcohol was secreted in a drawer in her desk and she gradually drank her way through it during the day. As I had rarely seen her when she was leaving the building after work and the Doctor for whom she was working had made no complaints I had no idea that she might often have been somewhat under the influence when going home.

The problem needed resolution via the Director and led to counselling for the secretary and then to early retirement on ill health grounds. Sad to say she never really recovered and was to pass away after only a very few years. A shame because she was a really nice woman underneath all her problems

As it was I was disappointed in that I had succeeded in annoying one of my colleagues by leaving him with a problem on each occasion that I had gone overseas on company business. The fact that I had no knowledge of the woman's problem as she never exhibited it in front of me wasn't good enough.

CHAPTER 54

FUN WITH FRANCHISES

Through the nineteen eighties the airline industry began to change rapidly. National airlines such as British Airways, which had been Government owned and therefore had their losses subsidised by the tax payer were sold into private hands and had to become cost effective.

Stand-alone airlines were too small to gain the benefits of scale and so began a round of consolidation and route sharing which eventually resulted in the formation of liaisons such as the One World group and the Star Alliance.

British Airways, whilst leading the One World group also embarked on setting up a series of franchises where small independent airlines, mainly in Europe, were encouraged to operate services on behalf of BA.

Utilising small aircraft, flying in British Airways colours and supported by BA sales and marketing they operated into airports in regional areas where passenger loads wouldn't have been large enough to have been profitable for larger BA aircraft but were instrumental in feeding passengers into the BA network.

These operations, some of which proved very successful, provided more challenges for me and my team. Although generally small, the franchise airlines were expected to provide a service which matched the normal BA standard. Their aircraft flew in British Airways colours, their crew wore BA uniforms and the flights carried BA flight numbers so to all intent they were British Airways and passengers expected the same level of service as they were used to receiving on the mainline services. They expected to be offered a food and beverage service even if the flight was relatively short. This in turn meant that the service had to be vetted to ensure that food safety standards were being maintained.

As a result, I was to visit a number of unusual and interesting airlines and places, sometimes with amusing consequences.

My first sortie was into Germany. Following the ending of the 1939-1945 war and the partition of the country into East and West the Germans were not allowed to operate their own airline within Germany. In order to provide a domestic airline service within West Germany, the British Government along with the French and Americans, had set up an internal German airline whose services were operated independently by British European Airways, Air France and Pan American Airways and were totally separate from their other airline operations. In the case of BEA, the flights were operated using British pilots seconded to the German service and backed up by German nationals as cabin crew and support staff.

The reunification of Germany in 1990 brought about an almost instant change. The Internal German Service as it had always been known in BA was now redundant as Germany could now be served by its own airlines.

At the time, British Airways had a small fleet of dedicated aircraft and a large number of German staff who had been operating the Internal Service for many years. Rather than making them redundant BA saw an opportunity. Looking around they quickly found a small German commuter airline called Delta Air, based in Friedrichshafen and operating local services. They bought it and renamed it Deutsche BA.

Their facilities had to be audited so one Monday evening in late Autumn I flew from Frankfurt to Friedrichshafen on a Lufthansa twin-engined Fokker F27 accompanied by a number of German business men returning from a day's work. The aircraft laboured through a darkening sky and landed around 7.00pm. Coming down the short set of steps at the front of the aircraft I arrived just a few feet from a small airport terminal building. I looked around, expecting to see someone waiting for me but amongst the melee of disembarking passengers and staff beginning the aircraft turn round procedure I couldn't see anyone who was obviously looking for me.

I walked into the airport building carrying my overnight bag. There was a small carousel around which were a few people waiting for their luggage to be delivered but the majority of the business men, like me, only had hand luggage. There were no airport staff visible so I moved to the door and walking through it found myself unexpectedly in the street outside. This wasn't a large airport terminal. Numerous men were hurrying away into the dark either towards the car park or to waiting cars where wives had come to pick them up.

I took a few paces along the building and walked through the door marked departures. It was a small but busy area with last minute passengers for the final flight to Frankfurt being marshalled at the departure gate. A young woman in airline uniform stood behind a desk next to the window. I walked across and introduced myself. "Ah, yes Mr Kelly. The manager apologises. He can't be here this evening but will meet you at your hotel at 08.30 in the morning. Do you know which hotel you are staying in?" "Yes thanks." "OK" She looked out of the window. "The taxi has gone so I'll just make a call and get him to come back."

The taxi, singular. I smiled to myself. This must be a really small place. In a few minutes the taxi returned and a short drive later I was in a town centre hotel. Clean, comfortable but very quiet, I had the feeling that I was the only person staying there. Later when I went for a short walk, I felt that I was alone in the town since it appeared to be deserted. There were no people and no traffic. I could have lain down in the road and nothing would have run over me.

The following day however I awoke to find that I was in a beautiful little city on the banks of Lake Constance close to the border with Austria and Switzerland and surrounded by lovely countryside. The town's claim to fame was that it had been the headquarters of the Zeppelin Company and later became an important aircraft manufacturing centre.

This in turn had made it a target for the RAF during World War 2 and somewhat to my embarrassment on this particular day when I was meeting some German colleagues for the first time, the local newspaper was announcing the recovery of a British Lancaster bomber which had crashed into the lake just a short distance from the town centre. To the great credit of my colleagues they didn't mention it.

Deutsche BA was the proud owner of a small but neat flight kitchen which was a pleasure to visit. Unfortunately however, like a number of these initial ventures by BA to expand and consolidate within Europe the venture was doomed to failure and was sold a few years later.

Deutsche BA was followed later by a foray into France in 1997 when BA bought two airlines, Touraine Air Transport, (TAT) and Air Liberte. The merged airlines were based in Orly airport in Paris and operated an internal French network linking a number of major towns and cities.

Once again the new airline was expected to comply with BA standards and so one morning I made my way to Orly airport to meet the Catering manager of the new airline. Stephan, a smart young French man, welcomed me to his office and we soon got down to business. "I've come to have a look at your catering facilities." He looked a bit bemused. "That's not a problem. Come with me."

We walked down the stairs, out of the building and along the concrete apron, eventually coming to what appeared to be an engineering storage hangar. Stepping inside Stephan walked towards a set of shelves. He reached into a large box and taking out a package handed it to me. "Here you are."

I looked at the package. It was shrink wrapped and contained a small bottle of orange juice along with what appeared to be a small sticky bun. I read the label on the outer wrapper. The contents were what we in the food safety profession call a "shelf stable long life" product. In other words, it wouldn't support the growth of bacteria, didn't need to be held in refrigeration and would last for a very long time.

This at least was a positive point. In all other respects the product was not one which would normally have graced a British Airways flight. "What meal is this used for?" I queried. Stephan looked at me with a smile. "Well if it's eight o'clock in the morning it's breakfast, if it's one o'clock in the afternoon it's lunch and if it's seven o'clock in the evening it's dinner." I was stunned. This was all that they had. "Do you have any alternatives and how often do you change it?" "No, there are no alternatives, this is it and we don't change it." Stephan replied. He seemed somewhat surprised that I should consider that a change in the passenger offering should be considered. At least from my point of view it was safe.

SunAir of Scandinavia was a totally different type of airline. A privately owned company set up in 1978 by Neils Sundberg it operated commuter flights from its home base in Billund, Denmark to other Danish towns and to Norway and Sweden using small twin-engined turbo prop aircraft. It became a British Airways franchise in 1996 and as with all such operations I had to go and have a look at what they were doing.

Billund wasn't an easy place to get to but having contacted Kristian Tvergaard, the Commercial Director at the airline he suggested that he would meet me at Aarhus airport on a Monday morning at 9.30. Aarhus could be reached by direct flight from Copenhagen but the timing of our meeting meant that I had to fly from London on Sunday afternoon, catch a connecting flight from Copenhagen to Aarhus and stay overnight at a hotel near the airport.

It followed that on Sunday evening, having arrived from London at 4.30pm and walked across from International Arrivals, I was sitting in the somewhat small domestic departure area at Copenhagen airport with little better to do than look at the airport operation through the window. The building was single storey and whilst functional, appeared to be almost of a temporary nature.

Being a Sunday, it wasn't very busy but I watched as a few small turbo prop aircraft destined for local airports, slowly filled their passenger complement before lazily disappearing into the bright evening sunshine. I was somewhat surprised however when around 6.30pm a McDonnell Douglas twin-engined jet was towed into sight from around the corner. I wondered casually where it might be going. My flight was due to depart at 7.30pm and knowing that it was a short flight I was expecting to be departing on one of the small propeller driven aircraft that I had been watching. By seven o'clock the gate area had become more crowded and suddenly the flight to Aarhus was called.

As I got up to head for the gate I realised to my great surprise that the passengers were being directed to the large jet aircraft. Not only that but they appeared to be using the aircraft as a local bus service given the assortment of hand baggage that they were carrying. One lady dressed very elegantly was accompanied by a small lapdog on a lead. On boarding the aircraft, I found to my surprise that it was almost totally full and was amused to see the small dog placed carefully on the floor under the seat in front of its owner.

I took my place by a window and listened as the Captain introduced himself. "Welcome on board this SAS flight from Copenhagen to Aarhus. Our flight time will be 17 minutes." Seventeen minutes! I couldn't believe my ears. I have to admit that I hadn't looked too closely at Aarhus on the map at home before leaving so although I knew roughly where it was I hadn't thought too much about the distance. Seventeen minutes! It's hardly long enough to get airborne and it can't be financially viable to use a jet aircraft for such a short distance.

I was still thinking about it as the aircraft roared into the clear blue sky and turned away from Copenhagen. We were hardly off the ground before a flight attendant appeared beside my seat. She had an armful of small packages and was literally throwing one into each passenger's lap. I took mine and opened it. It was a cup sealed in a wrapper. Inside the cup was sugar, milk and a small biscuit. I had hardly got the lid off the cup when a second flight attendant appeared beside the row of seats. "Coffee?" It wasn't so much a question as an order. I proffered my cup and it was instantly filled. She moved rapidly forward, dispensing her coffee with practised speed.

I was barely half way down the cup of scalding hot coffee, I drink it without milk which can prove to be a disadvantage, when I became aware of another flight attendant rapidly making her way up the aircraft aisle with a large black polythene bag into which she was throwing the remains of the coffee service as she grabbed it from the tables in front of the passengers. "You have to be pretty quick on this one" I thought to myself as I quickly drained my cup. Within seconds the aircraft engines wound down and we began a steep descent into Aarhus. It was all over in minutes. What an experience, I thought, as I left the aircraft to a chorus of "Thank you" from the crew lined up at the door.

Aarhus airport was built by the Germans during the 1939-45 war and is some twenty-eight miles from the city so as I had to be at the airport in the morning I stayed overnight at Ebeltoft, a small seaside town which was somewhat closer. The following morning I made my way back to the airport and duly presented myself to the young woman behind the Sun Air check in desk. "Ah Mr. Kelly, nice to meet you. Welcome to Denmark. Kristian is on his way and will be landing here shortly. If you would like to come into the office? Perhaps you would like a coffee?"

It was all very civilised and I sat down to wait. I didn't have very long. The door opened and a young man entered, hand outstretched. "Mr. Kelly? Nice to meet you. I'm Kristian." "Hi I'm Mike" I responded. "I believe you want to see all our catering uplifts is that correct?" He was quite formal but in a pleasant manner.

"Yes" and I began to explain to him. "I know that you are a small operation but now that you're flying as British Airways I need to be sure that any food uplifts that you're picking up are safe and are being properly handled." "That's fine. I've spoken to all our caterers and they will be happy to meet you. I've arranged that we fly to the smaller stations today and we will visit Billund tomorrow where SAS Service Partner caters for us. If you're ready, we can get started?"

"That's fine with me." I picked up my bag and we walked outside. I wasn't quite sure where we were off to but I followed Kristian. However, I was more than a little surprised when we left the building and walked out on to the aircraft apron.

There in front of us stood a single-engined small passenger aircraft sporting the original Sun Air red and black logo on the tail. As we reached it Kristian turned to me and smiled. "OK, you're in the right hand seat. I thought it was easiest if I flew us into each of the stations. That way we'll get to all the small ones today and finish up this evening in Billund where I've booked you a room at one of the airport hotels for the night."

I grinned at him and thought to myself well this is a first. I've done thousands of audits in hundreds of places but never before have I arrived by personal aircraft.

We climbed aboard and I sat in the right seat as told. "You've been on the flight deck before?" Kristian looked expectantly at me. "Yes, I've often been grateful for a seat on the flight deck when the aircraft has been full so I've covered quite a few miles up the front and I've also personally flown a small aircraft on one occasion."

"Great, so you'll understand a bit about it then. Put on the headset." I complied quickly. "Here's the map." He leaned across and set a reasonably large scale map of Denmark in front of me. "This where we are and this is where we are going to." He pointed to the map. I obviously knew where we were starting from but he was now pointing to a small town to the North West. "You can navigate." He grinned at me. "You'll find this a much different experience to the flight deck on a BA aircraft, for a start it's much easier to see an airfield when you're at 30,000 feet than it is when you are somewhere below 10,000."

Settling down into the Captain's seat on the left he began to go through all the procedures necessary prior to take off. He's obviously filed a flight plan sometime earlier I though as I listened to him contacting the control tower, asking for permission to start the engine and taxi. Clearance was given. A short taxi to the runway and within a few moments we climbed rapidly into a clear blue sky.

It was a beautiful September day and as we climbed the view became spectacular. We flew West to Skive for our first audit then North to Thisted and on to Aalborg, the largest and most Northerly of the places we were to visit before ending the day by flying South to Billund, the Headquarters not only of Sun Air, but more importantly to many children in the world, also the Headquarters of Lego.

The airfields were small but catered for relatively large regional areas with Sun Air providing an important link between towns not only in Denmark but also in nearby Sweden and Norway allowing people to travel across the area without always having to pass through Copenhagen in order to make connections. The Sun Air staff at each airport welcomed me warmly. The catering facilities were simple consisting mainly of the airport manager's wife making sandwiches, tea and coffee to order with last minute figures for the passenger numbers being delivered to her as the inbound aircraft arrived and the last passenger for the outbound flight checked in. As passenger numbers would normally not exceed a dozen people this wasn't difficult but it was all being carried out in a spirit of friendly co-operation and local banter, and there was of course a number of flights at each airport through the day.

With everything made freshly and the conditions in the small kitchens generally acceptable there was little cause for concern from my point of view.

Taking off from Thisted provided the only excitement of the journey. We were only about fifty feet off the ground when a sudden and unexpected down draught hit the aircraft and we lurched seriously downwards and to the left. "Whoa!" I heard Kristian exclaim as he expertly twitched the control column and regained control. "I wasn't expecting that. Are you OK?" he looked across at me. "Fine" I replied, quietly marvelling at the quick skills which he had applied to rectify the situation. It could have been a great deal worse I thought.

In the evening as we headed South towards Billund, Kristian took the opportunity to give me a bit of history about the airline. "Our owner Niels Sundberg lives up here in the North. He has his own landing strip by the house so that he can fly home in the evening after work. He has an automated landing light system on the runway which he can activate from the aircraft." "Marvellous what you can do when you own the Company" Kristian grinned at me.

Billund is the second busiest airport in Denmark and was originally built by the Lego Company, the makers of the world famous children's building blocks. As we left the aircraft which Kristian had parked outside the Sun Air building he pointed out the Lego theme park right across the street from his office. "There aren't many theme parks which have their own airport right outside the gate" he laughed.

The Sun Air head office was a modern, bright and cheerful building and Kristian took me on a tour of the facilities. "This is our main engineering base." He walked me through a hangar in which one aircraft was being stripped down whilst another stood waiting. A small Mitsubishi twin jet stood in a second hangar. "We use that for private charter work" he explained. "A Formula one racing driver at the moment" he carried on. Entering another area, I spotted a glider parked on one side. "Why the glider?" I asked. "We sometimes use it for a bit of fun on a quiet day, flying it out of the airport" Kristian replied. I was amused. "I can't quite see that happening at Heathrow airport."

The joys of working for a small Company were brought home to me again on a subsequent visit to Billund brought about by Sun Air opening a service which would connect Billund to Manchester. Once again I had to fly into Aarhus the previous day and stay overnight in a local hotel. Reporting at the desk at Aarhus airport at 09.30 the Sun Air receptionist welcomed me and said "You're being picked up and flown to Billund. The flight from Oslo to Billund is being diverted to land here and pick you up. It will be arriving in a few minutes so I'll take you out to meet it." Without further ado she walked briskly towards the door and a few moments later we were standing in the sunshine. "Here he comes." The young woman pointed towards the end of the runway where I could see the landing lights of a British Aerospace Jetstream approaching.

The aircraft landed and taxied up to us as we stood somewhat incongruously on the apron. The door opened and the flight attendant dropped the steps which were built into the aircraft door. She motioned me forward and I picked up my bag and climbed aboard. The Sun Air ground receptionist waved goodbye. The door closed behind me and the pilot looked over his shoulder from the open cockpit door. "Welcome on board" he smiled at me. As I took my seat I was aware of the other passengers looking at me curiously, probably wondering who this person was that had caused their normally nonstop flight from Oslo to Billund to be diverted to Aarhus to pick him up. Landing at Billund a very short time later the Captain called me to the flight deck as the other passengers were disembarking.

"I've just had a call from Kristian. He's operating the flight behind us and is just landing. He's asked you to stay here on the aircraft and he will drop by and pick you up." I then spent a few minutes talking with the Captain who was interested to know who I was and what I did before Kristian appeared in the aircraft door. "Hi Mike. Are you ready?" and off we went to the flight kitchen. An interesting experience but obviously the easiest way for Sun Air to handle the situation.

Not all the franchises set up by BA through the nineteen nineties were as successful as Sun Air which is still operating at the time of writing but all of those with which I came into contact were fun to work with or provided extraordinary experiences.

One small airline with which BA had a brief flirtation in the nineteen nineties was Air Exel which operated out of Eindhoven in the Netherlands, the headquarters of the Philips electronics company and therefore perceived to be a good business route.

Operating as British Airways, the flight from Heathrow Terminal 4 departed at 6.30am and on a cold, wet and extremely windy Monday morning I joined a collection of somewhat sleepy looking businessmen trudging across the wet tarmac at Terminal 4 towards a small twin-engined aircraft, the plane being too small and inconsequential to be boarded via an air jetty. Small enough in fact for me, when walking down the aircraft to my seat at the rear, to have to step over the metal spar which held the two wings together running at right angles across the aisle!

It was an ungodly time of the day to be going anywhere in mid-winter and to add to the early start I had suffered the not unusual problem of being placed on standby when checking in an hour earlier. Fortunately, at the last minute a seat had been found for me otherwise my already grim start to the working week would have become even more intolerable.

Having boarded the small aircraft, I realised from the chatter going on between some of the passengers that these were regular travellers on the route and surmised that they worked for the Philips Company and were weekly commuters. Rather them than me I thought if this is their regular Monday morning start.

Without much ado the doors were shut and the female Captain announced herself to the assembled mass on board and explained that our flight time would be short due to strong tailwinds. We took off into a slowly brightening sky and bounced our way through the low cloud which had enveloped Heathrow. The flight was short as forecast by the Captain and we barely had time to gulp down our breakfast coffee before the seat belt sign came on and the disembodied voice from the flight deck announced our impending landing.

What it didn't warn us was that the winds at Eindhoven were stronger than those which we had left behind in London. The aircraft pitched downwards and began a series of twists and turns, successively rising and falling through down draughts and up lifts which would have been spectacular had I been on a ride at a theme park. It was a definite white knuckle ride and I could see that even the most seasoned of passengers were gripping the arms of their seats as we corkscrewed down to the runway. I realised that the motion was being exaggerated somewhat by the small size of the aircraft but despite the plunging around I was enjoying it.

We landed and having taxied to our stand were disembarking through the forward door. The door to the flight deck was open and the Captain turned towards me as I passed and with a smile wished me a good morning. I realised that for her it had been a perfectly normal flight and she had probably not found the approach to the airfield particularly unusual.

It reminded me of a previous occasion a few years earlier when on a BA shuttle flight from Heathrow to Glasgow we had arrived on the tail of what had been a hurricane when it had left the American coastline but had deteriorated to a very strong storm by the time of its arrival in Scotland. Our departure had been delayed due to the strength of the winds but eventually it was deemed safe for us to fly and as we approached Glasgow airport I was enjoying the view of the Campsie fells when the Captain warned us that due to the strong winds our landing might be a bit bumpy.

A bit bumpy was an understatement as we rocked and rolled in our Boeing 757 towards the runway. Sitting by a window I could see the wing tips rising and falling through several feet as the pilot flying skilfully touched down on the concrete with a very solid thump. My fear as we approached the runway was that one of the more vicious twists would bring a wing tip into contact with the ground and we would cartwheel.

I could hear the sigh of relief from many passengers as we rolled down the runway. The Captain's reassuring voice came across the address system. "Well ladies and gentlemen, welcome to Glasgow and I hope that you enjoyed the landing every bit as much as we did here on the flight deck!"

In 1993 British Airways bought Brymon Airways, a small Regional airline operating services out of Plymouth to London. As with other BA Franchises it was operating in British Airways colours using Bombardier Dash 8 twin propeller aircraft. Full catering was being provided on the flights so I contacted my colleague Gerry at Alpha Flight Services at Gatwick and we agreed to travel to Plymouth on the first service out of London on the following Friday morning to carry out a joint audit.

It was a miserable, grey, wet day as we took off. Gerry and I were seated close to the rear of the plane which was to prove interesting as the breakfast service commenced. I glanced over my shoulder and watched as the stewardess took the breakfast omelettes out of the oven, carefully placed them on the work surface then tested the temperature by sticking her finger into one of them. Then she licked her finger. I felt a nudge from Gerry. "Did you see that?" I nodded. "Just as well none of the other passengers did?" I replied over the constant whine of the aircraft engines. "I'll have a word with the Chief Stewardess when we get there. She's meeting us off the flight I believe."

Breakfast was duly served as we trundled West. The meal was a standard BA bacon and egg breakfast and despite what we had seen, Gerry and I enjoyed it. However, the bad weather outside was causing the aircraft to corkscrew around quite a bit and this was having an effect on a few of the customers who weren't looking exactly at their best.

We had completed our meal when the stewardess came back to us and asked if we would like some more coffee. "Yes please" We spoke in unison. Gerry held out his cup. The girl had a large coffee pot in her hand and was balancing herself carefully as the plane rolled around. "Hold it over here" she indicated a space over the aisle. "I would prefer that you drink the coffee rather than wear it." She grinned as she matched the aircraft movement up and down to her pouring the coffee into the cup which Gerry was now holding at arms-length over the aisle.

She looked at both of us. "You've done this before. You've obviously got good stomachs as well since you're the only passengers who've enjoyed the breakfast and asked for more coffee. Do you fly this route often?" She looked expectantly at us. "No. This is a first for both of us but we fly regularly to a lot of other places" I replied.

At that moment the public address system burst into life with the news that we were shortly going to land so I didn't have to explain any more as to what Gerry and I were doing. The plane sank rapidly on to the runway and appeared to stop very quickly. Looking out of the window it seemed as though we had landed in the back gardens of some local houses as I could see fences, garden sheds and washing lines, all very close to the aircraft. A short taxi to the terminal and Gerry and I were quickly disembarked to be met by the Manager of the flight kitchen.

"Hi Gerry, nice to see you" he stuck his hand out first to Gerry and then me. "Nice to meet you Mike, I've heard a lot about you. Are you expecting anyone else to be here?" He looked at the two of us. "Well the Chief Stewardess of Brymon will probably show up later but I don't know when, however she can catch up with us." "OK. Just follow me."

We walked away from the aircraft and headed towards some hangars a short distance from the modern terminal building. It was a damp, grey day in Plymouth, just as it had been in London and as I looked around I could see that the airport was small and did indeed lie adjacent to some housing. The taxiway running towards the hangars ran down a slope and as we walked down the hill I saw what appeared to be two "Portacabins" sitting in the corner. As we approached them I could see the Alpha Flight catering logo on one of the doors.

"Well this is it" the manager said, looking at the both of us. "Come inside and see what we've got." Gerry looked at me then without saying a word stepped inside. The building was exactly what I had suspected at first sight. It was two lightweight temporary single storey buildings sitting side by side and bolted together at the middle.

Looking quickly at the structure I noted that the two units were jacked up off the ground but that the rear jacks seemed to be sinking and as a result the buildings were tilted slightly backwards. I was to find out later that this was beneficial. Stepping inside to join Gerry I passed through a small lobby which was crammed with equipment and entered the kitchen.

It was a single room with food preparation tables occupying the centre. Work benches lined one wall whilst on the other stood a sink unit which whilst used for food washing also had a small dish washing machine fixed on to the adjacent drainer, with a hosepipe discharging its waste water into the sink.

A small wash hand basin stood nearby but was what I always referred to as "the legal minimum." It was there because food safety legislation required there to be one, but it was actually far too small to be of any practical use in a production kitchen. The average worker couldn't have got their hands into it.

The room was cramped to say the least. It was almost impossible for two people to pass in the space between the centre tables and the outer walls, but from my point of view the saving grace was that the menu for the flights was fairly simple and given the lack of storage space the food couldn't be prepared too far in advance of the flight for which it was destined.

Walking back towards the centre lobby between the two sections of the building the manager pointed out the refrigeration. It was working well enough but like everything else it had to be small enough to fit into the space available. "The equipment storage is through here." He pointed into the second half of the unit and we looked into a room crammed with galley and kitchen equipment. "Mind your feet, it gets a bit wet, we have a leak in the roof" he continued. Looking up I could see the signs of water penetration. I followed the marks down the wall and could see where the water ran across the floor, but this was where the tilt of the building from front to back came into its own. It allowed the rainwater to flow neatly to the rear wall where a hole had been drilled into the back wall to allow the water to escape, thus preventing any flooding. "Neat drainage system" I remarked, not to anyone in particular. I looked at Gerry. He didn't comment.

A few steps later we arrived at the staff toilets. One male, one female adjacent to each other. Both were generally clean and provided with all the necessary facilities but to my concern the entrance lobby to the ladies was packed with catering equipment, totally in breach of food safety law.

"Yes I know" the manager said before I could say anything "but I've nowhere else to put it." We quickly completed the audit and as we walked slowly out of the building Gerry turned to me. "Would you mind if I took our Company name off the door?" he said quietly. "Not a chance" I replied. "If we're in it so are you."

We walked back up the slope towards the airport Terminal. "What do you reckon we can do with it short of using a bulldozer?" Gerry looked at me again. "We'll work something out but it will have to be quick. Let's look at the menu first of all and make sure that we don't allow anything on it which might be a problem given the food safety issues."

We spent the next half hour working through the issues and by the time the Chief Stewardess arrived we knew what had to be done. A nice woman, she was very helpful. She also had a sense of humour. When, after we had discussed the problems with the kitchen, I mentioned the stewardess on the morning flight testing the omelette temperatures by sticking her fingers in them, she looked at me then replied in her wonderful Devon accent. "That's no problem my lovely. I can easily sort that out. I'll have a curtain put across the front of the galley so no-one can see what's happening in there." Her eyes twinkled as she sat for a moment letting me digest her wisdom. "No" she said "on second thoughts I had better have a word with the team and do a bit of retraining."

In 1997 British Mediterranean Airways joined BA as a franchise. It was a small independent airline set up by Lord Hesketh whose previous claim to fame had been his sponsorship of James Hunt the successful and flamboyant British Formula 1 racing driver.

My introduction to BMed as it was known came via my colleagues in the Catering Division. They wanted me to meet with the woman responsible for the airline's catering, particularly on its route to Bishkek in Kyrgyzstan which according to them was fraught with difficulties.

On the appointed day my secretary Judy ushered a youngish woman into my office. She introduced herself in a strong Scottish accent and sat down opposite me. "OK, tell me all about BMed." At that moment I really had very little idea as to what the airline actually did. She very quickly gave me a brief outline as to how the airline operated. "What about Bishkek?" I queried. "Ah well that's a difficult one. Although it's shown as a scheduled service it's actually more of a charter" I was intrigued. "Go on."

She continued. "Well there is a very large gold mine about an hour or so flying time out of Bishkek. It's being operated by a Canadian mining company and we fly the miners from London to Bishkek." "I take it that the miners fly into London from Canada on a scheduled service?" "Yes they come from West coast Canada, fly in to London, have a few hours in London and fly overnight with us to Bishkek. I think that they work six weeks at the mine then go home for a rest before returning." "So how do you cater the flight? Is there a flight catering unit in Bishkek?" I looked at her hopefully.

"No, there's no catering unit there so we use a local hotel." "They cater the flight then?" "Well not exactly." It was beginning to feel as if I was pulling teeth one by one. She obviously wasn't very keen to tell me any more than she felt she had to. "So what happens?" I pushed for an answer. "Well we take the catering from Sky Chef here at Heathrow to Bishkek where it's taken to the hotel. Then a Russian woman organises it in the hotel for the return trip. We have a Canadian woman of Ukrainian background who is out there as the mining company agent and she oversees the arrival and departure of the aircraft."

"Does the aircraft turn round and come straight back?" I was thinking about the length of time that the food would be sitting around both on the outbound flight and before the return. "No. It arrives about nine thirty in the morning and leaves to come back around midnight." This I've got to see, I thought to myself. It's about a ten hour flight to Bishkek by my reckoning and there's not likely to be much refrigeration on the aircraft for the return meals.

"OK. I think I've got the picture so how soon can you arrange for me to go out there and have a look at the operation?" "It'll take a couple of weeks because I will have to talk to the mining company to release a seat then tell the Ukrainian woman to expect you."

It was Wednesday morning a couple of weeks later. My phone rang and picking it up I heard the familiar voice of John, a colleague of mine who worked for a catering company on the airfield. "I hear you're off to the wilds of Kyrgyzstan tonight" he chuckled. "Who told you that then?" I questioned him. "Ah, you know what it's like on the airfield, the drums are beating."

He carried on. "There's a certain lady frantically calling round every caterer to ask if they have any polystyrene food boxes that she can borrow to ship her food out in tonight on a flight to Bishkek. The story goes that she normally just packs the food in cardboard boxes for the trip but she knows that you're going out on the flight tonight to see the operation and you won't be happy." He laughed. "You get to go to all the best places don't you? You'll be pleased to know however that she says that she needs to get it right because you're not bribeable."

"Well she got that right anyway. Actually if you're talking to the said woman you could suggest that there is nothing that she has that she could bribe me with." "That's a bit harsh" John replied, continuing to chuckle. "She can't be that bad" "No don't get me wrong she's a nice enough

331

person but I just don't like the idea that anyone could think that I could be open to a bribe."

Later that night I made my way to Terminal 3 at Heathrow to pick up my ticket at a British Airways desk in the departure area and join the flight to Bishkek. It had been some considerable time since I had departed from Terminal 3 as BA had long since moved operations to Terminal 4 and it took me a few minutes to locate where I was supposed to go. Eventually I found the Customer Service desk, picked up the ticket and without looking at it, walked across to the desk where the flight to Bishkek was checking in.

A British Airways uniformed check in agent greeted me and without much ado issued the boarding pass and wished me a pleasant journey. I looked at it and realised that the seat I had been allocated was at the very rear of the aircraft. I turned back to her. "Wrong seat" and gave her back the boarding card. She looked at it then looked at me. "I'm sorry?" she questioned. "Have a look at my seating priority" I said. She looked back at my passenger details. "Oh yes Mr Kelly, I'm sorry but I'll have to speak with the BMed supervisor." She got up and turning to her rear called another girl over and had a quick whispered conversation with her, all the while looking backwards towards me. The supervisor approached me at the desk. "I'm sorry Mr Kelly. I'll improve your seat but I'm afraid I can't put you in First Class since there's nothing available."

"That's fine" I smiled at her. "It's only that I'm going out to work there all day tomorrow and then come back on the same flight so I need to get as much rest as I can on the way there." "That's a bit rough" she said looking at me in a somewhat different light. "You're out and back on the same aircraft and having to work all day in between?"

"That's it in a nutshell." I replied and smiled at her. "They must pay you a lot for that" She responded whilst looking at her computer screen to see what seats were available. "I wish" I grinned at her as she looked up. "I'd rather you than me then but maybe this will make it a bit better" she handed me a Club Class boarding pass. "It's the best I can do." "Thanks, I appreciate your help." I said as I walked off towards the departure gate. "Have a good flight." The words rang in my ears.

Boarding the aircraft, I was surprised to find myself on an Airbus 320, a small aircraft for what was to be a long flight. I was even more surprised to find that there were only four flight attendants on board who between them had to oversee three cabins and an almost full passenger load. We took off into the night heading East towards Europe and I rapidly realised that despite my upgrade to Business Class the aircraft was not equipped to BA standards and my seat was one of the most uncomfortable that I had ever travelled in.

Dinner was served out of London and the four crew worked admirably to look after their passengers. Unlike most other flights they had to keep the curtains separating the cabins open so that they could each see what the others were doing and what might be required.

I dozed off after dinner to be woken by a change in the aircraft engine note as we began to descend. I looked at my watch. It's the middle of the night so we can't be landing at Bishkek. The Captain's voice came across the across the cabin. "Ladies and Gentlemen as we are about to land at Schonefeld airport to refuel please ensure that your seat belts are fastened."

We landed and taxied across the airfield to a refuelling point. It was pitch black and I could see nothing outside the aircraft. I could hear noises but no-one was visible. I knew that we were in Berlin and on an airfield which had originally been in the Eastern sector and therefore under Russian control but I had never been there before. I was also surprised that we were refuelling with the passengers on board but as most were asleep I could understand why a low key stance was being taken by the crew.

Forty-five minutes later we were on our way again and I desperately tried to get some sleep. It was all to no avail and I tossed and turned all night which was unusual for me. We landed into a grey day at Bishkek on to a runway which appeared to undulate like a ploughed field. As we came to a stop one of the crew came to me. "Mr. Kelly?" "Yes" "Would you please stay on the aircraft when the passengers disembark. The company agent will come on board and meet you." "Thanks, that's fine."

I waited until the passengers had disembarked and was surprised on looking back down the aircraft to find that there were two others who had also been told to stay behind. A young man accompanied by a young woman of Indian appearance and dressed in a very smart business suit. The young man walked up the aisle to me and putting out his hand said "You must be Mike Kelly." He introduced himself and his companion. "We're from Sky Chef and we've come to see how they handle our food."

As we were chatting a woman walked purposefully down the aircraft towards us. "Mr Kelly?" She looked at me for confirmation then introduced herself. "Welcome to Bishkek. I see that you've met your work colleagues." This must be the Ukrainian airline agent that I'd been told about. I quickly explained that we had only just met and that whilst we would be working together through the day we didn't actually know each other and we worked for two different companies.

"No matter" she dismissed the situation quickly. "As none of you have visas for entry into Kyrgyzstan you will be landing here as crew members. You will stay on the aircraft until the military have examined your passports and then you will disembark the aircraft and leave the airport on the crew transport. I'll travel to the hotel and will meet you there." With that she was gone.

A few moments later several young men dressed in army greatcoats and wearing the familiar looking Russian style large wide topped flat military caps boarded the aircraft via the front door. Marching down the aircraft aisle they each took up a position in front of one of us. No words were spoken but a hand was held out and I took this to mean that a passport was required. I handed mine over. The young man scanned it page by page then looked me carefully in the face as I stood unmoving. He went back to scanning the passport then with a grunt he nodded his head towards the door at the front.

I assumed that this was my permission to leave so quickly gathered my possessions and headed down the aircraft steps. Standing at the bottom I looked around. The crew were standing as a small group to one side. The terminal building was a short distance away and looked fairly modern which was more than could be said for a line of passenger aircraft standing nearby. They were biplanes!

I couldn't believe it. They appeared to be Antonov 2 aircraft and the last time I had seen one of those was in an aircraft museum in Hungary. Were they still in use?

The aircraft Captain walked across. "Are you the guys from Sky Chef?" "These two are." I introduced them and went on "I'm Mike Kelly from British Airways Health Services."

"Ah yes, I was told you were coming with us. You're here to look at the catering aren't you?" As we spoke I could see the catering being unloaded from the aircraft hold. As I'd been led to believe it was in a series of large cardboard boxes which were being placed on an open flatbed lorry of uncertain vintage but looking like something which would have been operating in England in the nineteen thirties or forties. "You're coming with us to the hotel" the Captain continued. "It's going to be a tight squeeze I'm afraid but we'll manage." He pointed at a four-wheel drive Land Cruiser style vehicle. "Come on let's go" and he made his way across to it.

Looking at the group I could see that there were ten of us in total. Two pilots, a flight engineer, four cabin crew, two male and two female and three of us from catering. The vehicle was only designed to take seven crew and their luggage but the Captain was up to the challenge of getting us all in. "No standing on ceremony. It won't be comfortable but we don't have too far to go. If the blokes can have the girls sitting across their laps, we'll make it fit."

And so we all squeezed in. I had a half share of a stewardess as she sat partly on my knee and partly on the First Officer's lap. I felt sorry for the cabin crew. It had been a long night and they must have been exhausted but there were no complaints. As we drove out of the airfield I thought to myself that I couldn't see a mainline BA crew opting to share their transport like this. The girl on my knee was quite chatty to start with. "What are you here to do?" she asked over the noise of the engine which appeared to be working very hard to cope with the extra load. I explained what we were doing.

"So you'll be staying at the crew hotel?" "Yes but I doubt that we'll get much rest as we have to oversee the preparation of the food for the return flight tonight." "What's the hotel like? I've been told that it's brand new?" "It's a lot better than where we were staying before" she smiled at me. "Where was that?" "We used to stay in what was a boarding house of sorts but it was pretty awful. As we only have a daylight rest period here we have to sleep through the day and it was very difficult. There were people coming and going all day. Doors banging, people yelling. There was no peace. And it wasn't clean. One of my friends was getting into her bed when she found a used condom in it!! Absolutely disgusting. Ugh."

I had to agree with her of course. "So what about the hotel?" "Oh it's much better, new and well equipped." That made me feel much better about my chances of finding somewhere hygienic for the food preparation.

We continued in silence for a while then looking down I realised that she had fallen asleep on my shoulder.

Soon we arrived at the city. It wasn't what I had expected but then again I wasn't really sure what to expect. It seemed to be more of a large town with most buildings being only a couple of storeys high and many with corrugated iron roofs.

Arriving at the hotel we disembarked outside a modern multi storey building. Our Ukrainian friend was outside to welcome us. "Come in, come in" she greeted us enthusiastically, waving us towards the reception desk.

Check in was quick and efficient and within minutes I was being ushered in to the lift for my journey to the seventh floor. The lift was full and as it arrived at my floor I was more than a bit surprised to feel the firm pressure of a hand squeezing my rear. Looking over my shoulder I got a broad smile from my Ukrainian hostess. I can't say that I hadn't been warned as the Scottish catering manager from BMed had told me with a grin on her face to expect a feisty woman. I turned at my bedroom door. "I'll meet you in the lobby in fifteen minutes and we can begin work. Can you ask my two colleagues to be there as well please?" She smiled her acceptance and left.

Fifteen minutes later my colleagues and I were introduced to the manager of the hotel and ushered into a food service area between the kitchen and the hotel dining room. As I stepped inside I almost gasped in amazement at the sight which greeted me.

Lunchtime was just beginning and the room was very busy. A host of women were rushing around taking food out to the restaurant and returning with the used plates and cutlery to be loaded into the large new dish wash machine standing proudly on one side of the room. It wasn't the number of women in the room which amazed me but the fact that they were all young and dressed in what can only be called a bizarre collection of clothing modelled on Western style youth fashion. What was more amazing was the extremely short skirts. So short in fact that when many of the women bent forward their underwear was readily visible.

Added to this their hair colouring was amazing. They were all the colours of the rainbow from bright red to blue. I had assumed that the majority of the population in the country would be Muslim but obviously I must be wrong. I looked sideways at my Asian female colleague. She was standing with a look of shock on her face. She couldn't believe what she was looking at.

Well at least the facilities were modern, well equipped and well staffed which gave me some confidence for the production of the aircraft meals. The manager walked us through and opened the door of another room. There on the floor stood the cardboard boxes of food, last seen being unloaded from the aircraft. Bang went my confidence. They were obviously defrosting. "Can these be moved into a refrigerator?" I looked to the Ukrainian woman for help. She spoke quickly to the manager who nodded his head. "Yes, the manager will organise that." "Thank you. Well I don't think we will be able to do anything until after the lunch service is completed so perhaps we should leave the staff to get on with their work and we can come back later. When does the Russian woman who does the flight catering turn up?" "She'll be here around three o'clock." "OK so we'll aim to be back here at three o'clock and will watch what happens."

As my two colleagues and I moved back into the lobby of the hotel we thanked the manager for his help. The Ukrainian woman turned to us. "Good bye. I've finished now." and having shaken our hands she left the hotel. "Well what did you think of that?" I asked my companions. "Amazing. Did you see those hair colours and those skirts?" The two of them had been as surprised as me. "I suppose it's what they see in magazines because I doubt that they can buy these things in the local shops. They must make them themselves."

"Well what will we do now?" I asked. "We can't do anything much for the next couple of hours so I suggest that we take a bit of a walk around the local area and see what it's like."

We walked outside and immediately became something of a curiosity to the locals. It was a cold, grey, miserable day with light rain beginning to fall but there were a lot of people in the street and all of them were taking a good look at us. They were a mixture of ethnicity ranging from Oriental through Middle Eastern to Western Russian. We must have seemed somewhat incongruous to them. Two Western European men accompanied by an Indian woman, immaculately dressed in business suits. Looking around I could see little of modernity. The buildings were drab and mostly no higher than two storeys. There was little greenery but to be fair it was Winter so what could I expect. The city or what little we could see of it, bore all the hallmarks of its former Russian history.

As we walked along I was struck by the obvious poverty. The street was lined with people sitting squat legged on the ground, each behind a piece of cardboard on which stood a variety of items which they were trying so sell. From fruit and vegetables to small second hand spare parts, it was all there. The sellers were mainly middle aged and sat looking dourly through the drizzle at the passers-by. There was no obvious attempt to encourage people to buy. There was none of the colour and life to be found in a similar African market. I found it all quite sad. For most, the contents of their piece of cardboard probably represented their entire family wealth.

Come three o'clock I and my two companions were back in the hotel. After the lunch time rush it now seemed quiet and deserted. We walked through the lobby and into the food service area. Where was everybody? It was deserted apart from one woman dressed in a grey skirt and top and wearing an apron. She looked up and smiled. I walked over and introduced myself. She smiled again and said something in what I assumed to be Russian. It seemed that she spoke very little English. "Where is everyone?" I looked at her. I indicated the area around us. "Who is making the aircraft meals?" I looked at her again. She obviously understood some of what I had said as she pointed at herself. "Just you?" I replied pointing at her. She nodded and carried on working, stripping the waste food off the plates from the flight on which we had arrived and stacking the dirty dishes beside the sink.

My colleagues and I stood and watched for a while whilst she sorted them out and then began to wash them by hand in the sink. I walked across and asked why she wasn't using the large modern dishwashing machine standing a few feet away. "It belongs to the hotel and I don't know how to work it" she suddenly said in broken English revealing that her knowledge of English was better that we had at first thought. "Who will be working with you?" I carried on. "My daughter will come in one hour" she replied and went back to her dish washing.

I went back to my two Sky Chef colleagues who had been watching from the sidelines. "You're not going to believe this but this is it. This is the entire aircraft catering arrangement. One woman and possibly her daughter.

They looked aghast. "You're joking?" "I wish I was" I replied. "You mean she is going to wash and strip the entire off load and then set up the flight?" "Looks like it."

For the next hour we watched as the woman assiduously unpacked the dirty equipment from the flight and began to wash it in the two sinks available to her. The overnight flight had served dinner in three different cabins on the aircraft out of London followed by a small continental breakfast before our morning arrival. Given the large passenger load this amounted to several hundred individual dishes, glassware and pieces of cutlery. A pretty large task for a team to wash up let alone one person.

An hour or so later and a daughter turned up. A slight, pretty girl she immediately put on an apron and got stuck into the washing up. Mother having completed about half the washing now left her daughter to finish it whilst she turned to putting together the meal for the return flight.

She took a number of small starter dishes and laid them on a table. She looked at them carefully then added a few more. Next she walked across to a pile of food and equipment standing on one side and selected a large catering size can. Bringing this across to the table she picked up a can opener and removed the top then, sticking her hand into it removed a handful of the contents, squeezed it hard to remove the liquid in which it had been canned and began to place a portion on each of the first plates. She then repeated the process, gradually working her way along the row of dishes.

Looking more closely I realised that what she was plating up was a Julienne of vegetables which was to make up part of the dinner starter. As she worked her way down the can her arm went further and further into it and I could only imagine how much of her skin was in contact with the food, and with it, the likelihood of one or more meals being contaminated.

From time to time she stood back to admire her work and to check that each dish had the right amount of food on it. Obviously she had never had any instruction as to decanting the food and weighing or measuring portion sizes. The work proceeded extremely slowly. Later in the evening, around seven o'clock a second girl appeared. "My other daughter" the woman smiled at me.

She was a big girl with a very large and obviously unrestrained bosom which swung wildly every time she turned around and threatened on more than one occasion to topple the pile of cleaned dishes which her sister was stacking beside the sink. It also soon became obvious that not only was she not wearing a bra but she wasn't wearing any form of deodorant as the air became ripe with her body odour.

Come the middle of the evening it became apparent to me that despite their non-stop work the women weren't going to get the meal completed on time. Turning to my companions I said "Get your sleeves rolled up, we're going to have to help here." And so we began to put it all together. We quickly set up a production line system with each person having their own job to do. At first the three women looked bemused but then began to realise what we were doing and set about doing it with us.

It still took us all evening. We finished just after 11.30pm. "We'd better get a move on. Pick up is at midnight in the lobby." I reminded my colleagues. "Don't be late." We dashed for our rooms to pick up our things. At five minutes to midnight, showered and changed into fresh clothes, I walked out of the lift into the lobby and bumped into the Captain. "Hi, how are you? Did you have a good day? What time did you finish?" he looked at me cheerfully. "About half past eleven." I replied. "Oh so you've had most of the day to yourselves then?" "Not quite" I said "half past eleven this evening" and proceeded to tell him what we'd been doing. Watching the miners devouring their meal on the aircraft some two hours later I was thinking "how little you know!!" But all in a day's work.

National Jet Italia was another short lived franchise venture that BA got involved with in the early part of the new Millenium 2000. Designed to operate local routes in Italy and flying in BA colours I was invited by Anne, one of my catering colleagues to join her and a member of her team on an audit of two flight catering units in Sicily. I already had an audit planned for Genoa so it fitted in quite well as I could fly from Genoa to Palermo to join the others but like all such things it didn't go exactly to plan.

My evening flight from Genoa, operated by the local airline Meridiana was late and when it eventually arrived I was somewhat amused to see the Captain and crew of the small turboprop walk from their aircraft into the airport departure lounge where they happily stood and had coffee whilst their joining passengers watched and waited. As a result of all this I arrived at Palermo airport very late in the evening. Having collected my bag, I made my way to the taxi rank in the almost deserted airport and gave the driver the address of the hotel to which I was going.

It was close on midnight. I had never been to Sicily before but was aware of its reputation and Mafia connections so was a little bit on edge as we drove rapidly through the dark and empty streets into the city. I had no idea where we were going and could only hope that the driver was an honest man and I wasn't being taken on an expensive tour of the island, something which had happened to me many years previously in Manila, when after arriving in the dark I was given a forty-minute taxi ride which turned out the following morning to have been 30 minutes longer than it should have been!!

I wasn't reassured when the car came to an abrupt halt in a darkened street and the driver indicated that I should get out. I clambered out with my bag and paid for the ride. The driver pointed at a doorway then drove off into the night leaving me standing in the street. I looked at the door. There was no illuminated sign and the door had a metal gate across the front. Walking towards it I spotted a bell pull and on pulling it heard a bell ring inside.

I waited and heard noises behind the door. Bolts were being pulled and then light appeared as the door creaked open. A young man looked at me through the metal gate. Obviously satisfied with what he saw he took a key from a large number hanging on a ring which he was holding and unlocked the gate. It opened outwards so I had to step back quickly. Looking at him I got the impression that he "wasn't the full shilling" as the saying goes.

At the risk of sounding unkind I felt that I had arrived in some horror movie and Quasimodo had just opened the door. He ushered me into a small lobby with a reception desk a few feet away. A man standing behind the desk looked at me and said "Good evening Mr Kelly? May I have your Passport." He had obviously been waiting for me.

I handed it over and with a quick flourish he handed a room key to the young man telling him to take me to my room. He then turned to me and said "Your companion waited up for you but she has gone to bed and left you this message." He handed me a note. "Good night" he said and turned away.

Realising that the conversation was over I turned to pick up my bag only to find that the young porter already had it in his hand. He gestured towards a small lift and we got in. The lift groaned slowly upwards to the floor level which he had selected, the doors opened and he waved me out in front of him. I stepped out of the door and stopped. I had no idea as to what my room number was so didn't know which way to turn. He pointed me along the corridor and I started to walk but as I didn't know which room I was looking for I slowed down and waited for him to take the lead. However, he was reluctant to do so and every time I let him get a step in front he stopped to let me pass him again. It was a slow walk! Eventually we came to a door which he was happy with and taking the key he opened the lock, carried my bag in and without a word was out and gone before I could even offer him a tip. Very strange.

The room was small and the bathroom was tiny. So small that I could virtually touch both side walls whilst standing in the middle of the floor but it was only for one night and as it was already after midnight I just needed to get to bed. I read Anne's note which confirmed what the receptionist had told me but added that she would meet me at 8.00am for breakfast.

Waking in the morning I got up quickly and made my way to the shower. Stepping back into the room I suddenly realised that the door from my room to the corridor had a large gap running round the frame. So large in fact that I could see fully into the corridor and likewise anyone passing could see me. Just at that moment Anne walked past. "Morning Mike. I'll see you downstairs." She glanced casually at me standing scantily draped in a towel but didn't turn a hair and didn't mention it when I reached the dining room a few minutes later and described my trip from Genoa much to the amusement of her and her colleague.

We were joined at Palermo by Jennifer, the Senior Cabin Crew member from National Jet Italia, who, once I'd completed my audit was going to drive us to Catania on the other side of the island where NJI also operated services. The catering units were relatively small so we were able to audit Palermo in the morning and Catania in the afternoon.

Catania was a nice little town sitting on a sparkling sea but over shadowed by Mount Etna which was spewing out volcanic lava a sight which became more spectacular as darkness fell and the fiery embers were blasted into the night sky. Having finished our work in the flight kitchen the owner suggested that he would like to take the team out for a meal and said that he would pick us up at our hotel around 7.30pm

As good as his word he arrived accompanied by with several men and one woman in two large black limousines. Looking at the men Anne turned quickly to me and whispered in my ear "Don't leave us in a car with the men, whilst you go in the other one!"

We were ushered into a car and I made sure that the three girls and I were together much to Anne's relief as we set off and headed into the dark towards Taormina. It was a long drive and although we had been told that were going to a lovely part of Sicily in the dark we could see very little.

On arrival, having parked the cars, we walked up hill to a local restaurant and were seated around a very large circular table. There were twelve of us in total and it was an entertaining meal made more so by the fact that the woman whom the flight catering owner had brought with him spent the entire evening fawning all over him whilst he in turn ran his hands casually up and down her legs. Anne thought it was hilarious and had trouble keeping her face straight. "She's not his wife you know" she whispered to me although I already knew because we had met his wife during the audit.

The food was good and I thoroughly enjoyed it. When we had finished and were walking back to our car the owner suggested that we went for a night cap. I was strolling along as part of the group but suddenly realised that I was being accompanied by the young woman friend of the owner. She began to talk to me in strongly accented English. "Come with me and look at the view" She began to angle me towards a side street. "There are lovely views across the straits towards the mainland."

She was being very persuasive and took my arm to guide me away from the rest of the group. I looked over my shoulder to see Anne trying to stifle a laugh as she watched my predicament. I had no wish to be rude but at the same time I realised that there was an ulterior motive being played out. The woman walked me a short distance to a balcony which must have overlooked the sea but at ten o'clock at night there was little to see. She spoke to me again. "Isn't it beautiful?" I nodded my head. "Yes and it must be really wonderful in the sunshine during the day."

"We Sicilian women are not very beautiful but we are very passionate." She gave my arm a squeeze as she looked expectantly up at me. "I think we ought to catch up with the others." I turned and began to walk back along the street. Turning at the end I saw Anne standing waving to me from outside the doorway of a small bar. "Over here."

"Thanks" I said as I reached her. She laughed. "What was she offering, as if I couldn't guess?" She laughed again. "She was obviously trying to get her claws into you." "You could have walked along with me to keep us company" I looked at Anne "What and spoil your fun" She laughed again. "Just you wait. I think I might just let you go back to the hotel in the car with the other men." "You wouldn't" Anne replied looking suddenly serious. "Try me" I laughed but of course she knew that I wouldn't.

CHAPTER 55

CORFU, AN
AMUSING INTERLUDE

Other social occasions over the years also provided amusing incidents. In the early nineteen eighties British airways operated a Charter Division under the name British Airtours, flying out of London Gatwick airport to a number of popular holiday destinations in the Mediterranean.

One of the most popular was the island of Corfu where, as the aircraft were catered at the local flight kitchen for their return flight, I had to visit to assess the food safety standards.

The premises were owned by a local business man who also owned a hotel set on a small hill overlooking the airport runway. He spoke little English but following my audit was willing to do what was required in the kitchen and we got on well. On my return visit a few weeks later to check that my recommendations had been followed he invited me to join him for dinner in his hotel after work.

At the appointed time I turned up at the hotel to find it awash with people. The Catering Manager spotted me and came across. "Mr Kelly our apologies but due to flight delays at the airport we are having to cope with an excess of delayed passengers so the owner sends his apologies but he will be unable to join you. However, he hopes that you will stay and enjoy your meal. Please follow me." He turned and swept me imperiously into the dining room. Behind us came a small entourage of waiters. The dining room was packed with holiday makers having dinner and making the most of their unexpected delay who watched as I was led to an individual table set in the middle of the room, conspicuous not only because of the flowers on the table but also the large ice bucket standing beside it in which was a bottle of Champagne.

All eyes were on me as I was walked to the table. I sat down and there was a flourish as the Head Waiter deftly swept my napkin on to my lap. "Enjoy your dinner" the manager said as he left me. I was somewhat mortified by my position in the room and the fact that I was getting so much attention. My ideas of a quiet meal and chat with the owner of the flight kitchen had gone out the window. I was handed a menu by the Head Waiter who then proceeded to open the Champagne and poured me a glass.

I ordered my meal and as I glanced around I became aware that the table next to me was occupied by two middle aged couples, husbands and wives. Judging by their sun tans they were part of a delayed flight. One of the women was watching me closely as the waiters delivered my food. She was obviously trying to work out why it was that I was being given some extra attention. Eventually her curiosity got the better of her. "Ought I to know thee?" Her strong Northern accent came across. "Are you on the TV or something?"

I smiled across. "No, I'm not anybody famous" I replied with a smile. "What's it all about then?" She waved her arm towards the table. "I'm in the Travel business and they do some work with us" I responded without giving too much away.

"I knew it had to be something." She turned to her companions. "I knew he was something special" as if to vindicate her interest in me.

I smiled across and said again. "I'm nobody special" then I looked at the bottle of Champagne. "Would you like a glass of Champagne to help you pass the time whilst you're waiting for your flight? I'll never drink a whole bottle on my own." They looked at each other, obviously not too sure as to what they should say.

"Come on I'll get some glasses." I looked across and caught the eye of one of the waiters. "Would you bring me four wine glasses please?" "Are you sure?" the woman said. "Of course." "Well that's really nice of you." She was made up as they say up North and we chatted about their holiday whilst they enjoyed the Champagne and I ate my meal. It was certainly more pleasant than sitting eating on my own.

A subsequent visit to Corfu the following year to check that standards were being maintained had a somewhat different ending. Once again, following the day's work, I was invited to dine with the owner of the kitchen. This time we were going to the Greek Folk Village Museum on the island for dinner and a concert. The village was made up of a collection of cottages, houses etc. brought from all over Greece and rebuilt in Corfu to provide tourists with a view of life in Greece. but on this particular evening it was being used for a concert by two famous Greek singers flown specially from Athens for the event.

I was picked up at my hotel by the BA Manager in Corfu and in getting into rear seat of his car, found myself beside a young English girl. The Manager was accompanied in the front by one of the girls whom I had seen in the BA office earlier in the day. Following introductions, I was chatting to my companion. She seemed somewhat tense and I asked her what her connection was with BA. "I'm a holiday representative on the island." "So you know the flight caterers?" I asked "No, I've no connection with them." I obviously must have looked a bit baffled. "I'm here to look after you." "Look after me?" I queried. She looked somewhat uncomfortable. "Yes. I'm here to provide you with whatever you may want." I was horrified. "You're joking?"

She shook her head. "I'm the rep on the island and my job may depend on my doing what I'm told." "Well I'm not going to ask who arranged this but I've got a good idea and I'll be having a few words about it in the morning. Meanwhile, just forget all about looking after me and enjoy yourself." She looked very relieved and began to relax.

The evening passed well. The dinner was good, the caterer and his wife were excellent company and the concert although in Greek was entertaining. The most dangerous aspect was the fact that we were seated at a table at the front and near to the stage. As the Greek audience became more and more excited by the singing, plates began to be thrown towards the stage by the audience as a sign of appreciation and it became imperative to keep one eye on the stage and one on the audience behind so as to be able to duck some of the oncoming plates!!

CHAPTER 56

TRAVELLING COMPANIONS

One of the more pleasant aspects of my travels was meeting a variety of people, some during the flight and many others as a result of the audits which I was carrying out. On boarding an aircraft one is never sure of who is going to be in the adjacent seat. Being a staff passenger could sometimes make things a little difficult, particularly when travelling in the front cabins in either Business or First class. Given that I was effectively travelling at no cost whilst the person sitting beside me was paying a considerable sum of money for their seat I always avoided telling them that I worked for the airline unless directly asked the question. Most passengers therefore considered me to be their equal, which sometimes had unexpected consequences.

Travelling across the Atlantic early in my career and seated in First Class I had a youngish man sitting beside me. This was in the days before the bed seats were designed as a result of which passengers became more segregated. The original first Class seats were like very large and comfortable armchairs and were positioned two by two through the cabin.

The young man had spoken to me when he had boarded the flight but thereafter there was no conversation. That was fine with me. I always left it to the passenger to begin any conversation. Some were happy to converse through a flight whilst others just wished to settle down in their own quiet world.

We were about half way across the Atlantic when suddenly without any warning he looked up from the magazine he was reading and said "Excuse me, but do you think that these people would take an offer on this property?" Looking across I saw that he was reading the Real Estate pages of Country Life. He pointed to the advertisement that he was looking at. It was showing a large house with a price tag of well in excess of £1,000,000. This was the early nineteen eighties so we were looking at a large amount of money. "I'm sure that they would" I replied whilst thinking to myself "this is well out of your league, what would you know about it."

He looked up at me again and felt that he owed me an explanation. "I'm the newly appointed lawyer for Reuters and am just in the process of moving to London from Sydney." I recognised the Australian accent as he spoke. "I'm looking for somewhere that will be around twenty minutes from my office in the city so where would you suggest?"

I thought quickly. "Well you couldn't be much further North than Hampstead, or further West than Chelsea. You might want to look at the new developments in the old London docklands area. That's the up and coming future of London."

"Thanks, and who would you suggest that I approach? Are these the right sort of agents?" I looked again at the magazine and saw the name Knight, Frank and Rutley, this being before Rutley's name was removed. "Yes they're amongst the best who deal in quality property. You might also like to talk to the Harrods Estate Office. They may also be able to help." "Thanks, I appreciate that" and he went back to studying the advertisements. I sat back in my seat and thought "I think I dealt with that fairly well." It's a strange life.

Travelling home from an audit in Dubai again quite early in my career the aircraft, an L1011 Tristar landed in Dammam in Saudi Arabia to pick up more passengers. I was seated in a window seat at the front of the aircraft and watched as the new joiners made their way down the aisle. The aircraft was filling up rapidly when I became aware of a young woman being escorted by a steward. Walking behind her he looked across at me and winked at me in a conspiratorial fashion as if saying "look what you've got."

The young woman was ushered into the seat beside me and I looked at her in some amazement. Not because she was particularly attractive although that was very much the case but more because although obviously from an Arab family she was wearing a very modern European style black dress, trimmed with red around the hem and sleeves and with the words "I'm foxy" inscribed across her left breast. Quite startling coming out of Dammam where Muslim standards were very much in effect and I could only surmise that she had kept herself covered in an Abaya prior to boarding.

She smiled and said "Good morning" as she sat down and I smiled and returned the compliment but added "Does it mean what it says on your dress?" She looked at me and laughed. "You've got about six hours to find out haven't you?" It was the start of a very interesting conversation as she continued by looking around the aircraft cabin and then saying "I much prefer these wide bodied aircraft to the one we have at home." "What do you have? " I asked, expecting to be told that it was a Lear Jet or similar small business aircraft and was somewhat amazed when she replied "A Boeing 727."

"What do you use it for?" I queried "We use it to travel to the West coast and my mother goes to Paris and London to shop." It's a different world I thought.

It appeared that the young lady was on her way back to college in the USA, somewhere in Iowa she told me much to her disgust. She had apparently originally been in a college in California but her father had moved her as he thought she was learning a bit too much, according to her.

She was a lively companion and the flight passed quickly as I learned about the Middle East way of life and her political thoughts on what was happening in the West Bank. As we arrived in London she told me that she was staying over for a few days to meet her younger brother who was attending a famous Public school before continuing her trip to America and asked if I would like to join them for dinner at the Dorchester Hotel.

I declined politely claiming a prior engagement but in reality I didn't think that my wife would be too happy about such a meeting nor would my bank manager if I had to pay the bill!!

A subsequent flight, this time from Los Angeles provided more in the way of entertainment. I had just completed a two day audit and on the overnight flight home was fortunate to have been given a seat in the First Class cabin. Settling into my seat which was next to the window I was welcomed by the Purser who knew me as I was travelling back with the same crew which had brought me out from London two days before. He asked me how the audit had gone and if there was anything I needed before making his way back to the door to greet more oncoming passengers.

A few minutes later he was back alongside, ushering a passenger into the aisle seat next to mine. I looked up and immediately recognised Joan

Collins, the actress who was enjoying a wave of fame on both sides of the Atlantic having starred in the TV series Dynasty. I acknowledged her arrival with a brief "Good evening" and a smile which she acknowledged.

The purser was more forth coming. "Miss Collins, what a pleasure it is to have you on board with us tonight. Please let me know if there is anything that I or other members of the crew can do for you." She smiled graciously. "Do you know the gentleman seated next to you?" He looked enquiringly as she turned to me. "He's world famous. May I introduce you to Mr Michael Kelly." "You so and so" I thought to myself whilst turning to Miss Collins and extending my hand. She took it whilst looking at me with a quizzical look that said "Should I know you?"

The Purser moved away quickly and we settled back into our seats. A few minutes later he reappeared, this time with a tray of pre take off drinks. He moved to the front of the cabin and began the service at rows one and two. Seated in the first two rows were four Arab women whose male companion was seated at the rear. They were obviously very high ranking and probably part of the ruling family of one of the major Arab countries.

The Purser wasn't going to let that get in his way. "Something to drink ladies?" He knew perfectly well that the ladies wouldn't drink alcohol and had both Champagne and orange juice on the tray but thought that he would amuse them. "A glass of Champagne perhaps?" he leaned conspiratorially towards them and placing the back of his free hand across the side of his face said in a stage whisper "It won't do any harm, anyway he's not watching" he said nodding toward the rear of the cabin.

I couldn't believe what I was hearing and feared for the worst but the women started to giggle. The Purser had obviously gauged it right. Perhaps they had travelled with him before. Working his way down the cabin he offered a glass of Champagne to Miss Collins then having delivered it said "I don't suppose you would have a small part in your next film for an up and coming aspiring actor?" He moved away from the seat threw his head back and flicked the front of his hair with the back of his hand. Joan Collins chortled. "Just a small walk on part will do" he continued.

He obviously knew his audience well. By the end of the dinner service he had managed to promote himself to the lead male in the movie much to Miss Collins' amusement. It was very funny and his audience thoroughly enjoyed the performance.

Leaving London late one night on a flight bound for Durban via Harare I was given the inside seat in the last row in First Class. An elderly gentleman was seated in the aisle seat next to me. He was doubled up with arthritis and had a young woman travelling in the business cabin behind who regularly came up to ensure that he was all right.

As the evening progressed, through the dinner service and after a few glasses of wine, he became quite chatty. "And where are you going to?" He enquired. "Harare" I replied. "Strange place to be going to. What do you do there?" Not wishing to tell him that I worked for the airline I replied "I'm in the travel business."

He didn't question it further but continued "I'm on my way to Durban to visit my wife. I go down a couple of times a year. I'm ninety-four now so I can't go too often." "And what did you do before you retired?" I asked. "I was a cobbler all my life but my sons threw me out when they reckoned I was too old for it" he said with a smile. Later when I left my seat to go to the toilet I spoke to one of the crew looking after us in the Cabin. "Can you tell me the name of the gentleman that I'm sitting beside?" I asked.

She knew that I was a staff passenger so she whispered in my ear "His name is Clark." Some cobbler I thought as I made my way back to my seat. Clark's Shoes was one of the biggest and best known shoe manufacturing companies in the UK.

It was interesting to know that old Mr Clark considered himself to be a cobbler rather than the owner of a major company. I wished him well as I left the aircraft in Harare the following morning.

I always enjoyed my visits to Australia. A fascinating country with wonderful fauna and flora much of which cannot be found anywhere else. To add to this, has several cities all of which are different in their own way but are modern and cosmopolitan. Sydney to my mind is one of the best cities in the world with a fabulous location on its enormous inland harbour. The pleasure of being in Australia was dampened by the fact that it is so far away from the UK and as a result the journey time was arduous sometimes taking more than twenty-four hours as the aircraft had to make several re-fuelling stops along the way.

Whilst Australia was a long way New Zealand was even further. On my first trip to Auckland my departure from London was around 10.00pm on Sunday and my arrival in Auckland was 3.30pm on Tuesday afternoon. Travelling for that length of time, then having to look bright and cheerful when coming down the aircraft steps to meet the local BA Manager on arrival could be quite difficult.

Auckland in the late nineteen seventies reminded me somewhat of my native Northern Ireland, being somewhat rooted in the past. A brand new Sheraton hotel had just been opened at the top of the hill leading up from the city and looking into the restaurant at lunchtime I was amused to see ladies dining out whilst wearing hats and gloves, reminiscent of a time long gone in London.

Coming home from Australia felt marginally better if only because I knew that at the end of the journey I would have a little time to recover in my own bed. The journey time was in no way decreased by this fact and after ten days of continuous work it was often a tough flight. Leaving Sydney as the sun set around 7.00pm on a Friday night then flying through the dark for 24 hours with the obligatory stops to refuel before arriving at 05.30am on Saturday morning into the pitch black of a cold winter in London was always horrendous. Twenty-four hours with no sunlight totally disorientates the body.

Some trips were better than others. Finishing one Australian set of audits in Perth I was boarding the flight for home. Both the BA Customer Services Manager Australia and the Manager Perth had been with me throughout the audit and were happily chatting to me as I was given my boarding card at the departure desk. "You're going to have a great flight home. Enjoy yourself." They seemed very enthusiastic. "Thanks but I really hate the trip and can never look forward to it." I responded, hoping that I didn't sound too disgruntled. "No, don't worry you'll have a good flight" they continued enthusiastically. I couldn't quite figure out their thinking.

I waited in the departure area for the flight to be called then made my way down the jetty to the aircraft. Half way down my two colleagues met me and again were keen to wish me well and hoped that I had a good flight. I shook their hands, boarded the aircraft and was escorted to my seat by the stewardess. As I placed my hand baggage in the overhead locker I looked at my travelling companion already seated in the window seat. It was Elle Macpherson the Australian super model, often known as the body!! Now I understood!! The flight was a pleasant experience.

Some years later on a similar flight home from Perth I had the pleasure of meeting Geoff Merrill the Australian winemaker. On boarding the aircraft, I found that there were only the two of us in First Class on the flight to Singapore. The Stewardess in charge of the cabin introduced us and having shaken my hand Geoff's first question was "Do you like wine?" I replied in the affirmative at which point he looked at the menu then asked the stewardess to open each of the wines that were on board so that we could have a tasting.

"I like to see what the competition is doing" was his explanation to me. I then had the wonderful experience of tasting a number of quality wines under the guidance of an expert in the field. It was a good flight to Singapore and I slept like a log on the long second leg to London.

It wasn't always like that. Flying home some years later I departed from Sydney with a single stop scheduled in Singapore. As the more modern aircraft could now fly longer distances there was no longer a requirement to fly via the Middle East to refuel but although the flight time had been reduced somewhat it meant a long 14 hours non-stop from Singapore to London.

I travelled in the First Class cabin as far as Singapore but had been warned on departure that the flight was full for the second leg. It came as no surprise therefore when the Cabin Services Director came to my seat before landing to tell me that I was being moved down the aircraft when we reached Singapore. After we had landed and those passengers leaving at Singapore had collected their bags and departed, the local station dispatcher came on board. "Sorry about this Mr Kelly I'm going to have to move you back into Business Class as we're totally full tonight" and handed me a new Boarding card. "That's fine, I fully understand" and began to pick up my bits and pieces.

As I did so the Purser came across and said "Don't worry about your hanging suitcase, just leave it in the front wardrobe. You can pick it up in London. I'll tell the joining crew when they come on board." "Thanks, that saves a bit of bother." "Have a good trip" he said as I moved towards the back.

I moved quickly into Club Class, found my new seat and sat down. The new crew boarded and having settled themselves in began the round of pre take off drinks. "Champagne, Sir?" The Steward proffered a glass which I happily took whilst quietly passing him my business card and asking him to give it to the Cabin Service Director. It was a standing instruction to my team to always make themselves known to the crew and to take time during the flight to chat to them and find out what was going on in their areas and what problems they may have come across. It was one way of gaining useful information about what was happening in the company.

"Fine Mr Kelly, I'll let him know that you're on board. I'll come back for your jacket in a moment." True to his word he came back shortly, picked up my blazer and took it to hang up in one of the Club wardrobes. I had just settled back in my seat when a young lady from the flight dispatch team arrived alongside my seat. "Mr Kelly?" She looked at me "Yes?" I replied.

"I'm sorry but we have to move you again." She handed me another boarding card and in an instant was gone. I looked at it. Row 55, right at the back!! I didn't believe it but it was too late to ask any questions. The doors were being shut as I stood up to make way for the last passenger.

I knew that my seating position was wrong because in the previous few minutes I had seen a couple of my Catering Operations colleagues joining the flight and taking their seats in Business Class. It seems churlish now but I knew that I was the most senior staff passenger on the flight and therefore according to the rules I should have stayed in Business Class.

Ah well, too late now I thought and, carrying my briefcase I wandered to the back to find row 55. Looking along the seats I realised quickly that they were all full. This is going to be fun I thought as I walked rapidly back to the front to find the cabin Services Director.

"Sorry Chief, but you've got a strap hangar." He looked at me. "How come?" "It's a long story but I started at the front and have made three seat changes to the back only to find that there's no seat." He looked at my boarding card. "There must be one somewhere. Wait here while I have a quick look." He rushed away. A few minutes later he was back "Yes," he said, "it's upstairs so follow me." The aircraft had already pushed back from the stand and was beginning to taxi to the runway so I didn't hang around. We moved quickly to the stairs and went up to the upper deck economy section. "Here you are." He pointed to the vacant middle seat in a block of three. "Thanks" I said and squeezed past the man on the outside seat.

My companions for the next 14 hours introduced themselves. In the window seat was a girl in her early twenties with a Jimmy Hendrix hairstyle that threatened to take over the whole area. She had been visiting her sister in Australia. My male companion in the aisle seat was a BA Steward positioning back to London and was very obviously gay. I then had a slight dilemma as to how I would manage to stay bolt upright in my seat without leaning either one way or the other!

After the meal service I quietly dozed off. I don't know how long I actually slept but woke to find myself enveloped in the Jimmy Hendrix hair which was threatening to suffocate me. The girl next to me was happily asleep with her head on my shoulder. Should I waken her? I knew only too well how difficult it was to sleep on an aircraft so thought it best to let her sleep on. In any case she might be terribly embarrassed if I woke her since she would realise that she had been responsible for me waking up. Better to let her sleep since she would probably naturally turn over to her other side sometime through the night. I just hoped that she wouldn't dribble on my shoulder!! And so to London through a long night.

The following morning I had to retrieve my belongings. My hanging suitcase was in the First Class wardrobe, my blazer was in Club Class and I was on the upper deck. The joy of staff travel!!

Some years later I was on my way to Hong Kong to audit the station. Having advised the caterers that I was coming, I was surprised to get a message in return inviting me to dinner on the night of my arrival. It appeared that they were holding a function at a local hotel and would be pleased if I would attend. Given that I would have flown for thirteen hours or more and would arrive around six in the evening I really didn't feel up to going out to a social event so I sent a note thanking them for the offer but politely refusing.

They were persistent however and suggested that they would meet me on arrival at the airport, transport me to my hotel where they would wait whilst I checked in, showered and changed then escort me to the event. Given their insistence I felt obliged to say yes.

On the Sunday night of my departure as I checked in for my flight the young woman behind the desk apologised and gave me the bad news. "I'm afraid that both First and Club are overbooked so you've been put into Economy but I've put you in an aisle seat in a block of four. There's one person on the aisle seat at the other end of the row so you have two spare seats in the middle and that'll give you a bit more room." I thanked her for being so thoughtful.

Boarding the flight, I made my way to the rear cabin and settled myself in. It was going to be a long night. We took off into the night and almost immediately I dozed off. It could only have been a couple of minutes when I suddenly became aware of someone beside me in the aisle.

Waking with a start I realised that there were two large young African woman standing beside me. One of them indicated the two seats in the middle and it became obvious that they wanted to move in. I had no choice. They were paying passengers and there was no reason why I should deny them the seats. Reluctantly I moved into the aisle to let them pass.

I settled down again and waited for the dinner service, ruing my bad luck. Dinner and a couple of drinks later and once again I drifted off to sleep despite the more cramped conditions that I now had.

I don't know how long I had been asleep, nor exactly what had woken me, but I suddenly became aware of something moving around my feet. The main cabin lights had been switched off so it took a moment for my eyes to focus. Looking down I suddenly realised that another pair of eyes was looking up at me!

One of the women had decided that she would be better off sleeping on the floor so had dropped off her seat and squeezed herself into the space between the seats with her head almost directly under my feet. She was smiling happily at me although this was the most normal thing in the world to do. It was just bizarre.

"I'm sorry but you can't sleep down there." I spoke quietly so as not to waken the rest of the sleepers in the cabin. She looked up at me with a query in her eyes. "No, I'm sorry, it's now allowed, you'll have to get up." I moved my feet with a fairly positive action which, whilst I didn't actually touch her, gave her an indication that it might not be too safe to stay where she was. With great reluctance and a lot of pushing and squeezing, not to mention some words of invective which she threw at her companion, probably telling her exactly what she thought of me, she heaved herself back into her rightful position.

The night passed uncomfortably into daylight although since most of the window blinds remained closed it was hard to tell. Eventually another meal was served and then the aircraft began its descent into Hong Kong where dusk was falling. As I made my way off the aircraft on to the air jetty a man stepped up beside me. "Mr Kelly?" I'm not sure how he recognised me, "I'm from LSG Skychef. I have a car waiting for you and I'll walk through Immigration and Customs with you."

It took only a short time for me to clear the formalities and collect my bag. We exited the Terminal and I was guided quickly to a large black car waiting at the kerbside. "I'll take you to your hotel, the Excelsior isn't it and I'll wait whilst you check in and change. It will only take a couple of minutes to get to our destination." I confirmed that the Excelsior was the correct hotel. It had been the British Airways crew hotel for more years than I had worked for the company and as such was an icon. I felt absolutely shattered. Although I had slept for some time during the night it was the uncomfortable, twisting and turning sort of sleep that comes with trying to make one's self comfortable in a space which seems to have been designed to be anything but comfortable.

My initial stay at the Excelsior was short. A few minutes to check in and find my room. A few more minutes to shower, shave and change into a suit and I was on my way again. It was only a short distance to my next stop. The car pulled up and I was whisked through a hotel lobby into a large reception area where a number of people were milling around, chatting and holding glasses of Champagne in their hands. "Mike, how are you, it's good to have you with us. How was your trip?" The manager of the Flight Kitchen came towards me, hand outstretched. We had met on several previous occasions in other Sky Chef facilities. Within minutes I had a drink in my hand and was being introduced to others. Many of the people I already knew, including one or two from competitor airlines and I began to realise that this was quite a big occasion.

Hotel staff were quietly gliding amongst the guests proffering canapes and topping up drinks. After a while I began to mellow and was just thinking this isn't too bad, I'll have another couple of canapes and then I can quietly slip away to my hotel and get some well needed sleep when suddenly a Master of Ceremonies appeared and having gained the attention of the audience said, "Ladies and Gentlemen please welcome your host for this evening, the Chief Executive of LSG SkyChef.

The Chief Executive stepped forward and taking the microphone welcomed the guests and invited us to join him for dinner. At that moment the side walls around the room began to move and to my horror I realised that we had been standing outside a very large dining room which was now being revealed. As the guests began to move towards the tables a

German band bedecked in lederhosen marched into the room playing a typical Bavarian song.

We sat down and began to work our way through a very large meal. It was the last thing in the world that I wanted but I couldn't figure out any way by which I could escape without appearing to be rude. It was a long night. Food course followed food course and to my now half dead brain it appeared to be never ending.

The meal ended only for the speeches to begin. It must have been close on eleven pm when it finally began to draw to a close but the worst was still to come. The Master of Ceremonies stood up to announce that all the guests had been entered into a raffle competition and he was about to announce the winners, each of whom was to make their way to the stage to be presented with their prize by the Chief Executive. I watched and waited as a number of people were called to receive their prize.

Finally the MC got to the main prize of the evening which he announced with great gusto. "Our star prize for this evening goes to someone who only landed in Hong Kong at 6.30 this evening and has made a special effort to be with us here. I'm very pleased to say that our prize goes to Mike Kelly of British Airways."

I was stunned and wished that the ground would have opened up and swallowed me. It was the last thing I wanted and my first thought was "should I turn it down?" In a brief second I realised that that might just make the whole thing even more embarrassing. I stood up and made my way to the front, to the applause of the many people there and having shaken hands with the LSG Chief Executive was given a very large hamper containing an assortment of food and a bottle of wine.

A staff member from LSG helped me to carry it back to my table. It took a few moments whilst I received the congratulations of my table companions and then, finally, I was able to make my excuses and head to my hotel and bed.

The following morning when I woke up, it all seemed like a bad dream, but no, there on the floor was a large food hamper. I had no idea what to do with it. It was far too big for me to take with me on my next flight out of Hong Kong in two days' time. Eventually I thought that the best thing for me to do was to take it with me to the BA catering team at Hong Kong airport and share it amongst them, which is what I did, much to their surprise and pleasure. Thinking about it long afterwards and becoming more cynical in my old age, I wondered whether or not my receipt of the main prize was a veiled attempt to bribe me into giving the kitchen a good score. If so it failed abysmally.

Hospitality was the norm in the industry but I normally always made a point of having completed my audit and given the Flight Catering Manager the result before I accepted an invitation to a meal. This one had been an exception.

Whilst many of the meals were light hearted and entertaining, others could be quite hard work, particularly if my hosts weren't English speaking and I always had to remember that I was representing my Company and had to keep my mind alert to what was being said.

Many other flights through my career produced entertaining or memorable moments but one which amused me was on a long haul evening departure out of London when the diminutive passenger seated next to me asked the Stewardess whether he might be allowed to climb into the overhead luggage bin and sleep up there!

CHAPTER 57

HUMOROUS INCIDENTS

During my career in the airline I came across many humorous situations, some during my audits and others whilst travelling on board aircraft. In my early days in Europe I had to get used to the vagaries of local customs and practices something which was brought home to me very suddenly one morning in Germany.

I had just spent the night in the crew hotel in Dusseldorf and waking early decided to have a swim before breakfast. The hotel which we used at the time had a large indoor pool on the top floor and it being very early I had the place to myself.

Having completed sufficient lengths of the pool to earn myself a decent breakfast I made my way to the changing area and the showers. Standing under the cascading hot water, eyes closed whilst soaping myself I was suddenly shocked rigid by a distinctly female voice saying "Guten morgen."

Opening my eyes I realised to my horror that I was now sharing the showers with a middle aged German woman who, like me, was stark naked. I smiled weakly and returned the greeting, then thought to myself "well if it doesn't bother her then why should it bother me and come to think of it we could both do with a good ironing!"

It was my introduction to the fact that many European countries have a very open and relaxed view of the human body and don't find total nakedness in any way unusual, unlike we British who tend to have a very closed mind about such things.

Aircraft crew could also produce their own moments of hilarity. One morning I was on the first flight to Rome, seated by the aisle towards the front. The flight was very full and as a football match between England and Italy had been played the previous evening there was a number of Italian football managers on board returning from the game.

Suddenly Paul Gasgoine the English midfielder, then playing for the Italian team Lazio appeared, making his way down the plane. He was wearing a very lurid green suit and as he progressed down the aisle he was being stopped and spoken to by a number of the managers who knew him.

The resulting build-up of passengers behind him caused the Purser in charge of the flight to call down the aisle. "Excuse me Sir, is there a problem?" Paul Gasgoine looked back at him. "No" he answered in his best North Eastern Geordie accent and moved on.

The Purser then said in a quieter voice "I thought maybe he hadn't paid for the suit." The passengers in the surrounding seats chuckled but laughed even more when the Purser continued "I wouldn't have!"

The Captains on the aircraft weren't averse to adding their sense of humour to proceedings. A very early morning departure to Amsterdam was livened up when the Captain began his pre departure talk to the passengers by saying "Good morning ladies and gentlemen, I'm your pilot and this is my first flight" then paused just long enough to allow a slight sense of unease before continuing "this morning."

He continued on landing at Amsterdam by saying "Ladies and Gentlemen welcome to Amsterdam. I always think it's great when we find it first time."

Other classics included the Cabin Service Director's comment after a particularly heavy bounce on landing "Sorry about that Ladies and Gentlemen. Had I known that we were about to reach such a high altitude again, I would have saved the dinner service until now."

The more commonly heard commencement to the pre-flight safety briefing was "Ladies and Gentlemen, Paul Simon says that there are fifty ways to leave your lover. This may be so but there are only four ways by which you can leave this aircraft in an emergency so if you want to know how to get out then please listen carefully to what I'm about to tell you." This usually got peoples' attention.

As we taxied down the runway on landing in Paris one morning the Purser welcomed the passengers to Paris and added "in my experience it's pointless to try to get to the arrival gate before the aircraft so please remain in your seats until the aircraft has come to a complete stop and the seatbelt signs have been switched off." This touch of humour was appreciated by the customers.

One other incident indirectly involving an aircraft has remained memorable. It began with me having a disagreement with my boss Peter. He had scheduled me to carry out an audit in Dubai after which I was to fly to Islamabad in Pakistan to audit the facilities there. I was happy enough to do the audits but said that I didn't wish to fly from Dubai to Islamabad with Pakistan International Airways (PIA). This followed from a minor incident which had happened on a previous flight that I had made with them.

For some reason Peter felt that I was trying to override his authority and he insisted that I do what he told me. After some strong words I left his office feeling somewhat disgruntled. The following morning when I picked up my daily paper I was amazed to see a front page picture of a PIA Boeing 747 which had landed on a runway with its wheels up. Fortunately, no-one had been badly injured.

Taking the paper in my hands I stormed into Peters' office and placing it in front of him said "This is why I don't want to fly with PIA!" Faced with the evidence he agreed that I could fly from Dubai to Islamabad with Emirates, the newly formed airline of Dubai.

On the morning of the flight I walked up the steps of the aircraft, resplendent in its Emirates livery and was greeted by a smiling stewardess who welcomed me on board. Settling into my seat I thought to myself that she didn't looked very Arab but I then remembered that Middle Eastern airlines generally recruited their crew from a range of countries. Looking around I saw other cabin crew who didn't appear to be of Arab ethnicity. I shrugged it off until we were ready to depart and the Captain spoke to the passengers. "Good morning Ladies and Gentlemen, this is Captain Khan speaking. Welcome on board this Emirates flight to Islamabad, operated by Pakistan International Airways on behalf of Emirates Airline."

"The best laid plans of mice and men" I thought to myself as we taxied to the runway.

Amusing incidents didn't only happen on the aircraft however. Even the most mundane of audits could sometimes produce bizarre or humorous moments.

In the mid nineteen eighties the BA crew hotel in Kuwait was opposite the Embassy of the USA which had been subjected to a suicide bombing.

Auditing the hotel some time afterwards I found that the main kitchen which was on an upper floor and faced the Embassy, was in a disgustingly dirty condition with food debris and dirt readily visible along floor edges and under equipment. Raising the issue with the manager I was amazed by his response. "This is because when the Embassy was bombed the hotel was moved backwards by several inches." I didn't know quite how I was supposed to believe that.

Auditing sometimes provided other surprises such as a kitchen in London which produced kosher meals specifically for Jewish travellers. As I progressed through the food production area the owner of the business was at great lengths to tell me how good the product was and how strictly the production methods complied with the requirements of the Jewish religion in the separation of various foods. He obviously hoped that I would be suitably impressed but his hopes were due for disappointment when on reaching the despatch dock I pointed to a stack of large plastic trays being used to transport completed meals to their final destination. "What does the Rabbi think of those?" Each of the plastic trays was imprinted with the name of a major well known British food production company at that time, "Pork Farms Ltd." He was speechless for a moment before saying "Those have been sent to us by an airline so that we can transport their food."

Staying in a hotel in Tehran in which our crew were accommodated I was somewhat perplexed by a peculiar smell coming from the fire escape stairwell right next to my room on the eighth floor. All was revealed when I walked down the staircase during my audit to check the facilities. The smell became noticeably stronger with each floor that I descended until on reaching the third floor I was faced with a staircase totally covered in loose onions. A vast number being stored there for subsequent use during the winter months. Heaven help anyone trying to escape a fire and rushing down the stairs I thought. There was a strong possibility that they would have lost their footing and slid a fair way down on their back.

Hotel fire escapes were a problem not least in the fact that they often didn't exit where people may have thought they should.

One hotel in a Caribbean resort was built on the side of a cliff above a beach. The reception lobby was at ground level but whilst some of the bedrooms were on upper floors, six of the floors went down. Whilst the rooms may have had wonderful sea views the staircase going down to the lower floors ended at a brick wall some height above the beach outside. The only escape route was up the stairs but there was no signage to explain this to guests and my view was that in the panic of a fire alarm in the middle of the night the reaction of most people would be to run down the stairs rather than run up?

When auditing hotels, I always checked the fire escape provisions at night as well as during the day. It was not unusual to find all sorts of things casually left on the staircase after dark. Beds, chairs, equipment etc. all of which would be hazardous to escaping guests.

More frightening was finding the fire escape doors in a hotel in Nairobi padlocked when I checked at midnight. The explanation from the manager was that if they weren't locked burglars might get in! When asked what would happen if a fire broke out I was told that the duty manager would arrive with a key to open the doors. Not much chance of that happening in the middle of a real fire I thought.

The expectations of some hotel managers as to what their staff would be capable of during an emergency were often somewhat ambitious in the extreme. For example, on asking a hotel manager in a European city what happened when a fire alarm sounded his reply was that one of the staff at the front desk would run up the stairs to check if the alarm was genuine or not. If not, then the alarm would be stopped before any evacuation of the hotel was ordered. The hotel alarm system was connected directly to the local fire station so if the alarm wasn't cancelled within three minutes the fire crew would turn out to the hotel which would prove expensive if it was a false alarm as the hotel would incur a hefty charge. Looking at the staff behind the reception desk, who were built more for comfort than speed, I suggested that it was highly improbable that any of them would be able to run up to the ninth floor of the hotel to check the source of an alarm in less than three minutes.

Hotels could also be perplexing as well as humorous. Given that I spent more than thirty years staying in hotels of all shapes, sizes and locations around the world, I like many other regular travellers, rapidly became used to the idiosyncrasies that they often threw up.

After my first few years I used to tell my friends that if they named a hotel I would tell them what was on the coffee shop restaurant menu.

It was fairly easy. The main hotel chains, because of their branding, would always try to produce an identical product in each hotel from room design to menus, no matter where in the world it was. Often when waking in the morning somewhat jet lagged in a hotel room and not sure of where, looking around me in the room would give little clue as to which city I was in.

The hotel looked exactly like the last one that I had stayed in. The décor and furnishings were the same and looking out of the window revealed a grey city which if there were no visible distinctive landmarks gave me little information. The joys of jet setting!

The fun of any hotel room was in finding out how things worked. Having checked on arrival outside my room door as to where the fire escape was and where it led to, the next question on entering the room was how do the lights work?

The light switch was sometimes controlled by the door key entry card which had to be placed into a slot on the wall near the door before the lights would work. Turning them on was one thing then turning them off was another.

Some room lights were often left partly switched on by the chambermaid and would turn on in full when the door switch was activated. Normally they could be controlled by switches on the bedside cabinet. Sometimes however there was a remote switch positioned somewhere in the room but not obviously by the bedside and there was nothing more infuriating last thing at night when after climbing into bed there followed a game of hunt the switch.

Once found it may not provide the answer as switching it "off" meant that one set of lights was extinguished but perversely another light would come on. Who in their right mind designs such things?

Similar rules applied to the television. Did it have a remote power switch somewhere which needed to be activated or was it controlled purely by the remote control unit and how were the channels changed? Many frustrating minutes have been spent searching for the answer.

The shower in the bathroom could also provide hours of entertainment in trying to make it work. I'm sure that many of them were designed by people with sadistic tendencies who wanted me either to get drenched in freezing cold water or alternatively scalded.

Not for them an obvious on/off tap but a variation in turning the hot water tap one way and the cold water tap the other or providing one set of taps for the bath but conveniently hiding the single tap that would turn on the shower. Whose idea was it to cunningly conceal the tap beneath the external edge of the bath in one hotel or design it to look like something completely different in another? Whatever the problems I survived them all.

The different cultures in the many countries that I visited also provided me with some entertaining moments. On a visit to Sydney I was invited by my British Airways colleague based there to join him after work for a drink and a bite to eat at his local sports club where he was due to meet his brother in law who was visiting from England. "He'll want to buy the drinks so just go along with it. He runs his own business in the UK and he likes to throw his money around a bit."

We met at the club where the brother in law lived up to his reputation. Walking up to the bar his first words to the barman were "Do you have any Champagne and I mean the real thing not your Australian rubbish?" Not the way to introduce yourself in an Australian bar I thought to myself but the barman didn't seem perturbed and brought out a bottle of chilled Champagne. "This do?"

Having been joined by another friend of John we got through the bottle fairly quickly and the brother ordered another. Coming back with the new bottle the barman asked "Are you fellows celebrating something? Did one of you get divorced?" We laughed.

One audit took me to Stavanger in Norway to review a salmon production unit. Seven o'clock in the morning saw three of us waiting for a taxi at the door of our hotel. The cab had been pre-booked to enable us to get to the harbour in time to catch a ferry due to depart at seven thirty. By seven fifteen it became obvious that the taxi wasn't coming so we hailed a passing vehicle and having piled ourselves into it urged the driver to get us to the port as quickly as he could. He was equal to the task but despite his efforts we arrived on the quayside just in time to see the large ferry beginning to move slowly away from the jetty.

The taxi slid to a halt and Peter was first out of the door, running down the pier, shouting and waving his arms at the ferry. The crew saw him and to our surprise put the ship into reverse. As it moved back towards the jetty a crew member appeared at the ship side and operated a lever which caused a side panel in the rail to open and a gangplank automatically swung out and downwards towards the quay.

I had followed Peter running towards the ship whilst Mike Marchant shouted "I'll pay the taxi." Arriving breathlessly at the gangplank I followed Peter up to the deck. The crew member, who hadn't seen Mike, who was now also racing down the pier, pushed the lever to cause the gangplank to begin to rise again and at the same time the Captain opened up the engine and the ship began to move.

"Wait for me!" Mike cried then realising that the boat wasn't going to stop he jumped for the gangplank which was now some three feet clear of the side of the pier. He made it although as he told us later had he thought about the danger he would never have jumped. "You bastards" he stood there looking accusingly at Peter and me. "You might have told him, looking at the crew member, that there were three of us." Peter and I were convulsed with laughter. "I didn't think you could move that fast" Peter said "Or jump that nimbly" I added.

Our visit to the salmon farm and processing factory was very informative. The salmon were grown in the sea in large circular nets, each of which held upwards of 40,000 salmon. An operative spent his working shift sitting on a small, old, defunct car ferry anchored some distance from the shore to which it was connected by a long floating walkway.

His job was to watch a video from cameras in each of twelve or more nets showing the salmon swimming slowly round and round. From the pictures he could identify any problems or illness that the fish might suffer and this could be dealt with. He also fed the fish using a large floor mounted gun by which food pellets could be fired with considerable accuracy directly into any one of the nets of fish. At the end of his shift he had a long walk back to shore on the walkway.

When the fish were the correct size the nets would be towed individually and very slowly to the shore alongside which stood the modern processing factory. The towing could take up to three days in order not to upset the fish. Once alongside the fish were sucked out of the net, humanely killed and then processed into individual salmon meals, packaged for the airline industry. The whole process was remarkable.

I thought that the job of the worker watching the salmon must have been one of the worst jobs in the world until I visited a lobster producing company in Nova Scotia, Canada. The factory was only open for sixteen weeks every year during which short time they processed thousands of lobster for consumers across the world.

Whilst auditing the factory I came across a young man standing in front of a table on which there was a one metre tall vertical pipe into the top of which lobster claws were fed. The claws dropped down the pipe and fell out on to a V shaped piece of metal pointing upwards. As each claw arrived the young man hit it with a hammer in order to crack the shell before placing it into a bin to be taken for further processing. What a dreadful job. Sixteen weeks of standing there hitting lobster claws with a hammer.

On my way back from this audit I was flying initially via a local airport to connect with a BA flight in Montreal. On arriving at the small modern airport there was nobody at the check in desks and I appeared to be the only passenger but I could hear voices from an office at the rear and on my calling out, a young woman appeared. She apologised saying that she hadn't expected anyone to be there so early as my flight wasn't due to leave for an hour. "You're not having a busy day then?" I said. "Oh no," she replied "this is our busiest day of the week. We have seven flights today." Thinking of Heathrow, I had to smile.

CHAPTER 58

INTRODUCING ANGOLA

Whilst the franchise airlines often provided me and my team with some interesting experiences often the mainline BA operation was no different, particularly when it came to opening new routes.

Those in the company who were responsible for finding new lucrative routes only had one thought in mind, a destination with a long enough runway and large numbers of passengers with money to spend on airline seats. They had no concerns about the need for a catering supply, mains drinking water and crew hotels. These were someone else's problem.

The Republic of Angola was a case in point. A large African country situated in the South West of the continent, bordering on Namibia, Zambia and the Congo it is rich in minerals and oil.

Formerly a Portuguese colony it gained independence in 1975 and almost immediately became embroiled in a civil war which lasted from 1975 to 2002. By late 2002 it became obvious that the war was virtually over. The world's major oil companies were exploring in the country and BA saw the opportunity to open a new route to its capital Luanda.

I was immediately approached by the Route Catering Manager for Africa and asked to go down and have a look at a flight kitchen which he understood was operational at Luanda airport. Almost simultaneously I had a call from the hotel procurement team asking if I could have a look at a possible crew hotel.

I had barely put the phone down when it rang again. Picking it up I heard the familiar Irish tones of my colleague John O'Sullivan, the Head of Fire Protection. "I hear you're going down to Luanda" he said. "You're quick off the mark John, I've only just been asked a couple of minutes ago" I replied. "News travels very fast."

"Well I knew that you would be asked so I thought I'd get in quickly.

I'm planning to go down next week and I'd be happy if you would come with me then we can look at whatever there is together." "That's fine with me."

"Great. I've been looking at flights. We'll probably have to go with Air Portugal out of Lisbon. If we leave here after work on Tuesday and fly to Lisbon, they have a flight that leaves about 1.00am on Wednesday morning and gets to Luanda at around 09.30am. We can do a days' work and come back on the return flight on Wednesday night and be back here by lunchtime Thursday." John had obviously been doing his homework.

"Well that sounds absolutely wonderful" I said with some irony. The thought of some twenty-four hours of non-stop travel and work didn't exactly thrill me. "Well you wouldn't want to be staying in Luanda overnight would you?" John replied.

The following Tuesday after work I met John in the airport Terminal to catch the BA 504 to Lisbon. "I hope that this is going on time otherwise our connection may be a bit tight." I remarked as we checked in. "It won't be a problem. We've got a couple of hours to spare in Lisbon to kick around the transfer area."

John was absolutely right. Our flight actually landed a bit early and as we only had carry on bags we were checked onto the TAP flight within a few minutes.

There wasn't much to do at Lisbon airport as we hung around waiting for our late night or was it early morning departure. A European Nations Cup football match was playing on a small TV screen at high level on one wall but there was nowhere to sit anywhere near it, so we sat by the bar and drank a beer whilst discussing what little we both knew about our destination.

"A typical Operations idea this one" John snorted indignantly. "Middle of nowhere this place but all they can see is people with wads of money." He felt even worse as we boarded our aircraft and found that our seats in economy were in the middle of a centre block. The aircraft was absolutely packed and there wasn't an inch of spare space. "Why on earth are all these people going to Luanda?" John looked at me as a large woman seated next to him wedged herself in alongside. "You can see now why Operations are so keen for us to start a service. Anyway it was a Portuguese colony so they probably still have a lot of family connections down there." We settled down for an uncomfortable night.

Our arrival was on time and as we taxied to our disembarkation point I was trying unsuccessfully to see what was outside.

The doors opened and after some considerable time due to our position at the rear of the aircraft, John and I were able to extricate ourselves from our seats and join the throng of passengers walking across the apron towards the Terminal building.

As I got to the top of the steps and looked around I could see a very busy airfield with numerous aircraft mostly military, in process of taxiing to the end of the operational runway where there was a large queue waiting for take-off clearance.

It was bright and sunny outside but the arrival Terminal was dark, thronged with people, and noisy. "Sunil is supposed to be picking us up" John remarked as his eyes roved across the waiting crowds. Sunil was the newly appointed BA Manager in Luanda but as neither of us had ever met him we didn't know exactly who we were looking for. Suddenly a man was by our side. "Mr Kelly, Mr O'Sullivan" a voice said. "Come this way." He moved positively and quickly through the crowds. "Sorry I was a bit late. How was your flight?" "You want an honest answer" John looked at him quickly.

"It was about what you would expect" I answered "I certainly didn't expect it to be so full." "They're all full" Sunil replied. "This place is booming and we're awash with oil men and geologists hence why Head Office is so keen to get a service up and running as quickly as possible. All of the passengers at the front end of the aircraft are business travellers, many are American and we're the only airline that will be able offer a one stop service to most of the US destinations that they want to travel to."

By this time we had exited the building. "Are you both fit to start work?" "Yes, no problem. We could do with a shower but we can probably get that when we get to the hotel?"

"I wouldn't bank on it but we'll see what we can arrange. I thought we could start with the flight kitchen. It's not too far. After that we'll see the airport Manager for the Fire Protection then we can go into town to look at the hotel. Is that OK?"

Jumping into a car we set off. Driving out of the airport terminal area it looked much like many other African airports I had been to. Hundreds of people all over the place, most of them showing the signs of third world poverty but all looking very busy although doing what I couldn't tell. Within a few moments we were drawing up outside a large beige coloured building which instantly was recognisable in shape and size as a flight kitchen. From the outside it didn't look too bad so at first glance I was encouraged.

We were ushered inside, up a flight of stairs and into a first floor office where a well-dressed young Angolan woman was waiting to greet us. "Good morning and welcome to Luanda." She spoke perfect English. "Would you like a coffee?" Within minutes we were discussing the requirements of BA flight catering and food safety in particular.

She answered all my questions fluently and I complimented her on excellent English and asked where she had learnt it. "I studied at University in Belgrade and all lectures were in English so I had to learn very quickly" she smiled. "If we're ready to go down to the kitchen I'll get some white coats."

I was impressed. Protective white coats, obviously freshly laundered were produced for us followed by protective hair covering. "This is all pretty good" I was thinking as we made our way out towards the stairs leading down to the kitchen.

My positive thoughts didn't last long. Walking down the stairs I had my first view of the kitchen through the glass panels on the side wall. As I looked I could see numerous mice cavorting through the dust and debris visible on the tops of the refrigerators and cold rooms beneath us. They were kicking up small clouds of dust as they ran. My heart sank.

The door into the kitchen opened into a very large tray preparation area. It had tiled floors and part tiled walls but looked very tired and dark. Looking up at the ceiling I could see a number of holes across the roof. My food safety instincts immediately saw this as a problem since in the wet season heavy rain would come through the roof and become a hazard to the food being prepared on the trays beneath.

Suddenly however I realised what the holes were. The building had been strafed! I pointed up at them "Those are bullet holes aren't they?" I looked at the young woman. "Yes but there isn't a problem anymore. The war is very nearly over. The fighting is 200 miles away and the rebel aircraft cannot fly as far as here so we won't be attacked again." She was so matter of fact about it that I couldn't think to say anything.

We gradually worked our way through the building. Conditions were atrocious. Any thoughts I had harboured as to quality standards whilst upstairs in the office rapidly disappeared. There was no hot water supply anywhere in the building, the refrigeration was non-existent in that although there were many refrigerators in which food was stored there were none that I could find that were operating at a temperature below $15°C$.

The dish washing machine had a thick coat of mould attached to the fingers of the belt which carried the dishes through the machine and the staff toilets were abysmal. Smelling, dirty and with no hand washing facilities.

Arriving at the rear of the building where the prepared aircraft trolleys containing the food for departing flights was loaded on to the trucks to go to the planes I looked at the flight details on the doors of a line of trolleys standing on the dock. To my horror these showed that the trolleys were destined to leave on a flight at 10.00pm that night, some ten hours away. Apart from the fact that they had been prepared a long time in advance of requirement they were parked in a temperature in the mid-thirties centigrade.

"These should be in a cold holding room until departure time." I said to the manager. "We don't have anywhere to put them" she replied quietly. "You don't have a final cold holding room?" I was almost incredulous. "No" came the short reply, "but it will be better in our new kitchen." "You're building a new kitchen?" I looked at her expectantly.

"Yes, it will be open in a few months. You will be able to come back and see it." "Good, I look forward to that but can we not have a look at it now?" She shook her head emphatically. "No that's not possible. The builders are working in it and we would have to get special permission."

We eventually finished the tour of the building and after saying our goodbyes made our way back to the car. As we pulled away from the building en route back to the airport, John looked at me "We won't be eating much on the flight home tonight then will we?" He grinned.

We headed back to the airport Terminal and ten minutes later were in the office of the airport manager. A large man, he welcomed us with a cheery smile. "I understand that you want to see the airport facilities. What exactly do you wish to see?" His English was excellent.

"Well Mike needs to see the aircraft drinking water supply and the aircraft servicing arrangements and I would like to see the airport fire and rescue facilities." John looked hopeful. Past experience had taught both of us that it wasn't always easy to persuade airport Managers that you should be allowed to look at what actually happened on an airport.

"That's easy" the Manager beamed at us. "I'll come with you." He shouted a few orders to one of his staff loitering in the adjacent office. "Come with me" and with that he led the way out of the office, downstairs and out on to the active airport ramp towards a car. "Get in and I'll drive you wherever you need to go."

We set off to the aircraft drinking water fill point. The airport was amazing. It was awash with aircraft. The apron outside the terminal was covered with planes. A number of them were passenger aircraft in process of arriving or departing but the majority were cargo aircraft of all shapes and sizes. Many of them appeared to be of Russian origin, some large elderly propeller driven whilst others were modern jets.

The runway departure point was crowded and it seemed that there was an aircraft taking off every minute on the single runway in operation. These were interspersed with landing aircraft which having touched down had to negotiate a D shaped turning point at the end of the runway where they waited for a suitable moment before being allowed to taxi back towards the Terminal.

The apron was crowded not only with aircraft but also with people and vehicles. It seemed chaotic and there appeared to be limited control over what was happening. As I watched a large Russian aircraft lumbered around the corner and with propellers thrashing noisily proceeded across the apron passing in front of a recently landed passenger flight and straight through the line of passengers walking towards the building. No one seemed particularly worried about the safety risk.

"Here's the water supply." The Manager pointed to a fill point on the wall of the building. I took my test kit and in a couple of minutes I had assessed the facility and checked the chlorine level in the water. To my surprise it was good. Off to the toilet servicing point next and again I found it quite satisfactory. At least some things were workable I thought.

Back in the car we were now heading for the airport fire service which was in the middle of the airfield. As we travelled round the perimeter before crossing the live runway John and I were amazed at the number of aircraft parked or abandoned around the airfield. Neither of us could believe what we were seeing.

There were literally dozens of aircraft of all shapes and sizes. Some had obviously been parked for a very long time and looked unlikely ever to fly again whilst others looked almost brand new but appeared to have been abandoned due to a broken part, a missing flap or in some cases a missing engine. In many cases they seemed to have been just pushed off the taxiway into the grass at the side. A large helicopter park contained at a guess one hundred helicopters again mostly Russian built and in various states of disrepair and abandoned.

I presumed that all of this was a direct result of twenty years of war. It was an amazing sight none the less and had to be one of the biggest collections of used aircraft outside the obsolete aircraft parks in the deserts in the USA.

The Fire and Rescue service was expecting us and as we jumped out of the car we were received by the Chief Fire Officer who led us towards his men, lined up at attention in front of three fire trucks.

The men looked quite smart as I stood to one side whilst John went about his work. A closer look at them however revealed that all was not what it should be. To my amazement I noticed that their protective clothing consisted of a set of blue cotton overalls and a plastic builders' type hard hat. Not much good in the event of a blazing aircraft. The heat would set fire to the overalls and the hat would melt I thought to myself!

John looked at the three fire trucks. One was out of commission judging by the grass growing around the wheels. A second was undergoing repairs with spare parts lying on the grass beside it in an untidy heap. The third was in the shade of a rickety looking open sided shed. "Does it work?" John looked at the Manager. "Yes, Sir." "Can you start it up?" John asked. He wanted to see how quickly the engine would start.

The Manager said something and with a large grin the Chief Fire Officer and one of his men raced towards the truck. They leapt into the vehicle, the engine burst instantly into life and without warning the truck roared out of the shed, blue lights blazing, sirens going and careered towards the runway. Next moment an arc of foam appeared and covered a large area of grass.

"Bloody hell" John said. "I only wanted them to start the engine to check that it started first time. They've probably wasted half their supply of foam doing that and they've also scared the life out of the airport ground controller who's wondering where the fire is" he added.

As I stood watching, a small voice came from beside me. "Sir, Sir"

I turned round to find one of the airport staff standing beside me. He looked intently at me. "They're not always here Sir" he said quietly. I was surprised to hear him speaking in English but as he had spoken very quietly I didn't quite catch what he had said. "They're not always here Sir" he repeated. I looked at him questioningly. "When there's a large fire in the city they will go down to help to put it out."

He walked away without another word. The implication of what he had told me was frightening. It meant that there could be occasions when there was no fire cover on the airfield should an aircraft crash. I motioned to John to come over to me and I repeated what I had just been told. "You're joking" he said. "It's what I've just been told and why would he lie?"

John walked back to the airport manager to ask a few more questions. Eventually he finished and walked across to me. "That's it for now. I've seen all I need to and I'm not going to get any more answers. The Manager obviously denies that the Fire Team ever leave the airport but I'm not sure that I believe him, however it's not worth starting a row at the moment."

We walked to the car and were driven back to the Terminal building where we took leave of our host. He bade us a happy farewell as we left.

"Where to next?" our guide, Sunil asked us. "The hotel please." I had been told before leaving London that the BA hotel procurement team had located one possible hotel in the city which might be suitable for use for British Airways crew. "OK. That's in town, down by the harbour." Sunil said as he turned the car out of the airport complex. I was now to get my first look at Luanda.

I thought that I was used to Africa and that I had seen most things but this was shocking. Like most African countries it was colourful, full of people and busy. What I wasn't prepared for was the sheer poverty. All of the countries which I had previously visited on the Continent were poor but this was something else.

The population appeared to be living in a sea of rubbish. It was almost as it they were living on an enormous rubbish tip. There was garbage everywhere. Piles of paper, cardboard, plastic, glass, just about everything one could think of lying on the ground or stuck in the mud. Their shanty homes seemed to be built on the compacted garbage which stretched as far as I could see. The people were very poorly dressed and although there was an appearance of them being busy I couldn't work out exactly what

377

they were doing. There appeared to be little in the way of shops or market selling which were normally apparent in African countries.

I looked at John. He was as transfixed by what he was looking at as I was.

The road began to descend into what had at one time been a relatively large and probably prosperous city designed in a European style. The ravages of war were immediately obvious. I could see the scars of bullet and shell damage and in many cases buildings were partly demolished or there were gaps where buildings had once stood.

There was traffic in the streets but I was aware that most of the population was either walking or being transported in a variety of small vans designed as mini-buses and thronged with passengers. Each bus had a "conductor" who hung out of the door shouting encouragement to all and sundry in an attempt to get customers to join his bus whilst also shouting insults at his competitors. What was very noticeable was the lack of bicycles. I had never been in an African city which didn't have any bicycles.

We drove through the city and emerging at the bottom of a hill I saw the entrance to the harbour. An elegant stone archway stood as both the gateway to the harbour and as a reminder of the Portuguese who had once colonised the country.

"Here we are." Sunil smiled at us as he turned the car to the right and pulled up a short distance from a large multi storey and relatively modern looking hotel. The name of a well-known five-star international hotel group was visible on the front.

What was also immediately visible and instantly recognisable to me from my Northern Ireland experience was the car bomb protection provided by a collection of large concrete barriers strategically placed in front of the building. Between these and the front door were several guards wearing flak jackets and metal helmets and carrying what I could only presume were Kalashnikov AK47 automatic rifles.

As we walked towards the door I was very aware that we were being watched very carefully but even more aware that one of the guards was spinning his rifle carelessly in his hand. "I hope to God he has the safety catch on" I thought to myself. John let me lead as we entered the hotel. "I'll just follow you if you don't mind. This your area again."

Looking around the reception area and lobby I realised that the property was more than a little dated and hadn't seen any changes in style or décor in the last twenty years at least. We were welcomed by the manager and after the introductions and normal pleasantries we began a tour of inspection. What had once been a style icon in its early days, the hotel was now best described as basic by modern standards. The public rooms were old and tired, the bedrooms were small, not very clean, poorly equipped and poorly maintained. The walls were light weight construction and therefore not very sound proof.

We descended into the kitchens where conditions were much the same as those which I had seen at the airport flight catering unit. Food safety was non-existent. It was immediately obvious that cleaning standards were very poor with food debris and dirt readily apparent on floors and equipment and there were no sanitisers or modern cleaning aids.

Working my way through the poorly lighted food preparation areas I was horrified to find that in one room both raw and cooked meats were being handled simultaneously thereby ensuring a serious risk of cross contamination with the cooked meats being liberally coated with the bacteria from the raw products.

The butchers, for the room was indeed a butchery, handled the raw and cooked meat with no thought or knowledge of the danger involved. I immediately raised the question with the manager. "Why are the cold meats being prepared in this room?"

"Because it's the butchery" came the reply, coupled with a look which suggested that I was mad to ask such an obvious question. "All meat is handled in a butchery?" he questioned me, suggesting that surely this was normal practice.

I tried to explain that there was a serious risk of contamination but the shrug of his shoulders indicated that I was wasting my time and he wasn't really interested.

Refrigeration throughout the kitchens was just as at the airport, in that what there was didn't work very well. Food was piled into fridges indiscriminately with little covering of individual dishes to avoid contamination and no date coding to indicate how old any of the products were. The whole place was a nightmare which was compounded by the evil smelling staff locker and toilet areas which were absolutely devoid of any hand washing facilities.

John and I made our way back to the lobby. Having been travelling all night we were all too aware that we needed a shower and asked if we could have a room for a couple of hours. The manager was happy to oblige but only if we were prepared to pay a substantial sum of money.

"What did you make of that?" John looked at me as I closed the bedroom door. "Pretty appalling wasn't it?" he asked. "Where would you start" I replied. "It doesn't come anywhere near to what we require and I doubt that the owner is interested in making any changes. We're meeting him later according to Sunil so we'll have to wait and see."

Just to add to the serious unease which I felt about using the hotel, a heavy rumbling noise outside drew my attention to the window. I looked out and what I saw caused me to call to John to come and have a look. Crawling up the road which led from the harbour up the steep hill at the side of the hotel was a large convoy of flatbed trucks.

Each was heavily laden with boxes of ammunition, sitting on the top of which was an armed guard dressed casually in shorts, a dirty tattered shirt and a pair of flip flops, wearing a bandolier of ammunition and toting an automatic rifle.

The war was obviously still going on and although we had been told that it was now some two hundred miles away the thought of an indiscriminate shot being fired at one of these trucks and setting off a huge explosion made me cringe.

Our meeting with the owner later in the day proved as fruitless as we had expected. An elderly gentleman of Portuguese extraction he had lived in Angola for most of his life. He explained that his hotel was very busy and in fact even if BA wished to stay there he wouldn't be able to accommodate us since his hotel was 110% occupied each night. Effectively that meant that he was letting some rooms out twice in every twenty-four hours to different guests. He already had a number of airline crew staying there and didn't want any more. End of story.

John and I set off that night on our return trip to Heathrow. Squashed into the economy seats on the TAP aircraft I had a Portuguese woman seated next to me. After take-off I fell into a deep sleep and only awoke prior to landing at Lisbon. "You slept very well" the woman spoke to me in halting English. "You didn't even eat any of the food." How little you know I thought.

Back in London I wrote my report, stating that from a safety point of view both the flight catering operation and the hotel in their present condition were totally unsuitable for use by BA. A week later I was asked to attend a meeting of all departments concerned in the attempt to open the new route to Luanda. There were at least twelve people in the room including John and me. The Chairman was tasked with opening the route and his position was fairly simple. He would not consider any reasons why this route could not work.

He worked his way around the table taking each of the departmental representatives in turn and confirming how far each had proceeded with their task. Most, if not all, had not been to Luanda so were speaking from information available from other recognised sources. Eventually he got to me. "Thanks for your report Mike" he said. "I understand that catering operations are looking at ways to overcome the flight catering issues?"

I nodded in assent, knowing that my discussions with my catering colleagues had caused serious concern and were a long way from being resolved. "As regards the crew hotel, we'll have discussions with the owner and will offer him the money needed to improve the rooms. £75,000 should be enough to provide some sound proofing." He moved on to the next item without even coming back to me. As far as he was concerned that was it. Job done, crew hotel accommodation sorted.

I sat there thinking that's a classic example of British Airways arrogance. We're BA therefore everyone must want to have us, no matter what. "I'm sorry" I said "but that won't work."

The Chairman didn't appear to hear me so I spoke out again. "Excuse me but that won't work." This time he heard and came back to me. "What was that?" "That won't work. I've spoken with the owner and he doesn't want our business. He has the only hotel worth talking about in town and although it's a very long way short of what we require he doesn't need us. The hotel is 110% occupied every night. He already has airline crew staying there," I named the airlines concerned, "and he doesn't want any more. In any case his room rates are extortionate. He charged John and me US$242 for a half day use of a room to shower and change. John will confirm all of this."

I looked across the table and John chipped in. "Mike's quite right. Not only would you not keep your dog in that place, but the owner doesn't want us." Looking down the table I realised that at last I had got the message through. "Two hundred and forty-two dollars did you say?" The Chairman sounded somewhat incredulous. "Yes and we were actually only in it for an hour to shower and change purely because we had travelled all night having worked through the day before and then worked through the morning when we arrived." "OK we'll have to take that one away and have another think about it. And there aren't any alternatives?" "Not that I'm aware of" I replied.

A few weeks later I was asked to go back to Luanda again. This time I was to join a full BA team of representatives from a number of Departments including Operations, Catering and Hotel procurement.

Meeting on arrival at Luanda airport we were a motley crew. I knew a few through my connections with other departments. Gerard from Catering Operations and Dave from Crew hotel procurement, but others were unknown to me. One in particular looked somewhat incongruous in his sports jacket and grey flannel trousers in the steaming heat. Under his arm he carried a very large tape measure on a gigantic reel.

"What's that for?" one of the team queried. We all waited expectantly. "It's to measure the D at the end of the runway." The explanation obviously baffled a few of those on the bus that was transporting us. "After landing the aircraft have to turn into a D shaped taxiway at the end of the runway to wait for clearance to taxi back up the runway towards the terminal area" he explained.

"Your job's going to be a bit dangerous" I said. "Why?" he queried. "Have you seen how busy this airport is? There's barely time to backtrack the aircraft between take offs so I can't see the airport manager agreeing to you stopping the flights whilst you measure the space. Anyway isn't the information in the existing airport manuals?" I replied. "Well you can't always rely on what someone else has done some time in the past." He sounded a bit aggrieved that I'd queried his work.

Arriving at the airport we split up. Sunil told the driver to take me to the new flight kitchen whilst he took the operations people into the airport to meet the manager. I was accompanied by Dave and Gerard who looked impressed at the sight of the brand new building.

I have to say that at first glance it looked good but once again I was doomed to disappointment. We were accompanied on the visit by the same woman who had shown me around the original kitchen on my first visit. She seemed pleased to see me again but it wasn't to last.

It didn't take long for me to see the problems and to be honest I began to feel really sorry for the caterers. They had obviously paid for some form of consultancy when designing the building but the construction standards used in building the premises had undone many of the benefits that the new building should have provided.

It was pleasing to see that the refrigeration had been vastly improved with a number of blast chilling units provided to enable the cooked food to be rapidly cooled after cooking was complete, along with numerous cold rooms, but these were virtually impossible to use since for some strange reason they had been built on plinths which raised them above floor level. This meant that to get trolleys of food into the chillers they would have to be manually lifted off the floor.

To add to the difficulty, a copper water pipe was running across the front of the chillers at head height which meant that to get a trolley into a chiller not only would it have to be lifted off the floor but it would have to be tipped backwards to allow it to pass beneath the pipework. Given the weight of the trolleys and the fact that they were carrying hot food, this was just a nonsense. I felt sorry that the caterers had been let down so badly by whomsoever had acted as a consultant in the design and fitting of the building.

This wasn't the end of things however. Walking through the kitchen my colleague from hotel procurement looked at me and pointing at the water pipe running down the wall to the wash hand basin said quietly "Have you noticed? They've got no hot water supply." I nodded my head. I'd already spotted it. At first glance, the wash hand basins were equipped with two taps. One hot and one cold and to the unwary to all intent and purposes there was a hot water supply. However, a closer look revealed that a single water pipe was running vertically down the wall and behind the wash basin there was a T junction. Both taps were connected to the same pipe.

My colleague couldn't contain himself. "Excuse me" he tapped our guide on the shoulder. "Yes" she said turning round to look at him. "You don't have any hot water supply to your hand wash basins." Dave spoke accusingly. "Yes there is hot water" came the instant response. "But you've only got one water pipe connected to the two taps." Dave had walked forward and was pointing out the deficiency. The other members of our group were now listening intently. The young woman walked forward and pointing to the vertical water pipe ran her finger down the left side. "The hot water comes down this side and the cold water comes down here" she said, moving her finger to the other side of the pipe.

She gave Dave a look which suggested that she thought that he was totally dumb in not being able to understand the basic principles which she had just explained, before turning on her heels and walking away. Dave looked at me incredulously. "Did I just hear what I thought she said? The hot water comes down one side of the pipe and the cold water comes down the other?"

"Yep" I replied, "It would be funny if it wasn't so serious." "What are you going to do?" "There's not much I can do" I replied. "Despite being a new kitchen it's not fit for purpose until they make some expensive changes. It's just going to make the operation that bit more difficult" Gerard from Catering Operations joined in "It's a bit of a mess isn't it?" "It's still a thousand times better than the old kitchen" I said. "If you think this is bad you should have seen the old one."

We made our way out of the building and into the bus which was to take us to the city and the crew hotel. Driving down the city streets those, for whom this was a first visit, were looking intently out of the windows. "It doesn't look too bad." Gerard's voice came from a seat towards the back. "I was expecting worse."

"I don't think you're seeing it as it really is" I responded, slightly irritated by the casual approach that was being exhibited. "The empty spaces between buildings are where bombs or shells have exploded and the buildings have collapsed and if you look closely at the marks on the walls of the surrounding buildings you'll see that they're shrapnel or bullet marks where the fighting took place some time ago."

"Have you noticed anything else which may be different from other places that you've been to?" I looked around the bus. There was no response so I continued. "There doesn't appear to be anyone over the age of forty anywhere. There are no old people visible. Life expectancy is very low and there's something else missing." I stopped. People were now taking a closer look at the surroundings. "There aren't any bikes" one of my colleagues said suddenly. "Correct" I said. "When have any of you been to a third world country where you haven't seen a bike? It shows the level of poverty and deprivation that's here as a direct result of the years of fighting."

We arrived at the hotel. Nothing appeared to have changed in the few weeks since I had last visited. Some of my fellow team members seemed to be a bit taken aback by the armed guards and the concrete blocks protecting the entrance to the hotel. "Remind you of home?" Gerard grinned at me as he referred to my Northern Irish background. "Yes it was much the same in the bad old days in Belfast."

Inside, the hotel Manager walked Dave and me through the premises. Nothing had changed. The bedrooms still looked shabby and in need of an upgrade. Walking through the kitchens I saw Dave cringe as he witnessed at first hand the conditions which I had written about in my report of my first visit.

We reached the staff toilet and locker areas and as we walked into the ladies' toilets Dave was so busy telling me how bad he thought the place was that he wasn't looking where he was going and walked straight into a voluminous ladies' bra which was hanging from a make shift clothes line stretched across the room.

"Agh" he yelled whilst trying to disentangle himself from the heavy, wet piece of lingerie which had wrapped itself around his head. I fell about laughing as he eventually got free.

Walking into the first of six toilet cubicles I waited for Dave's comments which weren't long in coming. "There aren't any toilet seats" he said first, followed rapidly by "there isn't any toilet paper." He walked out of the cubicle towards the row of wash hand basins fitted on the wall opposite. "There aren't any taps!" His horrified voice reflected the thoughts going through his mind. Nonetheless he still asked the question. "How do they wash their hands?"

"They don't" I replied. "You must have read the report of my last visit?" He looked stunned. "I just didn't think that it could be this bad."

CHAPTER 59

CUSTOMER COMPLAINTS

Whilst overseas airports provided us with many problems many more came to us directly from the customers who travelled on our flights. Customer complaints were a regular feature of our daily routine. The majority of them came to us from the Customer Relations Department tasked with answering the many letters which they received daily. Not being experts in food safety and environmental health they relied on us to help them compose a suitable reply for problems that had arisen in those areas.

Others came directly to my desk via letters sent to the Director of Health Services, whilst some came via the office of the Chief Executive or from our colleagues in the Insurance Claims Branch.

The complaints ranged across a number of areas but the great majority of them were related to the food served on board and an allegation that the complainant had been ill after eating the meal. All of them, no matter how bizarre the complaint might be, had to be fully investigated before a decision could be made as to how to answer the complainant.

Most people have little or no knowledge of food poisoning organisms and their incubation periods, or to put it more simply the period of time that it takes between consuming contaminated food and beginning to suffer the effects. This can be anything from hours to days depending on which organism caused the problem.

It's not surprising therefore that when people are unexpectedly sick they will usually blame the last thing that they ate but this may not be the case.

With each complaint it was up to me and my team to prove what the possible cause might be, given the information which we were able to glean.

Often we started with a very basic letter from the annoyed passenger which said "I flew on your flight BA... on ... date. I ate the disgusting meal and after getting off the aircraft I threw up" or something similar. This was usually followed by a claim for compensation.

To investigate properly we needed to know what had been eaten, what the symptoms were and when the alleged sickness actually began. A check with flight catering would quickly give us the total number of meals provided for all flights on the day in question and the number and content of the meals produced for the specific flight.

Many passengers travelling on the same flight will eat the same meal, even when there is a choice and if one meal was contaminated then it would be likely that others in the same production batch would also be contaminated. If this was the case it would be probable that more than one passenger on the flight would be ill.

It also follows that many flights out of a busy airport such as Heathrow will have the same menu on board and once again if one meal was contaminated then a very large number of others would also be affected and passengers on a number of flights would fall ill. A good example of this was the outbreak of Salmonella which hit BA flights in 1984.

A lack of complaints of sickness from other passengers on the same or other similar flights made it a fairly simple, if time consuming exercise, to prove that the complaint was not viable. This would be compounded if the passenger had actually been sick whilst on the aircraft. If food on a particular flight had been contaminated by an organism which produced such a short incubation illness, then we would expect a number of passengers on board to have begun to vomit and perhaps suffer with diarrhoea at the same time. This would be very noticeable given that even on the largest plane there is a limit to the number of available toilets. If several passengers were taken ill simultaneously, the results could be quite disastrous.

To be absolutely sure, the production records from the flight kitchen which produced the meal, wherever in the world, were also checked to make sure that there were no disparities, and prove that the airline meal had not been responsible for any illness suffered.

The exercise became more simple in my latter years following the introduction of a Hazard Analysis and Critical Control Points (HACCP) programme in all of our caterers across the world. HACCP was an innovation in food safety which required a caterer firstly to identify all food safety risks in the production and handling of food within their premises, then identify and put in place the controls necessary to eliminate the risk. They then had to keep written records to prove that the controls were working.

This method of food safety control meant that things such as the cooking, cooling and handling times and temperatures for high risk foods such as chicken, cold meats, crustaceans, desserts etc. were monitored and recorded.

In the event of a food poisoning complaint we were able to analyse the food production records from the supplying kitchen in detail to see if there had been any discrepancies.

Introducing the HACCP concept was not an easy task. The system required a lot of training to explain what it was all about and we needed the co-operation of all the staff working in the catering units to ensure that it succeeded. Recording times and temperatures was totally alien to chefs and many of them didn't take kindly to adding the extra work involved to their already busy schedules. Converting them was to be an uphill task.

How many times did I hear the phrase "I've been in this business for twenty years and I've not killed anybody yet!" as an excuse for not getting involved? My answer was always "Well do you want today to be the first time that you kill somebody?"

In the early stages many of the staff involved in making and keeping the records tried to convince us that they were doing the work when in reality the figures that we were given as proof were being falsified. Realising what we were looking for, the temperatures and times were being written on to the required record sheets without any measurements having been taken.

This often was very obvious during an audit as the records were much too neat and tidy to have been written by a chef in a busy kitchen. The record sheets were too pristine. They didn't have the greasy marks and food staining on them which I would expect to see on sheets produced during the working shift in a kitchen. Not only that. Sometimes the neatly written figures covered more than one working shift and an investigation would show that the chef who supposedly carried out the work wasn't present during the second shift. Try hard as some of them did, they didn't have enough imagination to falsify the records with any great skill.

As the system became standard through the food industry we were able to change the way in which we audited our suppliers. Our audits now became a paper trail in the first instance followed by a physical check of the catering unit to confirm that what was written in the records was actually happening.

Normally I would begin an audit by asking for the records for a particular BA flight on a particular date. This could be any day in the past six months and as the unit Managers didn't know in advance which date I would choose they had to ensure that the record keeping was accurate but despite their best efforts it didn't always go to plan.

Visiting one large kitchen in the Southern hemisphere all was going well until I entered the blast chilling area in the hot kitchen. It was around 11.00am and there were numerous trays of food being rapidly cooled, having recently been taken from the oven. To comply with HACCP rules, the cooking temperature and time at the end of the cooking process had to be recorded followed by records of the time taken to blast chill the cooked product and its final temperature. These would show if the food had been correctly cooked then rapidly chilled to avoid the risk of survival of food poisoning organisms.

Temperature control would continue to be monitored and recorded whilst the food was stored in cold rooms prior to tray setting later in the day. Measuring and recording the temperatures and times wasn't difficult but it was time consuming.

Some of the food produced earlier in the shift was already in storage in a large cold room so I asked for the records of the cooking and chilling procedures for that morning and waited along with the manager for them to be collected and brought to us. The records took some time to arrive but when I eventually got them and read through what was on the sheets I could understand why. "It appears that your chef is a prophet and can foretell the future." The manager looked at me, not quite understanding. "According to these records he already knows the temperature of these trays of food at three o'clock this afternoon. The figures are already written on the sheets. Have a look." I showed them to him. He glanced at the figures then all hell broke out as he yelled for the chef.

I would add that this wasn't the only flight kitchen in the world which had a chef who could see into the future. I was to meet more in audits in other places.

One other incident proved amusing. The team in a flight kitchen in California had worked very hard to get their systems right and as the audit began the Executive Chef took great pleasure in wheeling into the board room a large trolley load of records. He had everything according to him.

As normal I picked a date a month or so in the past and asked for the BA Club Class production records. The Chef's assistant began rifling through the appropriate record box to find the paperwork. As I sat chatting to the management team I could see the assistant get to the end of the box. He looked a bit perturbed as he began to go through the box again. He obviously hadn't found what he was looking for. Getting to the end of the box again he now moved to the side of the Chef and had a word in his ear. The Chef got up and he too went through the box. He too was unsuccessful and following two more attempts was forced to turn to me and with a red face admit defeat. "We can't find the date you've asked for but we have every other date for that month."

"Sods law" as they say. He was absolutely correct. Every other day in the month was present and for the last six and when I checked the records they were excellent. Why one day was missing they couldn't work out and why I chose that particular day was just pure luck but it provided a good laugh at the Chef's expense as the rest of his team wouldn't let him forget it. "Why did you choose that date?" he asked. "It was my birthday" I replied, which provoked even more laughter.

But let's get back to our customer complaints. The fact that I could prove that the airline meal wasn't the cause of the passenger illness didn't necessarily convince the irate passenger. Having replied to the complainant through Customer Relations, often a further letter would arrive which basically said "well you would say that wouldn't you."

Sometimes this might be followed by a letter from a Solicitor which having re-iterated the original details of the case, which we had already investigated and found not proven, would still claim for compensation for the alleged illness.

If the law firm was particularly clever they would ask for a fixed sum of money such as "not less than £5,000 and not more than £10,000 in respect of the illness and suffering endured by my client." This was designed to get the airline to pay up because the solicitor knew that it would cost vastly more money in legal fees to defend the case than it would to pay a relatively small amount of money. That was always annoying and caused more work in refuting the claim.

Often people wouldn't accept the evidence which was provided and were prepared to take their complaint into court which led to my having to appear as a witness for the defence on more than one occasion. Two of these cases were noteworthy and both of them were defended in the USA.

The first wasn't related to food but was an allegation that a female passenger had been deliberately sprayed in the face with an aerosol insect spray whilst flying to a destination in Africa.

It's a legal requirement of many countries that aircraft arriving at their airports must be treated to kill any disease carrying mosquitoes which may accidentally be travelling on board. This is to avoid the transmission of malaria, yellow fever etc. from country to country. The process is called disinsection and is carried out under the guidance of the International Health Regulations.

It requires the aircraft to be sprayed by the crew with a prescribed insecticide at the point of departure from the originating airport. When everyone is on board and the doors have been shut the passengers are advised of what is going to happen and told to cover their mouth and nose if they think that the spray may affect them. This despite the fact that the insecticide has been designed to meet defined World Health Organisation standards to ensure that it is safe in use.

The woman bringing the case alleged that she had been sitting in her seat by the window when she saw in her words "smoke approaching." She claimed to have leapt into the aisle of the aircraft to remonstrate with the crew member who was walking down the aisle spraying the cabin air space above the heads of the passengers, in accordance with the required procedure. She then claimed that having confronted him he deliberately sprayed the insecticide in her mouth. This allegedly had caused untold damage to her which had resulted in a serious deterioration in her health for which she required damages in the sum of several millions of dollars.

As a result, one July day in the heat of summer I found myself in the Daniel Patrick Moynihan Courthouse of the Southern District Court of New York, prepared to face questions in defence of British Airways.

I had previously met with the British Airways defence attorney, Stephen Fearon of Condon and Forsyth, the company retained by BA for their legal work in the USA. He had come to London and gone through the details of the case with me, taken a written deposition and I was to arrive in New York the day before the case was due to be heard so that we could go through the final details in his office.

My journey over had not been without incident. Due to it being high summer our regular flights to New York were heavily overbooked and there was a strong chance that I might not be able to get on any flight on the specified day.

My Director therefore thought that it was important enough that I should fly across on Concorde in order to arrive in good time for my meeting. Happily ensconced in my seat on the morning departure from London and awaiting the arrival of my breakfast tray, as the aircraft climbed rapidly towards 50,000 feet, a sudden shudder in one engine put paid to that thought. The Captain's announcement of an engine failure meant a slow subsonic and much lower level flight back to Heathrow from a point off the West coast of Ireland.

Two hours later I was boarding a second Concorde which had been parked at an adjacent stand ready for the transfer of passengers and catering from the stricken aircraft as soon as we arrived back in London and a little while later we were airborne again. At that point the Senior Cabin Crew member walked down the aisle handing each passenger a letter of apology from the BA Chief Executive, a letter which contained a considerable sum of money to recompense the passenger for their late arrival into New York. After all, the reason for them paying a vast sum of money to travel on Concorde was to get to New York quickly. Looking at me as he reached my seat, and knowing that I was a staff passenger he quietly said "No chance" and whisked the envelope past me with a broad grin.

But all was not yet finished. Landing at John F Kennedy airport the aircraft came to a halt on the runway with a distinct list to one side. The pilot's voice came across the PA system. "I'm very sorry about this ladies and gentlemen but we've had a hydraulics failure on landing and I can't move any further until we have engineering support. This is the first time in my career that I've had two incidents with two different aircraft on the same day and I really can't apologise enough." And so I arrived in the offices of Condon and Forsyth some four hours late, despite travelling on Concorde, much to the amusement of all present.

The Courtroom proceedings in New York were very different from those that I had experienced in the UK. The Judge had his own courtroom which had his name on it almost as if it was his office. Well it probably was as far as he was concerned. The defence team sat at the back of the court matched by the plaintiff and her team sitting a little distance from us across the room. It was my first view of the complainant. She didn't look very unwell to my untutored eye.

The Judge introduced himself to the legal teams and then called in the prospective Jurors. Some thirty in all they filed into the body of the courtroom and sat down. The Judge then gave them a brief résumé as to what the case would be about. Each was then called to the witness box where they had to describe themselves to the Judge, tell him what they did by way of employment and give any reason why they felt that they shouldn't hear the case.

Gradually the group was whittled down as the Judge dismissed those whom he felt were unsuitable for this particular case for reasons such as working in the airline or travel industry or in the case of one girl, being a lawyer. "They'll never appoint a lawyer to a Jury" Stephen whispered in my ear, "just in case they use their knowledge of the law to pervert the Jury decision."

Eventually the Judge was happy with those that were left in front of him but now the two legal teams were allowed to have their chance to remove any person whom they felt might prejudice their case. It took all morning and into the early afternoon at which point the Judge decided that he'd had enough and moved the hearing to the following day.

Next day we started in earnest. I was a witness and wasn't allowed into the Court until I was called to give evidence so I spent most of the morning in a small witness waiting room accompanied by the Cabin Service Director of the flight in question who was also going to be called to give evidence.

Eventually my turn came. I walked into the room and was accompanied to the witness stand by a Court official who gave me a bible to hold whilst swearing me in. The Judge was behind me on my right side, the Jury was to my left and I was obviously expected to speak directly to them. A US Court stenographer sat in the middle to record everything that was said.

Stephen Fearon was standing in front of me and unlike in British Courts he wasn't dressed in a gown and wearing a wig but was dressed casually in a suit and tie. He introduced me to the Jury, explaining my role in British Airways and asking me questions to confirm each of his statements.

It was all going well until turning to me with a smile he suddenly said "Mr Kelly would you please explain the content and purpose of the International Health Regulations and their application in this case" and walked away from me.

For a second I was stunned. I hadn't expected this. I was used to the UK court system where I would be questioned in detail by the defence Barrister who would previously have appraised me as to what he was likely to ask.

I took a deep breath then looking straight at the jury tried to explain what it was all about. Twice Stephen stopped me in order to explain slight language differences to the Jury, the differences being a classic example of England and the USA being two countries divided by a single language, but otherwise it seemed to go well. The Judge also asked me some questions to clarify working points and then it was the turn of the plaintiff's team. Their attorney didn't seem to want to get involved in the workings of the regulations so was happy to let me off lightly.

The case ran for several days. I had to attend each day in case I was recalled but it didn't happen. Each afternoon when the hearing was adjourned, we watched as the plaintiff's defence team left the building with her and she happily trotted down the steps in front of the Courthouse showing no signs of any medical disability.

Her own evidence was almost unbelievable. In her own words she had seen the "smoke coming" before the crew member had reached her area of the cabin, which, given that the aerosol was effectively a can of fly spray, sounded implausible.

She had then "leapt into the aisle to confront him" notwithstanding that she was a large lady, seated by the window and had to get across two seats the outer one of which was occupied, before she could reach the aisle. And all this to meet a crew member walking down the aisle at a speed of one row of seats per second, which was the prescribed rate of application. It all sounded a bit far-fetched and that's what the Jury thought when they found in favour of BA.

A good week's work but an expensive defence for the airline.

The second memorable legal action in which I was involved didn't actually get into the courtroom but was notable for the work in which I was involved when putting the defence case together. It began one morning when I received a note from our Insurance Branch Claims manager Gordon Simpson, with which was enclosed a letter of complaint and request for compensation from an American law firm.

The basis of the complaint was that their client when travelling in Business Class on a British Airways flight from London to San Francisco had, whilst eating his meal, inadvertently swallowed a toothpick. This had lodged in his intestine and subsequently had to be surgically removed. Attached to the letter was a photograph or to be more precise a copy of an x-ray showing a toothpick firmly lodged in the duodenum.

I was intrigued. Looking closely at the photograph it certainly appeared to be a toothpick similar to those which formed part of the tray set up for our Club Class meals. However, for the life of me, I couldn't see how someone could accidentally swallow one.

The toothpicks in question were some two inches (5cm) long, made from hard plastic of circular hollow construction and shaped to have a point at one end. They were extremely hard and couldn't be cut through with a standard metal cutlery knife. I know this because as part of the investigation I got some of the toothpicks and tried to cut them.

To add to this, each toothpick was packed in a sealed wrapper when delivered from the manufacturer. This was placed in the cutlery wrap on each individual passenger meal tray. Therefore, each toothpick had to be taken out of the cutlery pack and unwrapped before use. Finding a toothpick in the food and then accidentally eating it seemed somewhat unlikely.

It seemed more probable that the passenger had taken the toothpick out of its wrapper and then for some unknown reason, whilst using it, had accidentally swallowed it. He may then have thought that it might pass harmlessly through him and he wouldn't have to mention it to anyone but when it lodged in his gut and required surgical intervention there would have been a degree of embarrassment not to mention that in the USA there would be a hefty medical bill to pay.

After some investigation and discussion, our Insurance and Legal teams agreed to fight the case on the grounds that the airline wasn't liable for something which the passenger may have caused to happen. The case was going to be heard in a San Francisco court and as was the norm, I and some of my colleagues would be asked to give written depositions prior to the case. This entailed us having to be cross examined by the plaintiff's lawyers whilst under oath.

It was decided that in order to reduce costs, I along with Stephen Glass, the member of my team who oversaw the food safety standards in the London catering unit which had produced the meal, would be cross examined in our office in London.

On the day in question we were accompanied by Rod Margo, a lawyer from Condon and Forsyth who, as the case was being heard in the USA, were once again representing BA. A US Court stenographer based in London was present to record all that was said as we sat in a closed office connected to a female lawyer in San Francisco via an open phone line.

It was somewhat surreal. A disembodied voice asking questions to which I had to respond whilst Rod, sitting beside me listened carefully to both the questions and my answers and occasionally jumped in with a loud "objection" followed by his reason and often a quick "you don't have to answer that" to me. On a couple of points his objection lead to some heated discussion between him and his counterpart on the phone. However, we eventually got through it all, although it had taken a full afternoon and was quite tiring.

A few days later I got a phone call from Gordon our Insurance team manager. "We have a problem" he started off. "You're not going to believe this but the lawyer who took your deposition last Thursday has died."

"You're joking" I said, somewhat shocked by the news. "How come?" I continued "She didn't sound as though she was that old although it's hard to tell over a phone line." "She wasn't" Gordon continued "Apparently she was in her early thirties and had a very unexpected heart attack." "Good grief. It just proves that you can never be sure of what's going to happen next. I'm very sorry to hear the news however even though I didn't get to meet her." "It's very unfortunate but it leaves us with a problem." Gordon continued "Apparently you're going to have to go through the whole deposition thing again."

"Oh no! How come?" I was a bit staggered at the thought as I really didn't want to have to do it again. "Well they will obviously have to change the lawyer and he or she will have to go through the case for themselves and ask the questions which they think are important." Gordon explained.

"Well if that's the way it has to be then I don't have any choice however this time I'll go to San Francisco and meet the lawyer face to face. It's a lot easier when you can see them and make eye contact when answering."

And so one morning a couple of weeks later I met Rod Margo in a hotel in down town San Francisco. He accompanied me into an upstairs room where a lawyer representing the plaintiff was waiting for us.

"Good morning Rod" he greeted us with a smile and then put his hand out to me. I was introduced and as he shook my hand he said "Which part of Northern Ireland are you from?" "Bangor" I replied, recognising his familiar Belfast accent.

"You went to Bangor Grammar school then?" came the next question. "No, I'm an Instonian." I said referring to the Royal Belfast Academical Institution, a highly respected Belfast city centre school. "Ah, an Instonian. I was at BRA." came his response, referring to the Royal Academy also in the City.

"Do you know anyone in the legal profession back home then?" he continued the questioning. "Yes, I know Colin Gowdy of King and Gowdy the Belfast Law firm and Patrick Coughlin. Colin was in my year at school and Patrick was a couple of years younger but lived down the road from me in Bangor."

"Yes I know Colin and Paddy." he replied. "Not Paddy, Sir Patrick to you now" I said with a grin. "He's a Judge these days and has been awarded a Knighthood." "Well I never."

At this point Rod intervened and took me to one side. He was worried that I was getting too friendly with the opposition and told me so. I couldn't understand why he was getting so excited. It was two people meeting a long way from their original homes and talking about their common background. I was well aware that once the legalities commenced the lawyer would be asking me a series of questions and trying to pry open any areas of dispute that he thought might be present and would be useful in his case. I for my part would answer all the questions as honestly as I could. Whilst the questioning might be a little antagonistic I fully realised that there would be nothing personal in it and that the lawyer would only be doing his job to the best of his ability.

At that the US Court stenographer arrived, introduced herself, set up her equipment and we were ready to start.

The questioning followed much the same line as it had previously. The lawyer was trying to prove that his client had swallowed the toothpick by accident because it had been in the food on his plate when he had eaten the meal. I on the other hand was at pains to point out that the toothpick would have been packed in its sealed wrapper and inside the napkin wrap on the tray. Had it been in the food how could it have been picked up on a fork, put in the mouth and swallowed without being noticed? Two inches of hard plastic? It was circular in cross section and wouldn't sit on a fork without rolling off. Placed in the mouth it was hard and couldn't be bitten through and because of its size it could only pass down the throat lengthways. Notwithstanding all this the lawyer was desperately trying to prove that the toothpick could have been in the meal when his client was eating it.

I answered all his questions about food production, explaining that during the plating up of the meal in question there were a number of people who would have looked at the plate and would have been expected to see any foreign item that was present on it.

He then began to question the dish washing process. "You say that all the dishes are washed when they return from the aircraft to the flight kitchen?" "Yes." "Can you explain to me how this happens?"

"OK. On arrival they are separated into their various types such as plates, glasses, cutlery etc. then each type goes down a separate stripping line into a specially designed commercial five tank dishwasher. The waste food is manually scraped off the plates before they are stacked vertically in racks and passed on a conveyor belt into the washing machine." I carried on. "Once in the machine they pass through high powered jets of water which give them a pre-rinse, wash, rinse and dry cycle."

He looked at me. "It's possible that not everything would be scraped off the plate before it enters the machine?" "Possible but not probable" I replied.

"And it's possible that a toothpick from a previous flight would be stuck on the plate?" Again I answered "It's possible but not probable."

"What happens when they come out of the machine?" "They are off loaded by hand and checked. The clean plates will be placed into storage racks and any which are marked or deemed to be unclean will go into bins to be reloaded into the machine."

"So a toothpick could be stuck on a plate when it leaves the machine and could accidentally be packed into the clean equipment rack?"

This was getting ridiculous I thought as I pondered my reply. Whilst some food items such as egg can be difficult to remove when stuck on a plate it would be hard to believe that a circular cross sectional piece of hard plastic stuck on a vertical plate could pass through a series of high pressure water jets without being washed off.

In my frustration at the continuing line of ever more ridiculous suppositions I replied "It's possible that Paul McCartney was offloading the dishwasher but it's not probable." The stenographer started to giggle then restrained herself. Rod glared at me, worried that I was antagonising his opponent.

"OK I think that we'll move on" said the lawyer and started a new line of questioning.

Two and a half hours later and we were finished. Rod and I went and had a coffee. As we sat in the coffee shop and discussed what had happened Rod asked me "What do you think happened. Did he swallow it accidentally?"

"It's fairly simple. According to the information that we've been given the plaintiff by his own admission drank a quantity of Scotch prior to eating the meal. He then had a couple of glasses of wine with the meal. He claims that he doesn't remember seeing or swallowing the toothpick. However, I would surmise that being an American, after eating his meal he took the toothpick out of its wrapper and placed it in his mouth and proceeded to chew on it. I've often see Americans chewing on a toothpick." Rod nodded in agreement. I carried on.

"Whilst doing this he dozed off as a result of the combination of alcohol and food and whilst asleep the toothpick slipped and he accidentally swallowed it. He would have had it lengthways in his mouth so it's quite probable." Rod nodded again.

I didn't have to go into court to be cross examined as the case apparently was settled out of court. However, some considerable time later I had to repeat my evidence, this time in London as the Insurance company who presumably had chosen to pay compensation rather than face the expense of going into court, were now trying to sue the Flight Catering contractors who had supplied the meal.

A bit bizarre I thought since my original evidence on behalf of BA was pointing towards the contractors not being responsible for the incident. If this was the case how then could the BA Insurers expect to reverse the scenario?

Once again the case went to the wire with me meeting a Queen's Counsel on a Friday afternoon to discuss my evidence with the case due to be heard on the following Monday morning. I was disappointed when it failed to go ahead and was settled out of court. It would appear from my experience that the people who make the most money out of such claims are the lawyers!!

CHAPTER 60

FOREIGN BODIES

Foreign bodies in food, unlike that in the case I've just described, are a problem for all manufacturers and no matter how stringent the controls are in trying to ensure that nothing untoward gets into the food they will always be an area of concern.

British Airways serves millions of meals every year with good quality food from reputable sources but despite the precautions taken it was inevitable that from time to time something would go wrong and a customer complaint would be received.

Often these would feature a small insect found in a salad. Despite the washing process through which the salad items were subjected it appeared to be impossible to ensure that everything was washed off in the thousands of salads that were produced worldwide. Naturally the complainant would be upset and our crew and subsequently our Customer Relations team would do their best to redress the balance and make the passenger feel better about their experience. My team and I would detail the complaint to the caterer in question and if there had been more than one complaint in a relatively short period we would schedule an unannounced visit to check what was happening.

Insects in the salad were bad enough but much worse was the appearance of a caterpillar or worse still half a caterpillar since when that was found the passenger wasn't sure where the remainder of the caterpillar might be! A rare but somewhat startling visitor in the lettuce was the miniature tree frog. Brightly coloured in green and red it was very tiny and had sticky pads on its feet thereby enabling it to stick to the salad contents and avoid being washed off. Passengers whilst not happy at finding one in their meal were often entranced by the small size and the colouration.

Sometimes the foreign body was much larger or much more repugnant. In one case a large metal bolt was found in a bag of pretzels served with drinks on a Club Europe flight. When the complaint arrived on my desk I was very surprised as I had read the Hazard Analysis and Critical Control Points programme for the factory which produced the snack only the previous week. It was an excellent document and appeared to have covered all eventualities.

It was a Thursday afternoon and having emailed a copy of the complaint to the company along with photographs of the offending object I asked for someone to come to my office on the following Monday morning to explain what had happened.

Monday morning at 10.00am and a young woman was ushered into the office. She was obviously somewhat nervous, visibly shaking as she introduced herself as Sara, the Company Food Safety Manager. Sitting down at the desk she started off by apologising profusely on behalf of the Company. "I can't tell you how sorry we are that this has happened and we have already taken steps to ensure that it can't happen again. When we saw your photos we recognised immediately where the bolt had come from. It's part of the gate assembly on the production line prior to the filling machine."

She went on to explain that as the factory produced a range of different products the production line had an adjustable bar on it which could be raised or lowered according to the depth of product passing through. The bolt was a hand tightened unit which held the gate in place.

"What we couldn't understand was that the metal detector on the filling line didn't apparently pick it up as it passed through." Apparently the product dropped down a chute as it passed into the film wrapper which produced the filled bags. A metal detector was positioned in the chute and when a fragment of metal passed through, an alarm was triggered which stopped the next set of bags being separated. This allowed the operator of the machine to identify the bags in which the piece of metal should be found. "We've worked all weekend to figure out what happened and if you open this bag you'll find another bolt exactly the same." She handed me another bag which on opening revealed another bolt.

"Well how did it happen?" "We reckon that when the bolt fell into the filler chute it triggered the alarm but then got jammed in the chute and didn't actually fall into the filler and into a bag. The machine would have stopped and the operator would have lifted off the five unseparated bags which should normally have contained the metal before restarting the machine. After restarting, the bolt was shaken loose and fell into the filler."

"It took us two days to work it out." "I'm not surprised given what you've told me." Sara looked relieved after having explained it all to me. She then went on to detail the actions taken to ensure that it wouldn't happen again. It was one of those rare events that you look at in hindsight and think "Why did we not see that this could happen?" she said.

Some other complaints however were more predictable and should have been foreseen and prevented. A series of passenger complaints about cigarette ends and other bits of unsavoury detritus being found in packets of nuts served with drinks took me to a packing factory some distance down the M4 from Heathrow. The owners of the factory couldn't understand how the "high quality" nuts they were providing could be contaminated until I pointed out that they were sourcing their product from a third world country and were not screening the contents of the jute sacks in which the nuts arrived before pouring them into their processing and packaging machines. Some of the nuts were likely to have been harvested at ground level and may have been raked up before being bagged. There was therefore every likelihood of foreign bodies being present in the sacks.

Sometimes however foreign bodies found in the aircraft meals didn't get there by accident but had been deliberately put into the food by a recalcitrant worker. On one occasion on a flight out of Australia ten passengers in Club World found pieces of metal swarf in their food. When the first passenger alerted the crew it was thought to be a "one off" incident but as other pieces of metal appeared in meals across the Cabin the crew realised that this wasn't a normal incident and advised the ground team at the departure airport. Fortunately, the passengers also realised what had happened and were very sympathetic towards the airline. Investigation later proved that the metal had been deliberately put into the food by a disgruntled employee at the flight kitchen.

One of the most unusual complaints I dealt with was received from a passenger travelling from Barcelona to London who on starting to eat his breakfast found a set of false teeth under his bacon and scrambled egg. It wasn't a full set of dentures but part of an old well used dental plate with some of the teeth missing, but a gruesome find in any circumstances. Apparently the passenger who found it had a sense of humour as when the flight attendant arrived to ask why he had rung his call bell he said "Is this meal so tough that I need extra teeth to eat it?"

In this case the problem was caused by a chef who had been dismissed and was taking his revenge before leaving the building. One good reason why any staff member who is dismissed shouldn't be allowed to go back into their working area as it gives them the chance to sabotage something.

CHAPTER 61

THE DETERMINED MAN

Food is a very subjective subject and most passengers will have their own views as to how good or bad a particular meal may be but whilst many will complain about the quality few will take it to extremes.

One winters' evening around 9.00pm I had a phone call at home. "Sorry to disturb you Mr Kelly but we have a problem with a passenger who has arrived from Oslo. He's complaining about the meal he was served and he won't get off the aircraft." "Can you tell me anything more?" I replied. I really needed to know a bit more if possible. "Sorry, that's all I've been told. Apparently the Captain of the flight has stayed with him." "What time did he arrive at Heathrow?" "At 7.30pm." "You mean he's been on the aircraft for nearly two hours?" "Yes."

I was flabbergasted. Surely someone in customer relations should have been able to deal with this. "OK. I'm on my way. Where is the aircraft positioned?"

Just before 10.00pm I arrived at the Terminal 1 stand where the aircraft was parked to find that the aircraft had been closed down as it wasn't going to be used again until the morning. Standing on the concrete apron below it in the cold evening air was a passenger in his overcoat, briefcase in one hand and an aircraft meal in the other. A Captain was standing beside him. "Mr Kelly?" the Captain looked at me. "Yes" I acknowledged.

"Thanks for coming out. I believe you've come in from home?" "It's all part of the job" I smiled at him. "This passenger believes that there is something wrong with the meal he was offered on our way across from Oslo. He wasn't happy with whatever he was told on board and after we arrived he refused to disembark. I eventually got him to leave the aircraft as it was being closed up for the night but he wouldn't go into the building. Perhaps you can help to sort it out? If it's all right with you

405

I'll leave you with him and make my way into the terminal to check out." With that he walked off and left me with the passenger.

Looking at him I saw that he was a very big chap and my first thought was that I wasn't going to get into an argument. We were on our own beside the plane with no help available should he turn nasty. I introduced myself and explained my role in the Company.

He was almost apologetic. "I'm sorry you've had to come into work from home but I got annoyed on the aircraft that no-one would take my complaint seriously." "What's the problem?" I still didn't know what I was dealing with. "I think that the meal is undercooked and as it's pork it could be dangerous." That was it? That was what had caused a major incident on the aircraft and had dragged me into work at 10.00 o'clock at night? I couldn't believe it.

"OK. Well I can't see it very well down here in the semi dark so let's move into the building." He was happy to follow me as I led the way up the stairs from the ramp into the gate lounge above. I took the meal from his hand and had a look at it. It was pork medallions as he had said earlier and yes they were a bit pink but they certainly weren't rare in the sense of being bloody and distinctly raw.

As I said before, food is subjective and if the customer thought that the meat was a bit underdone then I wasn't going to argue. "Fine, I can see your point. It may be cooked enough for those who like it rare but it may not be acceptable to others." He nodded in agreement and I carried on.

"I don't think that it will have been dangerous but I'll have the meal examined by our laboratory to check if there are any food poisoning organisms in it. There will be some bacteria in the food because it has been open and exposed to the air since you were given it on board but we'll be able to make allowances for that. If you give me your details, I'll ensure that you get a full report."

"Thank you." He said. "I only wanted somebody to take my complaint seriously. It was just laughed off by the crew. I'll give you my card." He delved into his jacket and produced his business card.

I responded by giving him mine. I walked him up to the main corridor and pointed him towards the terminal building. "If you make your way through to immigration I'm sure you know your way out." I shook his hand and he walked purposefully away.

Next morning in the office I had a phone call from the Chief

Executive's office. His PA said "I hear you had an entertaining night last night?" "Word gets around quickly. Who told you?" The customer rang the Boss this morning. Apparently he had some complimentary words about you but you'll never guess what else happened?" "Go on."

"We lost his bag!!"

"No!! Probably he was so late getting into the terminal that his bag would have been removed from the carousel and there would also have been a shift change. It must be in the building." "You're right. They found it this morning." She laughed.

As promised I sent the microbiological test results to the customer which confirmed there was nothing untoward in the food as I had suspected. Since I heard nothing further from him I had to assume that he was satisfied with what I had done.

I also had a word with my Catering colleagues to explain what had happened and suggesting that in future they might wish to cook the pork for a minute or two longer.

CHAPTER 62

ALLERGIES, INTOLERANCE AND GM FOOD

Apart from foreign bodies we also had complaints about the content of our meals. Allergies, food intolerance and genetically modified food began to become an issue and as always the food safety team were in the forefront when it came to dealing with irate passengers.

Allergies are a very serious issue especially in children and quite naturally people who suffer from an allergy and the parents of affected children are very sensitive about the subject but even with the best of efforts, there is a limit to what airlines can do to protect the individual from the foods to which they may be allergic or intolerant.

Peanut allergy is one of the most common and whilst were able to remove peanuts from the menu we couldn't ever guarantee that the aircraft would be "peanut free" as it was impossible for us to ensure that on any flight that there wasn't a passenger who had brought peanuts on board with them.

I had a classic example when returning on a flight from New York one evening. Seated in Club class I was somewhat surprised when as the pre-dinner drinks were being served the passenger next to me said "I don't like the snacks that BA provide with the drinks since they took peanuts off the menu so I bring my own." With that he reached into his pocket and brought out a handful of peanuts. "My own?" I thought as I recognised them as being from the Club class lounge in the Terminal building where peanuts were still available.

It was considered that the risk in supplying the nuts in the lounge was much less than when they were offered on the aircraft and it was a debatable point as to whether the requirements and in some cases the idiosyncrasies of an individual passenger should prevail over the preferences of all the other customers.

In some instances, passengers could become somewhat irrational in their views as to what the airline should do to protect them.

One letter of complaint which I received came from a father who was travelling to Florida with his family. His son had a peanut allergy and the father became absolutely incensed when, on the aircraft, a small boy sitting across the aisle from his son took a chocolate bar which contained peanuts, from his pocket and began to eat it.

Whilst I could understand his immediate anxiety over his son, the airline couldn't be responsible for the actions of every individual who flew.

Similarly, although each aircraft interior was cleaned after every flight we couldn't guarantee that if a passenger had been eating nuts on board that the cleaning would remove every vestige of peanut dust that might be present on the seat and surrounding area, particularly if we weren't aware that peanuts had been brought on board.

I often wondered how the allergen sufferers dealt with the rigours of everyday life? How did they deal with other forms of public transport such as trains and buses or going into shops where nuts were sold or were present on some of the products?

It must be extremely difficult and I have every sympathy with them in their problem but for some reason they always seemed to think that the airlines had some magic powers to deal with the issue better than other forms of transport. We tried our best but we couldn't guarantee total success.

I had similar problems with genetically modified foods. The threat of their introduction into the UK raised an enormous public outcry. The immediate reaction of some in the airline industry was to state categorically that "the airline doesn't use any GM food."

I knew that this couldn't be the case. Whilst we would be able to prove that there was no GM food in menus out of the UK this wasn't possible in the USA where no legislation existed to require food producers to disclose the GM content of their food. When BA Catering Operations in the USA asked the question as to whether particular foods contained GM ingredients the result was a blank wall. No-one would answer so we didn't know.

This was of little help to me in dealing with one passenger who bombarded me with phone calls over a number of weeks insisting that BA guaranteed that the food that he was eating on his regular flights across the Atlantic were GM free. Over and over again I explained that whilst we could track the content of the food supplied out of the UK there was absolutely no way in which we could do this on flights from the USA.

Still he continued to call until I finally had enough and after another prolonged conversation which lasted more than 30 minutes and which was going nowhere I eventually said "I'm very sorry sir. There is nothing more that I can do to change the circumstances but please remember that although BA provides food on the flight, there is no compunction for you to eat it. If you think that it may contain GM ingredients then you can refuse the meal. You are of course at liberty to bring your own food on board to eat during the flight. In this way you can ensure that you will not eat anything untoward. Thank you and goodbye."

At that I hung up. Surprisingly he never came back to me again.

CHAPTER 63

AMUSING EVENTS AND INTERESTING PLACES

On a trip to Malawi very early in my career when Blantyre was still the Capital city I was sitting in the upstairs restaurant in the airport Terminal having lunch with the BA station Manager when a Hercules C130 appeared on its landing approach. The aircraft was painted grey and had no distinguishing marks apart from its registration letters and numbers which I recognised as being from South Africa. I was surprised given that this was in the days of apartheid as a result of which South Africa was supposedly incommunicado with its neighbouring African countries.

"That's an interesting aircraft." I remarked to my colleague. "Yes" he replied. "It doesn't exist. It's officially not here. Watch." The aircraft taxied to a standstill at a point some distance from the Terminal building but adjacent to a number of cargo pallets sitting at the side of the taxiway.

As I watched a door opened in the belly of the aircraft and a set of stairs dropped out. A man descended and moved to the rear of the aircraft. He operated something and the rear door of the aircraft slowly dropped and two more men appeared and began to help him offload a number of loaded pallets followed by a small sports boat.

Having unloaded these, they then quickly loaded the collection of pallets in the pile adjacent to the taxiway and having done so the rear door was closed and the man climbed back up the stairs under the aircraft nose. The aircraft engines restarted, it taxied quickly to the runway and in a few moments was airborne. The whole performance had taken less than fifteen minutes. I looked at my companion with a raised eyebrow.

"You didn't see that happen" he said with a smile. "This country has no connection with South Africa so that flight doesn't exist, even if it turns up twice a week."

Shades of my days in Zambia when I watched the trains travelling from the Copper Belt, South to Rhodesia in the days when there was supposedly a trade embargo between the countries. The World works in mysterious ways.

Some of my experiences were more esoteric. Standing on the aircraft apron at Delhi airport watching as the sun rose, breaking through the early morning mist to reveal the British Airways aircraft on its final approach on a transit stop which I was there to audit.

Sitting in the catering manager's office in the flight kitchen in Mahe in the Seychelles at 9.00pm eating a scratch meal of steak and palm heart salad off a plate on the desk whilst waiting for the transiting BA flight from Mauritius to London on which I was due to fly. The meal was memorable for its content as well as the location.

The thrill of the aircraft breaking through the cloud layer into sunshine above the English Channel on a bright morning. Surfing along the top of the cloud layer giving a real feeling of speed.

The beauty of the lights of London viewed as the landing aircraft descended over the Thames before daybreak on a cold crisp Winters' morning.

Arriving in Venice on my first ever visit to the city on a February day, I was driven after work from the airport to the city by the manager of the flight kitchen. He dropped me off in a raging snowstorm at the bus/rail terminal which I was later to find out was at the end of the causeway which linked Venice to the mainland.

I had no idea as to where I was or where my hotel might be but following his instructions I walked down a jetty to a ticket office where I had been told I would get a boat to take me there. I struggled to explain what I wanted in my non-existent Italian to the man seated behind the window then after a few seconds was amazed when he spoke to me in a broad London accent. "That's all right mate. Just take boat number one or five. They stop right outside your hotel." I couldn't believe it.

I slipped and slid my way down the walkway and was fortunate enough to have a boat arrive as I got to the end. Boarding it I was transfixed as we edged out into the waterway and made our way into the centre of the city.

It was exactly as Canaletto had painted it and viewed through the falling snow it was magical. The vaporetto wound its way through a series of twists and turns, each one opening a new vista. Eventually I saw my hotel appearing and true to the directions I had been given the water taxi pulled in to a jetty just outside.

Disembarking I ran quickly through the snow storm to avoid getting too wet, dashed up the steps and into the hotel only to find my feet disappearing from under me as they lost grip on the polished marble floor of the lobby. I slid along the floor in an untidy heap coming to a standstill just short of the reception desk. "Good afternoon Sir," said the snooty looking reception clerk as he watched me pick myself up. "You have a reservation?"

Some events were more surprising. Realising one morning on arriving by taxi at the flight kitchen in Manila, having taken only ten minutes to get there from my hotel, that on arrival the previous night I had been taken for a very long and expensive taxi ride by an unscrupulous driver who realised that I was a newcomer.

This was par for the course. Many taxi drivers across the world are not averse to taking the unsuspecting customer for a ride. It wasn't unusual when getting into a cab at some airports to be asked by the driver "which route do you think we should take this evening? I'm thinking about it being rush hour." He was just trying to figure out if I knew where I was going and whether or not he could take a circular and expensive tour with me.

Meeting a French Executive Chef in an overseas kitchen who didn't think it wrong to walk around with a large cigar in his mouth was another interesting moment, as was watching a very large but totally unafraid rat running around the passenger departure lounge in Mumbai one morning whilst I was awaiting a flight. Other passengers in the lounge seemed unconcerned and a father pointed out the rodent to his young son saying "Look there's Mickey Mouse" and laughing. I sat there amazed thinking "That's not Mickey Mouse that's Roland Rat!!"

I had previous experience of rats in India, firstly being warned not to leave my first floor bedroom window open in a crew hotel in one city as there were adjacent roofs from which the local rat population could climb into the bedroom. Secondly when opening a new route into Madras or Chennai as it is now known I stayed in an upmarket hotel which had provided a bowl of fruit on the table in the middle of the room. Imagine my surprise and horror when in the morning, after a good night's sleep, I noticed that some of the fruit bore the teeth marks of a rodent which had obviously shared the room with me through the night.

It wasn't the only rodent to give me a bit of amusement. I was in Antigua in the Caribbean to audit the facilities and was sitting in the manager's office in the flight kitchen at the start of the morning's work. Pedro Corbin the kitchen manager was not on the island, having gone to a meeting at the Goddard Company head office in Barbados, they being the main supplier of food throughout the islands. As a result, his deputy was sitting nervously in front of me, very obviously not relishing the prospect of an audit.

The office was at the end of a long corridor which ran from the main kitchen and from my position I could see along the full length. The deputy manager, seated behind a desk couldn't see any of the corridor.

As I began to work I noticed out of the corner of my eye, a mouse, galloping at full speed along the corridor and heading straight for the office. I waited to see what would happen. The mouse raced into the office at full speed and as the deputy manager saw it his face turned at least three different colours as he realised what had happened and then wondered how he was going to deal with it. It was an absolute picture and I sat there trying to keep my face straight. I knew from past experience that this was a "one off" as the kitchen was generally very well run so we were able to sort out the problem fairly quickly.

Two days later I travelled on to Barbados for a further audit where I caught up with Pedro. He had already heard the story of the mouse and was chortling about it. "I wish I had been there to see his face" he laughed. "He was worked up enough when I left to come down here and he knew that you were about to arrive for an audit but I knew it would be good experience for him. How did he do?"

"He was fine. I checked all your pest control records and there was no cause for concern and no evidence of an infestation."

Later in the afternoon whilst I was going through the Barbados kitchen I got a call from Joe Nicholson the Director of Flight Catering at Goddard's asking me if I would like to join the team of managers from all the Goddard flight kitchens across the Caribbean at dinner in St Joseph that evening.

We were seated at a large long table. Suddenly without any warning another large party arrived. Looking up I realised with some surprise that it was the Rolling Stones complete with an entourage of young women and various hangers on. Apparently according to a couple of the managers they were in Barbados to record some new music at Eddie Grant's studio on the island.

They began to party alongside us and soon the evening was in full flow. Charlie Watts amused everyone by constantly getting up and wandering off into the garden outside, each time causing someone in the group to have to get up and go and retrieve him. He was obviously as high as a kite on something.

The following evening, I was standing in the queue for security at Barbados airport, about to join the BA flight home when a voice beside me said "Did you enjoy the dinner last night?" I looked up and to my surprise found Mick Jagger looking at me. Immaculately dressed in a very expensive looking leather jacket and jeans he was totally on his own. No security, no BA staff accompanying him. He travelled in First Class of course and contrary to reports of his wild life style was the model passenger, causing no problems whatsoever to the crew.

A number of notable moments in my travels came courtesy of the flight crew on the aircraft. Flying into the famous or should it be infamous Kai Tak airport at Hong Kong, I was invited by the crew to join them on the flight deck for the landing. For those of you who may not be aware, Kai Tak was one of the most challenging airports in the world to land at, situated as it was in the harbour below the adjacent Kowloon hills and apartment blocks of Hong Kong.

I listened as the Captain made an announcement to the passengers to advise them as to what was about to happen and sat transfixed in the jump seat as we made the descent, dropping to a height of 500 feet at the top of a hill to make a sharp right angled turn at the huge red and white checkerboard which implausibly marked the turning point for the final steep approach to the airport, then down through the apartment blocks, so close that it was possible to see inside through the windows, to touch down impeccably on the runway.

It was a fearsome approach and over the years more than one aircraft missed it and came to grief in the harbour. Kai Tak was replaced by a new airport in 1998 but is still fondly remembered by those who landed there in the past. I was privileged to see it from the Captain's viewpoint.

Despite rumours to the contrary the flight deck crew often had a great sense of humour. Flying out of Stuttgart in Germany one winters' evening I was grateful to be offered the jump seat as the flight was full. It was a filthy night, dark with low cloud and falling snow. The handling pilot was the First Officer seated in the right hand seat. We taxied away from the Terminal building towards the de-icing zone to join the queue of aircraft waiting to be sprayed with de-icing fluid. Our turn came eventually and we moved into our allotted parking space. Two de-icing trucks approached, one on each side and began to spray the aircraft, working their way carefully from the tip of the tail down all the surfaces. It's a vitally important job since accretions of ice on an aircraft can cause it to lose its ability to fly.

We were three quarters complete when the operation suddenly came to a stop. "Bugger. One of the trucks has run out of de-icing fluid and is going to have to go and refill. That's going to delay us." said the First Officer. We sat and waited, watching as the snow fell and by the time the truck returned the whole procedure had to start again from the beginning. It seemed like an hour but probably was only half of that before we were eventually cleared and made our way to the end of the runway. "Clear for take-off." The disembodied voice of the controller came through the headphones. The Captain and First Officer had completed their take off checks and we started to roll. Looking through the windscreen I could see very little. The Terminal building wasn't visible and the aircraft headlights were straining to pierce through the falling snow. The aircraft gathered speed sluggishly at first as it ploughed through the slush and water on the runway slush then began to pick up. "V1" came the call from the Captain who was monitoring the instruments. This was the point of no return when the flying pilot still had time to stop the aircraft on the runway should he think that there was a problem. "Rotate." The First Officer eased the control column back and the aircraft took its leave of the runway.

The next few moments were busy as he flew the aircraft through the first few hundred feet and it climbed away. Then settling back in his seat he turned to the Captain. "That wasn't bad was it? No panic, no hysterics, no shouting." He gave a stage glance out of the side window. "We are off the ground aren't we??" The Captain grinned." Yes. I think so." We all laughed.

Coming out of Faro in Portugal one busy summer evening I was once

416

again on the flight deck, this time accompanied by another staff passenger in the adjacent jump seat. We had just taken off when the Captain began to make his first in flight announcement to the passengers.

"Good evening Ladies and Gentlemen. Now that we're on our way from …" he stopped, switched off his microphone and looked at the rest of us. "Where have we just taken off from?" Faro came the united reply. Looking somewhat guilty he continued his chat to the customers. As he finished and switched off the microphone again he turned to the rest of us "I was down this way yesterday. Did a flight to Lisbon and I just went blank for a minute and couldn't remember where we were today."

About twenty minutes later the Purser came on to the flight deck. "Excuse me Captain. I've got a passenger down the back who wants to know where we're flying over at the moment." "Let's have a look. Anyone got any idea?" the Captain asked. "The First officer looked out of the window. "Looks like the Douro valley to me" he said. The Captain took out a copy of High Life, the magazine produced monthly by the airline and provided at every passenger seat and opened the map section. The maps in the rear of the magazine had recently been changed and in my opinion they weren't as good as their predecessors. The Captain seemed to echo my opinion. "These are worse than useless. They don't really show you anything."

"Hang on a minute I've got a better map in my bag" the First Officer responded. He started to scrabble in his flight bag then began to pull out a series of map pages. I had expected to see some form of professional map but to my surprise these turned out to be the map pages torn from an Olympic Airways In-flight magazine! "These are a lot better and yes by the look of it we're over the Douro valley." "Thanks I'll tell the passenger" and the Purser disappeared from the flight deck again.

Later on the same flight we approached the island of Guernsey. It was a beautiful evening and the island was very visible in a calm blue sea. The Captain spoke to the passengers. "Ladies and Gentlemen for those of you on the left side of the aircraft if you look out you will get a wonderful view of the island of Guernsey."

He waited for a few minutes then went back on to the PA and said "Ladies and Gentleman that was a little unfair to those of you seated on the right side of the aircraft so I'm just going to turn the aircraft slightly so that you can also see the island." He then proceeded to to make a left turn followed a few moments later by a right turn to take the aircraft back on to its original course. I'm sure that it pleased the customers but I wondered what the air traffic controller thought seeing the aircraft making a small S shaped turn over the Channel Islands.

One evening, flying back from an audit in Germany I heard a familiar voice addressing my fellow passengers. It was Gill, a flight attendant whom I had met when we were both selected by BA to study for a Master's degree in Business Administration at Bath University. Although we had never met before the first day of the course we found that we lived within ten minutes of each other. As a result, in order to save costs, we and a third course member shared transport when we had to attend the University campus and we had become good friends.

I was seated in an aisle seat in Club class and Gill was operating at the rear of the aircraft so hadn't seen me. After the meal service had been completed Gill walked past me pushing the Duty Free trolley to the front of the aircraft to start the sales routine. She then began her progress back down the aisle. "Duty Free, Duty Free" she called as she passed the rows of passengers. As she reached my seat row she still hadn't seen me until I looked up and with a grin said "Is that the best you can offer me after all these years?"

She stopped her tracks. "Hi, I didn't realise that you were on board." "No reason why you should" I replied. We chatted for a few seconds then she said "I'll come back to you when I've finished this" and proceeded down the aircraft. True to her word she came back to me some five minutes later, squatted in the aisle beside me and as we hadn't seen each other for some time chatted about what our respective families were doing. "We've changed our phone number" she said. "I'll find a piece of paper and write it down for you. I'll be back in a minute."

She scampered off down the aisle again only to return a few moments later. "Here you are" she said as she wrote her new number on a scrap of paper. "That's my number give me a call." The whole things had only taken a few minutes but whilst Gill and I had been chatting the man seated next to me in the window seat had been intrigued and vainly trying to hear what we'd been saying over the noise of the aircraft.

As Gill walked away he turned to me and said "She's very attractive, I wish I had been sitting in the aisle seat, maybe I might have got her phone number." I didn't explain to him that I already knew her but just left him wondering.

CHAPTER 64

THE WAYS OF THE WORLD

On my first visit to Bombay my British Airways colleague, Ashok Bagley, the Catering Officer met me in the hotel in the evening after work and shared a meal with me. Having finished he asked me if I would like to have a look at some of the city. "It's not all like this" he said as we walked towards his car. "I'll take you to see the tougher side of the city and it's not very far away" he added.

We drove a short distance, passing the Gateway to India, a large monument on the seafront close to the Taj hotel. Turning away from the sea we arrived in a street which was a hive of activity but what I was looking at made my eyes open in astonishment.

The street was full of girls. Hundreds of girls aged I guessed probably between twelve years and maybe thirty years of age although many of them looked older. In all stages of dress and undress they were filling the pavements and the roadway.

Along the side of the street were rows of what would normally have been expected to be shops but here the windows had been removed and replaced by vertical bars which turned the windows into jails or cages. Each of the cages contained numerous girls and it was very obvious that we were in the red light district and the girls were all on offer. Many of the cages were divided between front and back by a curtain and it became apparent to me that the space behind the curtain was where the action took place. It was appalling.

Men thronged the street and the traffic was forced to drive through at a crawl. Ashok looked me. "I just wanted you to see what it can really be like here in Bombay. This is Falkland Road and as you can see it's part of the red light district as you would call it in the UK. It's a lot different from your hotel and the seafront isn't it?"

"I've never seen anything like it" I replied. "How much would one of these girls cost? Not that I'm interested" I added quickly. "I don't know for sure" he replied "but I would guess that it would cost less than a can of Coke in the hotel." Horrendous was all I could think.

My first face to face or should I say hands on experience of "ladies of the night" as they are euphemistically called, came about somewhat unexpectedly in Nairobi. My catering colleague Tony and I were having a drink and chatting in the bar in the Hilton hotel after work when suddenly Tony said "Look out we're about to be cruised."

I didn't know what he meant but on turning round from the bar I realised that we were being approached by two local girls. "Hi guys, why don't you buy us a drink?" The leader of the two was looking intently at us. She was elegantly dressed in a floor length red cocktail dress split down the middle to her waist and with a hair style which made her look remarkably like Diana Ross of the Supremes. "No I don't think so" Tony replied. "Of course you will, you know you really want to" she said insistently. I was standing with my back to the bar and she moved up close, face to face with me. "You look really nice. You'll buy us a drink."

"No, you heard my friend" I said with a smile. At that moment her hand moved like a flash and before I knew what had happened she had slid her hand down the inside front of my trousers and grabbed my genitals. I would add that I was very slim at the time. "Are you sure that you won't buy me a drink?" she repeated whilst squeezing me firmly. "No. Get off. Get your hands off me!" I yelled in a slightly higher voice than normal whilst looking across at Tony for help. A waste of time. He was so creased up laughing that tears were coming down his face.

The girl realised that she was getting nowhere and her hand was removed as fast as it had previously gone into my trousers and without another word the two women walked out of the bar. "Thanks mate, you were a lot of help." Tony was still doubled up laughing. "I've not seen anything that funny in years" he gasped "You should have seen your face!! Anyway I did warn you that they were coming. Are you all right? She hasn't damaged you?" "I'm fine although no thanks to you."

I was to see similar girls in European cities such as Amsterdam and Hamburg although perhaps on a slightly higher level and through the years I never failed to be surprised when I was approached either in the street or in my hotel by some woman who was looking for business. Sometime the approach was subtle and came from the most innocuous looking woman who just happened to bump into me as I was crossing the hotel lobby although on one occasion it was much more brazen and somewhat humorous.

I was in Budapest and having come back to my hotel after a days' work was having a meal in the coffee shop in the lobby on the ground floor. It was early evening and the restaurant was in an elevated position with a view of the check in area and the hotel entrance.

I had ordered a goulash and as I was waiting for it I noticed a woman who had come through the door and was walking across the reception area. One look at her told me exactly what she was. She wore a very short skirt which revealed not only her stockings but also the suspenders that held them up, coupled with a blouse opened down the front to reveal a large expanse of cleavage, added to which was the very heavily made up face. A single glance was enough and I looked back at my meal which was just being delivered.

I had just started to eat when suddenly to my horror the apparition which I had seen in the lobby appeared in front of me and without a word pulled out the chair opposite and sat down. "Two hundred dollars" the voice came in English with a thick heavy accent. I looked at her. My first thought was "I hope that there is no-one in here who recognises me and thinks that this horror is with me." She looked even worse close up than she had from a distance I thought.

"Two hundred dollars" she spoke again looking at me intently. "No." I said "Five hundred dollars." She looked slightly puzzled. "Two hundred dollars" she said firmly for the third time. "No" I said again. "Five hundred dollars. I don't come cheap. If you want me, you have to give me five hundred dollars." I smiled at her and put my hand out, indicating that I wanted her money.

She was stunned. "You pay me?" she said questioningly. "No you pay me" I said firmly. At last she realised what I was saying. She looked at me as if I was mad, shook her head, said no in her thick accent, got up and walked away.

I went back to my dinner but this story had a follow up. A number of months later when doing a follow up visit to Budapest I was accompanied by my Secretary Del who was with me as part of a Company team building exercise seeing how our audits were carried out.

I had told her the story of the woman in the restaurant although at the time I think she thought that it was a bit of a tall tale. However, after dinner in the evening we were sitting in a small annexe off the bar in the lobby when suddenly without warning there appeared the female apparition dressed much as before. Short skirt, with suspenders and stocking tops readily visible and ample bosom exploding out of her blouse. She took a quick look at us and just as quickly disappeared from view.

"Oh my God" said Del. "Was that her?" I nodded my head. "I don't believe it. I didn't believe what you had been telling me. I've never seen anything like it." Del was virtually speechless but it made an entertaining end to the day.

Bangkok in Thailand could also be a problem. A large city set on the banks of the Chao Phraya river it seethed with people and traffic. It was noisy and dirty and having been a rest and recreation centre for American troops during the Vietnam war it had a large carry over of seedy bars, massage parlours, and markets. Walking along the street outside the crew hotel in the middle of the afternoon I would be approached by girls offering their services, men offering their services or the services of girls or boys. Often the approach would be less than subtle with a girl standing face to face with me and it could be somewhat intimidating. I also imagined that the many middle aged couples walking along on holiday, many from Australia or the UK were looking at me, a lone male and thinking paedophile !!

Nothing in Bangkok was ever what it seemed. The market stalls were piled high with fake designer goods, some of which were really good imitations and difficult to tell from the real thing. At one of the many stalls the young woman behind the counter was extolling the virtues of the watch she was trying to sell me. "It very good watch. It waterproof. Look it says on back." She turned it over and offered it to me. "Yes, I can see but it doesn't mean anything. It says Rolex on the front but it's not a Rolex. It's a fake." She looked at me in disgust, took the watch back and without a word plunged it into a bucket of water standing on the ground beside her. "Look it still working!!"

American women always appeared to be entranced by a British accent. On several occasions in different cities in the USA whilst seated at the hotel bar having a quiet drink on my own after work I attracted the attention of the woman sitting on the bar stool next to me. "You're British?" was always the opening question followed immediately by "I just love your accent."

On turning around, I usually found the question being posed by an attractive well-dressed woman in her thirties. Call me an old cynic and I may well be mistaken, the women could have been visiting the city on business as I was and just wanted someone to have a chat with but although I was never openly propositioned I worked on the basis that as I wasn't George Clooney or Robert De Niro then the ladies were working girls and I was a target. Apart from the fact that I was happily married I had no idea as to whom these women may have been with the previous night. It could have been the whole of the US Marine Corps as far as I knew.

Over the years I became more savvy and realised when walking into a hotel bar that the woman sitting on her own in the corner was there for a purpose. From her well-chosen vantage point she could see everyone who entered and would carefully watch any unaccompanied male who made his way to the bar, waiting to see whether he was genuinely on his own or was expecting to meet someone. Given sufficient time to assess the situation she would then discreetly make her way to the bar and order a drink before attempting to strike up a conversation. It was all very cleverly done.

One American girl was a bit more forthcoming. I was auditing Boston and had flown in from New York somewhat late having been delayed by the tail end of hurricane David which had shut down La Guardia airport for a few hours. It was early afternoon when I walked into the BA airport manager's office at Logan airport. The girl behind the desk wasn't the usual secretary who apparently was on vacation. The replacement was a young woman in her early twenties who introduced herself as "Dinah" which she pronounced as "Deena."

"You must be Mike? I've been expecting you. You're here to audit the station?" She looked at me with a smile. I confirmed who I was and asked if I could see the manager for a few minutes. Whilst I waited Dinah continued to talk, asking me a lot of questions about where I came from, what my job entailed, who I worked with etc. Eventually the manager was free to see me and welcomed me into his office. "Hi Mike, good to see you again how are things?"

We sat down and discussed the arrangements for my audit. It was pretty straightforward and I suggested that as I was running late I should start by auditing the airport terminal restaurant immediately. "Good idea. I'll get Deena to take you up and introduce you to the manager. Hey Deena" he called out through the open office door, "would you take Mike up to the restaurant upstairs?" "Yes" came the immediate reply "but I'd rather take him out to dinner tonight." "I'm not asking you to take him out for a meal but just to introduce him to the manager. Mike has to audit the facility."

"OK" Dinah walked me out of the office through the terminal and as we stood on the escalator on the way up to the next floor turned and said. "The invitation to dinner still stands. I know where you're staying as I made the reservation so I'll pick you up at the hotel when I finish here after the flight has departed."

I was somewhat amazed by the brash approach but thought why not and as a result had a very pleasant meal in my hotel with a young woman who only wanted to have a conversation with someone British to find out what the UK was like and how our countries differed. At the end of the meal I said goodbye and put her into a cab never to see her again as her shift pattern didn't coincide with my work over the next two days. Such was life in the aviation world. Here today, gone tomorrow.

CHAPTER 65

ADVENTURES IN RUSSIA

My rare visits to Russia over the years provided some amusing and pleasant experiences. Early visits prior to the break up of the USSR were to a country which was bleak in the extreme. Cold featureless hotels which were basic, where there would be no soap or other amenities provided and often no plugs in the washbasins or baths. Poor quality food and the knowledge that you were being monitored constantly not only by the ubiquitous "watcher" sitting at the end of each corridor in the hotel, watching you come and go but also possibly through your room being bugged.

A couple of visits to both St Petersburg and to Moscow towards the end of my career showed the great changes that had taken place.

St Petersburg is an interesting city with a wealth of history and culture. On one visit I was shown round the flight kitchen by the operations Director, a French man on loan from the French Catering company Servair. He had been in the city for some years and having suffered the death of his wife was now married to a younger Russian woman.

After work was done he invited me to join him for dinner later in the evening and around 7.00 pm he picked me up at the hotel. We drove to the river and boarded a large sailing ship which had been converted into a restaurant. As we sat down the young waitress handed the menu to each of us. Looking at it I realised not unexpectedly, that it was written in Russian and turning to my companion said "You'll have to translate this for me as I don't read a word of Russian." To my surprise he replied "Neither do I."

I couldn't believe it. Here was a man who had been in Russia for a number of years and was married to a Russian woman yet he didn't understand the language. There then followed an entertaining few minutes as the young Russian waitress valiantly attempted to translate for us using her schoolgirl English.

A year later I was due to revisit St Petersburg and when I contacted the BA airport manager Julia, an interesting woman not least because her two eyes were different colours, to advise her that I was coming, she sent me a message asking me if I liked music. I said yes and when I arrived at the airport she told me that she had booked tickets for a concert that evening.

After working all day in the flight kitchen Julia was waiting to drive us into the city to the concert hall where she had booked seats in a box on the upper floor. I don't know what I expected but looking around the auditorium I felt that I could have been in the Albert Hall in London. The audience was every bit as cosmopolitan as in London and dressed similarly.

It was a good concert and as we filed out with rest of the crowd Julia said "We're just going down the road to a small restaurant. Are you happy with that?" I enjoyed the experience of eating a local meal with local people but was surprised when at the end of the meal Julia suddenly said "Let's go" and without another word she was off. I followed her out of the restaurant and along the street. "Where are we going?" "On to the bridge. It's the week of the white nights and we're going to watch the sunset." I thought for a second and then realised that it was the 21st of June and the longest day of the year in the Northern hemisphere

We strode on to one of the bridges crossing the wide river and joined a throng of people who were obviously there for the same reason. Julia delved into the large bag which she had been carrying all evening and to my surprise brought out a small bottle of Champagne and two glasses. "Here you are" she handed me a glass. We stood and watched as dusk began to fall then gradually the light began to grow again as the sun rose to begin another day.

There was a happy buzz of animated conversation amongst the crowd on the bridge as everyone enjoyed the pleasure of the long warm evening. Although twilight had come it had never actually got dark. It was a surreal experience, made more so by the fact that I wasn't expecting Julia to have gone to such lengths to let me enjoy it.

"We try to make the most of this particular week" she explained. "Our summers can be hot and the days are long but our winters are severe and very dark." I had never previously been this far North in mid-summer

426

so had never before experienced the twenty-four hour daylight but I had experienced the cold, dark, bleak Winter days on visits to Finland so knew what she was talking about.

This wasn't to be my only surprise on a visit to Russia. Towards the end of my career I had to visit Moscow to audit the facilities at Domodedovo airport to which British Airways flights had just been moved from the older airport at Sheremetyevo. I was accompanied on the trip by Tony Lytras from BA Operations and as the new airport was some distance from the city we were booked to stay overnight at a hotel nearby. Having been to Moscow some years before I well remembered the cold bleakness of the place. This time I was to be pleasantly surprised at the improvements which had taken place in the intervening years.

The airport had recently been updated to become the new International airport and was well equipped with all the facilities necessary for our aircraft turn round so Tony and I were very satisfied with what we saw. Our hosts from the Russian handling company who handled the British Airways flights were very welcoming and went to great lengths to make sure that we were able to see everything that was needed.

As we got towards the end of the day Tony asked if it would be possible for us to go into Moscow in the evening as he had never been there before. The local manager was a bit hesitant. "It's a long way into the city and you have to go by train" he explained. "How far?" I asked. "It's 46 kilometres, that's about 26 miles" he replied.

At that point one of his colleagues offered to take us in by car. "I live in the city so I can easily take you in and drop you off." So after work, armed with full details as to how to catch the train back to the airport and when the last train left we set off by car. Arriving in the city centre, which was noticeably very quiet in comparison with similar European cities our companion pulled up outside an elegant block of apartments.

"I'll leave the car here and just walk you into the main street and show you which way to go." We walked round the corner and made our way up the slight hill into Lubyanka Square. "What's that building?" Tony asked, looking at a very large four storey red stone block overlooking a flag bedecked grass roundabout in the centre of the square.

Our host said nothing so Tony asked again. Again there was no reply so I turned to Tony and said "That's the KGB headquarters. You'll have heard of it." Then added jokingly "You'll find that the American Embassy is some distance away on the other side of Red Square but they can still listen to each other." Our host turned to me and smiled. "I'd forgotten that you'd been here before."

We walked past the KGB building, magnificent as it looked with its pillared first floor frontage and he pointed us in the direction of Red Square. "Don't forget how to get to the train" was his last comment and as left us to enjoy the visit.

Walking into Red Square Tony was amazed, as I had been when I first saw it, to find that it was cobbled and ran over the top of a hill running down towards the famous St Basil's church with its onion domes. "I had expected it to be much bigger" he exclaimed. "It looks bigger when you see it on TV with the troops marching through it."

We strolled around. Lenin's mausoleum stood coldly on the pavement backed by the enormous Kremlin buildings whose walls stretched round the corner and downhill. Having walked along the walls, admiring the size of the building we crossed the square and entered what had previously been the State Department Store, Gum which faced the Kremlin.

The store was in many ways very like Harrods in London. The architectural style was similar although the building wasn't as tall. My memory of it was of a cold empty space with little or nothing on the shelves but how it had changed. It was now a Mecca of upmarket shopping, the aisles lined with world renowned names such as Gucci, Armani, Dolce and Gabbana etc. We had a coffee in a cafe suspended across one of the wide aisles, then conscious of the time and our need to catch the train back to the airport we headed down to the Metro station.

We had instructions as to how to get to the office in the city where staff would direct us to the airport train. The trip wasn't going to be easy as none of the signs in the stations were in English but our hosts had told us where to go and at which station to get off. Three stations down the line we left the train and made our way up the escalators, being scrutinised at each level by a babushka dressed in a long grey army style greatcoat whose sole job appeared to be to stand and watch what was happening. Reaching ground level, we turned into the street and made our way into the office to which we had been directed. Three young women were sitting behind a desk. We explained who we were and that we wanted to travel back to the airport in the train. They looked at us in some confusion and there was a barrage of Russian between them before one turned and said "But you've missed the last train to the airport. It left at 9.00pm."

We were flabbergasted. "We were told the last train was at 10.00pm?" "Only in mid-Summer" the girl replied. "So what do we do?" The young women conferred then came back to us. "You can take the Metro out to here" one of them pointed to a station on the map "then you catch a bus to the airport from outside the station. You will need to be quick however as the last bus leaves just before midnight." "I'll take you back into the Metro and show you the way" said the girl who spoke the best English.

We left the office and went back down into the Metro, back to the platform at which we had only recently arrived. Standing amongst the crowd of people waiting for the train, we attracted some strange looks from our fellow travellers who were wondering just who these two men were, given that we were accompanied by a good looking young woman dressed in a very smart airline style uniform.

A train rumbled into the station and the young woman said "This is for you" as the doors opened and saying "Good bye" she ushered us on board. Tony and I stood in the crowded train as it travelled down the line. I looked at the map on the wall and tried to make out where we were and which stations we were travelling through. None of the signs were in English and I didn't speak any Russian but the language is Cyrillic and the alphabet is not dissimilar to Greek which I had studied, without any great distinction I would add, at school.

I had never thought that my small understanding of Greek would ever become valuable but here it came into its own. I could recognise some of the letters and from that could work out which stations we were passing through.

"Have you any idea as to where we are?" Tony said in a worried voice. "Yes I can read some of the station names." "How come? Do you understand Russian?" he was incredulous. I was watching the names carefully as I had noticed from the map that the track divided a couple of stations later with one line going towards the airport and the other going off in the wrong direction. I didn't know which line this train was going to take and had to hope that the girl had put us on the right one.

The train rattled out of a station and as it reached the next one I realised that we were on the wrong line. Sods law I thought. "Come on Tony we have to get off we're on the wrong train." We pushed our way to

429

the door and jumped out as the doors began to shut. The train departed and we were left on our own on the platform as other passengers who had got off rapidly left. "What do we do now?" Tony looked at me. "We have to go back one stop then change trains again and go back up the other line."

I looked around. I couldn't see which platform we needed to be on to catch a train back to the last station. "I'll have to ask." I walked towards a uniformed woman carrying a baton who was standing further down the platform. "Do you speak English?" "Niet" It wasn't the answer that I had hoped for. "Airport?" I said hopefully. She burst into a torrent of Russian with a smile and gesticulating with her hands appeared to explain where we had to go. I thanked her and went back to Tony. "Up the stairs then three platforms across. At last that's what I think she was telling me." "Are you sure?" "No but it's the best I can do."

We hurried up the stairs then along the upper corridor across the tracks counting the platforms and came down on the third. A train was just pulling in so we jumped on board and I held my breath as we travelled to the next stop.

As we pulled into the station I strained for a sign showing the station name and breathed a sigh of relief when it showed the name I was hoping for.

"This is it." I pushed Tony ahead of me and we jumped out on to the platform. I looked for the railway attendant and spotting the woman in uniform walked quickly towards her. "Airport?" I looked at her hopefully. She pointed to the adjacent platform. "Da" "Thank you" I said then added "Which station?"

She looked at me and then showing an understanding took me by the arm and walked me over to a map on the wall. She pointed at a station then counted, in Russian of course, but also using her fingers, the number of stations up to the one at which we should leave the train. "Thank you" I said again and was rewarded with a large smile and a pat on my arm.

I went back to Tony and told him what I thought she had said. He wasn't convinced but we agreed that it was the best we could do. The next train pulled in and the woman waved at us to get on board. I waved my thanks back to her. Tony and I counted each station that we went through and once again I recognised the name on the sign board at the station where we had been told to get off. Leaving the train, we were alone on the platform except for another woman in uniform, carrying a baton.

I walked over to her and smiled. "Bus to the airport?" She looked at me uncomprehendingly so I tried again. "Airport?" This time it registered but once again I got a tirade of Russian accompanied by a lot of arm waving. Tony turned to me and said "Did you get any of that?" "Well I think she was indicating that we go outside then cross the road to where the bus is." I wasn't convinced but we had nothing to lose.

Leaving the station in the direction that the woman had indicated we walked into a square through which ran three parallel roads. A small group of people were standing together at what looked like it might be a bus stop about fifty yards away on the third road across.

"That looks like it might be it. We can walk over and ask." I started to walk across the road and Tony followed. Approaching the group, I saw that they were mostly young, a mixture of men and women. They looked at us with interest. I smiled and asked "Airport?" One of the men said "Yes" in English then turned back to his friends. As we waited more people joined the group which was becoming somewhat animated then a mini bus appeared round the corner.

The man who had spoken to me turned and pointed at it. "Airport" he said and motioned for Tony and me to get on. We clambered in and found two seats whilst the rest of the crowd joined us and carried on their animated conversation. One of the men pulled a brown paper bag out of his coat pocket and turning to us offered us a drink from the vodka bottle concealed inside. I smiled at him and politely refused. The bottle was passed happily around the rest of the customers who appeared to have been enjoying a night out.

The road was dark and thickly wooded on both sides and as it was now after midnight there was little traffic around. From time to time individuals would indicate to the driver that they wished to get off and he would pull in to the roadside to let them out. I couldn't see where any of them were going as there appeared to be nothing much more than occasional tracks running into the forest.

Tony and I carefully watched the road ahead for any sign of the airport and were rewarded when gradually the forest thinned and we began to see buildings. Then suddenly and somewhat unexpectedly our hotel appeared on the left side of the road. I indicated to the man that I'd spoken to earlier at the bus stop that we wanted to get off. "At the hotel?" he said in good English. "Yes please." The bus drew up outside the door and with a thank you to everyone on it, Tony and I hopped off followed by several calls of "good bye" and walked into the hotel.

"Well that was a bit different then wasn't it?" Tony nodded in agreement. When we told our colleagues the following morning what had happened they couldn't believe that we had managed to find our way back to the hotel without any knowledge of Russian. But the people that we had met along the way couldn't have been more friendly and helpful and it was certainly a bit of an adventure which whilst somewhat hair raising at the time turned out to be quite entertaining in retrospect.

CHAPTER 66

DESIGN MANAGEMENT?

Through my airline career the aircraft types on which I flew changed considerably. I had my first flight as a lad on a DC3 Dakota known as a Pionair when in service with BEA. A workhorse from the second World war still flying well into the nineteen eighties.

Changes in aircraft design often involved Health Services and the Hygiene team and one or two were memorable because of the problems which they threw up rather than the improvements which they made. For example, the arrival of the second generation of Boeing 747 or Jumbo jet raised the thought that the service offered to those passengers who suffered from a disability should be improved.

It was decided that a toilet for disabled people should be put on the new aircraft and as a result Jim Dunlop, one of our Senior Doctors and I should visit the manufacturers to see a mock-up of the proposed toilet. We were joined at the factory by a number of other BA staff and after the introductions were walked through to a workshop in which stood a model of the toilet.

Jim had brought with him a folding wheelchair which had been designed to be used on board the aircraft, being narrow enough to fit in the aisle. "OK Mike, you sit in the chair and I'll wheel you into the toilet." I climbed into the seat and Jim wheeled me to the toilet door and swung the chair into the gap. It came to a sudden halt. Jim wasn't used to pushing a wheelchair but he made every effort to get the chair to fit through the door. It wouldn't budge. The door was too narrow.

One of the company engineers stepped up. "That's OK" he said quickly. He looked at me. "Just lift your feet up and we'll swing the footrest out of the way, then it will go in." "No" I replied looking him straight in the face. He looked surprised then a little angry. "What's wrong?" he demanded.

"I can't lift my feet up. That's why I'm in the wheelchair!!" I said looking up at him. Jim added "That's why we brought it. To see if it would fit but obviously it doesn't. You'll have to widen the door frame to allow access for the chair." "But that will destabilise the door" came the engineer's reply. "Well in that case you'll have to redesign it" Jim replied firmly.

I hopped out of the chair and the rest of the group began to look at the internal design of the toilet. "What are you going to do about the mirror?" one of the BA team asked. "What do you mean?" came the response. "Well if you're sitting in a wheelchair you won't be able to see yourself in the mirror as it's above the wash basin."

The engineers looked at each other. "We could put it on the back of the door" one suggested brightly. "That's a good idea" said one of his colleagues. "No I don't think so. Some people might object to sitting on the toilet and watching themselves in a mirror on the door facing them" came the reply. "How about keeping it in its normal position above the basin but tipping it forward at the top so that it's angled?" I suggested. "That might work" was the general conclusion.

"The toilet will need a handrail inside to aid people when they need to pull themselves upright" Jim said. "Something like this "and he produced a picture showing a suitable rail. He passed it around. "No we can't do that "said one of the engineers. "Why not?" said Jim "What's wrong with it?" "Well that's an Airbus fitting and this is a Boeing." I thought that Jim was going to throw a fit!!

On the way back to the office he was almost incandescent. "Would you credit those people? Firstly they build a mock up without checking that a wheelchair will fit into it and then they argue about a handle because it's made for a different aircraft. It was the basic principle I was after, not what the handle looked like."

I was to have similar problems with the toilets a few years later, but this time with the design of the waste system. In the early aircraft the toilets were designed much the same as those in a caravan. The toilet bowl was sitting on top of a large tank into which the waste passed. The toilet was flushed after each use by means of an electric motor which recirculated the liquid in the toilet, having first passed it through a filter to remove any gross contents.

The tank was emptied at every turn round stop and was refilled with a small amount of water and a chemical which was designed to kill the bacteria which might be present in the waste and would work even when the toilet was virtually full. The chemical was coloured, usually deep blue or green, and had a perfume in order to disguise what was happening when a passenger flushed the toilet. It all worked reasonably well although there were occasional blockages of the system when unthinking people threw things such as baby nappies into the toilet.

As aircraft were modernised a new method of waste disposal was introduced. The vacuum toilet, first patented in 1975 made its way in to BA aircraft toilets in the late nineteen eighties. The system was fairly simple. Instead of each toilet having a waste tank beneath it the tanks were now placed in the rear of the aircraft. The waste products were no longer flushed down the pan but were sucked to the rear via a small diameter pipe with the suction being provided via the differential pressure available between the inside and outside of the aircraft, or at least that was what I was told.

A set of drawings of the new system had been sent to me for comment prior to installation in our newly ordered aircraft. It didn't take too long to spot a possible flaw. Some of the small diameter waste pipework running from the front to the rear of the aircraft had bends in it to enable it to pass round structural parts of the aircraft framework. This could cause a problem.

I pointed it out to the engineering department. "What if someone throws something large into the toilet and then flushes it? It will travel along the pipe until it reaches the first right angled bend and gets stuck. We'll then have a blocked pipe which will eventually back fill with sewage and will probably leak into the cabin?"

"That's not a problem. We'll put a notice in the toilet asking people not to throw things into it" came the response. "How many languages would you like to put it in?" I replied "and what about the child who goes into the toilet but can't read particularly well?" It very obviously wouldn't work. The answer was to re-route the pipework and provide more rounded corners to try to avoid blockages as much as possible.

The newly designed toilets duly came into service and despite the changes, my colleague John had to deal with a couple of blockages in the first two weeks. These came about through a source which we hadn't foreseen. The design engineers had recognised that the waste from the toilets would be travelling at some speed when it reached the tanks in the rear of the plane so in order to avoid any damage they had installed a braking mechanism which utilised a flap fitted in the pipe just before the entrance to the tank.

What they hadn't thought of was the possibility that a woman would flush her panties down the toilet. These travelled at speed to the brake point where they instantly got caught on the flap mechanism and provided a bag which collected all subsequent waste and caused the pipework to block up. John had been called across to the Engineering bay where the pipework was being cleared in order to see what had happened as it was considered so bizarre. More so when a second incident happened a couple of weeks later and was found to be due to the same problem. Perhaps it was the same woman on a return flight?

Despite our best design efforts toilets would block from time to time. There had always been problems on the earlier systems and these would continue into the modern era. People had a habit of accidentally dropping things into the toilet. Spectacles, watches, jewellery and false teeth were regulars. If something fell into the old style toilets it would drop into the tank beneath and there were numerous occasions when a passenger would approach a crew member on board to say that something had been lost in the toilet and "could we find it?"

When this happened the aircraft, after arrival, would be positioned to a remote area away from the Terminal, the toilet could then be emptied directly on to a concrete surface and the contents would be gone through in order to find the missing item. It was usually successful and the item was returned to the customer.

I'm not sure however that I would have been too keen to put my false teeth back in my mouth, knowing where they had been!!

CHAPTER 67

WORLD STANDARDS

As a result of the catastrophic food poisoning experience that BA had suffered in 1984, the Association of European Airlines, a trade organisation of the major European carriers, set up a working party to examine airline food safety and formulate some common standards which each of the airlines could apply across the world.

The working party was a mixture of food safety professionals and catering managers employed by the airlines and my predecessor Peter Jerram had sat as a member of the group on behalf of BA.

On taking up my post as Head of Food Safety in 1992, I naturally assumed his seat and at the first meeting which I attended, hosted by KLM in Amsterdam, I was to meet a number of individuals whose work over subsequent years was to prove influential in the improvement of food safety in airline catering.

The first of these was Steen Christensen. A graduate Veterinarian who had specialised in food safety, Steen was originally employed as Head of Food Safety with SAS the Scandinavian airline but subsequently headed the food safety division at Gate Gourmet, the catering company which bought the airline catering division when it was divested by the airline.

Steen's knowledge of food safety was extensive and he had a great ability to get into the detail in subjects such as microbiology in a way which didn't drag our meetings into lengthy irrelevant semantic discussions but concentrated our minds on what was immediately necessary. Over the years we were to become good friends as well as good working colleagues.

Sam Ritzman was another Gate Gourmet member of the working party. He had originally been employed by Swissair as a food safety adviser in their catering operations but like Steen had found himself in Gate Gourmet following their purchase of the business. Like other members of the group Sam was a fluent English speaker but often amused me by his eloquent use of the English language. His choice of words, whilst always correct, often used words or phrases from an earlier generation of English which took me back to my formative years.

On my first meeting held in Amsterdam I found that I wasn't the only new attendee at the meeting. Ulrike Enneking the representative of Lufthansa was also new and both she and I were welcomed by the Chairman. Later that evening, after the conclusion of the day's work the group went for dinner at a local restaurant. Seated at a circular table I found myself next to Ulrike. "Hello" she said, putting her hand out. "I'm Ulrike Enneking. I'm from the country whose greatest claim to fame is that we are always first to get to the beach chairs in the morning."

I laughed. It was a standing joke in England that in all the holiday destinations across Europe the Germans were always up first thing in the morning to race out and grab all the best sunbeds by the swimming pool at the hotel, ahead of the British.

I introduced myself, thinking "A German with a sense of humour?" We spent the evening getting to know each other and over subsequent years Ulrike was to prove a strong force in the working party and she and I were to become firm friends. Others in the group were to change through time as people and airlines came and went but Steen, Sam and Ulrike along with me were to remain as core members until my retirement in 2006. During this time the group developed a comprehensive guide to Food Safety in Airline catering which became a standard reference within the industry.

A similar group existed in the USA. The International Flight Service Association (IFSA) was the representative body for airline food service providers as distinct from the Association of European Airlines which represented all facets of the airline industry. My connection with IFSA came through Carol Heaver-Norton the food safety adviser at the catering unit in New York which supplied BA who in her role as Chairperson of the Government Affairs Committee at IFSA asked if I would be willing to join the group. "Your expertise in food safety across the international arena would be very valuable to us" was how she put it to me. I was suitably flattered and agreed to attend the next meeting.

The group was very influential as its members represented the majority of flight caterers in the USA plus a number of airlines and suppliers. It also had good contacts within the US Government Food and Drugs Administration (FDA) and had regular dialogue with them which proved interesting in so far as it let me see how Food Safety legislation was dealt with in the USA.

I rapidly made myself useful in the Group meetings using my knowledge of how food safety was applied in many other countries. A large number of my colleagues on the committee had very limited experience outside the USA and little understanding of how farfetched or impractical some of their ideas might seem when taken beyond the American mainland.

My most interesting experience as a member of the Committee was when a delegation was invited to Washington DC to meet with the FDA to discuss a proposed new Code of Practice for the Food Industry. I was surprised to be invited as one of the delegation but pleased to attend.

The meeting took place in an imposing Government building and after introduction to a number of very senior members of the US Administration we spent hours in animated and productive discussion. As a "non American" I felt very privileged to be part of a group which was formulating a Code of Practice which would affect the whole of the USA. More so when I realised that I was being invited to pass comment on the work previously carried out by the Government team and my comments were being acted upon. It made me feel quite humble but pleased at the same time in that I was making a positive contribution to food safety.

IFSA also organised an annual trade exhibition and conference which provided a networking opportunity and sales possibility for the many hundreds of people involved in the industry. Each year a different US venue was chosen and the highlight of the event was the keynote speaker, who regularly provided entertaining, thought provoking and witty speeches.

One conference held in Salt Lake City, the home of the Mormon church, lasted over a weekend and on the Sunday all attendees were invited to visit the Mormon Tabernacle at the top of the main street to take part in the weekly service led by the world famous Tabernacle Choir and televised and broadcast worldwide. I decided to go, if only to listen to the choir.

Arriving at the church I was greeted and welcomed by a gentleman formally dressed in a suit and tie. He was one of a number of men all welcoming visitors and I was invited to step inside the church where I was welcomed again, this time by a woman, one of another team, all of whom were probably the spouses of the men outside.

The service was a revelation of organisation and skill. A full professional television and broadcasting team was working inside and the whole thing was extremely slick. As the live broadcast began the TV anchor man's voice echoed through the church, deep and treacly.

The choral singing was magnificent. We were told that the choir membership of three hundred voices was made up from the Mormon community and each member had to live within one hundred miles of the church so as to be able to get to rehearsals each week. Aged between 25 and 55 when recruited they had to undergo interviews and stringent singing tests before being accepted and they retired at age 60.

All too quickly the service ended and as I walked out of the Church I came face to face with a young blonde woman, probably in her early twenties. She smiled. "Did you enjoy the service?" "Yes, it was very good." "Would you like to take a walk round our facilities here and see what we do?" I realised instantly that given that I was old enough to be this girl's father, this good looking young woman had not decided to speak to me because of my youthful good looks but was about to embark on a sales promotion to get me to join the Church.

Looking around I could see a number of her colleagues doing the same thing to other visitors and thought it interesting that all the men were approached by young women whilst all the women were being approached by young men.

"I would be delighted to" I said looking at her closely "but only if you will join me for a cup of coffee before we start?" I had heard that the Mormons didn't drink coffee so my offer was instantly turned down and she walked away to try to catch someone else.

This particular conference was also memorable for an amusing incident on my way home. I had attended the keynote speech, delivered by a veteran of the industry, who took the opportunity during his presentation to castigate some of the aspects of being an airline passenger.

Showing a picture of a snack consisting of a filled wrap he commented "Who in their right mind would want to eat that at seven o'clock in the morning?" provoking laughter in the audience. He then followed by showing a picture of an Embraer regional jet, a small aircraft with limited internal space, "and who would want to fly in one of these with your knees jammed between the seats for more than two hours?" provoking more laughter.

I had flown from Phoenix to Salt Lake City in an Airbus so on my return trip, the day after listening to the speech, I was surprised to find myself boarding an Embraer regional jet exactly as had been portrayed the previous day.

The smart looking modern little aircraft was fitted out with two seats on each side of the aisle. I was seated next to the window and watched as a very large woman walked down the aisle towards me. Arriving at the vacant seat beside me she slowly and carefully looked around then as she sat down said in a loud voice "I haven't been this close to a man in years!" The passengers around burst into laughter and I smiled in appreciation of the joke. We introduced ourselves and chatted happily together through the flight.

Other IFSA conferences produced similar amusing moments. The Executive Chef at Dobbs Flight catering was one Dirk Brakebusch. A lively entertaining man he oversaw the food production in the numerous flight kitchens which the company operated across the USA and further afield.

Dirk was known for his sense of humour. On one occasion, having just arrived for the annual conference this time in Albuquerque, New Mexico, I bumped into Dirk in the hotel lobby as I was checking in.

"Hi Mike, good to see you. Would you care to come to dinner with me tonight?" Having known Dirk for many years I was happy to agree and at 7.00pm I was in the lobby with a group of others waiting for Dirk. Suddenly the door opened and he bustled in from outside. "OK you Guys, come along the bus is waiting." We followed him as he led us to a large coach. Once boarded we were quickly on our way, driving through the city streets and out into the suburbs, eventually pulling up at a very large roadside Mexican restaurant.

Ushered inside we joined a larger group of people and were shown to our seats. The meal was typically Mexican. The tequila flowed and the conversation got louder and more animated. I didn't recognise many people in the room but they were all in the industry one way or another and were very friendly. Suddenly with a couple of quick taps on a glass to get the gathering into order a gentleman at the top table stood up and began to welcome us all to the meal. It was at this point that I realised that the dinner hadn't been organised by Dobbs Flight catering but was in fact a dinner held by a major food supplier to thank their customers. Dirk had hijacked a complete table to bring along his own customers!!

I tackled him about it the following morning. "What was all that about last night? I thought I was going to a Dobbs dinner and was somewhat embarrassed when I found myself at someone else's party." Dirk grinned. "Forget it. They asked me to come along and said I could bring a friend. I just extended it a bit." "Yes I don't expect that they thought you would bring a coach load!"

On a later occasion at another annual event Dirk was at it again. Rumours were circulating at the Conference that Dobbs Flight Catering was being bought by another company. There was no concrete evidence and no-one was saying anything, however around 7.00pm when various groups of people were setting off for dinner and a line of buses was parked outside there was much amusement when the bus marked for Dobbs' guests was seen to have a sign on the side which read "Under new management."

No-one owned up to having stuck the sign on the bus and the top management at Dobbs weren't best pleased but Dirk was the prime suspect.

I very much enjoyed my membership of the IFSA Government Affairs and Education committee and hoped that the time which I spent working with them, particularly in the drawing up of what the Americans chose to title "The World Food Safety Guidelines" for airline catering, was useful to them.

I certainly enjoyed the friendship, camaraderie and experience which I gained from my exposure to this influential American organisation and was extremely surprised and honoured when in 2008, some two years after my retirement from BA, I was invited to the IFSA Annual Conference in Orlando, Florida where I was inducted into the President's Roll of Honour in recognition of my "Outstanding contributions to the Flight Services Industry" as written on the presentational plaque.

CHAPTER 68

9/11

Tuesday 11ᵗʰ September 2011. A date which will never be forgotten in World history. A day which changed the World when the twin towers of the World Trade Centre in New York were attacked by Al-Qaeda terrorists using hijacked airliners. An event which in the long term was to seal my retirement from British Airways a few years later as its aftermath changed the way in which airlines were operated.

On that day I was in the Renaissance Hotel at Atlanta airport, Georgia having been invited to present a paper at a Food Safety conference organised by the Government Affairs Committee of IFSA. It was the second such event at which I was invited as a speaker, the first having been held a couple of years previously in Seattle, and was well attended with more than one hundred delegates present from the USA and abroad.

I was the opening speaker and had just finished my presentation at around 9.45am when the Chair of the meeting, Carol Heaver Norton walked on stage and told the audience that New York was under attack. At first we couldn't believe what she was saying but as it sank in the conference was adjourned for fifteen minutes to allow delegates to catch up with what was happening. I went to my room, turned on the television and couldn't believe what I was seeing. It was horrendous as I watched the first of the Twin Towers burn and then collapse.

The conference reconvened and continued in a desultory fashion through the morning but as news came through that all US airspace was being closed down and all flights were being grounded there began a mad rush of delegates clamouring to get away and head for home. Within a very short time every available mode of transport from Atlanta had been commandeered and the hotel emptied.

All that remained of the conference were five of us from overseas who had attended and had now been abandoned to our own devices. Our hotel overlooked the runways at Atlanta International Airport, normally one of the World's busiest airports, and we sat looking at the sea of parked aircraft on a totally quiet non moving airport. It was surreal.

The next four days became something akin to "Groundhog Day." Each day was exactly like the day before. As we came down to breakfast the same waitress would come up to the table and say "Are you guys still here?" There were very few other guests in the hotel and any who were there were stuck just like us. It was very strange and somewhat disconcerting as for once in my life I had no control over what was happening and what I could do to change things. I couldn't get out of the country as there were no flights and I had no idea as to when they were likely to restart.

As I had been due back in the UK to present a short paper on Friday morning to a group of airline medical Directors at a meeting hosted by my boss, Dr Sandra Mooney, I had to phone to appraise her of my situation but given the circumstances most of her guests were unlikely to make it to London due to the fact that flights across the world had now been totally disrupted by the US airspace closure.

The next three days passed very slowly and as each progressed I began to try to work out how I could get home. I appeared to have two choices. I could either try to make my way South to Mexico and get a flight from there or alternatively travel North to Canada but as each involved a lengthy overland journey I thought it best to give it a couple more days to see what happened.

Saturday arrived and suddenly things began to change. The US Government realising that the lack of air travel was causing problems to the US economy, decided to lift the ban on flights and aircraft began to move on the airfield outside the hotel. Out of the blue I got a phone call telling me that British Airways would be operating their service that night from Atlanta. I was elated and quickly caught up with my four friends in the hotel to tell them, knowing that if BA was on the move their flights home would also become available pretty quickly. They were pleased for me but there was some ribald comment about BA and how they were looking after their own people!!

I made my way to the airport terminal in the evening and joined the throng of people waiting to be processed at the check in desks by the BA staff. I wasn't hopeful of getting a seat so wasn't surprised to be told by the check in staff that they would hold my ticket and call me later if a seat became available.

I moved away from the desk and as I waited at the back of the crowd I saw the aircraft crew making their way to the check in desks. I recognised them as the same crew that had brought me out from London on the previous Monday and like me, had been stuck in Atlanta.

One of the Stewards looked across, recognised me and walked over to have a word. "Hi, how are you. You got stuck same as us then? Pretty grim wasn't it. Are you on this flight?" It all came in a rush. "On standby because of the number of people" I explained. "Don't worry I'll have a word with the CSD and we'll find a seat for you." I was relieved. I didn't really want another night in the Renaissance hotel. Fortunately I didn't need the help of the crew as shortly afterwards I was called to the desk and given a seat. My relief was palpable.

I was glad to get back home and was surprised when looking back at the event, just how stressful it had been. The loss of control over my life hit me harder than I could have imagined but I suppose that was because I had always previously been able to plan exactly what I was doing in order to fit my work and home schedules and being unable to do that left me in a void.

The result of the terrorist outrage was to leave British Airways along with most other airlines, struggling. Passenger numbers, particularly to the US dropped dramatically with a subsequent fall in cash flow. Senior management meetings with the Chief Executive Rod Eddington brought the reality sharply home as the airline at one stage was haemorrhaging money at the rate of £2m per day. Serious cost cutting began, resulting in staff reductions and cutbacks on food and on board services.

Concorde was the most obvious casualty. The aircraft was just too expensive to run and was retired from service to the intense disappointment of many people. Changes in the food service on board led to all food on short haul European flights being supplied from London and return catered. Out bound aircraft carried the food for the return flight and meals in the economy section of the aircraft were reduced to drinks and a tiny snack.

This obviously had implications on my team as we no longer had to check the standards in European catering units but it increased the workload in the UK as a lot of the food product was now being manufactured in food factories rather than in the flight kitchens. There was also a greater tendency to buy on "price" and with no prior knowledge of the producers it behove us to audit them all to ensure that the product was safe. Some of what we found was interesting to say the least!! It's enough to say that very often you only get what you pay for and if you want good quality products prepared in hygienic conditions you may have to pay a bit more for them.

CHAPTER 69

AND FINALLY

Through my years of working in British Airways I had the pleasure and privilege of visiting more than half of all the countries in the World and all the continents bar one. I also had the pleasure of meeting and working with a vast number of people all of whom were connected in one way or another with the airline industry.

One of my former colleagues once worked out that each of us in the Hygiene Team met some four hundred new people every year through our work. If that was true, then I have met some twelve thousand people during my airline career. Added to these were all those that I met when working in Africa and in Local government.

My biggest regret in writing these anecdotes is that I never kept a diary. My memory of many of the people has dimmed with age and although I can recall numerous incidents through the years, the names of some of the participants and the time scales are somewhat more difficult to remember.

Africa was challenging, difficult and exciting but although my time there was short, looking back at it I felt that I achieved something, if only in giving the possibility of a longer life to those children that I vaccinated.

My short spell in Hillingdon was educational and took me back to the basic roots of my profession but my long time career in British Airways proved exceptional.

Like Africa, it too was challenging, difficult, exciting and ever changing. No day was exactly the same as the last and whilst it provided many disappointments along the way, it gave me a job which in my mind couldn't have been bettered.

Yes, I may have been able to have worked in a job which paid more money but where would I have had the same job satisfaction? Meeting challenging targets across the world to enable the airline to operate safely, making a difference by improving standards in the many countries through which the airline flew, experiencing the geographical and cultural problems which had to be overcome were all in a day's work.

Many would say that you have to be mad to work in the airline business and that may well be true but those that I met along the way were resilient, hard working professionals, usually with a good sense of humour and a great loyalty to the Company for whom they worked. This applied equally to those who managed the many hotels in which our crew and other staff were accommodated across the World and which I and my team audited.

The countries which I visited were vastly different in many ways although bound together by the airline operation which was governed by a set British Airways routine and didn't vary although through the years it had to adapt to the rapid improvements in aircraft type and technology.

There was a lot of history in the way that things were done, much of it redolent of the early days of commercial flying and often referred to as "Custom and Practice" or alternatively "Old Spanish Customs." Don't ask me where the latter came from.

My retirement in March 2006 came somewhat earlier than I might have wished but wasn't unexpected. It not only brought to an end my career in the airline industry but my career in Environmental Health. Looking back at it all I can only marvel at the wonderful life and experiences that I have enjoyed.

From Local Government to industry, from Ulster to Africa, from Belfast to Bishkek from elephants to Jumbos and pythons to pilots.

These musings contain only a small part of it but I would like to thank all those people whom I have met along the way and who helped, often in no small part, to make my career as enjoyable and fulfilling as it was.

Thanks to you all.

Mike Kelly
2015